John Williams's Film Music

WISCONSIN FILM STUDIES

Patrick McGilligan
Series Editor

John Williams's Film Music

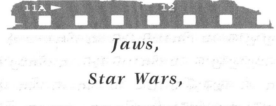

Jaws,

Star Wars,

Raiders of the Lost Ark,

and the Return of the

Classical Hollywood Music Style

Emilio Audissino

The University of Wisconsin Press

The University of Wisconsin Press
1930 Monroe Street, 3rd Floor
Madison, Wisconsin 53711-2059
uwpress.wisc.edu

3 Henrietta Street
London WC2E 8LU, England
eurospanbookstore.com

Printed in the United States of America

Library of Congress Cataloging-in-Publication Data

Audissino, Emilio, author.
John Williams's film music: Jaws, Star Wars, Raiders of the Lost Ark,
and the return of the classical Hollywood music style / Emilio Audissino.
pages   cm — (Wisconsin film studies)
Includes bibliographical references and index.
ISBN 978-0-299-29734-3 (pbk.: alk. paper)
ISBN 978-0-299-29733-6 (e-book)
1. Williams, John, 1932–Criticism and interpretation.
2. Motion picture music—History and criticism.
3. Jaws (Motion picture).   4. Star wars (Motion picture).
5. Raiders of the lost ark (Motion picture).
6. Boston Pops Orchestra.
I. Title.   II. Series: Wisconsin film studies.
ML410.W71335A83   2014
781.5'42092—dc23
2013033116

publication of this arrangement

is made possible by a grant

Figure Foundation

To

Vittorio and Silvia

i miei carissimi genitori

There is nobody in my experience who made the kind of impact on my career and my films than this man. This man has absolutely transformed everything that I have done into something that I could not imagine ever having done. And he does it because he communicates so well with all of you. He has re-discovered something that was very popular and important in the 1930s and 1940s. . . . And I know of no one who knows how to write film music that goes straight to your heart and straight to your soul than my good friend John Williams. . . . And John is actually one of the greatest storytellers of all time.

Steven Spielberg

"Hollywood Bowl Hall of Fame Ceremony,"

23 June 2000

Contents

Illustrations

Musical Examples

Acknowledgments

There are many people who have accompanied me throughout the preparation of this book. My appreciation goes to the Dipartimento di Storia delle Arti at the University of Pisa, Italy, where I completed the three-year doctoral program in which I had the chance to refine and complete the necessary research work. Special thanks to Pier Marco De Santi, Cinzia Sicca, and Sandra Lischi. A tip of the hat also goes to Giulia Carluccio at the University of Turin, Italy, who was the supervisor of my master's thesis (again, on John Williams) and my very first cinema teacher.

Part of this book is based on fieldwork carried out in Boston, Massachusetts. On the one hand, it consisted of my regular presence at all the John Williams concerts with the Boston Pops from 2007 to 2013. On the other hand, it consisted of archival research at the Boston Symphony Orchestra Archives and at the WGBH Educational Foundation Media Library and Archives. Many thanks for their advice and assistance go to Bridget P. Carr and Barbara Perkel (BSO Archives) and to Keith Luf, Nancy Dillon, and Leah Weisse (WGBH Archives). My warmest thanks to my dear friends at Boston's Symphony Hall: Doreen M. Reis, Vincenzo Peppino Natale, and Adam Castiglioni for their constant friendship and support, and to Ron Della Chiesa for our delightful conversations about the history of the Boston Symphony Orchestra and the Boston Pops. A special acknowledgment goes to my Bostonian friend Victor Brogna, who lent a very helpful hand both with legal issues and with the proofreading of the book manuscript. This book originates from my Italian PhD dissertation. Since I wanted to present Maestro Williams with a copy of said dissertation upon our meeting in June 2012, my seven-hundred-page work had to be translated from Italian into English. I must thank my friend Alessandra Voi for sharing with me the burdensome work of translation under a very tight schedule, thus helping me meet the deadline.

My friend John Norris deserves my warmest gratitude and a central niche of his own. He is a thorough connoisseur of film music and John Williams's works, and was an invaluable assistant in my archival research in Boston. He was also my eyes and ears at those concerts that I was not able to attend, and consequently provided me with detailed reports and lots of material. Moreover, he did a remarkable job of language revision, having been part of the translation team that had worked on the English version of my dissertation. *Grazie,* John!

As for the form and appearance of the book, I wish to express my appreciation to the many people who gave their contributions at the various stages of the process. First of all, I'm grateful to the University of Wisconsin Press for giving me the opportunity to bring this book to life. My sincere gratitude goes to Executive Editor Raphael Kadushin, who has always believed in the project's potential and has been encouraging from our very first e-mail contact, to his assistant Matthew Cosby, to my editor Sheila McMahon, and to all the other nice persons I worked with at UW Press. My thanks—in alphabetical order—also go to George Burt, Vincent LoBrutto, Jeff Smith, and Larry Timm, who read the manuscript in its first version and offered insightful and enhancing comments and pieces of advice. For their competent legal advice on U.S. Copyright Laws and on the Fair Use doctrine, my deepest appreciation goes to attorneys at law Redenta Enne and Bill Lee. As for the visual part, my appreciation goes to Vincent Hardy, Jonathan Player, and Mark Zastrow for providing and kindly allowing the reproduction of their lively concert and backstage photographs, and to Mrs. Samantha Winslow Williams for giving the permission of featuring her exquisite John Williams portraits.

My deepest gratitude to Jamie Richardson for his patience and kindness in replying to my (many, many) requests, and for his indispensable advice.

Heartfelt thanks, praise, and love go to my family: my father, Vittorio, my mother, Silvia, and my sister, Sara. They have always been constantly loving, supportive, and reassuring.

Dulcis in fundo—last but not least—my most sincere appreciation to Maestro John Williams for the friendliness, graciousness, and interest with which he has always received me in each of our meetings. Having known him personally, I can say that he is not only an exceptionally talented artist but also an exceptionally nice human being.

Boston, Massachusetts
12 June 2013

Preface on Methodology

It has been twenty years now that I have been studying John Williams's music. Along the journey, one thing has kept striking me as extremely odd: there was no English-language book on John Williams. So, I resolved that I should try and fill the gap. The book you are about to read is, hopefully, my answer to the problem.

This book is the result of the revision of part of my PhD dissertation that centered on John Williams's neoclassicism. The text has been "de-academized" and many hard theoretical parts removed. However, since it stems from theories and employs methodologies that might not be familiar to everyone, a few explanations are in order at the outset. Moreover, some terms that are commonly used in film-music studies are deliberately discarded or employed with reservations, while new ones are proposed, which are more precise to express my point—among them, a custom-made method to analyze music in films. In order not to burden the following chapters, all such terminological, methodological, and theoretical points are gathered here.

Methodology

The methodological approach adopted is David Bordwell's and Kristin Thompson's neoformalism.[1] The film is seen as an artwork created according to specific norms in a specific historical context in order to produce specific aesthetic effects. Unlike semiotics, neoformalism sees the film not so much as a text conveying a message to be studied in terms of its communicational strategies, but rather as an artifact to be studied in terms of its perceptual strategies.

Each film is a formal system consisting of an interplay of a series of devices. Devices are all those elements of a stylistic, narrative, or thematic nature that combine to shape the film's overall form: three-point lighting, tracking shots, fades, costumes, settings and scenery, flashbacks, montages, crosscutting, characters, extratextual allusions, philosophical/political ideas, and so on. These devices fulfill a specific *function* within the film and their presence must justify itself by some *motivation*.

There are four types of motivation for the presence of a device in a film: (1) *compositional motivation*—a device is in the film because it is essential to build either the causal, temporal, or spatial system of the narrative; (2) *realistic motivation*—a device is in the film because its presence is plausible according to our experience of how things are in the real world; (3) *transtextual motivation*—a device is in the film because it follows the conventions of a given genre; and (4) *artistic motivation*— a device is in the film for no other motivation than an aesthetic one.

Music is one of the many devices used in films and its presence in a given scene is explained by one or more of the above-mentioned motivations. The opening scene of *The Abominable Dr. Phibes* (Robert Fuest, 1971) is a good example. The film tells the story of a disfigured theologian who retaliates against the doctors he holds responsible for his wife's death. The plot consists of a series of *Grand-Guignolesque* deeds of deathly revenge inspired by biblical episodes. The film opens with a black-hooded figure seen from the back—Dr. Phibes, we will soon find out—playing some music on a reddish neon-lighted plexiglass pipe organ. The presence of the opening title organ music is motivated *realistically*, since there is someone onscreen playing an organ. The choice of organ music is also motivated *transtextually*, since the pipe organ has not only had a long association with horror films but is also an overt quotation of *The Phantom of the Opera* (Rupert Jullian, 1925), in which the similarly disfigured and vengeful Lon Chaney character is used to playing such instrument. Moreover, the musical piece being played is Felix Mendelssohn's "War March of the Priests" ("Kriegsmarsch der Priester" from *Athalie*, incidental music, op. 74, 1845) and the *compositional* motivation of such a choice is to anticipate what the film is about: the war of a priestlike theologian against his wife's murderers. Finally, in the scene, Dr. Phibes's hands swipe the air in histrionic gestures mostly unsynchronized with the music he is supposed to be playing, and such flamboyant and unrealistic moves can be motivated *artistically* so as to introduce compellingly this larger-than-life villain.

It goes without saying that music operates powerfully in films. On the narrative level, music contributes to the clarification of the narrative events, not only for the narrative logic (e.g., suggesting the thoughts of a character and thereby motivating the reasons for his actions) but also for time construction (e.g., providing the fragments of a montage sequence with some linking and temporal continuity) and space construction (e.g., hinting at the nationality of a place through the use of a representative tune or anthem). Similarly, music's contribution can reinforce the stylistic level: through the use of dark timbres, music can enhance the dark shadows of low-key lighting, as Bernard Herrmann's score for *Citizen Kane* (Orson Welles, 1941) does. Music can also reinforce the thematic level: the grotesque version of "La Marseillaise" in *Metropolis* (Fritz Lang, 1927) accompanying the workers' wild rebellion may suggest a negative interpretation of revolutions in general. Music can fulfill many functions, and a methodology for analyzing film music should therefore aim at pinpointing them.

The following sections use a grid developed to best suit my needs, especially for the analysis of music that is designed to duplicate the visual actions—as is the case with classical Hollywood music. The framework blends neoformalism with Leonard B. Meyer's studies on style, emotion, and meaning in music and with psychomusicological scholarship.[2] The resulting format consists of the following functions, named after the three levels of engagement of the viewer: emotion, perception, and cognition.[3]

Emotive Function (macro and micro)

The *macro-emotive function* is what unifies the aesthetic experience of the film for the viewer. It performs the function of the frame in a painting. By presenting the theme in the opening titles, then reprising it in variations throughout the film, and finally presenting it again at the end of the film, music helps the shaping of the perception of the film's formal unity. It acts as a conventional indicator of the boundaries of the narrative, marking the initial and final limit.[4] Emotionally, the feeling of an overall cohesion is given by the pleasure of recognizing recurrent musical themes throughout the film, with which we come to be progressively familiar.[5] An example is provided by the famous "Tara's Theme" by Max Steiner, which opens, closes, and runs throughout *Gone with the Wind* (Victor Fleming, 1939), reinforcing its formal cohesion.

The *micro-emotive function* is the solicitation of a particular emotional response from the viewer in a particular moment of the film. Music transfers to the images its emotional component. The most common—and banal—examples are love scenes accompanied by sentimental violin music. However, there are many more instances in which the micro-emotive function can significantly affect the success of a scene. A famous example is the opening scene of *The Lost Weekend* (Billy Wilder, 1945), where Ray Milland is "fishing" a bottle of whiskey out of the window. Before Miklós Rózsa's stern music was put on the scene, that incipit had induced many viewers to expect an urban comedy instead of a drama on alcoholism.[6]

Perceptive Function

Music guides or modifies the perception of the viewer, pointing his attention to a particular element inside the framed space (*spatial* perceptive function) or by altering or enhancing the perception of the visual rhythm and speed of the cutting (*temporal* perceptive function). An example of *temporal* perceptive function is the car chase in *North by Northwest* (Alfred Hitchcock, 1959) in which Cary Grant's drunken character is trying to keep his car on the road and avoid crashing into the precipice. Bernard Herrmann's frenetic *fandango* punctuates the rapidity of the editing pace, making the action appear more frantic. An example of *spatial* perceptive function appears in *The Sea Hawk* (Michael Curtiz, 1940). In one scene, a harp chord resounds in the silence to direct our attention to an event occurring in the film space: Erich Wolfgang Korngold's score uses the chord to punctuate the change of facial expression of one of the Spaniards when he sees in his chalice the reflection of Captain Thorpe and his men, freed from their chains and eager to retaliate.

Cognitive Function

Since it acts on time, space, and narrative logic, music also contributes to the understanding of denotations and in the interpretation of connotations. Music may unite the fragments of a montage sequence and aid the understanding of the progression of time; it may denote a place or a historical period by referring to some repertoire pieces; it may link fairly disconnected shots thus making the film's space look as a consistent whole; it may reveal the thoughts of a character presenting a musical theme previously associated with another narrative element, thus clarifying the reason for his action; it can link two distant narrative elements and suggest an implicit meaning. For example, in *The Treasure of the Sierra Madre* (John Huston, 1948), when the ceiling of the mine collapses on Dobbs—one of the three gold diggers—and buries him, his partner Curtin comes to rescue him but suddenly stops and lingers at the entrance of the gallery. Max Steiner's music proposes the motif associated with gold, thus guiding our understanding.

Curtin is thinking that if one of his partners dies, the share of the remaining two will be bigger. Solidarity, however, eventually takes over greed, and music shifts from the "gold motif" to the melody associated with the friendship between the gold seekers: Curtin banishes his temptation and saves Dobbs. In *Taxi Driver* (Martin Scorsese, 1976), Bernard Herrmann's music closes the film with the same three-note "madness motif" that closed *Psycho* (Alfred Hitchcock, 1960), suggesting that despite the circumstances, Travis is not a hero but a psychopath no less dangerous than *Psycho*'s Norman Bates. *The Adventures of Robin Hood* (Michael Curtiz, William Keighley, 1938) opens with a royal herald saying: "News has come from Vienna." Korngold used as the main theme his own waltz "Miss Austria," which colors Robin Hood's story with a Viennese flavor and thus contributes to give contemporary political connotations—the *Anschluss* had just been proclaimed and Hitler's invasion of Austria just begun—to a film that is otherwise about a medieval legend.[7]

Some Terminology

In film-music studies there is a traditional distinction between music at *diegetic* level—music comes from a source within the narrative world and can be heard by the film's characters—and at *non-diegetic* level—music comes from some sort of narrator outside of the narrative world and only the viewers can hear it, not the characters.[8] These terms originated from literary studies, leading to much debate about the legitimacy of their application to music in film.[9] For clarity's sake, though, the traditional "diegetic/non-diegetic" couple is employed hereafter, instead of the more correct and less controversial "source music/background music."

The use of *leitmotiv*, drawn from Richard Wagner's works, in cinema has been similarly criticized, both for being an inadequate practice for this medium and for being an imprecise term to refer to the technique as it is used in films;[10] the alternative term "leitmotivic function" has been proposed.[11] The issue, however, is still being widely debated.[12] Nonetheless, we use the term *leitmotiv* here because it is more convenient than other periphrases although we are perfectly aware of its difference from Wagner's idea.

In general parlance, *sound track* is used to define all the music composed for/featured in a given film, but this is incorrect. The sound track is the part of the filmstrip on which the sound mix comprising all the acoustic components is impressed: the dialogue track, the sound-effect track, and the music track. When referring to the musical component of a film the correct term will be used: *music track*.

The terms *theme* and *motif* will indicate respectively an eight-bar melody and shorter melodic lines, both having their own musical "personality." *Cells* are one- or two-bar fragments deriving from a theme or motif already presented. Further classifications will be avoided, which are more accurate from a musicological point of view but which also risk being confusing.

I use *wallpaper music* to define a non-diegetic musical background, which is neutral to the action and dialogue, that is, music that fills an otherwise silent background. For example, it may be some kind of light waltz underscoring a dialogue—think of Lubitsch's early sound operettas. I contrast "wallpaper music" with "functional accompaniment," where non-diegetic music fulfills other functions than simply filling the silence, and it is composed so as to follow the developments of the actions and dialogue closely and meaningfully.[13]

On "Style" and "Classical"

The first section of this book provides a chronicle and definition of the classical Hollywood music style. Here, it is necessary to clarify the meaning of the terms "style" and "classical" as they are used.

When talking about music, there is a tendency to think of style in a narrow sense, that is, as the language used to compose a certain type of music: *baroque* style, *classical* style, *romantic* style, *atonal* style, and the like. In this work, a broader meaning of style will be used. Indeed, classical Hollywood music is both a musical piece of work, one that employs a certain "musical style" in the narrowest sense, and an industrial product, one that responds to precise standards, is realized according to specific techniques and procedures, and utilizes the musical means provided by the "industry." Therefore, when I refer to the classical Hollywood music style I do not only refer to its musical language but also to the techniques, musical means, and the typical formal functions that the classical Hollywood music style is expected to perform in films.[14]

When referring to *style in the narrower sense*—that is, the musical language employed—I adopt, after Meyer, a three-term subdivision:[15] *dialect*—a shared musical language employed within a school; *idiom*—the idiosyncratic musical language of a given composer; and *intra-opus style*—the particular musical language that characterizes a single film score. For instance, consider Max Steiner and Erich Wolfgang Korngold, two key composers of Hollywood's Golden Age. Both worked at Warner Bros. within the overarching classical Hollywood music *style*, following those institutional practices required by the industry. For example, both used the leitmotiv technique. They wrote in the same *dialect* largely favored within the Hollywood music departments, that of late Mitteleuropean romanticism. Even if they used the same style and the same dialect, their *idioms* were different, one characterized by fragmentation and extreme adherence to the visuals (Steiner), and the other by extended melodies and strong motivic-thematic linking of operatic nature (Korngold).[16] Moreover, within their own production, the *intra-opus* style could change significantly from one work to others—from flowing tonal melodies as in Steiner's *Gone With the Wind* (Fleming, 1939) and Korngold's *The Adventures of Robin Hood* (Curtiz and Keighley, 1938) to darker and more dissonant writing, as in Steiner's *King Kong* and Korngold's *The Sea Wolf* (Michael Curtiz, 1941).

The adjective "classical" that I use to identify the music style of the Golden Age is a loan from Bordwell, Staiger, and Thompson's famous study, *The Classical Hollywood Cinema*. Music is one of the many devices used by narration in order to construct a film within the norms of the classical Hollywood paradigm.[17] Consequently, the term "classical" as used here must not be confused with the linguistic category of "classical" used in music historiography, meaning the music of the second half of the eighteenth century, of Haydn and Mozart. Hollywood music style was not "classical" in that sense. It was romantic, drawing its dialect from the late nineteenth-century music. In fact, music classicism was seldom used as a dialect. This happened mostly in period films to convey musically the flavor of the past—as in *The Three Worlds of Gulliver* (Jack Sher, 1960, music by Bernard Herrmann). Hereafter, "classical" is meant as a historical film category and refers to an idea of music molded according to the needs of the classical film style of the studio system. Some of Meyer's remarks on classicism in music can be of help to better understand the difference between "classical" as a linguistic classification and "classical" as an approach to music making:

> Classicism has been characterized by a valuing of shared conventions and rational restraint, the playful exploitation of established constraints and the satisfaction of actuality (Being), the coherence of closed forms and the clarity of explicit meanings; while romanticism has been characterized by a valuing of the peculiarities of the individual innovation and the yearning arising from potentiality (Becoming), the informality of open structures and the suggestiveness of implicit significance. . . . In the eighteenth century . . . unity of expression is significantly dependent upon kinds of dance steps, rhetorical figures, syntactic processes, and other conventional means. . . . Classic composers use such means to represent sentiment shared by humankind. Romantic composers, on the other hand, reject convention in order to express—to present, not *re*present—their own personal and individual feelings.[18]

A *classical* conception of music making based on "shared conventions" and seeking to communicate "sentiment[s] shared by humankind" was fundamental in the classical Hollywood system that aimed at reaching the largest audience possible. The term "classical" is thus helpful in underlying not only the universality sought by that musical style but also its exemplariness: classical Hollywood music, like all classical works, has come to be a model and a reference point, either to be followed or to be rejected.

John Williams's Film Music

Introduction

John Williams is probably the most successful composer in film history. His name is associated with many of the major Hollywood box-office block-busters of the last forty years. In a career spanning more than fifty years, John Williams has won four Golden Globes, five Emmys, twenty-one Grammys, seven BAFTA Awards, a number of Gold and Platinum Records, honorary degrees from twenty-one American universities, and five Academy Awards. Even more staggering, with forty-nine Oscar nominations, he currently holds the record for being the most Oscar-nominated living person, the second most nominated person in history, ranking just behind Walt Disney. His film scores have sold millions of copies, with *Star Wars* still being the best-selling symphonic album of all time.

Williams's success and fame is not confined to the film industry. For fourteen years he served as conductor-in-residence and artistic director of one of the most famous American symphony orchestras, the Boston Pops. As Boston Pops conductor, he performed not only in the United States but also in three tours to Japan. As a "Boston Pops Laureate Conductor" since 1994, he still maintains a busy concert schedule, both with his annual appearances in Boston and as a guest conductor with other famed orchestras. John Williams also pursued a career as a concert composer, receiving commissions from such important institutions as the New York Philharmonic, the Chicago Symphony, and the Boston Symphony. Plácido Domingo even tried to lure him into composing an opera for the Los Angeles Opera House.[1]

Over the years, John Williams has become America's "Composer Laureate." In particular, the number of celebratory pieces commissioned for many important events of American history and life have made him a modern-day American version of George Frideric Handel. His fanfares, marches, miniature pieces, and overtures have been performed on worldwide TV broadcasts; they accompanied the Los Angeles Olympics in 1984, the centennial celebrations of the Statue of Liberty in 1986, the Atlanta Centennial Olympics in 1996, the Salt Lake City Winter Olympics in 2002, and President Barack Obama's first inauguration in 2009. In 2012 he wrote the "Fanfare for Fenway" to celebrate the first centennial of the Red Sox and his beloved Boston's Fenway Park. As the London *Times* reported, "Williams' work is often described as quintessentially American. He writes big music for big studio movies. He has been called 'the king of grandiosity.'"[2]

In contrast to this huge success, Williams has received little attention from essayists and critics, and sometimes a kind of ill-concealed animosity from scholars. As of December 2013 there are only four books on him worldwide: two in Spanish, one in German, and one in French.[3] There are no books in English so far. Such a lack may derive from suspicion about the composer's enormous success and from some ideological prejudices, both of which I discuss later in the book. Similarly, European academic studies probably neglect Williams because he is judged to be too commercial and a symbol of the "imperialistic" Hollywood film industry: "If, as some argue, American cinema has conquered the world, then Williams can lay claim to have written the victory march."[4]

John Williams attracts as many admirers as detractors who look at his work with condescension and spite. Because of his success, many critics have categorized and dismissed Williams simply as a "commercial composer." They often deliberately focus on his most commercially successful works, such as *Star Wars* (George Lucas, 1977); *Superman: The Movie* (Richard Donner, 1978); or *Raiders of the Lost Ark* (Steven Spielberg, 1981), as if to imply that the score's success is merely a consequence of its lucky association with a successful film. Most critics also neglect or ignore his more experimental scores, such as *Images* (Robert Altman, 1972), or more sophisticated ones, such as *Jane Eyre* (Delbert Mann, 1970) and *Memoirs of a Geisha* (Rob Marshall, 2005). Such a biased attitude is rarely found to such an extent toward other similarly successful film composers, Ennio Morricone for one.

This prejudicial stance has caused a serious consequence, namely the absence of a thorough study of Williams's most important contribution to the history of film music: the revival of the classical Hollywood music style. Besides his single scores, commercial success, and artistic achievements, Williams is a pivotal figure in Hollywood history because he has been almost single-handedly responsible for bringing back the classical Hollywood sound, updating it to the requirements of the contemporary blockbuster film, and, more important, leading people to rediscover and appreciate the music of Hollywood's Golden Age. In the 1970s, Williams revived some then disused features of the classical style and consequently launched a neoclassical film music trend, of which he has been and still is the most representative composer. Moreover, in the 1980s, as conductor of the Boston Pops Orchestra, Williams acted as the leading promoter of film music by presenting its best achievements in concert, which contributed highly to its acceptance. This book studies how Williams brought back the classical Hollywood music, and to what extent, and analyzes the historical landmarks of the process.

Part I focuses on the classical Hollywood music style. This style is given an articulate definition and its history charted for its temporal borders, its main authors, its language, its compositional techniques, and the musical means typically utilized. The formal functions that this style used to perform in classical films are also described. Williams is not yet mentioned in this part, but a preliminary review of the classical Hollywood music is in order here, although a number of books have already dealt with the topic. For the already well-informed film-music specialists and enthusiasts, this section traces a custom-made account of the classical Hollywood music, which stresses the thin red line of influences, historical events, and stylistic traits that connect Williams to the classical period. For those readers not familiar with the film-music literature, it is a handy summary that provides the proper background.

Williams's role as the composer who revived the classical style and founded the film-music neoclassical trend is fully covered in Part II. First, I describe the context of the New Hollywood where the "Williams revolution" took place. Then I analyze Williams's style in terms of neoclassicism and focus on the 1975–83 period, the peak of the neoclassical trend. The *Star Wars* case—aka *Star Wars: A New Hope* (George Lucas, 1977) after the 1997 edition—is analyzed as the most influential neoclassical work. As a case study to close the survey and strengthen the point, this book offers a full, in-depth film/music analysis of *Raiders of the Lost Ark* (Steven Spielberg, 1981), a perfect example of Williams's neoclassicism. The part ends with an overview of Williams's conductorship of the Boston Pops Orchestra, a highly influential period in which Williams brought the classical film-music repertoire into the limelight. Finally, a few remarks are presented on the present-day Hollywood music and on what remains of Williams's neoclassical influence in the contemporary film-scoring practice.

This book is not written from a musicological perspective but from that of film studies. Nor does it give an exhaustive account of Williams's music output, covering all his scores and each period of his career. Although a few themes and motifs are analyzed musically, extensive music analysis is not at the core of this book. As the first English-language book on Williams, its aim is to present a micro-history within the larger Hollywood history, more than simply providing a musicological essay on Williams. It centers not so much on Williams the composer as on Williams the "restorer" of a part of Hollywood's classicism. There are many film composers who can be studied and appreciated for their fine musical achievements, and perhaps such studies can be undertaken more efficiently by musicologists. However, Williams is a unique figure for his competent retrieval and clever updating of a piece of Hollywood's history, and here the film historian can perhaps say more than the musicologist.

Focusing on the peak of the neoclassical trend, the analysis is deliberately narrowed to three films, considered the key historical moments and the most fitting examples to illustrate Williams's neoclassicism: *Jaws* (Steven Spielberg, 1975), *Star Wars: A New Hope*, and *Raiders of the Lost Ark*. There are many more films that can be listed in the neoclassical Williams canon, such as *Superman, 1941* (Steven Spielberg, 1979), *E.T. the Extra-Terrestrial* (Steven Spielberg, 1982), the other chapters of the *Star Wars* saga, and a few others. They all would deserve a similarly in-depth analysis, but here they are given only a brief overview. There is no need to analyze each Williams neoclassical score but instead to illustrate the historical account with a limited number of selected examples. For the same reason, Williams's scores that are not strictly neoclassical—for example, the piano-based *Accidental Tourist* (Lawrence Kasdan, 1988) and *Stanley & Iris* (Martin Ritt, 1989)—are mentioned only briefly in appendix 1. Each of the three aforementioned films is dealt with differently. *Jaws* is analyzed in search of the hidden hints of neoclassicism, that is, how many elements in the score and the use and placement of the music differ from the established practice and models of the film music of the 1970s. *Star Wars* is not given a musical analysis but is studied as an anomaly within the context of the late 1970s film music, so as to underline its unexpected success and unprecedented impact on the present and future of film music. Finally, *Raiders of the Lost Ark* has been chosen as an outstanding specimen of Williams's neoclassicism and is the object of a full "film/music analysis"—a detailed film analysis based on the description and explanation of how the score works in each scene and within the overall film's form.

This book is not meant to be the definitive "Williams bible," but it seeks to lay the first brick to fill a gap in film-music studies. The impact of John Williams's work on the history of film music—past and future—is too important not to be considered in a scholarly study.

Part I

The Classical
Hollywood
Music Style

Fine symphonic scores for motion pictures cannot help but influence mass acceptance of finer music. The cinema is a direct avenue to the ears and hearts of the great public and all musicians should see the screen as a musical opportunity.

Erich Wolfgang Korngold

1

"The Classical
Hollywood Music"

A Chronicle

Music
in the Silent Era

The regular presence of music as an accompaniment to film projections during cinema's infancy—between 1895 and 1905—is not certain.[1] At that stage, cinema was seen as a kind of carnival amusement, a low-brow draw based on "attractions" presented in simple single-shot tableaux running a few minutes.[2] Music, however, became an essential part of the film experience in the 1910s.

With the rise of nickelodeons—those urban storefront theaters specializing in film projections at popular prices, usually a nickel—from 1905 on, and then the spread of the posh picture palaces in the teens,[3] the duration of films increased and the phase of the "narrative integration" began.[4] In order to meet the burgeoning demand and to guarantee a longer life for the individual films, it was no longer sufficient to resort just to isolated antics, short vaudeville skits, inventive optical tricks, and scenics and topicals (short travelogues and prototypical newsreels). Cinema could no longer settle for and live on the novelty effect given by reproduction of moving images but had to rethink itself in terms of more structured products. Cinema needed to tell stories. The conversion to the narrative form was accompanied by the consolidation of the relationship between cinema and music.

Many explanations have been given to account for the reasons of this now-solid relationship between music and cinema, and good summaries are available.[5] Herein, one raison d'être will be privileged over the others: music's contribution to film narration. The attention and care for music in terms of thematic consistency and coherent integration with the film's narrative rose significantly when cinema turned from showing attractions to telling stories. Improvised, unwillingly comical, and incongruous forms of accompaniment such as those typical of the "cinema of attractions" were no longer tolerated. Practitioners now realized that a botched-up performance or an unsuitable musical accompaniment could be harmful to the film's reception and could radically modify the intended effects that the film was designed to have on the viewers.

In the 1910s there was a flourishing of articles that theorized and prescribed the manner in which music should be written and performed in order to serve the film in a proper way.[6] Ever since *The Birth of a Nation* (David Wark Griffith, 1915, music by Joseph Carl Breil)—considered to be the first case of an American score expressly compiled/composed to support the film's narration—music now proved to be able to connote the implicit meaning of the narrative.[7] In the case of *The Birth of a Nation*, this implicit meaning is the film's infamous racism: "Music lends insidious aid to emphasize the teaching of the screen, for the tom-tom beats from time to time to convince us that the colored man, well drest [*sic*] and educated though he may be, came from Africa."[8] Film music in the late silent era had already developed a number of techniques to become an integral tool of film narration.

Yet there was still a major problem: the arbitrariness of the live performance. The struggle of many critics and theorists for music that should be congruent with the film's narrative clashed with a technical issue: music could not be stably placed on the film strip as happened with the visuals, following the best possible standards and the producers' exact intent. The live performance was under the control of the individual exhibitors. Even if they had closely followed the list of music pieces—the so-called cue sheet—provided by distributors along with the exhibition prints, the actual performance would have varied significantly depending on the musical means available in each venue. Attending the screening of a film at the Roxy Theatre in New York with an orchestra of 110 players was quite different from attending the screening of the same film in a small-town, third-rate movie house. Here the same music would be played from a piano reduction on a perhaps out-of-tune upright piano by a perhaps drunk pianist. In short, from a musical point of view, a silent film was never the same from one venue to another.

Music
and the Coming of Sound

Sound technology was introduced with the aim of fixing the film's *musical* dimension, rather than of having characters talk. Alfred Hitchcock claimed that "the accompanying music came at last entirely under the control of the people who made the picture."[9] Now it was possible to bring the impeccable performance of a large orchestra, which one might have heard only in a luxurious picture palace, even to small provincial-circuit theaters. Therefore, in 1926 Warner Bros. could present its *Don Juan* (Alan Crosland, music by William Axt and David Mendoza) in every equipped theater with the flawless rendition of the New York Philharmonic Orchestra.[10]

In the early years of sound films, the use of non-diegetic music was not a widely accepted convention, although recent studies have shown evidence of a number of exceptions: *The Singing Fool* (Lloyd Bacon, 1928) has wallpaper music accompaniment under most dialogue scenes, and some early-thirties Ernst Lubitsch productions at Paramount, like *Montecarlo* (1930), have episodes of dialogue underscoring.[11] In most films non-diegetic music was rare, limited to the opening titles, to a couple of chords emphasizing the "The End" title, to bridging passages between two scenes, and to montage sequences. In the drama *Dishonored* (Joseph Von Sternberg, 1931), Marlene Dietrich plays an amateur pianist spy, X27, who manages to smuggle strategic information from the enemy by encoding it into musical notes. Her diegetic piano playing provides most of the musical parts of the film; there are even some unusually atonal pieces, which is what the codes would sound like if played. The only episode of non-diegetic music is a brief montage sequence summarizing some war actions. The final, dramatic scene of X27 facing the firing squad after being sentenced to death, has no music at all, which sounds rather strange to the ears of a present-day viewer. The same can be said of *Madam Satan* (Cecil B. DeMille, 1930), a comedy with only diegetic music, and *Anna Christie* (Clarence Brown, 1930), a drama that has virtually no music at all. The presence of music was mostly at the diegetic level: music had to seem to come from the narrative world and was synchronized with some kind of on-screen performance—a singer, an orchestra, a pianist—or had to be motivated realistically by showing or implying the presence of some kind of sound source such as a phonograph or a radio, hence the term "source music." For example, in a couple of scenes in the comedy *Indiscreet* (Leo McCarey, 1931), we see Gloria Swanson asking for some music; in the first scene her maid switches the autopiano on and in the second she herself turns on a radio set, so as to motivate realistically the musical background of the following action or dialogue.

Most directors—Von Sternberg being one of them—thought that non-diegetic music could be harmful to drama and realism. The composer Max Steiner provides an example of this "musical realism":

> But they [producers and directors] felt it was necessary to explain the music pictorially. For example, if they wanted music for a street scene, an organ grinder was shown. It was easy to use music in [a] nightclub, ballroom or theater scene, as here the orchestras played a necessary part in the picture. Many strange devices were used to introduce the music. For instance, a love scene might take place in the woods and in order to justify the music thought necessary to accompany it, a wandering violinist would be brought in for no reason at all. Or, again, a shepherd would be seen herding his sheep and playing his flute, to the accompaniment of a fifty-piece orchestra.[12]

How can this obsession with musical realism be explained? One clarification is of an aesthetic nature and connected with the new idea of cinema that derived from synchronized dialogue. In the silent era, the lack of words implied a more stylized conception of cinema as a kind of spiritual, paintlike art, a sort of visual symphony. Since reality in sound films could be reproduced with greater fidelity, the aesthetics of the medium slipped toward a greater realism, which obviously favored the dialogue over the artificial non-diegetic music.

Another motivation is of an economic nature. At first—in the years 1927–28—sound films were produced following the 1926 model of *Don Juan*. These films were basically silent with synchronized music tracks. Another famous example is *Sunrise* (Friedrich Wilhelm Murnau, 1927, music by Hugo Riesenfeld). After the huge box office success of *The Singing Fool* (1928, music by Louis Silvers et al.) and the first "all-talking" *Lights of New York* (Bryan Foy, 1928), it was clear that the novelty of synchronized sound was quite successful in attracting the audience, thus bringing in big profits. In such films as *Sunrise*, this innovation was less evident. Although music was indeed synchronized with the images from a technical point of view, from the audience perspective the innovation could hardly be noticed. The sound of the orchestra that once came out live from the orchestra pit now simply emerged through loudspeakers from a recorded support. At this point, the innovation could be better exploited if the synchronization process were explicitly displayed. This meant favoring dialogue, on-screen music numbers, and the diegetic use of music, visibly synchronized with an identifiable on-screen source. Consequently, Hollywood produced talkies having a realistic narrative and setting, like that in *Scarface* (Howard Hawks, 1932), a film with no music at all besides the diegetic whistling by Paul Muni/Tony Camonte. Another much exploited genre was the musical, where diegetic music prevailed, especially in the revue subgenre, which was made up of a string of musical numbers: famous examples are *The Hollywood Revue of 1929* (Charles Reisner, 1929, music by Nacio Herb Brown et al.) and *Paramount on Parade* (Dorothy Arzner et al., 1930, music by Howard Jackson).

The third factor that discouraged the use of non-diegetic music was a technical one: before 1932 sound editing and mixing were very difficult, and this could prevent the simultaneous presence of multiple audio tracks.[13] The result of this was the inability to blend music and dialogue in terms of acceptable sound quality. The technical limitations made feasible neither *postrecording* (later used to stage diegetic numbers in musicals) nor *dubbing* (later used to add non-diegetic music to the sound track).[14] In the earliest years of sound cinema, music was recorded during the filming at the same time as the dialogue. Music numbers had to be staged by shooting the action and simultaneously recording the orchestra and singers playing live on set. Having the orchestra and singers on set with actors, and having to handle the filming and recording of all the sound elements meant an increase in production costs and shooting time.[15] Because this process was so difficult, music was obviously used only when absolutely necessary and profitable, in other words, only in diegetic numbers, in which the innovation of synchronized sound could be patently shown off to attract the audience and offset the high costs.

The technical issues were solved in 1932, when sound editing and multi-track mixing became feasible. Non-diegetic music, called *background music*, could now find its place in the sound cinema. The economic reason disappeared in 1930, after the unexpected flop of musical films at the box office. The audience had had enough of all those songs and musical numbers that were partly a kind of revival of the primitive "cinema of attractions" rather than a narrative cinema. As a consequence, many producers decided to dismiss musicians and to reduce the production of musicals, with the intent of focusing on talkies without music.[16]

Max Steiner (1888–1971) had moved to Hollywood during the early years of sound films and was one of those composers in danger of being laid off. Eventually, though, he managed to invert the trend in Hollywood. His non-diegetic score for *Cimarron* (Wesley Ruggles, 1931) is quite short and covers only about 3 out of the 120 minutes of running time. According to the prevailing poetics, most of the music pieces are diegetic. In the last shot, however, "there is not diegetic justification for the orchestral music which swells the sound track transcending the film's diegetic boundary and spilling over into the final credits. The importance of Steiner's score for *Cimarron*, however, rests not only upon its transgression of the industry's priority on diegetic realism in a dramatic context (it was not the first or only film to do so), but also upon recognition within the industry of Steiner's departure from the accepted norm."[17]

The last obstacle to the emergence of the classical style—the poetics of musical realism—was removed by Steiner with four subsequent RKO films that finally convinced the producers on the effectiveness of non-diegetic music in a sound film. The first film was the drama *Symphony of Six Million* (Gregory La Cava, 1932), then came *The Most Dangerous Game* (Ernest B. Schoedsack, Irving Pichel, 1932) and *Bird of Paradise* (King Vidor, 1932), two very different dramas— the former being a dark thriller, the latter an exotic Polynesian melodrama— that strengthened Steiner's reputation and increased the producers' confidence in background music.[18] Finally, the film that completed the collapse of the musical realism poetics was *King Kong* (Merian C. Cooper and Ernest B. Schoedsack, 1933), for which Steiner, despite the slim musical budget, insisted on composing an original score, instead of using preexisting music pieces.[19]

King Kong is definitely a *non*-realistic film, and the most important function of Steiner's music is to give credibility to Kong, a fairly rudimentary stop-motion animated puppet. Without Steiner's score the audience could have derided the monster, instead of being scared at the beginning of the film and feeling pity for him at the end: "Here the music is required, perhaps for the first time in an American film, to explain to the audience what is actually happening on the screen, since the camera is unable to articulate Kong's instinctive feelings of tenderness towards his helpless victim."[20]

The Classical Hollywood Music:
The First Generation

For its historical and stylistic importance, *King Kong* can be identified as the inaugural film of the classical Hollywood music style. *King Kong* was also the first case to reveal a general trend in the use of film music: genres that are best at ease with music are the least realistic ones. Music is more easily placed in films about the past, distant places, fancy romances, and exotic adventures, where the narrative is more in need of music to suspend the disbelief of the audience and to ensure the formal cohesion of the film, all of which confirms what Jack Warner used to say: "Films are fantasy—and fantasy needs music."[21]

In the 1930s the genres where music is most present and often takes a leading role are "adventure films" like *Captain Blood* (Michael Curtiz, 1935, music by Erich Wolfgang Korngold); *The Charge of the Light Brigade* (Michael Curtiz, 1936, music by Max Steiner); *The Prisoner of Zenda* (John Cromwell, 1937, music by Alfred Newman); *Lost Horizon* (Frank Capra, 1937, music by Dimitri Tiomkin); *Beau Geste* (William A. Wellman, 1939, music by Alfred Newman); and *Captains Courageous* (Victor Fleming, 1937, music by Franz Waxman); "period dramas" like *The Private Lives of Elizabeth and Essex* (Michael Curtiz, 1939, music by Erich Wolfgang Korngold); *Gone with the Wind* (Victor Fleming, 1939, music by Max Steiner); and *Notre Dame* (William Dieterle, 1939, music by Alfred Newman); "melodramas" like *Stella Dallas* (King Vidor, 1937, music by Alfred Newman) and *Wuthering Heights* (William Wyler, 1939, music by Alfred Newman); "horror movies" like *The Bride of Frankenstein* (James Whale, 1935, music by Franz Waxman); *The Invisible Ray* (Lambert Hillyer, 1936, music by Franz Waxman); and *The Devil-Doll* (Tod Browning, 1936, music by Franz Waxman). If we think of the comedies of the 1930s, such as *Bringing Up Baby* (Howard Hawks, 1938); *Mr. Deeds Goes to Town* (Frank Capra, 1936); *Ninotchka* (Ernst Lubitsch, 1939, music by Werner R. Heymann); *His Girl Friday* (Howard Hawks, 1940); *The Awful Truth* (Leo McCarey, 1937, music by Ben Oakland); and *My Man Godfrey* (Gregory La Cava, 1936), we realize that they tell contemporary stories and the screenplays are strong enough to provide a formal cohesion: when music is present it has a minor role—mostly diegetic—and in many cases it is not present at all.

To grasp the difference between the previous realistic trend and new trend, compare *Frankenstein* (James Whale, 1931) with its sequel, *The Bride of Frankenstein* (1935). In the former—like in other horror films such as *Dracula* (Tod Browning, 1931); *Murders in the Rue Morgue* (Robert Florey, 1932); and *Island of the Lost Souls* (Erle C. Kenton, 1932)—music is present only in the opening and closing titles, while the monster's appearances or the suspenseful scenes have no music.[22] But in *The Bride of Frankenstein*, Waxman's score is fundamental in supporting the narration for the entire running time, with color effects, timbre inventions, and a network of musical motifs associated with the various characters. Only four years separate these two films, both directed by the same person. The difference, however, could not be more radical.

If 1933 can be seen as the year of the beginning of the classical Hollywood music, it is in 1935 that this style reached its maturity and a pervasive spread. Three films—all veritable milestones in film music history—attest to the strength of the classical style. The first one is *The Informer* (John Ford, 1935, music by Max Steiner), a drama about betrayal and remorse, and often singled out as the most extreme example of the classical close adhesion of music to visuals.[23] Another influential score is Waxman's for *The Bride of Frankenstein*, which set the basis for horror film music. The third is *Captain Blood*, with which Erich Wolfgang Korngold made his official debut as a Hollywood composer. Korngold did not only institutionalize the way a score for an adventure film should sound—late-romantic dialect, lush orchestration, prominent brass section—but brought to the task the sensitivity and mastery of an opera composer and the formal strength that lacked in Steiner's fragmentary idiom.

Classical Hollywood music style was now well grounded. Film studios formed music departments, according to the assembly-line logic that characterized the studio system. A musical director was in charge of the entire operation, facilities, and branches of the department, which included a musical archive, a legal department for contracts and copyright clearance, and a casting office to recruit singers and musicians. There were also singing staff and instrument instructors, and a technical team in charge of recording, editing, mixing, and dubbing. The artistic workforce included composers, orchestrators, arrangers, conductors, piano accompanists, copyists, proofreaders and an in-house symphony orchestra.[24] The composers were payrolled; they were given a fixed weekly salary, rather than being paid for each individual work, and they would not own the music they wrote, as it was the property of the studio that could use and reuse it without the author's consent. They had to do office hours, often supplemented by overtime to meet the short deadlines. In 1939 Steiner worked on eight films, including the mammoth score for *Gone with the Wind*, which alone contains three hours of music. Some of Hollywood's first generation of composers in the years from 1933 to 1945 were Franz Waxman (1906–67), Victor Young (1899–1956), Dimitri Tiomkin (1894–1979), Hugo Friedhofer (1901–81), and Alfred Newman (1901–70), the powerful and influential music director of 20th Century Fox.[25]

The young craft of film music attracted the suspicion and disdain of many art composers, but it also aroused the interest of others. Among the preeminent art composers who worked in Hollywood, we should mention Aaron Copland (1900–90), although he was only sporadically involved.[26] However, it is the Mitteleuropean art composer Korngold (1897–1957) who gave the most fundamental and lasting contribution to the classical style and deserves more space:[27]

> Korngold arrived in Hollywood in 1934 with a shining reputation.
> Hailed as a second Mozart, he had astounded the music world with his

concert works and his operas. As a teenage composer, pianist and conductor he had the most prominent composers of the day shaking their heads in disbelief. Richard Strauss said: "This firmness of style, this sovereignty of form, this individual expression, this harmonic structure—one shudders with awe to realise these compositions were written by a boy." When Korngold was ten, his father took him to Gustav Mahler for a critical judgment. The boy played from memory a dramatic cantata as Mahler walked up and down reading the score, his pace quickening with growing excitement. At the end he looked at the father and said, "A genius," and made suggestions for education. A few years later, with a pair of one-act Korngold operas playing all over Europe, Puccini remarked, "The boy has so much talent he could easily give us some and still have enough left for himself." That Strauss, Mahler and Puccini should feel this way about the music of Erich Korngold was not surprising because they were the three strongest influences upon it. An analysis of Korngold reveals a Straussian orchestral colour, a Mahlerian feeling, and the melodic concepts of Puccini, all of them somehow melded and dominated by a strong Viennese character—plus Korngold's own personality.[28]

The highly talented Korngold penned some of the best film scores in history, examples of how film music can be good *music for films* while also being good music per se: *Captain Blood*; *Anthony Adverse* (Mervyn Le Roy, 1936); *The Prince and The Pauper* (William Keighley, 1937); *The Adventures of Robin Hood*; *The Sea Hawk* (Michael Curtiz, 1940); and *Kings Row* (Sam Wood, 1942). Korngold's touch consisted in treating the film score as an opera score. Korngold would see a film as a libretto to be scored and applied to the film work the same energy, creativity, and expertise that he would devote to his art music. *The Sea Hawk* score has a true operatic presence, especially in the sequence where Captain Thorpe and his men unchain themselves from the oars and take possession of the galley, singing "Strike for the Shores of Dover." The ambush sequence in Sherwood Forest in *The Adventures of Robin Hood* is very much like a ballet. Korngold was able to compose highly functional music without necessarily following every turn of the action too closely, which would give the music a fragmentary form—typical of Steiner's music, for example. He showed, more than anyone else, how to compose scores that successfully served the film while maintaining full-bodied phrases and a proper overall musical solidity of form and development.

In the 1930s, Hollywood music took form and institutionalized its practices, soon becoming part of the classical Hollywood cinema paradigm and giving a seminal contribution to the formation of Hollywood's conventional image: glamour, positive feelings, and happy endings.

The Classical Hollywood Music: The Second Generation

In the 1940s the world situation changed, and a series of events affected the film industry as well. First, there had been World War II and its horrors, but there was also the rapidly changing sociocultural context: the Cold War instilling suspicion and fear in American society; the baby boomer generation reshaping demography and urbanization; the growing success of television creating a new competitive entertainment medium. Films increasingly began to feature more controversial, negative, and even unpleasant stories and characters. The rising genre of those years, which would become the symbol of the decade, was the *noir* film, characterized by existential malaise, moral ambiguity, and a creeping sense of disorientation. The low-key cinematography and menacing shadows inherited from German Expressionism—used in the previous decade for horror films—now trespassed on contemporary urban space. Its high-contrast *chiaroscuro*, dark spots, and slashes of violent light replaced the well-balanced middle tones of the soft-focus, high-key style previously used. *Découpage* and selective focus—signs of a narration that guided the viewer's attention and understanding around the pro-filmic space and the narrative's causal chain— were replaced with *plan-séquence* and deep-focus cinematography, which made the viewer's experience freer and more self-directed but also the orphan of a reliable narrational guide.[29]

This social uneasiness influenced film music too. The symptoms were a shift from the late-nineteenth-century romantic dialect to twentieth-century modernism, with a decrease of consonance, soothing melodies, and heroic fanfares giving way to a rise of angular melodies, unstable harmonies, and more grating dissonance. The main authors emerging during this period—the second generation—introduced into film music some dialectal traits of the twentieth century, and updated the style of the previous decade in outstanding films like *Citizen Kane* (Orson Welles, 1941); *Double Indemnity* (Billy Wilder, 1944); *Laura* (Otto Preminger, 1944); and *The Lost Weekend* (Billy Wilder, 1946).

The most influential composer of this second generation was Bernard Herrmann (1911–75). He made his film debut at the age of twenty-nine with his groundbreaking score for *Citizen Kane*. In Welles's film, musical ideas are linked to concepts or characters—Xanadu, Death, the Chronicle—but they can hardly be defined as themes; they are rather shorter fragments or motifs and they lack the typical "hummable quality" of romantic melodies. The motivic writing is Herrmann's most prominent trademark. Think of the scores for *North by Northwest* (Alfred Hitchcock, 1959) and *Psycho* (Alfred Hitchcock, 1960) to notice how they are based on the repetition and variation of brief recurring and obsessive motifs. The famous *Psycho* prelude is built on the alternation of a major-seventh chord (which Royal S. Brown calls the "Hitchcock chord"[30]) with a two-bar "hysterical" fragment for violins and a longer melodic line that does not resolve to anything and has no final destination.[31] Everything sounds almost juxtaposed, without melodic or harmonic development, often floating in a tonal uncertainty. In *North by Northwest*, the main motif of the film is not even a melodic fragment but just a rhythmic *fandango* figure, reprised in different orchestral thicknesses and colors. Another characteristic of Herrmann's idiom is indeed his mastery in the use of expressive and evocative orchestral colors. The rapid pace of film editing and the fast shifts from one atmosphere and tone to another make it difficult to use the traditional harmonic and melodic development techniques, because they require a longer time to unfold properly. Herrmann then opted for "coloristic development": he responded to these fast cinematic transitions by modifying the orchestration in order to obtain fast music reactions. Because of this approach, Herrmann's music comes with an innovative orchestral color palette. *Citizen Kane* opens with unusually turbid bass writing—bassoons, contrabassoons, bass clarinets, alto flute, vibes—with no clearly distinguishable melody but rather a slowly creeping movement. Another recurring Herrmann trait is the use of classical forms and dances, more as rhythmic patterns than full-bodied forms. Besides the already mentioned fandango, we can find a habanera—actually, the rhythmic pattern of a habanera—as Carlotta's motif in *Vertigo* (Alfred Hitchcock, 1958). The *Citizen Kane* score is almost a suite of dances and traditional forms: "Hornpipe Polka," "Scherzo," "Waltz," "Gallop," a kind of *Grand Opéra* aria specifically composed for the scene of Mrs. Kane's debut—"Salaambo's Aria"—and a "Theme and Variations" as a sarcastic accompaniment to the montage where we see the gradual deterioration of the relationship between Kane and his first wife. Another example of a suite-like score is *The Three Worlds of Gulliver* (Jack Sher, 1960), which contains an overture, a minuet, and several marches in the eighteenth-century dialect, as well as a love theme that uses the modal dialect of old English folksongs.

Miklós Rózsa (1907–95) was an art composer with parallel careers in film and concert music.[32] Born in Hungary, Rózsa was influenced by the popular forms of his land, gypsy and Magyar songs, much like his countryman Béla Bartók. His idiom is chromatic and characterized by a rhythmic incisiveness, metrical irregularities, and dissonant harmonies. In Hollywood, Rózsa's name became associated with two large trends. In the 1940s, after *Double Indemnity*, he worked mostly for films dealing with crime, self-destruction, and madness: *The Lost Weekend, Spellbound* (Alfred Hitchcock, 1945); *The Strange Love of Martha Ivers* (Lewis Milestone, 1946); *The Red House* (Daves Dalmer, 1947); *Secret Beyond the Door* (Fritz Lang, 1948); and *The Asphalt Jungle* (John Huston, 1950). Rózsa's dissonant, harsh music was ideal for the new problematic topics of postwar cinema. He was the first composer to use the theremin in Hollywood; this electro-acoustic instrument was the ancestor, along with the Ondes Martenot, of modern synthesizers.[33] Its ethereal, trembling, and eerie sound was extremely effective in conveying the characters' mental disorientation and moral disorder. In the following decade, Rózsa changed hats and became the undisputed master of biblical-historical colossals like *Quo Vadis* (Mervyn Le Roy, 1950); *Ivanhoe* (Richard Thorpe, 1952); *Plymouth Adventure* (Clarence Brown, 1952); *Julius Caesar* (Joseph L. Mankiewicz, 1952); *Knights of the Round Table* (Richard Thorpe, 1953); *Ben-Hur* (William Wyler, 1959); *King of Kings* (Nicholas Ray, 1961); *El Cid* (Anthony Mann, 1961); and *Sodom and Gomorrah* (Robert Aldrich, 1962). In preparation for these films, Rózsa would research the music of the period in order to reach a sort of philological accurateness, employing archaic modal harmonies and ancient-sounding instrumentation.

David Raksin (1912–2004), after years of hard work at 20th Century Fox, won visibility in 1944 with his score for *Laura*, whose unforgettable theme soon turned into a successful popular song. This melody is interesting not just for the harmonic complexity when compared with coeval songs but also because it is the only theme present in the film. Indeed, this is one of the earliest examples of a "monothematic" score. In Preminger's film, everybody is obsessed or in love with Laura, a "ghost-woman" whose haunting presence is aptly represented by this obsessive melody. "Laura's Theme" is everywhere and appears throughout the film alternately shifting from the diegetic level to the non-diegetic, floating through the "walls" of the various narrative levels, just like a ghost would do. The theme becomes Laura's musical substitute. The dead woman cannot be seen, but her presence floats constantly in the air as her music theme does. Raksin's idiom is refined and harmonically sophisticated; his writing is more complex than the Hollywood standards, with a penchant for the variation and development of the musical material. Moreover, the *Laura* music track contains an occurrence of electronically distorted piano—a rare instance in the classical period—to depict the male protagonist disturbingly falling in love with the late Laura.[34]

Stylistic Changes and the End of an Era

In the 1950s, Hollywood entered a period of crisis. In order to differentiate their products from those of television, film companies resorted insistently to technological innovations with great spectacular impact. The idea was to lure moviegoers into theaters with the promise of big shows that could not be seen, or properly appreciated, on the small screen of the TV sets. Such gimmicks consisted of various types of wide-screen format (Cinerama, Cinemascope, Todd-AO, Vistavision);[35] stereophonic sound (with the introduction of the magnetic sound recording);[36] color cinematography (the swan song of the tripack Technicolor process before being overpowered by EastmanColor in the following decade);[37] and short-lived technical curiosities: 3D, as in *Dial M for Murder* (Alfred Hitchcock, 1954), or the bizarre "Percepto."[38] This particular gadget—a sign of how Hollywood producers were badly in need of bringing people back to theaters—consisted of electrical buzzers attached to the underside of the seats that would vibrate to increase the startle of the audience during a sudden horror shot.[39] Percepto was used, for example, in *The Tingler* (William Castle, 1959). In this kind of film, music would not deviate significantly from the dialect of the previous decade.

A genre that took on great importance in this period was the musical, consistent with Hollywood's concentration on spectacular films. For its rich music, charming songs, lush set design, and spectacular pieces of choreography, the musical became one of the decade's most popular genres, especially in the "Arthur Freed Unit" output at MGM, from *An American in Paris* (Vincente Minnelli, 1951); *Singin' in the Rain* (Stanley Donen, Gene Kelly, 1952); *Seven Brides for Seven Brothers* (Stanley Donen, 1956); to *Gigi* (Vincente Minnelli, 1958). In musicals, songs were foregrounded and presented in musical numbers at diegetic level, while film music sensu stricto—background non-diegetic music—had a secondary role. Nonetheless, we should mention some arrangers and orchestrators working in musical films whose contributions have left an indelible mark: Conrad Salinger, Saul Chaplin, Adolph Deutsch, Alexander "Sandy" Courage, and Johnny Green, music director at MGM in that decade.

The main musical innovations of the 1950s can be found in the least spectacular films, that is, in realistic dramas dealing with contemporary life. Such innovations, which were not just incorporations of other dialects but had started to affect the overall style and were thus the first signs of the forthcoming "modern style" of the 1960s, were the introduction of jazz, atonality, and even twelve-tone music.

Jazz, in its various forms and subclasses, had been used up to this time as diegetic music, to give a negative connotation to criminal characters or disreputable clubs. For example, think of the "Drum Boogie" musical number sung and danced by Barbara Stanwyck, the gangster's moll, in *Ball of Fire* (Howard Hawks, 1941), or "dirty" jazz to characterize the vice and immorality of the slimy jazz drummer played by Elisha Cook Jr. in *Phantom Lady* (Robert Siodmak, 1944). Jazz was also associated with African Americans as a race connotation as in *King of Jazz* (John Murray Anderson, 1930); *Hellzapoppin* (Henry C. Potter, 1941); *Cabin in the Sky* (Vincente Minnelli, 1943); and *High Society* (Charles Walters, 1956). In some 1950s films, jazz was used for the first time even at the non-diegetic level, losing the racial connotation but sometimes keeping the criminal one. Alex North (1910–91) applied the jazz dialect to a symphonic score in *A Streetcar Named Desire* (Elia Kazan, 1951). North's carnal music is the perfect aural complement of New Orleans's torrid setting where the sordid story of Blanche, Stella, and Stanley takes place.[40]

Leonard Rosenman (1924–2008) ushered in the twelve-tone dialect in Hollywood in *The Cobweb* (Vincente Minnelli, 1955). This choice, however, can hardly be seen as the advent of the "new music" in cinema—replacing the old late-romantic music—as advocated by Theodor W. Adorno and Hanns Eisler in *Composing for the Films*.[41] Rather, the twelve-tone dialect entered the classical style because it was appropriate for narrative reasons. *The Cobweb* is set in a psychiatric hospital, and twelve-tone music was the musical equivalent of madness as opposed to tonal music, which in turn corresponded to normality, in the Hollywood framework. Similarly, Rózsa wrote the only twelve-tone piece of music of his entire career for Satan's appearance in *King of Kings*; it was "perverse" music for a perverse creature, and this seemed to be the equation in Hollywood.[42] The use of jazz in *A Streetcar Named Desire* and twelve-tone music in *The Cobweb* was not a straight revolution but merely the acquisition of new dialectal tools and their integration into the paradigm, in order to better respond to new expressive needs.

Elmer Bernstein (1922–2004) brought in a more substantial innovation. With the music for *The Man with the Golden Arm* (Otto Preminger, 1955), he did not just adopt the jazz dialect as North had done but also recorded the score with the drummer Shelly Manne and a jazz combo, instead of the traditional symphony orchestra. This choice prefigured the modern style of the next decade and put the score outside the classical style.

As to negative connotations, the usual association of jazz with the criminal underworld, for example in *The Man with the Golden Arm*, a story about drug addiction, is abandoned in *Anatomy of a Murder* (Otto Preminger, 1959), whose music was composed by Duke Ellington, also appearing in a cameo role. Here, jazz music is finally no longer associated necessarily with outlaws but with a lawyer—Paul Biegler, played by James Stewart—an amateur pianist who loves that music.

As for other genres, the change of dialect in the music for Westerns must be mentioned. This type of music used to be based on folk inflections and quotes contained in the otherwise classical Hollywood late-romantic symphonic dialect. At most, the dialect was colored with some threatening modal topics conventionally used as "Indian music"—as in Max Steiner's score for *The Searchers* (John Ford, 1956).[43] Examples of folk influences are the ballad "Do Not Forsake Me, Oh My Darling" written by Tiomkin and Ned Washington for *High Noon*, or the *degüello*, a slow Mexican figuration for trumpet announcing the imminent battle, which is heard before the arrival of Burdette's gang in *Rio Bravo* (Howard Hawks, 1959) and is also used in *The Alamo* (John Wayne, 1960). Dimitri Tiomkin, a Russian native influenced by Rachmaninov, became the most important composer of Western genre music in classical Hollywood. Between this "Russian" period and Ennio Morricone's revolutionary approach—which overthrew all the Western stereotypes by bringing in elements of rock, archaic modalism, and onomatopoeic sounds before becoming itself a stereotype—a dialectal innovation took place in Hollywood. Jerome Moross (1913–83), an art composer of ballets, symphonic, and chamber music, and Aaron Copland's collaborator, brought Copland's twentieth-century idiom—a kind of pandiatonic neoclassicism that retrieves the oldest American musical heritage and its modal harmony—into the Western genre. This way, Moross proposed a tonal dialect that was authentically American and far from both the turgid old late-romanticism and from the "perverse" twelve-tone music. With Moross's *The Big Country* (William Wyler, 1958) the American genre par excellence found a congenial, truly American music. The modal harmonization, pentatonic melodies, syncopated rhythms, and bright orchestral sound of *The Big Country* was and still is a model, distinguishing the tradition-oriented Westerns—*The Magnificent Seven* (John Sturges, 1960, music by Elmer Bernstein); *The Cowboys* (Mark Rydell, 1972, music by John Williams); and *Silverado* (Lawrence Kasdan, 1985, music by Bruce Broughton)—from revisionist or postclassical Westerns like *The Wild Bunch* (Sam Peckinpah, 1969, music by Jerry Fielding), whose model is Morricone.

The studio system, which had been suffering an income crisis since the 1950s, fell apart in the 1960s. Film companies were being acquired by big corporations for which film production was just one of the many interests and business lines. Hollywood studios had to reduce in size; RKO no longer existed, having already been wound up in 1956, and many studios turned to what can be called survival strategies, if compared to the exuberant expansion strategies of the Golden Age. The last efforts to bring the masses back into film theaters, in particular the technological gimmickry and spectacular colossals and musicals of the 1950s, did not produce the desired effects. Hollywood was no longer the "dream factory," because of a number of factors, the most notable of which was the spread of television.[44]

The crisis also affected the music departments, which were severely reduced or closed down altogether. In 1958 a strike by the American Federation of Musicians (AFM), aiming at renegotiating the contracts between the musicians and the film industry, paralyzed Hollywood's music. The score for *Vertigo* was recorded in London, not conducted by Herrmann but by local specialist Muir Mathieson.[45] Eventually, the new contract was not signed with AFM but with a new union, the Musicians Guild of America (MGA). "Under the old pact with the AFM, the major studios had no choice but to hire 'contract orchestras.' . . . The new agreement with the MGA provided musicians with higher pay, but the pay was now determined by 'variable wage rates according to the number of musicians called for every three-hour recording session. . . . Certain musicians indeed stood to gain considerably from the MGA agreement. But the studios gained as well, for they no longer had to engage—or at least, pay for, whether they used it or not—a full orchestra for every recording session.'"[46]

As Hugo Friedhofer recalls, "All of the big studios had big orchestras under contract. And they had to utilize them. So the composer was forced to write more expansively and extensively than he might have liked."[47] From a stylistic point of view, this contractual renegotiation caused the progressive discarding of the symphony orchestra as the preferred musical means for film music. Smaller, less costly instrumental ensembles, which were closer to the musical tastes of the moment and indeed more trendy, won favor with film producers, a tendency anticipated by Bernstein with *The Man with the Golden Arm*.

The composer who guided Hollywood music from the classical to the modern style was Henry Mancini, who can be considered one of the leading representatives of the new style. Having grown up professionally in the music department of Universal Pictures, Mancini was perhaps the first person to perceive the new tide and to contribute to this change with his own work. He was very clever in integrating in his scores commercially successful songs like "Moon River" (lyrics by Johnny Mercer) in *Breakfast at Tiffany's* (Blake Edward, 1961), balancing the formal functions of the classical style with the trendy commercial appeal that music was supposed to have now.

As the classical style began to emerge before 1933 and reached its maturity later in 1935, similarly classical-style film music can still be heard after 1958, in films like *How the West Was Won* (John Ford et al., 1962, music by Alfred Newman); *Lawrence of Arabia* (David Lean, 1962, music by Maurice Jarre); and *Ben-Hur* (William Wyler, 1959, music by Miklós Rózsa). Classical-style film music became definitively obsolete only in the mid-1960s. However, 1958 was the year that marked the official suppression of the standard studio orchestras, and that date seems to be the most appropriate to mark the end of film music's classical style, which for the past twenty-five years had been strongly associated with those very orchestras.

2

"The Classical
Hollywood Music"

A Stylistic Definition

hat exactly is the "Classical Hollywood Music"? How can we distinguish a classical Hollywood score from, say, a coeval Italian score?
To answer the first question, we have to detect the typical characteristics that
define the "Classical Hollywood Music." In short, we have to define its style. To
give a definition as articulate as possible, film-music style should be subdivided
into four areas: *language, techniques, musical means,* and typical *formal functions.*

Language

In chapter 1 we saw the linguistic changes of the classical Hollywood music
throughout its history. Besides influences, updates, and the composers' idiomatic
differences, Hollywood music language is basically *tonal* and *romantic.* In particular, the model is the late-romantic art music bridging the nineteenth and the
twentieth centuries, the most prominent names being Richard Wagner, Richard
Strauss, Gustav Mahler, Giacomo Puccini, Pyotr Tchaikovsky, and Sergei
Rachmaninov. Linguistically, in the 1930s, Hollywood music was already old—
drawing from a dialect that was already considered outdated and "conservative."
The avant-garde twentieth-century music—atonality, polytonality, twelve-tone

music, and the like—was at first completely ignored and then integrated only partially and mostly for specific narrative reasons.

Why did Hollywood choose an old-fashioned dialect, rather than a contemporary one? T. W. Adorno and Hanns Eisler advocated the use of a twentieth-century modernist dialect because, as they explained, it was more flexible and responded better to the speed and fragmentation of film editing compared to the long melodies of the romantic tonal dialect.[1] Although that might be true, there were several reasons for opting for an outmoded dialect, some of which can be easily guessed.

For example, the producers, those who paid for the music, were notoriously uncultured musically—and not only musically. Testimonies on this point abound: "A motion picture producer is a man who knows everything there is to know about everything—except music."[2] Consequently, they preferred the dialect with which they were familiar, namely the accessible romantic tonal dialect as popularized by musical theater and popular songs. For the same reason, it is easy to see how products like Hollywood films—aiming at reaching as wide an audience as possible—obviously tended to use well-known "easy" formulas, familiar to the vast majority of viewers. Instinctively, those who were in charge of film production used themselves and their own tastes as a model of the average viewer.

Even more, the conservatism of the Hollywood music departments relied on the very musical education of the founding fathers of the craft, as Christopher Palmer explains:

> [T]he main conservatory-bred composers like Miklós Rózsa, Erich Wolfgang Korngold and Bernard Herrmann were the exception rather than the rule: musical theatre was the cradle of Hollywood music, and the musical idiom of the theatre has always been conservative. Hence the fact that in Hollywood's formative years there grew up a deeply-entrenched conservatism which jealously guarded its prerogatives and was quick to suppress any "progressive" or "modernistic" tendencies among juniors or novices. . . . This musical isolationism was wholly typical: the "real" world would have decried the music of Korngold, Newman and Steiner as anachronistic and refused it a place, whereas the "fantasy-world" of Hollywood not only wanted it but encouraged its procreation in vast quantities. "Romantic" music, music of romance, of fantasy, dream, illusion: what more logical than that it should find a final refuge in the real world's dream-factory?[3]

This quotation suggests two additional explanations for the choice of romantic dialect: (1) the adoption of well-tested tools of nineteenth-century music theater—the leitmotiv being the most prominent—and (2) the "illusionistic" complicity that music was expected to have in the Hollywood "dream-factory." This illusionistic complicity is what we call "macro-emotive function." Music helps viewers enter the film's "possible world" and facilitates the "suspension of disbelief" necessary to accept the narrative conventions.

Another explanation of why the classical Hollywood music favored the romantic dialect has been given in terms of ideology and psychoanalysis. Caryl Flinn explains Hollywood's adoption of the romantic dialect music on the grounds of an asserted utopian and nostalgic nature of romantic music.[4] This "out-dated" music has a soothing effect on listeners since it evokes a "romantic" past, happier times in which people (supposedly) lived a simpler life in more cohesive communities, as opposed to the fragmentation, individualism, and complexity of contemporary society.[5] On the other hand, Flinn also explains the nostalgia effect in psychoanalytic terms. The hummable nature of romantic music with which film viewers are flooded allegedly makes it possible for them to recover the "lost maternal object" in a sort of pleasant regression. Romantic music nostalgically reenacts the fusion with the mother's womb where the fetus lives in a sort of sound envelope. Before seeing, the fetus can already hear his mother's voice, a hearing that is not yet semantic, but musical.[6]

The orchestra conductor and film-music specialist John Mauceri reflects on nostalgia and Hollywood music in historical terms. He sees Hollywood and its musical community as a sort of protected oasis in which romantic dialect and its performance practices were preserved:

> There is a real dynasty, a tradition that continues, and the tradition is based on a European tradition untouched by the horrors of the bombings of World War II. In fact, it [Hollywood] was the beneficiary of the people who escaped the war. The great European tradition came to Hollywood like that—suddenly. . . . Something horrible happened [in Europe] but something very good happened here to balance it. . . . I love working in Los Angeles. . . . There is a tremendous cultural tradition. . . . They [Hollywood musicians] sound more like the Vienna Philharmonic before the war than the Vienna Philharmonic today. People at the Vienna Philharmonic are people who have grown up after the war with all the changes of culture and style. In Europe, it became very wrong to play long notes, to play with vibrato, to play portamento, because this was considered emotional and maybe without

taste. European orchestras are much colder now. Boulez and Stock-hausen were just symptomatic of a change toward music. They played more schematic performances of Brahms; it is really inexcusable to take the emotion out of the music and to play a post–World War II twentieth-century style. Whereas in Hollywood one continues the great instrumental traditions of Europe because their homes were not bombed, they did not have to go into air-raid shelters, their children were not screaming in the night.[7]

Timothy E. Scheurer—from a semio-anthropological perspective—sees in Hollywood music, in its formulaic romanticism and its many clichés, conventional gestures and topics, a musical equivalent of those recurring elements that make Hollywood genres—also based on formulas and clichés—a form of popular myth.[8]

Perhaps more convincingly, a formal/functional explanation of Hollywood's tendency to use the romantic dialect lies in the narrative form of Hollywood films themselves. In the classical Hollywood cinema, the primary purpose was to tell a story. Consequently, filmmakers had to make sure that viewers were able to easily reach an empathetic connection with the characters, and to follow and understand the narrative in the simplest way possible. "Invisible editing," "invisible storytelling," "unobtrusive style" are some terms recurrently associated with the classical Hollywood cinema, where a well-constructed narrative is more important than the display of originality and personal style. Indeed, the narrative form is based on strong and proven formulas and norms: the "stair-step construction" that alternates propulsive and delaying narrative events; the "canonic story" that replicates the outline of the hero's journey typical of fairy tales; well-shaped characters who undertake well-motivated actions to achieve their well-defined goals; clearly specified deadlines; "closure effect" given by the closing of all the story lines and their channeling to the happy ending; neo-classical criteria of unity of time, space, and action linked by a strong causality.[9] The storytelling is foregrounded, while the stylistic level tends to become invisible because it works in the background. Devices should not draw attention to themselves as technical processes: for example, a camera movement or an editing match must not be gratuitous but should respond to a narrative function and have a proper motivation. Likewise, music should cooperate to the narrative without drawing attention to itself.

The criterion of "inaudibility" is somewhat valid for all film-music styles, meaning that film music is generally subordinated to the visuals. This is particularly true with regard to the classical Hollywood style. For instance, it is evident how Ennio Morricone's music in a Sergio Leone Western is decidedly more obtrusive than Dimitri Tiomkin's in a Howard Hawks Western. Both composers and scholars have widely commented on the paradox of a kind of music that is supposed to be composed in such a way that it be almost inaudible,[10] and have rejected the idea that not being audible means not being useful or valuable.[11]

In Claudia Gorbman's *Unheard Melodies: Narrative Film Music*, "inaudibility" is the starting point to explain the role of film music, again from a psychoanalytic perspective. Gorbman equates film music with "Muzak," the background music aired in elevators and supermarkets. The function of Muzak (rebranded since 2013 as Mood) is to soothe the consumers—in our case, the viewers—and to make them less problematic social elements: if they think less, they are supposed to buy more, either the goods in a supermarket or the story events in a film theater. Like Muzak/Mood in supermarkets and airports, film music is not intended to be listened to but is intended to make viewers less critical and to lubricate the cogs of the fictional machine. Music hides the technical "cinematic apparatus," makes it easier to accept the fictional world, unites all viewers in a homogeneous listening community.[12]

Cognitive psychology, unlike psychoanalysis, presupposes an active viewer who constructs the meaning of the film rather than passively receiving it;[13] then, the inaudibility phenomenon is explained within the "Congruence-Associationist" framework, on the grounds of music's two components: the acoustical and the affective. In Annabel J. Cohen's words:

> While music in the film serves as a vehicle used to transport emotional meaning, it is a vehicle that is often "inaudible" . . . , much as the font of this page is transparent until I draw attention to it. We can discriminate between Courier and Galliard, but when reading, we don't really much care whether it is one or the other, as long as it is legible. Similarly, the viewer-listener accepts the musical meaning, but acoustical properties of the music itself seem to function transparently as a kind of "acoustical font." . . . In this analogy, we can consider music to have two components: an affective component and an acoustical, structural component. When these two components of music are presented simultaneously with a visual image, the conjunction of the affective element and the visual image makes a new meaningful whole, a whole much closer to our sense of reality than the visual image alone, or than the visual image conjoined with both the affective and acoustical components. Through the illusory conjunction process, the affect, originally carried via the acoustic properties of music, attaches to the visual

stimulus. . . . [M]usic is a vehicle transporting a variety of information, only some of which is relevant to a particular cinematic goal. The brain seems to be able to select what is useful for the goal at hand. . . . This framework explains the puzzling and paradoxical role of background music in film. Music adds information that is both consistent and inconsistent with the narrative. The affective quality is consistent; the acoustical aspects of the music are not. Although the affective associations produced by the music seem to belong to the corresponding images, the sounds that produced those associations do not. Somehow, the brain attends to this affective meaning, while ignoring or attenuating its acoustical source.[14]

This is why film music is inaudible: the acoustical/structural component—the one on which we generally focus our attention during a concert—becomes secondary in the audiovisual film experience, because our attention is focused on something else. Moreover, it is not just a matter of attention but also of two different cognitive processes located in different brain areas. For example, think of music underscoring a dialogue: Why is it "inaudible"? In the common right-handed nonmusician viewer, the left hemisphere, which processes analytically the structural component of sound stimuli, processes the meaning of the dialogue. On the other hand, music is passed to the right hemisphere, which is specialized in processing holistically the affective/emotional component.[15] In a dialogue scene, the average viewer's attention is focused on the analytical process of the verbal component of the sound track—dialogue—while the musical component passes through holistic processes, that is, it is perceived in its affective component and thus music is "inaudible." When the structural component is too obtrusive—for example, in film music with very elaborate counterpoint—the left hemisphere and the analytical process are also involved in the listening, which may draw the viewers' attention away from the dialogue or the narrative understanding. In case the listener/viewer is a musician, his knowledge of the syntactical/structural aspects of music causes the involvement of both hemispheres and therefore music can become not only audible but may even disturb the dialogue understanding in particularly musically receptive people. In the classical Hollywood cinema the viewer's attention and his analytical-sequential processes are focused on the unfolding of the narrative, and all the stylistic devices, including music, become unnoticeable. The average viewer does not notice the nature or even the presence of music as he does not notice either the number of cuts and kinds of editing matches in a scene, or the lighting pattern in a shot.

Hollywood's vocation for storytelling also explains why the tonal system is preferred to atonality. The tonal system, besides being based on universally shared intervals as the fifth and the octave, has a strong narrative nature.[16] In its moving to and from the tonic, it tells the story of a back-to-home journey across obstacles (dissonances), the clearing of such obstacles (resolution of the dissonances), and the final return to the home starting point (the return to the tonic, often with a IV–V–I authentic cadence, a sort of musical happy ending). This journey is exactly the archetypal journey narrated by Hollywood films.[17] Because of the widespread familiarity of its dialect, romantic music could better act as a neutral vehicle of the affective component and thus was the best choice to fit the functional transparency that cinematic devices were required to have. On the contrary, avant-garde music, with its esoteric dialect, can hardly be perceived as neutral and would draw the listener's attention to its structural component. That is why—pace Adorno and Eisler—modernist music had almost no use in the classical Hollywood cinema.

According to the musicologist Leonard B. Meyer, the universal appeal of romantic music is due to the importance given more to secondary parameters, such as dynamics, agogics, and expression rather than to primary parameters, which include overall form, harmony rules, syntactic relations between tones, and so forth.[18] Primary and secondary parameters are similar to the structural/affective distinction previously made. In romantic music, the affective component has a greater importance than the structural one. The classical dialect, as in the music of Mozart and Haydn, is also based on melody and tonality, but the primary parameters are more important than the secondary ones and are less suited to convey the affective/emotional component. However, according to Meyer, the modernist dialects inflate the secondary parameters to an extreme, to the detriment of the primary parameters that tend to lose any importance.[19] For instance, in aleatoric music such as that of John Cage there are only secondary parameters. In romantic music, primary parameters are still there to guide the musical understanding. In modernist music, on the contrary, the common listener has no guide to follow; the piece of music sounds simply meaningless and emotionally neutral to him, when not causing anxiety because of the frustration of expectations and the total lack of some kind of conventional orientation signs.[20] For this reason, unresolved dissonances and atonal writing are accepted in Hollywood when they can give their disorienting and distressing contribution to disturbing stories, creepy characters, and ominous places.

Another characteristic of the classical Hollywood music and of film music in general, apart from some modern instances such as Kubrick's films, is the almost exclusive use of original material instead of repertoire pieces, unlike the music compilations of silent cinema. The reasons are both economic and narrative. The economic reason can be easily explained: it was more affordable using original music—whose copyrights were owned by the studio—rather than undertaking the costly and often intricate legal paperwork required to secure the clearance for a copyrighted piece of music.[21] From a narrative viewpoint, a famous repertoire piece such as Beethoven's Symphony no. 6, op. 68 (the *Pastoral* Symphony) or any easily recognizable piece is likely to distract from the storytelling. If the viewer recognizes the piece, his attention can be drawn away from the visuals and the accompanying affective component of the music. In this case, the listener knows the piece; its general structure is present to his memory and can be retrieved, inducing him to follow the music flow, to anticipate its development, to focus on its structure. When hearing this music in a scene, the viewer would probably disconnect from the narrative and be led to metatextual considerations such as "Ah! They are using the 'Pastoral.' I wonder why they have chosen it," not to mention the connotations and extratextual associations that each famous repertoire piece carries along with it. In a hypothetical film where the Pastoral were used as a background for an amiable party conversation in a trendy Manhattan flat, the viewer might project the piece's traditional associations with shepherds and rural scenes on the visuals, and judge the music to be out of place.[22]

According to the Hollywood conventions, the use of repertoire music should have some kind of clear motivation. For example, in *People Will Talk* (Joseph L. Mankiewicz, 1951, musical direction by Alfred Newman), Cary Grant plays a professor who is also the conductor of the faculty's amateur orchestra. They are shown rehearsing, quite appropriately, Brahms's *Academic Festival Overture* (*Akademische Festouvertüre*, 1880, op. 80.) The film score presents Brahms's theme even at non-diegetic level, which is motivated both by the congruence of the piece with the academic locale and because this piece is also present within the narrative world. One of the most common uses of repertoire music, and a Max Steiner trademark, is that of using it to clarify in which geographical place or historical period the film is set. Think of Steiner's use of the Southern folk tune "Dixie" in *Gone with the Wind* (Victor Fleming, 1939), or "London Bridge Is Falling Down" in the opening sequence of *Top Hat* (Mark Sandrich, 1935), to denote the British austerity of the "London Thackeray Club, Founded 1864."

Techniques

In general, film music does not use the classical art-music forms of sonata, fugue, and the like. They are structurally too rigid, and their development requires too long a time and too foregrounded a position for the film's standards. Apparently with no form, film music actually has its own form in the film itself.[23] If film music cannot be said to have forms *sensu stricto*, it surely can be said to use structural techniques and formal strategies, the most widely used being *theme and variations*, *leitmotiv*, so-called *Mickey-Mousing*, and *dialogue underscoring*.

The *theme and variations* technique is borrowed from art music—it consists in presenting a theme, which will be later reprised and transformed in terms of rhythm, harmony, melodic shape, instrumentation, and so forth.[24] While theme and variations can be found in many styles of film music, two other techniques are characteristic of the classical Hollywood style: leitmotiv and Mickey-Mousing.

Leitmotiv—coined for Richard Wagner's *Wort-Ton-Dramas*—is the association and identification of each character, situation, or idea with a musical motif, which is reprised and developed narratively throughout the work. Probably also because of the founding fathers' familiarity with Wagnerian music, the leitmotiv was largely adopted in Hollywood. It is a very good fit for film narration, because it is an efficient aid to memorize and recognize characters and situations, it reinforces the film narrative through a parallel musical storytelling, and gives the overall score a coat of cohesion and formal coherence.

The other typical technique is *Mickey-Mousing*. In the American cinema, it seems to have been inherited from the musical accompaniment used in vaudeville, where the actors' antics and tumbles used to be stressed and punctuated by snare drum rolls and cymbal clashes.[25] Musically, Mickey-Mousing is completely informal and designed to adhere tightly to the visuals, and can be defined as a tight series of explicit synch-points. An explicit synch-point is that moment where a musical gesture and a visual action undoubtedly match, the composer having deliberately composed with that precise synch-point in mind. A typical example is a descending movement in the visuals mirrored by a descending gesture in the music, like someone falling down the stairs accompanied by a rapidly descending violins scale. As the term itself suggests, Mickey-Mousing derives from cartoons, where this technique is strongly present: think of Scott Bradley's scores for MGM's *Tom and Jerry* short films, in which the mouse's furtive footsteps are individually mirrored by plucks of *pizzicato* strings.[26] In other film-music styles, Mickey-Mousing is used for occasional comic effects, for example in Italian film music. In *What Scoundrels Men Are!* (*Gli uomini, che mascalzoni!*, Mario Camerini, 1932, music by Cesare Andrea Bixio) we see a montage showing unemployed Bruno/Vittorio De Sica checking his mailbox daily and slamming the door each time in growing frustration, as he finds that his job application continues to go unanswered. Music accompanies each slam with a sharp chord, marking Bruno's repeated disappointment. Herein, the term "Mickey-Mousing" is used each time the music closely duplicates the visual action, not just as a technique for cartoons or slapstick comedies. The term is used this way by practitioners too, and in classical Hollywood music Mickey-Mousing is employed, in a more or less marked way, for dramatic effect as well, not merely for comic episodes.[27] Steiner was the undisputed champion of dramatic Mickey-Mousing. For him, film music had to "fit like a glove"[28] and his point is clearly demonstrated in the score he composed for *The Informer* (John Ford, 1935). Even Korngold's music, which is less adherent to visuals, presents episodes of Mickey-Mousing: in *The Sea Hawk*, Alan Hale's character stuns the prison guard with a bang on the head, which is stressed by music. In *The Adventures of Robin Hood* (William Keighley, Michael Curtiz, 1938) the villain Sir Guy/Basil Rathbone is stabbed to death by Robin and falls down the stairs accompanied by a descending musical gesture. Typical of the Mickey-Mousing technique is the *stinger*, that is, a *sforzando* chord that dramatically underlines a crucial event, often a narrative twist as seen in *Casablanca* (Michael Curtiz, 1942), when Ilsa/Ingrid Bergman suddenly points a gun at Rick/Humphrey Bogart.

The preference of the classical Hollywood style for the leitmotiv and Mickey-Mousing techniques can be explained by the strong penchant for storytelling, which tends to have all formal devices invisible/inaudible and motivated compositionally so that they do not distract from the narrative. Consider the poetics of musical realism of the early years of sound cinema: it reveals a concern that the presence of music, not motivated realistically by showing a diegetic on-screen source, could indeed draw the viewer's attention to the music rather than to the narrative. Similarly, the tight adherence of non-diegetic music to the visuals can be explained by the attempt to motivate its source. These days, the Mickey-Mousing technique is obsolete and attracts the viewer's attention to the structural aspects of music rather than making the music transparent. Yet, following the aforementioned "Congruence-Associationist" theory, it can be argued that in the early days when non-diegetic music was suspected of not being transparent and motivated enough, Steiner had this idea: if music seemed to emanate from the actors' movements, maybe viewers would not be distracted by asking themselves where that music came from.[29] The same can be said of leitmotivs. A leitmotiv is so tied to the character that the music appearance is simply motivated by the character's arrival.

Another technique that sometimes showed a similarly tight correspondence between the music and what happened on-screen was *dialogue underscoring*, that is, music accompanying a dialogue scene. Virtually all dialogue—especially romantic ones—had a musical backing in classical Hollywood. However, one needs to distinguish the case in which some music was merely placed in the background to fill the silence—wallpaper music—from that in which dialogue underscoring was modeled around the actor's lines. In the first instance, music acted as a sound-coloring layer for the actors' lines; for an extreme example employing stock music just as a sound-filler, see *Glen or Glenda* (Edward D. Wood Jr, 1953). In the best, and rarer, cases, the composer would take into consideration the pitch of the actors' voices, their timbre, the content of the single lines, and the pauses in the dialogue, and he would write the music accordingly. He would write above or below the actors' pitches so that music would not interfere with the frequencies of their voices; he would make sure that the orchestral timbres blended harmoniously with those of the actors; he would meaningfully introduce a musical cell of an already presented leitmotiv to reinforce one particular line; and he would calculate when the dialogue paused, so that music could soar in those moments and retreat in the background as the dialogue resumed. For an example by the master of such technique, Korngold, listen to Robin and Marian's dialogue scenes in *The Adventures of Robin Hood*.

Musical Means

The score composed with all such aforementioned techniques had to be brought to life, performed through some *musical means*. The classical Hollywood standard was the richly orchestrated sound of the late-nineteenth-century symphony orchestra. However, while Wagner's, Richard Strauss's, and Mahler's orchestras had a hundred or more players, studio orchestras were assembled for recording, not for live performance, and consisted of a maximum of sixty players.[30] The symphony orchestra was the characteristical musical means for the entire period of the classical Hollywood music style. The first reason is historical. In the Nickelodeons of the silent period, projections were accompanied by a pianist or a couple of instrumentalists. Larger theaters had a chamber orchestra made up of a dozen players. Only the luxurious picture palaces had a full symphony orchestra, and the most ambitious and important film productions, such as *The Birth of a Nation* (D. W. Griffith, 1915), used to tour along with a large symphony orchestra.[31] Thus, the sound of the symphony orchestra began to be identified with quality screenings and first-class motion pictures. When introducing synchronized sound, Hollywood kept up with this association and also enlarged the string section. As a matter of fact, these instruments, mostly for timbre reasons, are those that better blend with dialogue without masking effects, but the predominance of the string section is again an aftermath of the silent period. A large string section was indeed typical of the symphony orchestras of first-class theaters and distinguished them from the smaller "salon orchestras."[32] And so this was the reasoning: the symphony orchestra meant prestige; a large string section meant a symphony orchestra; hence, a large presence of strings meant prestige.

The preference of the symphony orchestra as the musical means for film music can also be explained in narrative terms: it is the richest ensemble as to instrumental timbres and is capable of so many color combinations and hues as to make it completely versatile in meeting a wide array of narrative demands.[33] Finally, the use of such musical means until the end of the 1950s was also due to union agreements stating that each studio had to maintain an in-house orchestra. As things were, the studios, following a criterion of efficiency, obviously tended to utilize the tools already at their disposal.

Speaking of musical means, a few words must be said about orchestrators. In general, "to orchestrate" means expanding a piece of music—for example, one written in a condensed form on four staves—to a multiple-stave full score so that it is suitable for being played by a symphony orchestra, generally without making additions of harmonic or contrapuntal nature. An "arrangement," on the other hand, means orchestration plus heavier interventions on the original composition, such as rewritings, integrations, and cuts. Orchestration is a crucial step in creating the overall color and sound of the piece by carefully balancing the various timbres of the orchestra. It affects greatly how a piece of music will finally sound and is not a mechanical operation but an essential part of the art of composition—an art itself, as Maurice Ravel's *Bolero* shows. In the Hollywood music departments, it was not only customary but even stated by union rules that the composer had to compose and then hand the music to someone else to orchestrate it.[34] A biased view soon spread in less factory-like film industries such as those in Europe, where the composer was in charge of the entire process: the orchestrators were deemed to be the real authors behind Hollywood's symphonic scores.[35] Orchestrators were thought to be ghostwriters who would mend the elementary sketches of Hollywood composers, who themselves were considered amateurish practitioners incapable of really writing for orchestra. Of course, there were and are also cases where the orchestrator is indeed the ghostwriter behind the final result and the one who gives musical shape to the amateurish efforts of some would-be composer. A famous example is Charles Chaplin. Credited as composer of the scores for his films, he actually mostly whistled the tunes, which were then arranged for orchestra by a number of collaborators, among them David Raksin, who arranged Chaplin's melodies for *Modern Times* (1936).[36] However, inaccurate generalization should be avoided.

The use of orchestrators in Hollywood was mainly due to time constraints. To meet "punishing production schedules"[37] and allow the already-pressed composer to focus entirely on the key operation of creating the leitmotivs and composing the tight-timed single cues to accompany the scenes, all other technical and less-creative steps were assigned to collaborators, called "orchestrators." The orchestrator's task was to transcribe the condensed composer's sketches, a sort of shorthand score, to a detailed full score without adding anything substantial. These are Steiner's words about his work for *Gone with the Wind*:

> We were scoring all night all the time . . . we used to start at 8:00 at night and finish at 7:00 in the morning with the orchestra . . . because in the daytime I had to write. You say . . . when did I sleep? . . . I slept four or five hours, then a doctor [would] come in about noon to give me a Benzedrine injection so I didn't fall over.
> INTERVIEWER: Did you arrange *Gone with the Wind* also?
> STEINER: Arrange? No one arranges my music.
> INTERVIEWER: I had come across other information that said there were other arrangers working on it with you.
> STEINER: Well, certainly. But it's all from me. Nobody arranges anything from me. They just orchestrate what I write down.
> INTERVIEWER: I had the information that—Let's see . . .
> STEINER: There were five of them.
> IINTERVIEWER: Hugo Friedhofer, Adolph Deutsch, Morris Dupak, Bernard Kahn, Heinz Roemheld and Reginald Bassett.
> STEINER: Hmm . . . I don't remember him. Why sure, you got to have orchestrators. How are you going to write all that? [*laughs*] You couldn't do it. It's done from score. You see, I write six lines, or eight lines. The original. They take it off and put it in score. It's no great trick . . . [38]

Moreover, the composers usually wrote their sketches in a shorthand, often messy handwriting, which would have been unintelligible for a conductor to lead the orchestra from or for a copyist to extract the individual parts.[39] The orchestrator would transcribe clearly and expand the sketches, amending the possible errors that could have occurred in the hurry, such as a note not sharped or flatted. Each composer had his trusted collaborators, who were familiar with his idiom and idiosyncrasies, and knew how to read the composer's shorthand and what kind of musical effects he wanted.

However, in art music, using an orchestrator was and still is seen as a grave sin typical of a hack, a symptom of poor skills and artistic incompetence. Perhaps influenced by these prejudices, some film composers like Bernard Herrmann, Ennio Morricone, George Delerue, and more recently Howard Shore prefer to do all the work themselves, a choice that can be the result of an unconventional temperament, a lack of trust in collaborators, the desire to stand out, or a moral "categorical imperative" for an artistic integrity that would otherwise be threatened. With an art-composer attitude, Ennio Morricone strongly and vexedly rejects the idea of using an orchestrator: "Q: 'Have you ever had any collaborators?' A: 'Never, it is an absolute moral principle. . . . No, absolutely no collaboration at all. I like composing, it's my job, the only thing I can do. I cannot charge others with doing something that I feel deeply mine.'"[40] Morricone even stated: "To compose and to orchestrate are parts of a single moment. Whoever writes music for films without orchestrating each segment is nothing but a dilettante."[41]

This is an excessively broad generalization, and a very recurrent one. Even composers like Copland, Korngold, and Rózsa, who skillfully orchestrated their own art-music compositions, used orchestrators when working in Hollywood.[42] On the negative myth of orchestrators, Prendergast writes:

> The myth is simply that Bernard Herrmann is the only major film composer in Hollywood who does his own orchestrations. . . . This assertion has found its way into the film-music aficionado's lore and seems to owe its existence to two things: (1) An ignorance of the real relationship between the composer and the orchestrator in Hollywood, and (2) a blind faith in the word of Bernard Herrmann on this subject who is in no small part responsible for the propagation of the myth. There are numerous composers in Hollywood whose sketches are so complete and so detailed that the orchestrator really becomes, in effect, an intelligent copyist. Nor is this practice of orchestrating from highly detailed sketches restricted to the film-music world. Prokofiev, with the ironic exception of his score to the film *Alexander Nevsky*, had all of his scores orchestrated from detailed sketches. As Victor Seroff points out, "Prokofiev devised a system that permitted him not to lose time on the long trip across the country. Because the vibration of the train made it impossible to write the orchestral score, he did all his preparatory work by marking in his piano score which of the instruments was to play this or that melody or passage. . . . He was pleased with having perfected this method, for it allowed him to turn over the piano score to a capable

musician who could then easily transcribe it into the orchestral score."[43]

Functions

What is the typical formal function fulfilled by the classic Hollywood style? Claudia Gorbman sees Max Steiner as the epitome of the classical style and illustrates his style in these terms: "So while illustration to the minutest detail was a hallmark of Steiner's style in particular, our overall model of classical-era film music also must include the general tendency toward musical illustration."[44] Peter Larsen writes that "[t]he continuous accompaniment in *King Kong* . . . points forwards towards what was going to be one of the characteristics of Steiner and the other composers of the Golden Age: the exact synchronization of music and images.[45] Similarly, Mervyn Cooke adds, "One of two principal types of nondiegetic scoring in the Golden Age [was] the graphically illustrative music popularly known as mickey-mousing, or 'catching the action.'"[46] Fred Karlin and Rayburn Wright explain: "If you provide a musical accent for a specific moment in the drama, you are hitting the action. . . . Almost all film music from the thirties, forties, and fifties was conceived this way."[47] For Kathryn Kalinak the fundamental characteristic of the classical Hollywood music is the "musical illustration of narrative content, especially the direct synchronization between music and narrative action."[48] And so, there is a general agreement that the most peculiar characteristic of the classical style was the tight synchronization of music and image achieved through Mickey-Mousing, which is a technique, not a function. So, what is the function that Mickey-Mousing fulfilled? The classical Hollywood style has been called "excessively obvious"[49] since narrative information tended to be overstated in case viewers might fail to notice something important. Classical narration used music, among other devices, to help the viewer understand and interpret correctly and as effortlessly as possible the *plot* presented in the film so that he could mentally construct from it the chronologically and causally ordered *story*.[50] In order to have a correct mental *construction* of a certain world, a necessary prerequisite is to gain a correct and as complete as possible *perception* of that world. Music helped this perception: it pinpointed the important information and guided the viewers' attention, not only through Mickey-Mousing but also through leitmotiv. What Michel Chion says about sound in general can be applied to music as well:

> If the sound cinema often has complex and fleeting movements issuing from the heart of a frame and teeming with characters and the other

visual details, this is because the sound superimposed on the image is capable of directing our attention to a particular visual trajectory. . . . [Mickey-Mousing] . . . has been criticized for being redundant, but it has an obvious function nonetheless. Try watching a Tex Avery cartoon without the sound, especially without the musical part. Silent, the visual figures tend to telescope, they do not impress themselves well in the mind, they go by too fast. Owing to the eye's relative inertia and laziness compared to the ear's agility in identifying moving figures, sound helps to imprint rapid visual sensations into memory. Indeed, it plays a more important role in its capacity of aiding the apprehension of visual movements than in focusing on its own substance and aural density.[51]

The Mickey-Mousing technique thus primarily fulfills a *spatial perceptive function*. It makes viewers notice what narration wants them to notice by pointing their attention to a given action or visual detail within the framed space. For example, in *Casablanca* when French Captain Renault finally sides with the anti-Nazi cause and throws a bottle of Vichy water in the trash can, Steiner marks the fall of the bottle with a synchronized low chord to point our attention to the highly symbolic meaning of this action.

To summarize the four-point stylistic definition that has been articulated so far, the classical Hollywood style is characterized by the adoption of the late-romantic dialect (*language*); the use of leitmotiv and Mickey-Mousing (*techniques*); the use of the symphony orchestra (*musical means*); and although it also performed other *formal functions* typical of film music—such as the macro-emotive function, the micro-emotive function, the temporal perceptive function, and the cognitive function—its identifying one was the spatial perceptive function.

Portrait of John Williams (ca. 1977). Photograph by Samantha Winslow Williams. Courtesy BSO Archives/John Williams.

John Williams on the recording stage (ca. 1978). Photograph by Samantha Winslow Williams. Courtesy BSO Archives/John Williams.

Top: John Williams at the piano (ca. 1978). Photograph by Samantha Winslow Williams. Courtesy BSO Archives/John Williams. *Bottom*: John Williams at work in his studio (ca. 1990). Photographer unknown. Courtesy BSO Archives/John Williams.

Top: John Williams on the recording stage for *Jaws* (1975). Photographer unknown. Courtesy of John Williams/Universal Pictures. *Bottom*: John Williams on the recording stage for *Star Wars: Episode I—The Phantom Menace* (1999). Photograph by Jonathan Player. Courtesy Jonathan Player.

Top: John Williams in conversation with Zubin Mehta, with Steven Spielberg at his side (ca. 1978, probably at a *Star Wars* concert at the Hollywood Bowl in Los Angeles). Photographer unknown. Courtesy BSO Archives/John Williams. *Bottom*: John Williams with Leonard Bernstein on the stage at Boston's Symphony Hall (Harvard Night, 1989). Photographer unknown. Courtesy BSO Archives.

John Williams with George Lucas, Grammy Awards in 1999. Featureflash / Shutterstock.com.

Official Portrait of John Williams (1997). Photograph by Bachrach. Courtesy BSO Archives/Bachrach.

Top and bottom: John Williams rehearsing the New York Philharmonic Orchestra (2007). Photographs by Vincent Hardy. Courtesy Vincent Hardy.

Left, top, and bottom: John Williams conducting the New York Philharmonic Orchestra to film in a "multimedia concert piece" (2007). The conductor's monitor can be seen above, on which a specially marked version of the video runs, alerting to the forthcoming synch points to be caught by the orchestra. Photographs by Vincent Hardy. Courtesy Vincent Hardy.

John Williams at the AFI Achievement Award Gala, 2005. Featureflash / Shutterstock.com.

Author Emilio Audissino with Maestro John Williams, 2 June 2012. Photograph by Christine Dehil. From the author's collection.

John Williams
and the Classical
Hollywood Music Style

"Steven, for this film, you need a better composer than I am."
"You're right, John. But they're all dead."

John Williams and Steven Spielberg
discussing the music for *Schindler's List*

3

The "Modern"
Hollywood Music Style

The Context of Williams's Restoration

The change in contractual arrangements between musicians and studios in 1958 can be seen as the end boundary of the classical style. Film music underwent such changes in terms of language, techniques, musical means, and functions that the new style blossoming in the 1960s can be called "modern style."[1]

Cinema and Film Music
in the 1960s

In the 1960s, European cinema regained positions over Hollywood on the international scene. The up-to-date filmmakers of the time—the *auteurs*—were all from Europe. In modern art cinema, style and themes became more important than narrative. Consider Michelangelo Antonioni's idle moments and *temps mort*, in which the action slackens and narrative causality is weakened, or Federico Fellini's "excessive" and conspicuously idiosyncratic style, or Alain Resnais's narrative ambiguity, or Ingmar Bergman's "important topics."

> Specific sorts of realism motivate a loosening of cause and effect, an
> episodic construction of the syuzhet [plot], and an enhancement of the

film's symbolic dimension through an emphasis on the fluctuations of character psychology. . . . In the name of verisimilitude, the tight causality of classical Hollywood construction is replaced by a more tenuous linking of events. . . . The art film's thematic crux, its attempt to pronounce judgments upon modern life and *la condition humaine*, depends upon its formal organization. Unlike most classical films, the art film is apt to be quite restricted in its range of [narrative] knowledge. Such restriction may enhance identification (character knowledge matches ours), but it may also make the narration less reliable. . . . The narrow focus is complemented by psychological depth; art-film narration is more subjective more often than is classical narration. . . . To "objective" and "subjective" verisimilitude we may add a third broad schema, that of overt narrational "commentary." . . . Stylistic devices that gain prominence with respect to classical norms—an unusual angle, a stressed bit of cutting, a striking camera movement, an unrealistic shift in lighting or setting, a disjunction on the sound track, or any other break-down of objective realism which is not motivated as subjectivity—can be taken as the narration's commentary.[2]

Now cinema was no longer interested in the exterior development of actions linked in a straight line, oriented toward a final resolution and following tight cause/effect relationships, but it was focused on the visual representation of the characters' inwardness. Russell Lack states:

[M]usic becomes especially important since characters come increasingly to resemble feelings rather than having fully sketched-out biographies. Feelings rather than characters are transformed depending on what type of cinematic time they inhabit. This is something like a psychology of pure feelings as opposed to one rooted in characters or individuals. Accordingly, music acts crucially as a navigator of feeling dispossessed from bodies, from biographies. . . . Music in the modern cinema freely moves between the diegetic source that is revealed in the image and the non-diegetic music whose source is never revealed and vice versa. It comes more and more to symbolize the sublime in the most imaginative examples of its use.[3]

Many emerging European authors of the period were wary of using music, such as Michelangelo Antonioni or Robert Bresson: "How many films are patched up by music! Films are flooded with music. This prevents us from seeing that there is nothing in those images."[4] Some were even openly hostile; Eric Rohmer says that "With few exceptions, I reject the so-called film music, that is music that is not actually located in the space and time of the film. . . . Music is cinema's falsest friend, as it deprives film time of its peculiar exclusivity and objectivity."[5]

The new *auteur* cinema no longer needed music to sustain the narration step by step, as it now deliberately sought nonlinear and ambiguous forms. "When Alain Resnais hired Fusco to work for *Hiroshima, mon amour* (1959), the composer immediately decided that he would not work out fixed themes for the characters [i.e., leitmotivs], would not systematically emphasize the images, and would elude synchronism and carefully avoid any references to the Japanese locale."[6] Commenting on Georges Delerue's music for the film *Love on the Run* (*L'Amour en fuite*, François Truffaut, 1979), Russell Lack remarks, "The most notable difference from the Hollywood tradition of romanticism is that orchestral flourishes are not generally used to track movement but rather to set a scene."[7]

The Style of Modern Film Music

If we examine the works of Ennio Morricone (1928–), John Barry (1933–2011), and Henry Mancini (1924–94), three of the most successful representatives of this new style, it is patent that the classical-style "spatial perceptive function" (the case in which music directs the viewer's attention to a particular element inside the framing) holds a minority position in the new style. Consequently, the Mickey-Mousing and leitmotiv techniques became obsolete. Modern style favored the emotive function (adding or reinforcing the emotional tone of a scene) or the cognitive function (clarifying or implying the connotations and implicit meanings). The only kind of perceptive function retained is the temporal one: changing the perception of the visual rhythm, or temporally linking through a musical *continuum* events that might otherwise seem disconnected.

In the 1960s, Hollywood cinema was weakened by a severe crisis, and as it was strongly influenced by Nouvelle Vague (the "New Wave") and the European *auteur* cinema, so it was also influenced by the European music style. Compared to the classical Hollywood tradition, European style had always been characterized by a lower adherence between music and visuals and a minor use of leitmotiv.[8] Also, the European style distinctly favored the technique of the *closed musical number*. Instead of a continuous stream of music based on interwoven leitmotivs, the score was structured through a series of isolated set pieces closed in themselves. This is more similar to the Italian and French operas, constituted by musically self-sufficient arias clearly separated by *recitativi*, rather than to the continuous musical stream of Wagner's *Wort-Ton-Drama*, which had such a great influence on Hollywood music.

This modern stylistic feature can be found in the works of Nino Rota, for instance: "Another function of nondiegetic film music is to bind the incidents of a film together in a common ambiance. The thematic, instrumental, and stylistic continuities typical of film scores help to create a consistency of tone or feeling across the span of a film, especially where the events presented are not very tightly connected in a dramatic sense. Thus this, rather than any narrative task, seems to be the main function of Rota's score for Fellini's *Amarcord*."[9] Rota's score for *The Godfather* (Francis Ford Coppola, 1972) shows that his technique is not akin to the Hollywood style but rather based on closed musical numbers and little adherence to the visual action.

In the 1960s, this style spread internationally because of the worldwide success of European films; Rota's music had a vast diffusion and visibility thanks to his collaboration with Fellini. The technique of the closed musical number was also used by Ennio Morricone and disseminated through the enormous success of his scores for Sergio Leone's "Spaghetti-Westerns."[10]

Morricone is certainly one of the leading representatives of the new style, and he is equally far from both Italian and Hollywood classicism. He openly rejects the classical style: "The screen reflects a flat image that, *perhaps*, without music would remain flat. Music gives it a sense of vertical depth and horizontal dynamism, which can only be possible if music is surrounded by silence. This is necessary because our hearing, and therefore our brain, cannot listen and understand more sounds of a different nature simultaneously. We will never understand four people speaking at the same time. It is absolutely necessary, if the director wants to consider music *in the right way*, to isolate music and give the audience the time to listen to it in the best way."[11] Morricone not only rejects the dialogue underscoring technique but also all the classical techniques, such as Mickey-Mousing and leitmotiv, that do not give music a central perceptual position. In Sergio Leone's films, music emerges in closed musical numbers when there is no dialogue—similar to Italian opera: "I think that music should be present when the action stops and crystallizes; as in musical theater we can find the *recitativo* and the aria, music in cinema should be placed in correspondence with the aria, when the action stops and there are thoughts and introspection, not when the action has its own narrative dynamics."[12] As to the adherence to visuals, Morricone categorically rejects synchronism: "Music must follow its own discourse and have its own unity; encouraging synchronism means giving up all this."[13] In general, what Morricone rejects is the inaudibility of film music, which we have seen as being one of the cornerstones of the classical

Hollywood style, and the consequent *background music*: "In fact, Morricone's music can best be described as foreground music."[14]

Unlike the classical Hollywood style that undoubtedly influenced the practice of composition for film in general but was applied in its full form only in Hollywood, modern style was an international style, its features being present in films from different nations. Low adherence to action and closed musical numbers can be found in the scores by the French composers Francis Lai and Michel Legrand, the Argentinian Lalo Schifrin, the British John Barry, and the American Henry Mancini.

Consider the action sequences in many James Bond films. John Barry's music gives pace and suspense but compared to the classic adventure films it follows a freer musical development, one not tightly synchronized with the visuals. The difference is remarkable if we compare Monty Norman's score for the first James Bond film, *Dr. No* (Terence Young, 1962), with those composed by Barry for the following films of the series. In the *Dr. No* scene where Bond squashes the tarantula that his enemies had hidden in his bed, Norman uses many punctuational stingers and a kind of Mickey-Mousing to accentuate each time Bond hits the spider. Norman seems to still be following traditional techniques. Other occurrences of such explicit synchronism are not found in the following Barry scores, when the modern style was already well established.

As to the *musical means*, the symphony orchestra was no longer the standard in modern style. However, it was still used in some blockbusters or prestige films such as *The Lion in Winter* (Anthony Harvey, 1968, music by John Barry); *Ryan's Daughter* (David Lean, 1970, music by Maurice Jarre); *Tom Jones* (Tony Richardson, 1963, music by John Addison); and *The Godfather* (Francis Ford Coppola, 1972, music by Nino Rota). The choice now ranged from jazz combos to big bands to small chamber ensembles (*To Kill a Mockingbird*, Robert Mulligan, 1962, music by Elmer Bernstein) or even solo improvisation on the visuals (Miles Davis's music for *Ascenseur pour l'échafaud*, Louis Malle, 1957).[15]

As to the *language*, modern style included a wide variety, ranging from jazz to funk-soul, rhythm 'n' blues, rock, and "easy-listening" pop. It was open to any other languages that were either trendy or experimental, including dialects of twentieth-century art music such as atonality, modalism, and dodecaphonism—for example Leonard Rosenman's atonal score for *Fantastic Voyage* (Richard Fleischer, 1966) or David Shire's twelve-tone score for *The Taking of Pelham 123* (Joseph Sargent, 1974). These linguistic innovations were due not only to aesthetic or realistic reasons but also to an unprecedented phenomenon: the increasing commercial importance of film music in the 1960s. The adoption of contemporary and popular dialects in film music was an effective way to attract young audiences, which were now the basis of cinema attendance. Film music had to update according to the tastes of the new audience, which were certainly not in line with the symphonic late-romanticism of the classical style.[16] One of the reasons for this linguistic renewal, then—and certainly not the least important—was market orientation. The most obvious consequence was the growing importance of pop songs as core elements of the music track.

Modern Style and the Economic Motivation

The relation between cinema and songs is as old as cinema itself. The main reason is to achieve the maximum economic benefit by having the film and the music industries supporting each other. As early as the nickelodeon period, the fad of *illustrated songs*, a kind of "pre-karaoke," had been launched and was directly financed by music publishing houses.[17] Music composed to accompany such silent films as *The Birth of a Nation* (David Wark Griffith, 1915, music by Joseph Carl Breil) and *What Price Glory* (Raoul Walsh, 1926, music by Erno Rapée) was immediately adapted into songs and sold successfully.[18] In the early sound films the presence of music was either sparse and diegetic in the talkies, or assembled in a string of musical numbers in the all-singing musical revues. In either case, popular songs had the lion's share, and film studios either merged with music publishing companies or started their own subsidiaries in order to gain fully from the profitable song craze.[19] With the end of this trend and the emergence of the classical music style, songs continued to be featured in films, since their economic potential was still very important. All-symphonic film-music albums were rare and the market for film-music records was almost exclusively concerned with songs, which were consequently included in the films' sound track to promote the sale of the records.[20]

In the classical Hollywood cinema, the "economic motivation" for the presence of a song in a film was carefully masked with a realistic motivation: the song appeared at diegetic level as a live performance or as a broadcast coming from some on-screen visible radio. The proper locus to showcase a saleable song was the diegetic musical number by the female lead—a striking example of Laura Mulvey's "female-spectacle"[21]—often accompanied by some bankable musician. Such instances can be found both in comedies such as *Ball of Fire* (Howard Hawks, 1941), featuring Barbara Stanwyck singing "Drum Boogie" accompanied by drummer Gene Krupa, and in dramas like *To Have and Have Not* (Howard Hawks, 1944), where Lauren Bacall sings a couple of songs by Hoagy Carmichael, with the composer himself playing the piano. In the classical-style invisible narration, songs used at non-diegetic level were out of place because they were too noticeable. First of all, lyrics could distract from the narrative context or interfere with dialogue. Moreover, famous songs could evoke associations and connotations that were likely to disconnect the viewer from the film's narrative world. Also, a song is in itself less "inaudible" and less concealable than instrumental music: the structure of a song is rigid and cannot be bent and adapted to visuals, as is the case with orchestral music.[22] The use of a song at diegetic level—through the presentation of a musical number—put the narrative to a temporary stop, but it did not disrupt the narration invisibility because it was motivated realistically. In this way, it was possible to elegantly mask the actual motivation, which was to prompt viewers to go and buy tie-in records or sheet music when leaving the theater.

The balance between realistically motivated diegetic songs and compositionally motivated non-diegetic orchestral music broke down in the 1960s, when an extrinsic economic motivation became mostly evident and prevailed over intrinsic aesthetic and formal motivations. The first reason was technological. The introduction and rapid diffusion of the 33 1/3 rpm long-playing disc caused the blossoming of a massive record industry.[23] Whereas previous 78 rpm discs could contain just three to five minutes of music, the standard length of one song, the new format could store up to forty minutes, meaning that just one song was not enough to make a disc. Another reason was sociological. In the 1950s, film producers had discovered the potential of the teen audience and the importance of complying with its musical tastes, especially after the huge success of such films as *Blackboard Jungle* (Richard Brooks, 1955), which featured rock 'n' roll music by Bill Haley and His Comets, and whose LP album sold spectacularly.[24] Most important, the demise of the classical studio system in the 1960s caused a radical change in production practice. Whereas in the old days the decisive profits were the total net revenue of the studio, the sum of all the film projects, now—in the "package-unit system"—the decisive profits were those of the single films.[25] In the new highly competitive market the consequence was that each film had to be an economic success. To secure such a success, a good solution was to team up with the burgeoning record industry, balancing a weak box-office performance with the potentially better sales of the film's LP album. Controlling both the film and record industries and applying a carefully devised, synergistic cross-promotion not only advertised the film via the presence of the song on the radio and in record stores, but also promoted the song by having it showcased in the film. In the 1960s every major studio became an important shareholder in some existing record company or created its own subsidiary in order to collect profits from both markets. All these factors led to a new pop

song craze and prompted the rise of the modern style, of which the use of eco-
nomically motivated pop songs is a central feature.

If we compare the classical style with the modern style as to the way songs
were inserted in films, the difference can be seen in the move from the diegetic
to the non-diegetic level, that is, the "interpolated songs" phenomenon.[26] From
the 1960s, pop songs were placed at non-diegetic level and took over some of
the formal functions previously performed by orchestral music, such as linking
together the segments of a montage sequence or clarifying the emotional mood
of a scene. The film credited with having established this trend—thanks to its
big success both in theaters and in record stores—is *A Man and a Woman* (*Un
homme et une femme*, Claude Lelouch, 1966, music by Francis Lai).[27] Again, the
problem is that songs used at non-diegetic level are less flexible than orchestral
music and risk appearing as being arbitrarily inserted into the film for an overtly
economic motivation. Sometimes songs are indeed thematically congruent,
narratively functional, cleverly placed, and can function as effectively as an
orchestral score. The *American Graffiti* music track, for example, is made up of
early 1960s songs, with each scene supported by a different song—having a
formally consistent compositional motivation and being functional to the
nostalgic mood of the film. The music is also motivated realistically, not just
because of the time setting of the story but also because of the constant presence
of car radios in the pro-filmic space. This results in a subtly ambiguous play
between diegetic and non-diegetic levels: Are the songs broadcast by the radio
sets or are they non-diegetic? Can the characters actually hear the songs or,
because the songs are outside the narrative world, can they be heard only by
the viewers?[28] Other examples of songs included in a film for economic reasons
and yet well integrated into the narrative can be found in John Barry's works
for the James Bond series, starting with *Goldfinger* (Guy Hamilton, 1964). The
theme song ("Goldfinger") is showcased in a dedicated spot outside the narrative,
in a title sequence constructed like a "proto-video clip."[29] The lyrics tie in with
the film's narrative and themes, and its musical theme is recurrently presented
in instrumental versions within the narrative, thus fulfilling formal functions
similar to those once fulfilled by leitmotivs in the classical style.[30]

Nonetheless, a poorly motivated orchestral intervention is still less incongruous and obtrusive than a poorly motivated song. The minor flexibility of
songs resulted in debatable cases of incongruity and misplacement. Sticking to
the James Bond franchise, consider *Never Say Never Again* (Irvin Kershner, 1983,
music by Michel Legrand). Its music tried to replicate the successful commercial
formula of the series—a new song as the main theme of each film, presented in

the non-diegetic opening titles sequence—without being as congruent and functional as Barry's scores. The title song ("Never Say Never Again") is an easy-listening, lightweight piano-bar style tune, which would sound perfect as a musical wallpaper at a cocktail party. Instead of being placed in its own space outside the narrative, the song flows under the action prologue over which the opening credits are superimposed. In this sequence, Bond, here on a hostage-release mission, has to sneak into a South American estate surrounded by menacing armed men. The song is hardly consistent with what we are seeing and it certainly does not support the narration: its easy-listening, relaxed mood works against the suspense. It seems difficult to consider this case as a deliberate use of "anempathetical" music[31]—that is, the music is "indifferent" to the drama that unfolds in the visuals—or a kind of Kubrick asynchronism because no other stylistic elements seem to indicate such narrational intent. Another example is *The Graduate* (Mike Nichols, 1967), in which Paul Simon and Art Garfunkel's songs have little or nothing to do with what happens in the visuals. Even the lyrics of the only song expressly written for the film ("Mrs. Robinson") have nothing to do with the Mrs. Robinson portrayed in the film, as if the singer/songwriter duo was involved simply for a mutual commercial benefit and without even knowing what the film was about.[32] A textbook example is the bicycle-ride sequence in *Butch Cassidy* (George Roy Hill, 1969).[33] In this case, not only do the lyrics have nothing to do with the film sequence, but the music style is also inconsistent with that of the rest of the score. "Raindrops Keep Fallin' on My Head" just seems to have been forcefully inserted with the sole purpose of promoting Burt Bacharach's song. This type of unabashedly promotional sequence is brilliantly spoofed by Zucker-Abrahams-Zucker in *The Naked Gun: From the Files of Police Squad* (1988). We see a montage showing Lt. Frank Drebin and his new fiancée, Jane, involved in a series of clichéd romantic activities, accompanied by a merry song. At the end of the sequence, as in a MTV video, the song's title, authors, album name, and record company—"Herman's Hermits, 'I'm Into Something Good,' The Naked Gun Soundtrack, Wheelo Records Inc."—appear on-screen, hilariously baring the economic motivation of the presence of songs in such sequences. The ultimate result of this market-oriented approach was the phenomenon of the *compilation score*, a film-music track built out of repertoire pop songs instead of original instrumental music in symphonic, jazz, pop, or rock dialect.[34] This technique was largely adopted by the industry after the success of *The Graduate* and applied with successful results in such films as *Easy Rider* (Dennis Hopper, 1969); *Mean Streets* (Martin Scorsese, 1973); and *The Last Picture Show* (Peter Bogdanovich, 1971). In these cases, the risk that more attention is paid to the commercial allure of a song rather than to its actual functionality and consistency with the film is at its highest.

Henry Mancini, the most influential modern-style Hollywood composer, was perhaps the deftest "tunesmith" of the period, balancing the old-school sense of drama with a knack for staying in tune with or even shaping himself the current musical trends. He had a reputation for composing very successful songs, which found their right spot both in the films and in the record stores, and for having a keen understanding of how to put together a successful album.[35] Typically, "Mancini's scores emerge as collections of themes with one or two being more prominent than the rest. More importantly . . . his themes . . . retain the shape and formal character of individual musical numbers, and they typically function with a comparable measure of musical autonomy. Like the songs of a musical, Mancini's themes display a mastery of song structures, a plethora of musical hooks, and a surfeit of memorable melodies. In their orientation toward tunes, Mancini's multitheme scores proved eminently suited to the format of pop album."[36]

The closed musical number technique is clearly more functional than the continuous leitmotivic flow of the classic style if the aim is to have the film score also exploited in a marketable easy-listening album. Many Mancini scores, while working efficiently in the films, seem to be also composed with the very album in mind, as they are typically made up of a string of independent and well-defined musical numbers. Think of the party sequences in *The Party* (Blake Edwards, 1968), a slapstick comedy that once would have widely featured the Mickey-Mousing technique. On the contrary, the music track is a collection of cocktail and dance pieces, mainly diegetic.[37]

The Demise
of the Classical Music Style

The modern style and its innovations did not oust the classical style overnight. After 1958 and through the first half of the 1960s the last traces of the classical style can still be heard in films like *The Magnificent Seven* (John Sturges, 1960, music by Elmer Bernstein); *Spartacus* (Stanley Kubrick, 1960, music by Alex North); *The Alamo* (John Wayne, 1960, music by Dimitri Tiomkin); *King of Kings* (Nicholas Ray, 1961, music by Miklós Rózsa); *El Cid* (Anthony Mann, 1961, music by Miklós Rózsa); *The Guns of Navarone* (J. Lee Thompson, 1961, music by Dimitri Tiomkin); *Taras Bulba* (J. Lee Thompson, 1962, music by Franz Waxman); and *How the West Was Won* (John Ford–Henry Hathaway–George

Marshall, 1962, music by Alfred Newman).[38] The stylistic change became well established and strongly evident in the second half of the 1960s.

The landmark event was perhaps the infamous sacking of Bernard Herrmann by Alfred Hitchcock, after Universal pressed the director to include an easy-listening song in *Torn Curtain* (1966).[39] Herrmann, who had composed the scores for eight of Hitchcock's films, including some of his biggest hits, was notoriously against the use of songs in films.[40] However, he had accepted the practice in a previous Hitchcock film, *The Man Who Knew Too Much* (1956), the song being "Que Sera, Sera" by Ray Evans and Jay Livingston. Ten years later, Herrmann refused to follow Hitchcock along the pop path, and one of the most fruitful partnerships in film music abruptly came to an end. The comparison of these two episodes clearly shows how modern-style placement of songs in films radically differed from the classical style. The 1956 film had an orchestral score that served the film in the classical way. The marketable diegetic song featured in the film was motivated not only realistically—Doris Day's character is a singer and therefore it is highly plausible that she should sing—but also compositionally because the song is the narrative device that allows the kidnapped boy to be rescued. The presence of the song was not arbitrary, and its economic motivation was cleverly hidden. Using Herrmann's words, it was not "a pre-meditated attempt at song plugging."[41] On the contrary, in *Torn Curtain*, a tense and often crude portrayal of East Germany under the Stasi's yoke, there was no motivation at all to include a song, except that of selling tie-in LPs. Hitchcock replaced the uncooperative Herrmann with John Addison, who agreed to compose a singable love theme, which was adapted into the song "Green Years" by John Addison, Ray Evans, and Jay Livingston. Eventually, Hitchcock himself realized how the song would have been nonsensical in the film and decided not to use it and relegate it to the LP album.[42]

Mancini, Barry, and Morricone's growing reputation and the outstanding success in theater box-offices and in record stores of films like *A Hard Day's Night* (Richard Lester, 1964, music of the Beatles), *A Man and a Woman*, and *The Graduate* led to the prevalence of the modern style, pop idioms, and songs throughout the 1965–77 years. The young conservatory-trained symphonic composers active in those years, like Jerry Goldsmith, for one, were a discomforted minority: "Well, many of us composers are upset about this, because we get requests from producers that we've got to write a hit song. It's a real pain, because they forget what we're really supposed to be doing. It's a completely commercial device to try to promote the film. . . . It has nothing to do with anything dramatic in the picture, and this is a great annoyance to us all, but it's one of the syndromes of the business, and there isn't very much we can do about it."[43] Even Henry Mancini was well aware of the excessively commercial importance given to songs, to the detriment of narration: "The minute you put a song over the titles or in any part of the picture, you're unconsciously trying to play on the viewer's pocketbook—you're trying to get him to listen, to go out and buy. Often these songs don't really make the action progress or make any kind of comment."[44]

Symphonic orchestral film music did not disappear entirely in the modern-style years, but it definitely became less common, appearing in such films as *The Lion in Winter* (Anthony Harvey, 1968, music by John Barry); *Planet of the Apes* (Franklin J. Schaffner, 1968, music by Jerry Goldsmith); *The Reivers* (Mark Rydell, 1969, music by John Williams); *Patton* (Franklin J. Schaffner, 1970, music by Jerry Goldsmith); *Ryan's Daughter* (David Lean, 1970, music by Maurice Jarre); *The Wind and the Lion* (John Milius, 1975, music by Jerry Goldsmith); *The Omen* (Richard Donner, 1976, music by Jerry Goldsmith); and Bernard Herrmann's final contributions for *Sisters* (Brian De Palma, 1973); *Obsession* (Brian De Palma, 1976); and *Taxi Driver* (Martin Scorsese, 1976)—the only Herrmann score in the jazz dialect. What became marginal was the classical Hollywood music style. In particular, the old-style spatial perceptive function survived mostly in an exaggerated farcical form in some comedies such as *That Touch of Mink* (Delbert Mann, 1962, music by George Duning); *Send Me No Flowers* (Norman Jewison, 1964, music by Frank De Vol); and *The Glass Bottom Boat* (Frank Tashlin, 1966, music by Frank De Vol) or in the mannerist thunderous stingers of some horror/thriller B-movies such as *The Terror* (Roger Corman, 1963, music by Ronald Stein); *Strait-Jacket* (William Castle, 1964, music by Van Alexander); and *The Oblong Box* (Gordon Hessler, 1969, music by Harry Robertson).

Not until *Star Wars* did there appear patent signs that the old style could still have something to say.

4

Star Wars

An Oppositional Score

After his not very convincing debut with the Orwellian Sci-Fi film *THX 1138* (1971), the emerging film director George Lucas hit the box office with *American Graffiti* (1973) and became powerful enough to carry on with a big project that he had been contemplating for several years: *The Star Wars*.[1]

The idea was to make a film that blended sci-fi with mythology, technology with fairy-tale magic, comics with epics, future with past: "A long time ago, in a galaxy far, far away . . ." The main models were the *Flash Gordon* and *Buck Rogers* serials, the adventure films and B-movies produced by Monogram, Republic, and other minor production companies—the so-called poverty-row studios. Other models were *The Hidden Fortress* (*Kakushi-toride no san-akunin*, Akira Kurosawa, 1958) and *The Searchers* (John Ford, 1956).[2] Besides films, the influence of Carlos Castaneda's anthropological and philosophical theories and of Joseph Campbell's studies on the mythological archetypes were also seminal.[3]

Lucas's project was abandoned by United Artists and then rejected by Universal, to finally be taken over by 20th Century Fox, which, although skeptically, accepted to finance the pre-production.[4] Producers experienced some difficulty in understanding and envisioning Lucas's idea because of the confusing nature and constantly changing structure of the screenplay.[5] Most important, the main doubt about the commercial result of the project was that the sci-fi genre was out of fashion in 1970s cinema. Recent exceptions had been *2001: A*

Space Odyssey (Stanley Kubrick, 1968) and *Planet of the Apes* (Franklin J. Schaffner, 1968). As Lucas's collaborator Charles Lippincott recalls: "Kubrick's *2001* didn't break even until late 1975—and that was the most successful science-fiction film of all time. . . . You had to be crazy to make a science-fiction film when we wanted to."[6] Moreover, *2001* and *Planet of the Apes* were very different films from Lucas's project. They were adult sci-fi, dystopian tales with philo-sophical subtexts, while *The Star Wars* seemed to be a kind of expensive B-movie for kids. In 1975, in the midst of laborious pre-production first steps, screenplay rewriting, and budget discussions, the time came to decide what kind of music the film would require.

The Sci-Fi Genre and Music

Traditionally, music for the sci-fi genre would use a language inspired by twentieth-century musical modernism—atonalism, twelve-tone technique, aleatoric music, and so forth—or would use electronic instruments, timbres, or even *musique concrète* to provide the musical equivalent of futuristic or hyper-technological worlds.[7] Bernard Herrmann employed a modernist dialect for *The Day the Earth Stood Still* (Robert Wise, 1951), and also used the theremin, thus producing a shift in identification for that instrument's tremulous timbre from the psychotic 1940s thrillers to the sci-fi genre. In *Planet of the Apes*, Jerry Gold-smith used a traditional orchestra but adopted the atonal dialect, avant-garde instrumental techniques (key-taps on clarinets or horns played without mouth-pieces), and experimental timbres (a ram's horn and metal mixing-bowls of different sizes used as percussion) to produce the musical complement of the hallucinatory topsy-turvy world presented in the film.[8] In *Forbidden Planet* (Fred M. Wilcox, 1956) there is no music but rather "electronic tonalities" by Babe and Louis Barron.[9] Stanley Kubrick in *2001* chose to combine images of deep space and unseen worlds with a compilation of repertoire orchestral pieces—after having rudely rejected Alex North's original score.[10] The selection spanned from classic pieces like Richard Strauss's *Thus Spoke Zarathustra* (*Also sprach Zarathustra*, op. 30, 1896) and Johann Strauss Jr.'s *The Blue Danube* (*An der schönen blauen Donau*, op. 314, 1866) to contemporary art music like György Ligeti's *Lux Aeterna* (1966), *Atmospheres* (1961), *Requiem* (1963–65), and *Adventures* (1962). Kubrick chose to create a special "asynchronism" with the visuals. Music had to serve as an intellectual stimulus by pointing to extrafilmic refer-ences and creating an intertextual dimension, which would actively involve the viewer in deciphering this enigmatic film. Yet Kubrick's choice was also the consequence of a lack of trust in film composers: "However good our best film composers may be, they are not a Beethoven, a Mozart or a Brahms. Why use music which is less good when there is such a multitude of great orchestral music from the past and from our own time?"[11]

Lucas rejected the modernist and electronic options and chose Kubrick's approach. He wrote the script while listening to the late-romantic symphonic repertoire of William Walton, Richard Wagner, Gustav Holst, Richard Strauss, Antonín Dvořák, and Maurice Ravel along with the film music of Erich Wolfgang Korngold and Miklós Rózsa.[12] He resolved that the film should have an extensive musical coverage and, according to various sources, planned to have the music track made of preexisting symphonic selections, or at least to use preexisting themes arranged as leitmotivs for the film.[13] While pondering over such musical decisions, Lucas happened to have a very fruitful conversation: "I had known Steven Spielberg for a long time up to this point and, you know, we were talking about the film . . . and I said, 'I want a classical score, I want the Korngold kind of feel about this thing, it's an old fashion kinda movie and I want that kind of grand soundtrack they used to have on movies.' And he said, 'The guy you gotta talk to is John Williams. He made *Jaws*, I love him, he is the greatest composer who ever lived. You gotta talk to him!'"[14]

In April 1975 George Lucas had his first meeting with composer John Williams:[15] Williams remarked, "I looked at the movie and I liked it—I had no idea at the time it was going to be a trilogy—and I thought the film would give me the opportunity to write an old-fashioned swashbuckling symphonic score, so that's what I did."[16] Reportedly, Williams—contrary to his own habit—agreed to read the script,[17] and he was responsible for convincing Lucas not to use repertoire music but an original score instead: "*2001* and several other films have utilized this technique very well. But what I think this technique doesn't do is take a piece of melodic material, develop it and relate it to a character all the way through the film. For instance if you took a theme from one of the selections of Holst's *The Planets* and played it at the beginning of the film, it wouldn't necessarily fit in the middle or at the end. On the other hand, I did not want to hear a piece of Dvořák here, a piece of Tchaikovsky there, and a piece of Holst in another place. For formal reasons, I felt that the film wanted thematic unity."[18]

Finding the Musical Solution

Which music language could be suitable for a film like that? The modernist hypothesis had clearly been rejected, and Lucas, through his own temp track, showed Williams that his preference was for the late-romantic dialect, that of classical Hollywood.[19] *Star Wars* is in fact more a "super-genre" than a sci-fi film. Only a few elements of the sci-fi genre, such as robots, laser weapons, and spaceships, are present. *Star Wars* is rather a mixture of elements from Western, fantasy, and swashbuckler films and instead of being similar to the sci-fi films of its day, it was closer to the Warner Bros. adventure films directed by Michael Curtiz, featuring Errol Flynn's prowess and Erich Wolfgang Korngold's opulent music. Indeed, Korngold himself was Williams's main model, as he remarked, "[A] warm theatrical operatic almost kind of package. The kind of thing that Korngold in fact did so beautifully. He brought the Vienna Opera House to the American West. And in an odd way, in a similar way, it worked, I think."[20] Williams explains Lucas's choice to have very traditional music combined with a futuristic setting: "The music for the film is very non-futuristic. The films themselves showed us characters we hadn't seen before and planets unimagined and so on, but the music was—this is actually George Lucas's conception and a very good one—emotionally familiar. It was not music that might describe *terra incognita* but the opposite of that, music that would put us in touch with very familiar and remembered emotions, which for me as a musician translated into the use of a nineteenth-century operatic idiom, if you like, Wagner and this sort of thing. These sorts of influences would put us in touch with remembered theatrical experiences as well—all western experiences to be sure."[21]

This choice was not universally understood: some critics would label the score as "corny romanticism"[22] and wonder why, since the film was set in the future, avant-garde music had not been used instead.[23] This complaint is rather superficial: it cannot be simply said that since it features spaceships and robots, *Star Wars* is therefore sci-fi. The film begins with "A long time ago, in a galaxy far far away . . ." It begins as a traditional fairy tale set in a distant past: "[I]f one is writing music for a movie that is supposed to take place in the future, then futuristic music should theoretically suit the 'set' better than a score based on music from the late nineteenth and early twentieth centuries. But Williams hits closer to the mark when he points out that such films tend to cater to the audience's desire for escapism, 'and in that escapist thing is the whole romantic idea of getting away, of being transported into another kind of atmosphere.'"[24]

Williams provided a symphonic tonal score based on a dozen leitmotivs covering almost the entire film: Luke's theme, Leia's theme, the Jawas's theme, Ben Kenobi/The Force's theme, the Empire's motif, and many more. They all feature extensive and refined Korngold-like dialogue underscoring—think of the dialogue between Kenobi and Luke after they have watched Princess Leia's video message through R2-D2; old-fashioned heroic fanfares, as when Luke rescues Leia and, with her in his arms, crosses the chasm à la Robin Hood under the storm troopers' fire; and episodes of detailed Mickey-Mousing, for example, in the detention block ambush scene. Williams designed such clear-cut recognizable motifs and themes so as to support the film narration in a straight-forward way:

> I think in my mind, and possibly also George Lucas', when I was writing the score, I thought it was a children's film. I thought that it was some-thing that kids would go to on a Saturday afternoon, and that it had a kind of cartoon-like character, and the orchestra and the music should somehow be in that genre, whatever that is. But I thought, I have to grab the attention of the 10-year-olds with this. The emotion would have to be large, a sense of good versus evil made palpable. Simple tunes would be the key, though that was easier said than done. To say Darth Vader to a 10-year-old in clear, memorable and immediately affecting terms is a big challenge. And it's an opportunity probably that is, maybe sadly, found only in the craft of film scoring any more. I mean, where else can you do that?[25]

For such a prominent score, the services of a first-class symphony orchestra were required. Since the production took place in England, the world-famous London Symphony Orchestra was chosen. Famous for its skillful sight-reading and its powerful brass section, the LSO is, in Williams's words, "a very 'hot' orchestra, its decibel level is large, and the orchestra looms at the audience in a very vigorous, athletic way."[26] Moreover, the orchestra had a prestigious track record of film collaborations.[27]

In the years from 1975 to 1976 the choice of a full symphonic score was definitely against the tide and a very risky one: if the sci-fi genre was considered unfashionable, even more so was the classical music style. The studio feared that the film would have a disastrous performance at the box office and that, lacking an attractive pop score, such failure could not be offset by the sale of records. In fact, 20th Century Fox Records—believing that nobody would buy a symphonic film-music album—was planning not to release any tie-in disc.[28]

On 5 March 1977, at the Anvil Studios in Denham (UK), Williams conducted eighty-six musicians of the London Symphony in the first recording session of the more than eight-hundred-page score.[29] After eight days on the recording stage, the resulting *Star Wars* music track covered 88 minutes of the film's total 120-minute running time. Such an extended musical coverage coupled with such strong leitmotivic variety and interconnection was unheard of since Steiner and Korngold's heydays.

The very beginning of the film is a kind of manifesto of the restoration of the classical Hollywood music tradition. For the 20th Century Fox opening logo, the full Cinemascope version of the "20th Century Fox Fanfare" by Alfred Newman was resuscitated after a decade of less than sporadic use.[30] After a brief silence, the "STAR WARS" title flashes on the screen in tight synchronism with a startling *fortissimo* B-flat-major chord—"*Maestoso sffz*" in the score—in the same B-flat-major key as Newman's fanfare. This explosive chord affirms a continuity with the past: the deliberate tonal affinity with Newman's fanfare marks the recovery of the tradition and the score's affiliation with it. Moreover, the chord's precise synchronism with the visuals—the chord being like a stinger—and the fact that the chord is played by a full symphony orchestra mark the simultaneous retrieval of two other characteristic traits of the classical style: the tight adherence between music and images and the symphonic sound. Interestingly enough, the first "Main Title" version, rather than beginning with a bursting tonic chord, featured an upward *crescendo* leap from the dominant to the tonic. This was soon removed, probably because as the title appears suddenly from the black, so music should accordingly appear suddenly from the silence—a *crescendo* with a dominant-to-tonic leap would have better suited a fade in.[31] The overwhelming chord is followed by a canon-structured fanfare and finally by the film's main theme—the Luke Skywalker leitmotiv—followed by a secondary theme played by strings: "Like many of the overtures to old Hollywood melodramas, the *Star Wars* overture is divided into two sections, based on a musical contrast between a 'hard' masculine and a 'soft' feminine theme."[32] Williams describes his approach to the film's opening music:

> The opening of the film was visually so stunning, with that lettering that comes out and the spaceships and so on, that it was clear that music had to kind of smack you right in the eye and do something very strong. It's in my mind a very simple, very direct tune that jumps an octave in a very dramatic way, and has a triplet placed in it that has a kind of grab. I tried to construct something that again would have this idealistic, uplifting but military flare to it, and set it in the brass instruments, which I love anyway, which I used to play as a student, as a

youngster. And try to get it so it's set in the most brilliant register of the trumpets, horns and trombones so that we'd have a blazingly brilliant fanfare at the opening of the piece. And contrast that with the second theme that was lyrical and romantic and adventurous also. And give it all a kind of ceremonial . . . it's not a march but very nearly that. So you almost kind of want to [*Williams laughs*] [pat] your feet to it or stand up and salute when you hear it—I mean there's a little bit of that ceremonial aspect. More than a little I think.[33]

In such a film the score should not only support the narration but also have a mythopoeic function by strengthening those archetypal structures and references to the collective unconscious and mythical heritage inspired by Joseph Campbell's works.[34] Accordingly, Williams injected into the music hints, allusions, and quotations that could evoke past musical experiences in the listener and connect him with a sort of musical collective unconscious: "That's what in performance one tries to get with orchestras, and we talk about that at orchestral rehearsals: that it isn't only notes, it's this reaching back into past. As creatures we don't know if we have a future, but we certainly share a great past. We remember it, in language and in pre-language, and that's where music lives— it's to this area in our souls that it can speak."[35] This vision explains Williams's fondness for brass instruments, like the trumpets and the horns: "When I've tried to analyze my lifelong love of the French horn, I've had to conclude that it's mainly because of the horn's capacity to stir memories of antiquity. The very sound of the French horn conjures images stored in the collective psyche. It's an instrument that invites us to 'dream backward to the ancient time.'"[36] The memories of antiquity are also evoked by tone intervals, namely the perfect fifth, an idiomatic trait of Williams's that can also be found, for example, in *Superman: The Movie* (Richard Donner, 1978) and *E.T. the Extra-Terrestrial* (Steven Spielberg, 1982): "The interval of the perfect fifth also rattles our memories of antiquity,"[37] and "The interval of the musical fifth we use to celebrate has been with us thousands of years."[38]

Some scholars criticize Williams's music in general—and *Star Wars* in particular—for being allegedly too derivative and based on "stealing" from the great composers of the past.[39] The "Main Title," for example, is not only similar in spirit to many of Korngold's themes like *Captain Blood* (Michael Curtiz, 1935); *The Adventures of Robin Hood* (Michael Curtiz-William Keighley, 1938); and *The Sea Hawk*, but it is also almost a direct quote of the main theme of *Kings Row* (Sam Wood, 1942).

Top stave: Transcription of Erich Wolfgang Korngold, "Main Title," from the *Kings Row* film score (© 1942 ASCAP), published by Warner Olive Music LLC, administered by Universal Music (ear transcription from the film's soundtrack) [Used in compliance with the U.S. Copyright Act, Section 107]. *Bottom stave*: Transcription of John Williams, "Main Title" (mm. 3–10), from *Star Wars: Suite for Orchestra* (© 1977 BMI), published by Bantha Music and Warner-Tamerlane Publishing Corp., administered by Warner-Tamerlane Publishing Corp., printed by Hal Leonard, "John Williams Signature Edition," 044900057 [Used in compliance with the U.S. Copyright Act, Section 107].

The dissonant orchestral chords that can be heard right after the opening titles—during the attack by the Imperial ship—are similar to those of "Mars, the Bringer of War" from the suite *The Planets* (1916) by Gustav Holst.

Top staves: Transcription of Gustav Holst, "Mars, the Bringer of War" (movement 7, mm. 1–7), from *The Planets* (1921, public domain), originally published by Goodwin & Tabb Ltd., reprinted by Dover Publications, Inc., 1996. *Bottom staves*: Transcription of John Williams, "Main Title" (mm. 84–88), from *Star Wars: Suite for Orchestra* (© 1977 BMI), published by Bantha Music and Warner-Tamerlane Publishing Corp., administered by Warner-Tamerlane Publishing Corp., printed by Hal Leonard, "John Williams Signature Edition," 044900057 [Used in compliance with the U.S. Copyright Act, Section 107].

The derivative nature and the musical quotations are another method that Williams uses to evoke in the viewer/listener's mind some musical memories of a shared past: "[A] lot of these references are deliberate. They're an attempt to evoke a response in the audience where we want to elicit a certain kind of reaction. Another thing is that, whenever one is involved in writing incidental music—where you have specific backgrounds, specific periods, certain kinds of characters and so on—the work is bound to be derivative in a certain sense. The degree to which you can experiment, as you can in a concert work, is very limited. You're fulfilling more of a role of a designer, in the same way that a set designer would do a design for a period opera."[40]

Symphonic Music Rocks!

Lucas and many others feared that the film would be a box-office failure. On the contrary, *Star Wars* opened on 25 May 1977 and met a rapidly growing audience. Thanks to word-of-mouth advertising, it soon won huge success, even surpassing the highest-grossing film to date, *Jaws* (Steven Spielberg, 1975). Unexpectedly, the music was a resounding hit too: in mid-July, the double LP featuring seventy-four minutes of straight symphonic music and no songs at all had already sold 650,000 copies and grossed $9 million.[41] It would eventually sell more than 4 million copies, becoming the best-selling symphonic album of all time.[42] Lucas acknowledged the music's central contribution to the film's success to such an extent that he awarded the composer an extra bonus: a 1 percent share of the film's profits.[43] Meanwhile, Williams won his third Academy Award, one Golden Globe, and three Grammy Awards, and also received a Grammy nomination for "Best Album of the Year," unprecedented for an album of symphonic film music.[44]

Williams reestablished the symphony orchestra as a musical means for film music and as a stylistic device for film narration. And too, Williams's orchestra was a grand symphony orchestra. According to Lionel Newman, "[H]e has taught us to use full orchestra; in the old days, 50–60 men on a picture was considered a large orchestra—now, because of him, you can't think of a big movie without thinking of using a full symphony orchestra."[45] Williams's introduction of the big, full symphony orchestra was also made possible by technical innovations in sound recording, namely the Dolby Stereo process, which made it feasible to have a level of sound fidelity and clarity previously impossible.[46]

A sign of the new favor regained by the symphonic sound after the film's release was that the London Symphony resumed a steady involvement in film projects. During the 1960s and 1970s, when the modern style had ousted the symphonic sound, the London Symphony had exited the film market, with the exception of the Tchaikovsky biopic *The Music Lover* (Ken Russell, 1970, music by André Previn). Thanks to *Star Wars*, the London Symphony not only returned to work in films but also became sought after. In the following years, Williams himself worked with the LSO on various projects: *Superman: The Movie*; *Dracula* (John Badham, 1979); *Raiders of the Lost Ark* (Steven Spielberg, 1981); *Monsignor* (Frank Perry, 1982); and five additional films of the *Star Wars* saga.

Williams continued to compose music for the following *Star Wars* films and expanded the saga's musical catalogue over a period spanning twenty-eight years. Most notably, for *The Empire Strikes Back* (Irvin Kershner, 1980) he enlarged the orchestral setting to include up to 129 musicians and synthesizer touches for the magic tree scene.[47] Three new memorable leitmotivs are presented: a serene theme for the sage Jedi master Yoda, a threateningly imposing militaristic march for Darth Vader, and an expansive love theme for Han Solo and Princess Leia. Among the outstanding musical episodes are the battle of Hoth sequence, whose orchestration called for five piccolos, five oboes, an eight-percussion battery, two grand pianos, and three harps;[48] and the balletic accompaniment to the Millennium Falcon crossing the asteroid field. *Return of the Jedi* (Richard Marquand, 1983) saw the introduction of a malevolent motif for the evil Emperor, performed in dark timbre by a wordless male chorus; a brisk Prokofiev-like march for the teddy-bear-like inhabitants of planet Endor, the Ewoks; a slimy tuba leitmotiv for the space mobster Jabba the Hutt; and a warm and lyrical theme for the Luke and Leia sibling relationship. Memorable musical sequences are the majestic arrival of the Emperor on board; the highly kinetic, and again ballet-like, battle of Endor; and the climatic duel between the Emperor and Luke, with Darth Vader eventually siding with Luke, resulting in an unexpectedly poignant rendition of Darth Vader's theme as the archvillain gives his life to save Luke.

In the second trilogy, there are fewer new leitmotivs per episode. The first trilogy (1977–83) tells the story of a journey from tyranny to freedom, but the second one (1999–2005) is a prequel and concerns the events that had caused that tyranny, thus being a journey from freedom to tyranny. Consequently, the music for the first trilogy is more buoyant, optimistic, hopeful in tone, while in the second trilogy the music becomes more somber, doom-laden, desperate as the plot progresses and things get worse. For *Star Wars: Episode I—The Phantom Menace* (1999) Williams composed "Duel of the Fates," a *Carmina Burana*-like relentless piece for chorus and orchestra, which alternates driving *ostinato* writing with arresting *a cappella* choral salvos:

> This choral piece . . . is a result of my thinking that something ritualistic and/or pagan and antique might be very effective. I thought that the introduction of a chorus at a certain point in the film might just be the right thing to use. And, to take that idea of simplicity a bit further, I thought that I needed some kind of a text in order to do this. . . . One of my favorite books is Robert Graves' *White Goddess*, which is basically a history of poetry, but also has a lot to do with Celtic folklore. . . . I remembered the great Celtic epic poem *The Battle of the Trees*. . . . There is a stanza in that poem . . . which is roughly, "Under the tongue root a fight most dread / While another rages behind the head." And for no conscious sensible reason, the idea of a fight, something raging and imagined in the head more than anywhere seemed to be a good mystical cryptic piece of business. I collaborated with some friends at Harvard University, first asking them to translate it into Celtic, then into Greek, and finally into Sanskrit, just looking for good choral sounds and good vowels. The reason we like to sing in Italian is because it does not have consonant word endings, like our English, which is so hard to sing. Celtic does not work either for that same reason, nor does Greek. But Sanskrit is less well-known and has beautiful sounds. . . . I have reduced the stanza which was translated literally and used either single words or syllables or combinations of these things, the words "dreaded fight" for example, and repeated them.[49]

For the little boy Anakin Skywalker, who is doomed to become the archvillain Darth Vader, Williams penned a theme that already presents the "Darth Vader's Theme" concealed within: "It's the kind of theme you would have for a young boy, very innocent, lyrical and idealistic. But it's made up of intervals from Darth Vader's 'Imperial March' . . . an archetypical evil expression. I made Anakin's theme out of those intervals by inverting them or rearranging them rhythmically or accompanying them harmonically in a different way. It sounds familiar, very sweet. But if you listen to it carefully, there's a hint [of evil]."[50]

Star Wars: Episode II—Attack of The Clones (2002) features a passionate love theme for the illegitimate, ill-fated romance between Anakin and Padme. The theme, "Across the Stars," reworks the intervals of "Main Title" (Luke's leit-motiv/theme) to remind us that Luke will be the offspring of Anakin and Padme's love: "George [Lucas] wanted me to write a real old-fashioned love theme, and that is one of the hardest things to do—to write something that is melodic, accessible, and direct, able to take the lead but also able to be heard as an accompaniment to dialogue. There has to be a kind of space around it. In this case, there needed to be a tragic element in it, too."[51]

The central set piece of *Star Wars: Episode III—Revenge of the Sith* (2005) is a furious theme for chorus and orchestra, "Battle of the Heroes." It features violent wordless choral bursts and interweaves "The Force Theme"—associated throughout the saga with the Jedis and the good side of the Force—with an ominous horn motif based on the medieval sequence *Dies Irae*. Fittingly, the piece is showcased in the final duel between Obi Wan and his pupil Anakin, who has just betrayed the Jedis and passed to the "Dark Side." The duel results in the transformation of Anakin into Darth Vader and will eventually mark the demise of the Jedis—apocalyptically enough.

Musically, the *Star Wars* saga is a unique achievement. Williams explains:

> Well, the *Star Wars* experience has been, I think, unique in music history, film music history. Not because of me, there's no waving my own flag, but because of this simple reason. . . . I thought that *Star Wars* was just over and completed when I put the baton down at the end of the first recording. And a year or so later, he [Lucas] rang up and said, "I have the next installment. And we need the old music from the first film, but we also need new music for new characters, new situations." So a process started, that lasted over, I guess, 20-plus years, of adding bits and pieces of material to a musical tapestry that started . . . to pile up off the floors, quite an extensive library of music. Each film having over two hours of music. So there's about 12 to 14 hours, maybe 15 hours of orchestral music composed over a period of not 2 years but 20. And that, I think, is a unique opportunity for a composer, . . . to go back over and perhaps improve some of the things I'd done. And what's fascinating is, to me, that maybe some of the newer music isn't any better or as good as the earlier ones. That's one's own personal inner struggle, inner voice. When you write something when you're 40 years old, you wouldn't write it the same way when one is 70 and vice versa. One may be better than the other or a different kind of energy or different kind of acuity, whatever will go with it. So it's been a fascinating journey, *Star Wars*.[52]

During the years following its first release, the music for Lucas's space-opera has enjoyed great success beyond the screen. In 1994 the scores for the first trilogy were reissued as a 4-CD box set containing some additional previously unreleased material, which sold more than 150,000 copies, quite staggering a figure for a film-music re-release.[53] In 1997, on the twentieth anniversary of the first film's screening, BMG issued a series of double CDs featuring the complete score of each chapter of the trilogy. In 2004 the same double-CDs were reissued by Sony Classical. Over the years, there have also been huge numbers of suites and anthologies recorded by various orchestras around the world. In 2005 the American Film Institute chose *Star Wars* (1977) as the best film score of all time.[54] In 1999 "Duel of the Fates," the Williams piece for chorus and orchestra from *Star Wars: Episode I—The Phantom Menace* (George Lucas, 1999), was reportedly the first symphonic video-clip to be featured on the music channel MTV; excerpts from the film are alternated with shots of Williams conducting the London Symphony and the London Voices.

The presence on MTV shows how widely Williams's music spread, reaching unexpected targets for symphonic music. As Williams pointed out, "That's not a rock band on the sound track, not a Fender bass or a rhythm section. Yet even the kids liked the sound of it, they felt the need for this kind of communication."[55] One of the merits of the *Star Wars* score is that it has introduced many people to symphonic music, and thus one of the motivations for Williams having been awarded an honorary degree by Boston University in 1985:

> In an age when, in both popular and serious music, melody and harmony have had their backs to the wall, you have led millions to enjoy and appreciate music that would have been recognized as such by Beethoven or Brahms. This is no small achievement. We have watched and listened with delighted astonishment as you have ennobled anew the art of background music. But your cinematic music is more than background: it takes on an existence outside the movie house, selling millions of albums. Your suite from *Star Wars* has become part of the concert repertoire. Through your music . . . you expose children who have studied music neither privately nor in school and who hear little but single-note rhythms in popular music to ambitious melodies and to complex harmonic and rhythmic structures on a symphonic scale. In the tradition of Rachmaninov, Prokofiev, and Korngold, you have made orchestral music accessible to and enjoyable by the millions.[56]

Williams's score has been successful in concert halls too. On 20 November 1977 Zubin Mehta conducted a thirty-minute-long suite with the Los Angeles Philharmonic in front of 17,500 people in a sold-out concert at the Hollywood Bowl in Los Angeles.[57] This was the first one of the many "Star Wars concerts" to follow.[58] Williams himself was later invited to conduct his music by such musical institutions as the London Symphony Orchestra (16 February 1978) and the National Philharmonic (18 October 1980), both at the Royal Albert Hall in London. On 1 April 1978 Mehta repeated the previous year's program, adding Williams's suite from *Close Encounters of the Third Kind* (Steven Spielberg, 1977), and in that same month Williams conducted his music in San Francisco.[59] On 26 March 1978 Williams also appeared as a guest conductor on the TV show *Previn and the Pittsburgh* on PBS, in which André Previn invited him to conduct the Pittsburgh Symphony Orchestra in two extracts from the *Star Wars Suite*: "Princess Leia's Theme" and "The Throne Room and End Title." David Wessel's 1983 *Boston Globe* quote gives a better idea of the success of the *Star Wars* music in concert halls: "On *Star Wars*, according to his business manager, Williams has made almost as much money from performances as he did from record sales. After the film was released, Williams reworked the score into a 36-minute piece for orchestra. Fourteen sets of sheet music for full orchestra were prepared and rented to orchestras. Eiseman, then running 20th Century Fox's music publishing house, set a sliding scale rental fee that ran from $250 a performance for a 4500-seat auditorium to $1000 for one with more than 20,000 seats. 'We had close to 1000 concerts—maybe more than 1000 concerts now,' Eiseman said. 'Williams got half the money.'"[60]

This vast exposure and the success of his music favored Williams's appointment as conductor-in-residence of the Boston Pops Orchestra, a fundamental step toward the cracking of the "iron curtain" that isolates film music from art/absolute music and other types of applied music.

Star Wars proved that the traditional practice and models of Hollywood symphonic film scoring were still feasible and could also be successful for the present film industry; indeed, they could compete with the pop genre not only as a better way to help the narration but also in terms of revenue from soundtrack album sales.

Film Music Renaissance(?)

After *Star Wars*, the use of the symphonic score grew consistently in importance in the late 1970s and throughout the '80s.[61] Scholars, film-music historians, and experts are also more or less unanimous in giving Williams's score credit for launching a sort of "Film Music Renaissance."[62] Williams is typically humble and rather cautious in giving his score the merit of having single-handedly created such a thing: "Well, I don't know if it's fair to say the *Star Wars* films brought back symphonic scores per se. We've been using symphony orchestras since even before sound. Anyone interested in film knows that music seems to be an indispensable ingredient for film-makers. . . . I think if the use of symphony orchestras went out of fad in the '50s and '60s for some reason it was just that: it was out of fad. Someone would have brought it back. It's too useful and too successful not to have it back. I think that after the success of *Star Wars* the orchestras enjoyed a very successful period because of that. . . . I don't think we can claim that it was a renaissance really, more than just a change of fad if you'd like. . . . A little helping push."[63]

Williams perfectly understood what type of music was needed for a film like *Star Wars*; he possesses a deep understanding and a thorough knowledge of both the art-music and the Hollywood film-music repertoires, and he possesses such skills to be able to compose exactly the required type of music. He remarked, "In the sixties and seventies directors were interested in super-realism and a kind of proletarian leanness, where the cosmetic effect of a large symphony orchestra was just exactly what was not wanted. But now fantasy films have come back into fashion, and as a musician I'm very happy about it."[64]

However, Williams's aforementioned caution is acute and historically accurate. To state that *Star Wars* restored the classical Hollywood music style altogether is not correct, as it is not true to say that since *Star Wars* the symphony orchestra has become the dominant musical means in Hollywood cinema. Only six months after the release of *Star Wars*, the Bee Gees disco music used for the music track of *Saturday Night Fever* (John Badham, 1977) was not only a central factor of the box office success but also became one of the best-selling albums in history.[65] Similarly, Giorgio Moroder won an Oscar for his electronic pop music for *Midnight Express* (Alan Parker, 1978), defeating both Morricone's lyrical symphonic score for *Days of Heaven* (Terrence Malick, 1978) and Williams's rousing grand-orchestral score for *Superman: The Movie.*

In the following years, new idioms emerged as highly successful in Hollywood. Among them, disco music, New Age impressionism, ethnic influences (World Music), minimalism, and the like. In particular, the 1980s saw the wide spread of synthesizers and electronic music, preferred (also for economical reasons) by a number of emerging practitioners, such as Vangelis in *Blade Runner* (Ridley Scott, 1982) and *Chariots of Fire* (Hugh Hudson, 1981); Giorgio Moroder in *Midnight Express* and *Flashdance* (Adrian Lyne, 1983); Brad Fiedel in *The Terminator* (James Cameron, 1984); Harold Faltermeyer's "synth-pop" for *Beverly Hills Cop* (Martin Brest, 1984); the Angelo Badalamenti and David Lynch collaboration, starting with *Blue Velvet* (1986); and the director/musician John Carpenter in *Halloween* (1978). Even the past-generation French composer Maurice Jarre—formerly famous for imitating the lush symphonic Hollywood music in David Lean's *Lawrence of Arabia* (1962), *Dr. Zhivago* (1965), and *Ryan's Daughter*

(1970)—discarded the symphony orchestra and opted for the synthesizer in *The Year of Living Dangerously* (Peter Weir, 1982); *Witness* (Peter Weir, 1985); and *Fatal Attraction* (Adrian Lyne, 1987). All the examples above show that the 1980s were as much the decade of Williams's symphonic neoclassicism as the decade of the synthesized pop music.

The style of film music after 1978 is perhaps best defined as "eclecticism," which can be characterized by a freer, hybridized, and varied wide-range mingling of previous styles, languages, techniques, and musical means.[66] Cases of Mickey-Mousing, leitmotiv, electronic music, rock, pop, jazz, world music, and symphonic sound coexist not only in the general paradigm but sometimes also in the same film. For example, the *Flashdance* score is in a pop language and uses electronic means, but classical techniques such as Mickey-Mousing are also employed.[67] The contemporary style, which has also intensified the internationalism inherited from the modern style, can be said to be not only eclectic but also cosmopolitan. National film-music schools tend to disappear in favor of an international style that sounds similar everywhere.

The main contribution of *Star Wars* to the overall paradigm of the eclectic style is the large orchestra as the sound de rigueur for blockbuster films, regardless of the language, which can range from David Arnold's mimicry of Williams's idiom in *Independence Day* (Roland Emmerich, 1996) to Hans Zimmer's rock music arranged for orchestra in *The Rock* (Michael Bay, 1996). Moreover, *Star Wars* has promoted the revival of certain classical techniques like Mickey-Mousing, mostly used in adventure films and comedies, and leitmotiv used, for example, by Danny Elfman in *Batman* (Tim Burton, 1989) and *Batman Returns* (Tim Burton, 1992), and in the *Star Trek* series. As to the late-romantic dialect, even Williams's intra-opus style became more eclectic in the following chapters of the saga, including atonal writing and electronic-music episodes.

Even if there were not really a symphonic film music renaissance or a return of the classical style as such, how can Williams's work and idiom be defined within the post–*Star Wars* eclectic paradigm? The answer is that Williams has founded a "neoclassical trend" of which he still continues to be the greatest exponent. The peak of such neoclassical trend can be placed between 1975 and 1983, the years in which Williams composed the first *Star Wars* trilogy; *The Fury* (Brian De Palma, 1978); *Superman: The Movie*, *Jaws 2* (Jeannot Szwarc, 1978); *Dracula, 1941* (Steven Spielberg, 1979); *Raiders of the Lost Ark* (1981), and *E.T. the Extra-Terrestrial* (1981). Already in 1980 Williams had stated, "I don't expect what I have been doing for the last two or three years will last—nothing does; already in some studios they are calling for more pop music, for more youth-oriented pop noise."[68] The year 1983 has been chosen as the end of the trend:

in that year the album from the score of *Return of the Jedi* (Richard Marquand, 1983), the closing chapter of the first *Star Wars* trilogy, was not released as a double-LP but as a single LP, unlike the albums from the previous two films, even though more than 130 minutes of music had been composed for the film. And unlike the two previous albums, it had disappointing sales.[69] That same year also marked the last collaboration between Williams and the LSO, the "official" and most sought-after orchestra of the neoclassical trend. The second and third chapters of the Indiana Jones trilogy, *Indiana Jones and the Temple of Doom* (Steven Spielberg, 1984) and *Indiana Jones and the Last Crusade* (Steven Spielberg, 1989), were recorded in Los Angeles with a freelance studio orchestra. Williams would not work again with the LSO on a film until 1999, when he returned to Abbey Road Studios to record *Star Wars: Episode I—The Phantom Menace*. In 1984, for the adventure film *Romancing the Stone* (Robert Zemeckis), the emerging composer Alan Silvestri used electronic means and a modern pop dialect instead of following in Williams's neoclassical footsteps. In 1985 Silvestri's theme for *Back to the Future* (Robert Zemeckis) sounded more symphonic rock than neoclassical. Moreover, the songs "The Power of Love" and "Back in Time" by Huey Lewis and the News were the highlights of both the film and the album. A further proof of the anything-but-hegemonic role of neoclassicism is the case of *Legend* (Ridley Scott, 1985). The rich symphonic score composed by Jerry Goldsmith was removed from the American version and replaced with Tangerine Dream's electronic New Age music.[70]

The classical style did not actually rise again. With *Star Wars* and his subsequent works, Williams composed neoclassical scores in which he recovered many features of the classical style. After years of mostly market-oriented music, his narrative-oriented scores brought back to the general attention the importance and power of music as a device of cinematic art, and the fundamental help that it can give to film narration. This also caused a stronger awareness and interest for the rediscovery of Hollywood's musical tradition.

If *Star Wars* can be seen as the first clamorous manifestation of the neoclassical trend, the first signs of Williams's penchant for neoclassicism are already visible in his first 1960s film works.

5

Williams's Early Years

Spotting the First Traces of Neoclassicism

John Towner Williams was born in New York on 8 February 1932. His father, John Towner Williams Sr.—known as Johnny Williams—was a percussionist in the CBS Radio Orchestra and a member of the Raymond Scott Quintette.[1] Young Williams studied music and learned to play the trumpet, the trombone, the bassoon, the cello, and the clarinet, and used to follow his father into the recording studios and attend the sessions.[2] He soon decided to devote himself primarily to the piano, aiming to pursue a career as a classical concert pianist. He studied privately in Los Angeles with pianist Robert Van Eps, who was also an active Hollywood orchestrator, and this might be considered Williams's first contact with the world of film music.

Williams soon showed uncommon skills for composition and arrangement. During his years at the North Hollywood High School, he used to arrange music for the school band, applying to popular melodies the techniques he had learned from orchestration manuals. Later, he moved to the Los Angeles City College and the University of California at Los Angeles. Meanwhile, he was privately tutored in composition and counterpoint by Mario Castelnuovo Tedesco.[3]

In 1952 Williams was drafted and during his service in the U.S. Air Force he had the chance to work on his first film score:

I . . . spent two years with the Northeast Air Command Band in St. John's, Newfoundland. This was a wonderful experience, and it seemed I was the only one there who could write arrangements for that band. I conducted some of the rehearsals, and the band played summer concerts in a gazebo during which the base commander often requested his favorite songs. After the end of World War II, the Canadian government commissioned a German company, North Atlantic Films, to make a documentary about the Maritime Provinces of Canada. In 1953 the company was working in St. John's, and some of these people attended the summer concerts and heard my band arrangements. As a result they asked my commanding officer if I could write music for the film. He not only granted me permission but allowed me to use several band members. I discovered some folk songs of Newfoundland in the library and wove these into the score. This was my first attempt at film writing, and I used only winds.[4]

An article of the time was devoted to the young soldier-composer: "With discharge day coming his way in January 1955, Johnny plans to continue his studies at UCLA with a goal of writing and playing for motion pictures. If his advancement continues to be as rapid as it has been to this point, soon the words 'Music by Johnny Williams' will flash on the local screen and tell the realization of the goal of a former March airman."[5]

After military service, apparently not sure whether to opt for a career as a composer or as a pianist, Williams mused, "I guess I wanted to play Rachmaninoff with the New York Philharmonic."[6] Williams moved to New York, where he was admitted to the prestigious Juilliard School in the piano class of Rosina Lhévinne, where Van Cliburn was one of Williams's schoolmates.[7] To earn some money while studying, he worked as a pianist in jazz ensembles. However, his skills in composition soon proved his strongest talent: "I started to hear some of her [Lhévinne's] other students who were even younger than I was playing around the building . . . and I thought 'Well, if that's what the competition is, maybe I should be a composer.'"[8]

A Serendipitous Start in Hollywood

Back in Los Angeles in 1956, Williams became a father—after marrying singer/actress Barbara Ruick—and thus needed a stable job to sustain his new family. There happened to be a vacant pianist chair in the studio orchestra at Columbia

Pictures, and Williams auditioned for the post. He was hired, thus entering the world of film music as an orchestra member. Williams's piano playing can be heard in *Funny Face* (Stanley Donen, 1957, music adapted by Adolph Deutsch); *South Pacific* (Joshua Logan, 1958, musical direction by Alfred Newman); *The Big Country* (William Wyler, 1958, music by Jerome Moross); *Some Like It Hot* (Billy Wilder, 1959, music by Adolph Deutsch); *City of Fear* (Irving Lerner, 1959, music by Jerry Goldsmith); *Breakfast at Tiffany's* (Blake Edwards, 1961, music by Henry Mancini); *West Side Story* (Jerome Robbins, Robert Wise, 1961, music by Leonard Bernstein); and *To Kill a Mockingbird* (Robert Mulligan, 1962, music by Elmer Bernstein). Perhaps his most famous contribution is the piano riff that opens the title music in the TV series *Peter Gunn* (Blake Edwards, 1958–61, music by Henry Mancini). During this stint as a pianist, in addition to working for Columbia Pictures, he also played for the 20th Century Fox studio from 1958 on.

Williams gradually left the piano bench to undertake the typical career path in Hollywood's music departments: he worked as an orchestrator on *The Apartment* (Billy Wilder, 1960, music by Adolph Deutsch) and *The Guns of Navarone* (J. Lee Thompson, 1961, music by Dimitri Tiomkin) while also working in the record industry as an arranger and conductor for Columbia Records, with such singers as Mahalia Jackson, Doris Day, and Vic Damone. The next step was composition, and the gradual shift started in 1958, when he was offered a seven-year contract in the music department of the Revue Television Studios, later known as Universal Television Studios. He worked on such TV series as *M Squad* (1958–59), *Wagon Train* (1958–63); *Checkmate* (1960–62); *Bachelor Father* (1959–60); *Kraft Suspense Theater* (1960); *Alcoa Premiere* (1961–62); *The Crisis* (1963–65); *Gilligan's Island* (1964–65); and *Lost in Space* (1965). Meanwhile, he also stepped up to the podium to conduct recordings of his own music, not so much for ambition as for "self-defense" from lesser conductors.[9]

Television work in those years was good training for film composers. They had to deliver a steady output of music, always working under tight deadlines, and they had to learn to write fast and develop a quick, sure-fire instinct for what was suitable for the narrative needs of a given scene. As a staff composer, Williams had to work on thirty-nine one-hour TV shows per year, churning out scores of the most diverse kinds from comedies to thrillers to Westerns: "The shows I was assigned to were the hardest shows, the hour shows, which meant I had to write about 20 to 25 minutes of music a week, score it and record it. It was a tremendous learning opportunity for me. What I wrote may not have been good—it probably wasn't good; but the main idea was to get it done, and I got it done."[10] This work routine in television was very similar to that of the music departments in the old studios—although smaller in proportion. In this formative period, dividing his time between playing piano in studio orchestras and composing in the Revue Studio music department, Williams had the opportunity of mixing with, and learning the tricks of the trade from, some of the masters of Hollywood music: Alfred Newman, Dimitri Tiomkin, Franz Waxman, and Bernard Herrmann—with whom he became a close friend. Williams also acknowledges the important teachings of Conrad Salinger, one of the top arrangers and orchestrators in Hollywood, whose influence can be heard in Williams's arrangement of Cole Porter's "Anything Goes" that opens *Indiana Jones and the Temple of Doom* (Steven Spielberg, 1984): "[I] spent a lot of time with Conrad Salinger. [I] learned a tremendous amount from him—mostly from looking at his scores. As you know, he principally did musicals; he was the architect of what you might call the 'MGM sound'—that marvelous glow that the orchestra had. And it really came from his writing. His scores were highly idiosyncratic: he'd have the third trombone way up in tenor clef, and trumpets low down doing funny things—as if some Chinaman had written the score! And then you'd go on the sound stage the next day and hear the result . . . it was like a wonder. No one quite had his touch. . . . [O]f all the orchestrators . . . I think I learned more from Conrad Salinger than anyone else, even though I don't write anything like him."[11]

Most of Williams's career would be spent as a freelance composer in the post-studio-era "package-unit" system—each film project is a team-up of freelance artists and technicians assembled and contracted for that single project, unlike the typical in-house staff of payrolled people that used to work on each film of their studio in the old system. Yet Williams moved his first steps into the business during the last days of the studio system and in-house music departments, and he acquired an extensive training in the high-pressure schedules of television production. The relevance of this early "imprinting" within the old practice was of enormous importance in shaping Williams's neoclassical approach; it had a considerable influence on his work habits, which retain a number of old-school characteristics—as we shall see.

Johnny Williams, Emerging Composer

After television, he moved on to cinema. His first significant collaborations in feature films were with Don Siegel for the thriller *The Killers* (1964), with Frank Sinatra for the war film *None But the Brave* (1965)—the singer/actor's only directorial credit—and with Andrew V. McLaglen for the Western *The Rare Breed* (1966, starring James Stewart and Maureen O'Hara). After these multifaceted experiences, in the mid-1960s Williams was pigeonholed as a comedy com-poser.[12] Williams provided scores for such films as *John Goldfarb, Please Come Home!* (J. Lee Thompson, 1965); *Not with My Wife, You Don't!* (Norman Panama, 1966); *Penelope* (Arthur Hiller, 1966); *How to Steal a Million* (William Wyler, 1966); *A Guide for the Married Man* (Gene Kelly, 1967); and *Fitzwilly* (Delbert Mann, 1967). Most of them were somewhat spicy comedies in the typical post-Hays-code, liberated-mores style of the 1960s — "Lots of brass chords on cuts to brassieres," Williams recalls.[13]

In the next decade Williams was shifted to another genre and thanks to his previous collaboration with producer Irwin Allen for *Lost in Space*, he became the composer of choice for "disaster movies" like *The Poseidon Adventure* (Ronald Neame, 1972); *Earthquake* (Mark Robson, 1974); and *The Towering Inferno* (John Guillermin, 1974). He also worked in Europe on *Heidi* (Delbert Mann, 1968), co-produced by the Federal Republic of Germany and featuring a Richard Straussian *Eine Alpensinfonie*–like score performed by members of the Hamburg Opera; *Jane Eyre* (Delbert Mann, 1970) for British television, showcasing a sensitive score in the British idioms of Ralph Vaughan Williams and Frederick Delius; and *Story of a Woman* (Leonardo Bercovici, 1970), an Italian co-production to which he also contributed the song "Uno di qua, l'altra di là" sung by Ornella Vanoni and recorded in Milan.[14]

Besides demonstrating his ability to produce functional and well-written scores, Williams was already distinguishing himself from the average composers with a number of outstanding scores. For *The Reivers* (Mark Rydell, 1969), he adopted Copland's Americana idiom to paint a lively score imbued with nos-talgia, which is the perfect musical correlative of Faulkner's eponymous novel set in 1905. For *The Long Goodbye* (Robert Altman, 1973), he composed a mono-thematic score à la *Laura* in which the melody of the theme song (lyrics by Johnny Mercer) is skillfully arranged for different instrumentations and used at both non-diegetic and diegetic levels. And again, for *Jane Eyre*, Williams wrote a re-fined score that shows his thorough knowledge and love for British music. For *The Cowboys* (Mark Rydell, 1972), he provided a driving theme for full orchestra in line with the Copland-Moross-Bernstein Western tradition. The most notable and experimental work of the period is *Images* (Robert Altman, 1972), the story of the psychic double life of a schizophrenic woman, a children's book author, for which Williams composed a similarly schizophrenic score. A melancholic melody for piano and strings accompanies the woman's fantasies and the peaceful moments in which she works on her book. On the other hand, the psychotic episodes in which she sees her double self or talks with her dead lover are accompanied by disturbingly atonal and aleatoric music, performed by the percussionist Stomu Yamash'ta on metal and glass sculptures by the Parisian artists François and Bernard Baschet.[15]

In the first part of his career, Williams ranked among the most gifted and versatile composers of his generation. In addition to traditional symphonic scores for large orchestra—like *The Rare Breed* or *The Cowboys*—he composed a modern-style restrained score for *The Missouri Breaks* (Arthur Penn, 1976), scored for guitars, banjos, bass guitars, and harmonicas. Besides Copland's idiom and jazz dialect used in detective stories like *Checkmate*, Williams could also handle up-to-date pop dialects: rhythms and inflections typical of the current dance music can be found either in light-hearted versions in comedies like *A Guide for the Married Man*, or dramatically arranged for orchestra in thrillers like *Towering Inferno* and *Earthquake*. Williams's versatility was such that he followed one of the most characteristic practices of modern style as well, namely the incorporation of at least one pop song in each film. He wrote songs both for comedies—"A Big Beautiful Ball" for *Not with My Wife, You Don't!* or "Two Lovers" for *How to Steal a Million*—and for dramas—"None But the Brave" for *None But the Brave,* "Dream Way" for *The Man Who Loved Cat Dancing* (Richard C. Sarafian, 1973), and "Daddy's Gone A-Hunting" for *Daddy's Gone A-Hunting* (Mark Robson, 1969). In an early-1970s interview, however, Williams confessed feeling uncomfortable as a songwriter:

> Well, it has been overdone. God knows, it's a practice that I've been involved in on a few occasions myself. Not very happily, ever; some people seem to have a better touch at that than I do. Again, there I have mixed emotions. It's a practice that can be vile and obnoxious, and awful—very often. On the other hand, the commercial part of me says something has to do some business, and the music-selling business is not altogether a bad thing. . . . So on the positive side of it, this business of title song and popular success from film music is both a good thing and a bad thing. It isn't a great thing for the art of music vis-à-vis film scoring. But it does help the sort of general health of the music-publishing, revenue-creating areas of the music business—and the music "business" affects us all.[16]

Although versatility was a key feature of the young Williams, some neo-classical traits were already scattered within his 1960s works. As we have seen, the "spatial perceptive function" became obsolete after the classical period, surviving sporadically as mannerist bursts of Mickey-Mousing in some comedies. At that time, instead of embracing the up-to-date comedy musical style à la

Mancini, found for example in Burt Bacharach's and Quincy Jones's scores for *Casino Royale* (John Huston et al., 1967) and *Cactus Flower* (Gene Saks, 1969), respectively, Williams-the-emerging-composer opted for the illustrative and not-so-up-to-date musical approach featured in such comedies as *Gambit* (Ronald Neame, 1966, music by Maurice Jarre) and *The Glass Bottom Boat* (Frank Tashlin, 1966, music by Frank De Vol). Besides already showing a peculiar interest in explicit synch-points and Mickey-Mousing, Williams also showed a penchant for the leitmotiv technique. A close look at his 1960s films shows that he applied these classical techniques more extensively and systematically than most colleagues. Moreover, he applied them not only to comedies but also to dramas.

A Mancini/Williams Comparison

This section is a statistical survey of the recurrences of the spatial perceptive function in Williams's most important 1960s scores, comparing the number of occurrences in Williams's scores with those of Hollywood's most influential composer at the time and one of the main representatives of modern style, Henry Mancini. The survey compares some Mancini film scores composed in the period from 1962 to 1972 with some coeval Williams scores, choosing five comedies and three dramas by both composers. The Mancini sample contains:

- *Breakfast at Tiffany's* (Blake Edwards, 1961), a bittersweet comedy about nostalgia and loneliness concerning the serendipitous meeting between an eccentric and naïve prostitute (Holly) and a discouraged writer (Paul) maintained as a toy boy by a rich woman
- *Man's Favorite Sport?* (Howard Hawks, 1964), a screwball comedy in the spirit of Hawks's own 1938 *Bringing Up Baby*, the story of Roger, a successful author of fishing manuals who is forced to join a fishing tournament and has to conceal the fact that he is merely a theorist, having never fished before, while also having to cope with the relentless courtship by a troublemaking woman (Abigail)
- *A Shot in the Dark* (Blake Edwards, 1964), a slapstick comedy and the second chapter of inspector Clouseau's adventures, in which the inane detective falls in love with a blonde homicide suspect and tries to prove her innocent
- *The Great Race* (Blake Edwards, 1965), a cartoon-like epic about a car race set in the early twentieth century

- *The Party* (Blake Edwards, 1968), a slapstick humor-filled story of how a Hollywood extra is mistakenly invited to a big-shot party and ends up unintentionally destroying the host's mansion.

The dramas are:

- *Arabesque* (Stanley Donen, 1966), the story of university professor Pollock getting involved, along with a charming female spy, in the hunt for a mysterious code at the risk of his life
- *Wait Until Dark* (Terence Young, 1967), a thriller in which a blind woman (Susy) is trapped alone in her apartment with three criminals who want to retrieve a drug-stuffed doll they believe she is hiding somewhere in the apartment
- *The Night Visitor* (Laslo Benedek, 1971), a thriller in which a psychopath (Salem) escapes from an asylum to take revenge on those who had him locked up.[17]

As for the Williams sample, the comedies are:

- *How to Steal a Million* (William Wyler, 1966), a sophisticated comedy in which Nicole, the daughter of a forger, organizes the theft of a statue her father leased to a museum in order to prevent her father's forgeries from being discovered
- *Fitzwilly* (Delbert Mann, 1967), in which the austere butler Fitzwilliam coordinates thefts and cons to maintain the high standard of living of his oblivious old-lady employer in order to conceal from her the fact that she is now broke
- *Not with My Wife, You Don't!* (Norman Panama, 1966), about the jealousy of two ex-comrades (Tom and "Tank") who continue to contend for the same woman (Julie) even though she is now married to Tom
- *Penelope* (Arthur Hiller, 1966), in which the rich kleptomaniac Penelope resorts to psychoanalysis to discover the origin of her thieving drive but ends up robbing her own husband's bank
- *A Guide for the Married Man* (Gene Kelly, 1967), a farce concerning a clumsy would-be pursuer of extramarital affairs (Paul) who is instructed by an experienced friend on the supposedly successful techniques for cheating on one's wife.

The dramas are:

- *The Killers* (Don Siegel, 1964), the story of a penniless race car driver (Johnny) hired by a gang of bank robbers and then implicated in the ruthless pursuit of the lost loot—a remake of Robert Siodmak's 1946 film
- *Daddy's Gone A-Hunting* (Mark Robson, 1969), a thriller about a married woman (Cathy) who is stalked by her psychopathic ex-boyfriend (Kenneth) who wants to kill her baby to retaliate for her past abortion of the child he had fathered
- *Images* (Robert Altman, 1972), a tale about the psychic double life of a schizophrenic woman.

Comedies outnumber dramas because in the chosen time period, both Williams and Mancini worked more in that genre than in dramas. Each film has been analyzed by focusing on the presence of the spatial perspective function and of the leitmotiv and Mickey-Mousing techniques, but also taking into consideration other traits of the classical style vis-à-vis the modern style. (For brevity's sake, only the results of the comparison are given here, complemented with highlights from the films as evidence.)

First of all, the comparison confirms Mancini's preference for the closed musical numbers, typical of modern style. The comedies in the sample are for the most part directed by Blake Edwards, who used to model his comedic style on Jacques Tati: the viewer has to scan the frame himself to spot the gags, without being closely guided by the film narration—Tati avoided emphasizing the comic actions with non-diegetic music. Mickey-Mousing would be too intrusive and perceptually "coercive" in this type of comedy. Consequently, the Edwards/Mancini duo chose to accompany the comic scenes mostly with diegetic music, which flows independently in the background, as can be seen in *The Party* when Bakshi is clumsily trying to retrieve his shoe from the water stream. Apart from the director's artistic choice, this is also due to the modern-style, market-oriented approach. All films, except for *The Night Visitor*, contain one or more songs, skillfully placed in the right spot by Mancini to advertise them. *The Party* is a hilarious comedy in itself, of course, and since the film is about a party, the many diegetic pieces have a solid realistic motivation; but the film is also a clever showcase to promote Mancini's *cocktail music* and to advertise the tie-in LP album.

The same can be said of *Breakfast at Tiffany's*. In a scene, Paul pays a visit to Holly and they start a conversation only after Holly has put on a disc and turned on the turntable, the mellow light-dance music acting as a diegetic background for their dialogue. Similarly, the many party scenes are accompanied by fashionable dance music. The main theme—"Moon River" (lyrics by Johnny Mercer)—is presented in an instrumental version during the opening credits, sung by Holly at diegetic level with guitar accompaniment, reprised by the chorus at the end of the film, and it also appears as a diegetic "Cha-cha-cha" during a party scene. The only substantial occurrence of spatial perceptive function can be found in a short chain of synch-points in the shoplifting sequence. A stinger by the trombones emphasizes the shop assistant's suspicious look followed by an answering vibraphone chord underlining Holly's look of feigned innocence. Then, an upward harp glissando culminates on Holly playing the toy trumpet that she was about to steal. Oddly, when the two shoplifters flee and almost collide with a policeman, the music does not mark the event, as we might have expected; it keeps up uninterrupted with its excited flow accompanying the couple's escape.

A Shot in the Dark opens with a long sequence in which we see the inhabitants of a luxurious mansion engaged in a network of nocturnal stealthy visits to their secret lovers. The sequence is accompanied by the song "Shadows of Paris" (lyrics by Robert Wells)—the instrumental version of which serves as the film's love theme—and the song flows independently as a closed musical number, without following the visual actions. During the following opening credits, the theme associated with Clouseau's investigation is introduced—it is a jazzy piece akin to the more famous "Pink Panther Theme"—and is presented again arranged for big band as diegetic music during the nudist camp sequence. Clouseau's tumbles are rarely punctuated by music: when he falls into the fountain, when he inadvertently sets fire to his raincoat, or when he jumps out of the window, music places little emphasis on the action. Even the overtly comic fights between Clouseau and Kato are left without music. The only explicit synch-points are the strident bass chords that mark the appearance of the mysterious black-gloved murderer and the stingers that in the denouement scene introduce each close-up of the suspects' worried faces after Clouseau says, "One of you is a murderer."

The Great Race is a striking example, as Mancini rejects Mickey-Mousing in a couple of scenes that would have been a perfect place for this technique. In the sword fight between the Great Leslie and the Baron, everything harkens back to the classical duels starring Errol Flynn in Michael Curtiz's films: swash-buckling costumes, castle halls with chandeliers and stone walls, even the duelists' shadows cast on the walls—a typical Curtiz stylistic trait. Mancini, in spite of that, did not compose a Korngoldian score by treating the duel like a ballet but opted for a simple strings sound pad with slow modulations keeping the harmony unresolved. In line with modern style, he preferred the emotive function, that is, creating tension. Even the following custard-pie fight scene — a traditional slapstick comedy gag since the days of vaudeville, typically having each comic action accompanied by a musical gesture[18] — has no Mickey-Mousing accompaniment, but instead a spirited polka develops independently as a closed musical number throughout the scene.

Who was responsible for the musical choices of these three films? The director Blake Edwards or the composer Henry Mancini? It is clear that a composer has to meet the director's demands, but a director rarely ventures into detailed discussions on the nature of the music to be adopted in each scene; more often, a director will hire a trusted composer known for being in tune with his ideas on music. Therefore, the composer is mainly responsible for a particular musical solution, especially in the case of well-established collabora-tions like that between Mancini and Edwards.[19] Indeed, Mancini's stylistic choices were the same when he worked for Howard Hawks, whose comic style is quite different from Edwards's.[20]

In Hawk's *Man's Favorite Sport?* Roger's clumsy attempt to erect a tent is accompanied by non-diegetic dance music, as well as the gag of a bear ending up riding Roger's motorcycle. Most of the dialogue — like that between Roger and the two girls during the dinner on the terrace, or the conversation between the two girls in their rooms — are accompanied by dance music or piano-bar style Muzak, used at diegetic level. When non-diegetic music accompanies romantic dialogue, its style is modern, since the traditional strings are replaced by woodwinds — following the big-band influence — as in the final dialogue in the woods between Roger and Abigail. Only a few comic moments are high-lighted by explicit synch-points. When Roger catches his first fish, music builds an upward harmonic progression closed by a sharp chord marking the moment in which the man has to dive in to retrieve his fishing rod. Another case is the scene in which Roger's girlfriend unexpectedly arrives and finds him sharing the room with two women. When the bedroom door opens revealing Abigail, the supposed lover, in pajamas, a snare drumroll marks the surprise. Then, a cymbal clash, a plucked strings note, and a triangle tinkle respectively underline the consequent three close-ups on the astonished faces.

As for dramas, it can be noted that music, when not completely absent, performs, again, a purely emotive function. In *Wait Until Dark*, for example, the scene in which Susy, the blind woman, enters her house unaware of the three criminals waiting inside, takes place without music. The first dialogue between Susy and Mike, one of the criminals, is accompanied by a diegetic pop song coming from the on-screen turntable. Finally, the end credits are accompanied by the theme song.[21] There is only one effective episode of spatial perceptive function, when Roat, the boss of the gang, threatens Susy, then teases and disorients her by brushing her face from different directions with a silk scarf. Mancini underlines each scarf touch with a tam-tam rub, a sound that aptly conveys Susy's shivers.[22]

In *Arabesque*, explicit synch-points are more frequent, perhaps because of director Stanley Donen's background as a choreographer. Again, the tam-tam rub is used as a stinger to punctuate different events: the appearance of Beauchamp the "villain" in Professor Pollock's classroom; Pollock's image reflected on the coachwork of the prime minister's Rolls Royce; the threatening revelation of a gun holster under Beauchamp's jacket; Pollock being given an injection of Pentothal. During the chase sequence at the zoo, four shots of snakes are punctuated by four synchronized stingers. In one of the comic-relief moments of the film, Yasmin, the female spy, tries to seduce a Grenadier Guard: we hear a triangle tinkle when she winks and a flute trill when she blinks her eyes.

The Night Visitor score is interesting for the use of an idiosyncratic ensemble: twelve woodwinds, one organ, two pianos and two harpsichords, the two couples of pianos and harpsichords being tuned with a quarter-tone difference from one another, which creates a dizzy feeling.[23] The score does not have explicit synch-points at all, and its main function is emotive.

As for Williams's scores, the surface shows modern-style traits and the influence of Mancini's practices (e.g., the use of a title song on the opening titles of *Penelope*, *Not with My Wife, You Don't!*, *A Guide for the Married Man*, and the jazz dialect and big band sound for crime stories like *The Killers*). Yet, if we look closer, we can immediately see that Williams's idiom is far more classical. The use of explicit synch-points and spatial perceptive function is definitely more frequent, and the orchestral writing has a stronger symphonic structure when compared to Mancini's light/pop music orchestra writing.

Williams's writing is much more contrapuntal, as can be seen when comparing the main theme for *Breakfast at Tiffany's* with that for *Penelope*: unlike the former homophonic tune, the latter features a canon-like answer to the main melody by the horns, somewhat reminiscent of Miklós Rózsa. Williams also uses more insistently some classical techniques such as the leitmotiv or theme and variations. Mancini seems to be interested in variations mainly because they give musical variety to the tie-in album: think of the many multistyle versions of "Moon River" in *Breakfast at Tiffany's*. On the contrary, Williams seems to be interested in variations mainly in terms of functionality within the film. For example, the title song "A Guide for the Married Man" is sung in the opening titles of the film of the same name by The Turtles in a sunshine-pop style, accompanying images of voluptuous women and colorful graphics. Later in the film, when Paul finally has to move from fantasy (having an adulterous affair with a gorgeous woman) to action (fulfilling his desire by cheating on his wife), the music comically emphasizes the discrepancy between theory and practice: the theme of the title song is now presented in orchestral form, played clumsily and wearily by muted trombones.

In dialogue scenes Williams also shows his preference for the classical underscoring technique. Music makes room for the dialogue not just by having its volume turned down in the sound mix as is the case with Mancini's diegetic pieces. Williams makes room for the dialogue by thinning the musical texture and lightening the instrumentation. When the dialogue pauses, he inflates the writing and shifts the music to the foreground presenting melodic cells; as soon as the dialogue resumes, he shifts the music to the background again. In using this composing-around-the-dialogue technique, the composer is required to precisely follow what is happening on-screen when writing the piece. Like Mickey-Mousing, this is another technique that requires great attention to the adherence of music to visuals.[24] In an early 1970s interview, Williams talked about music and dialogue as Korngold would do:

> I think a composer should think of the dialogue as part of the score; he could write it as accompaniment for a violin concerto rather than compose a score to exist on its own. There are a few little tips, for example, low strings. . . . This isn't to say that one can't have high frequencies as well, but I think the choice of textures under the dialogue, the register of the speaking voices, and also the tempo of the dialogue— if a man says a line, and there's a pause, and the woman says the next line after another pregnant pause, it may be possible to color the music somewhat differently.[25]

The first sequence of *Fitzwilly* is an excellent example of extensive underscoring. After the main title sequence in which the main theme is introduced, the music starts again at the fifth minute of the film and accompanies the protagonist on his shopping activities around New York. Music continues uninterruptedly for the next five minutes: it accompanies the car journeys with variations of the main theme in march form; it gets thinner in the presence of dialogue, repeating cells of the main theme during the pauses between lines; it even emphasizes the shifts of place and marks the closures of the subepisodes with harp glissandos.[26] During the romantic scenes, Williams uses the classical strings and not Mancini's modern woodwind sound; similarly, strings are preferred in *The Killers, How to*

Steal a Million, and *Penelope*. As expected, explicit synch-points and even extensive episodes of Mickey-Mousing are considerably more present in the Williams sample. Some noteworthy examples follow.

In *Not with My Wife, You Don't!* the music replicates the movement of butter-flies flying out of a chocolate box; it duplicates the scattering of some roses in the wind during a funeral with a fast woodwind run; it quotes Mendelssohn's wedding march—as Max Steiner would have done—when we learn of the marriage between Julie and Tom.

In *Penelope*, when the protagonist exits through the revolving doors of Bergdorf Goodman, the music accompanies the door's rotation with a harp glissando and introduces the main theme. When Penelope tells her psycho-analyst that the trauma that caused her kleptomania was an attempt of sexual assault by a teacher during her college years, we see a flashback of the event in an overtly comic tone. The scene opens in a classroom and is given an appro-priately poised academic tone by the aloof sound of the harpsichord. Then, suddenly, the professor gets less poised and jumps on the girl. The harpsichord gives way to a wildly aggressive brass riff backed by relentless percussions and punctuated by "horny" horns rips. Mickey-Mousing underlines with a downward trombones glissando the fall of a book-stand that reveals the girl in underwear—the teacher had already torn her outer clothes off. This moment is immediately followed by a flute and piccolo trill that comically exaggerates the teacher's wildly excited gaze. Penelope—in her underwear—finally flees the classroom and runs along the lawns of the campus accompanied by her leitmotiv. Later, we see Penelope steal different items: a rapid harpsichord scale duplicates the rapid movement of her hand stealing a pair of earrings; Penelope's under-water theft of a precious brooch used to fasten a bikini top is scored with an upward scale that tracks the emergence of the loosened bra on the surface of the water, followed by a triangle trill when Penelope surfaces holding the loot.

In *Fitzwilly*, the sequence of the Christmas theft at Gimbels department store closes with Fitzwilliam—the head of the gang—entering the bathroom to take off the wig used as a disguise. From one of the toilet cubicles, a puzzled drunkard witnesses the scene. The music underlines the baffled man's face with a trombones glissando, then a second glissando marks the bout of sickness that makes him rush back into the cubicle. The music continues in a march arrange-ment that follows Fitzwilliam breezing into the elevator and showing the loot to his partners—the dialogue starts and the music texture thins accordingly. When the dialogue ends, music soars to become a triumphal march when Fitzwilliam exits the elevator and drops the self-addressed parcel containing the loot in the store's outgoing mail—the music closes the sequence and the successful operation with a *forte* authentic cadence in baroque dialect right on the cut-in on the address label.

In *How to Steal a Million*, during the heavily guarded transportation of the supposedly priceless (and actually fake) Venus statuette through the street of Paris, the music accompanies the action with a solemn march. When a group of gendarmes deferentially salutes the convoy, Williams humorously quotes "La Marseillaise," and when we see a group of priests looking on reverently, the solemn sound of a pipe organ comes in. Later Nicole's father—the forger—learns that his Venus will be examined by an insurance assessor—who will surely discover the fraud. The piece of bad news makes his heart skip a beat: a loud pedal-portamento hit by the timpani gives the idea,[27] and it is followed by a downward scale that mimics Nicole and her father fainting into the chairs. To spare her father the ignominy and imprisonment, Nicole comes up with the idea of stealing the Venus before the assessor can examine it and talks Simon into helping her, believing that he is a proficient art thief. In a later scene, a circular musical cell replicates the round test-flights of a boomerang—which will be a key element in Simon's ingenious plan. A bright triangle trill is used three times in the score to draw attention to Nicole's diamond ring—for example when Nicole is disguised as a humble cleaning lady, she suddenly realizes that she has forgotten to remove the conspicuously incongruous jewel. A tight Mickey-Mousing adheres to the visuals when the captain of the museum guards decides to set off the supposedly faulty alarm system: a pompous march accompanies his walk to the control panel; three dissonant piano chords emphasize the lowering of the switch and the turning off respectively of the upper and lower photocells around the Venus pedestal. Finally, a downward cellos and contra-basses scale marks the closure of the door of the closet where Simon and Nicole are hiding. After the theft, when Nicole walks away dressed as a cleaning lady, the music follows her closely. For example, music guides our view within a long shot of the main hall to focus our attention on a distant action: Nicole sneakily stretches her arm out of a door to get back the brush that she has left behind on the ground—a high-pitched piccolo trill being synchronized with the arm's swift gesture and the closure of the door marked by a short cellos and contra-basses *pizzicato* downward scale. Williams comments, "There's a chase in the museum and I treated it in a very burlesque way—sort of slipping on banana skins followed by a crash from the orchestra, and running semiquavers all over the place . . . I thought I'd gone too far but Wyler loved it."[28]

Equally rich in Mickey-Mousing episodes is *A Guide for the Married Man*, where music has a foregrounded position and an extensive presence, partly because of the film's farcical nature, and partly because of director Gene Kelly's dance background.[29] The pantomime-like nature of the score is evident from the outset. The title song starts on the shot of a buxom female neighbor wiggling her hips, the rhythm of the song synchronized with the woman's enticing walking. The film showcases many instances of Mickey-Mousing: the gestures of a worker who hooks up the phone and shrugs his shoulders—after lying to his wife—is ironically accompanied by the xylophone; a stereotypical gong hit points out the presence of a Chinese on the tarmac of an airport; an upward violins and harp glissando replicates the night breeze coming through the window; the Romanoff's restaurant scene is practically a silent film piece accompanied by music, which at one point renders a woman's enraged cries with furious *sforzando* horns rips. The cartoon-like scene in which an unfaithful husband hastily flees forgetting his shoes in his mistress's home also has, again, neither dialogue nor sound, but only foregrounded music: explicit synch-points stress his jumping off the wall, the surprise when he realizes that he is barefoot, his slapping his forehead in disappointment, and his taking off his hat to greet a shoe salesman when he enters his shop.

So far we have dealt with comedies, a genre in which the old practice of Mickey-Mousing is more tolerated. However, the Williams sample features explicit synch-points in the dramas as well.

In *The Killers*, romantic music for trumpet and strings underscores the dialogue between race driver Johnny and beautiful Sheila during their first meeting. The full string orchestra that accompanies the two lovers driving away gives way to an ironic episode of *staccato* woodwinds when we see Johnny's friend left alone on the racing track. After a ride in Johnny's car, Sheila playfully kicks him, and the score punctuates the gesture with a contrabasses *pizzicato*. When Sheila hires Johnny as a driver for a private job, woodwinds music underscores the dialogue. When Johnny asks about the job and his race opponents, and Sheila answers, "The police," three *staccato* notes of the cellos and contrabasses emphasize the reaction shot of Johnny's astonishment. In the final act of the film, when the chased Johnny slips into a ditch, the score accompanies his fall with a downward scale.

In the thriller *Daddy's Gone A-Hunting*, the deranged Kenneth stalks Cathy, his former girlfriend, who left him after aborting his child. Cathy is now married and is pregnant again. Kenneth is obsessed with his lost son and wants to retaliate; to get even Kenneth demands that Cathy have a second abortion. She refuses and decides to give birth to her child. As a consequence, Kenneth schemes to force Cathy to kill her baby. The musical interventions are limited and mostly of an emotive function: music is used to increase the suspense.

There are, however, two explicit synch-points: the first consists of low-pitched male vocalized tones that mark the shot of Cathy's womb when Kenneth appears dressed in a Santa Claus disguise; the second one is a contrabasses *pizzicato* punctuating the switching on of the red light during the scene in which Cathy agrees to meet Kenneth in his photography darkroom.

We have already discussed *Images* and the experimental nature of its score (see 90–91). There is no Mickey-Mousing here, and the only explicit synch-points can be found in the appearance of atonal-music bursts punctuating Cathryn's hallucinations. When comparing this film with a similar insanity-based thriller like *The Night Visitor* where Mancini's score has no songs and features a similarly experimental intra-opus style, it is evident that Williams's score is more close to the film's narrative structure. Thematically, *The Night Visitor* is also about madness and uncertainty between reality and hallucination: the village doctor is the only one to have seen Salem the psychopath, but no one believes him since Salem is still locked and guarded in a high-security asylum. Unlike the Mancini score, Williams's *Images* score is shaped on this reality/hallucination ambivalence. The peaceful dimension of Cathryn's fantasies linked to unicorns when she works on her children's books have melodic piano music, while atonal or even aleatoric music accompanies the scary hallucinations that will increasingly take over reality. As the woman's mental state degenerates, the melodic side of the score disappears, and the atonal/aleatoric one takes the lead.

Another observation arises from the comparison of the two samples. In Mancini's scores, explicit synch-points and episodes of Mickey-Mousing, besides being more rarely found, are usually placed as isolated elements; that is, they apply to the visuals as if they were sound effects instead of pieces of music. For example, think of the aforementioned appearance of the killer in the classroom in *Arabesque* or the girl coming out of the bedroom in *Man's Favorite Sport?* The various tam-tam rubs, triangle tinkles, and timpani hits punctuating these actions come in from the silence as individual sounds. On the contrary, in Williams's case explicit synch-points are musical elements embedded in the score texture, and they come in at the right moment as part of the musical phrases, emerging from a wider structure.

As for the musical means, Williams's orchestra during the period was not much different from Mancini's: it blended the traditional symphonic setting with big bands or jazz combos. Yet we have seen that Williams preferred classical strings to more modern-style woodwinds in dialogue underscoring.

As for the music language, Mancini was more interested in exploring the rhythms and colors of contemporary pop music (cocktail music, cool jazz, blues, Latin American). Williams also employed the musical dialect of the time in many instances—for example, in title songs, diegetic Muzak, and in action scenes scored with the contemporary Bond big-band style à la John Barry. However, a significant number of cases show Williams's preference for the dialects of both the art-music canon and the Hollywood tradition. Consider the cartoon prologue of *A Guide for the Married Man*. It is divided into three episodes of marital infidelity through the ages. In the first segment—the Stone Age—music is percussive and "primitive" in the manner of Stravinsky's *Le sacre du printemps*. In the second segment—Ancient Rome—Williams presents a modal organum-like parallel-motion march for brass mimicking Miklós Rózsa's *Ben-Hur*. In the last segment—Victorian England—there is an ironically dignified piece of *galante* music for harpsichord, celesta, harp, and flute. In the film, when Paul is asked to recollect the feelings he felt during his very first date with a girl, we are shown an overt parody: Paul runs with open arms, in an overly sentimental slow motion, toward a blonde girl in a bucolic meadow. Williams accompanies the ridiculous scene with a very kitsch Rachmaninov imitation—actually, a Rachmaninov-via-Tiomkin imitation. In another scene, when a shy man finally takes a chance and kisses the girl, we hear a heroic fanfare à la Korngold. The scene of the barefoot man fleeing his mistress's house is scored with a frenetic scherzo that recalls Scott Bradley's music for the MGM Tom and Jerry cartoons. In *How to Steal a Million*, the opening party at the museum is appropriately paired with a lofty baroque Handel-like overture. In a scene of *Not with My Wife, You Don't!*, Julie is in a movie theater watching a parody of an Italian-cinema stereotypical "jealousy drama," scored with passionate music evoking Mascagni's *verismo* operas. Finally, for the upper-class setting of *Fitzwilly*, Williams wrote an overture in baroque dialect—updated with comic dissonances and amusing polytonal episodes—played by trumpets, harpsichord, and tuba, the latter having an unusual number of prominent solos during the score.

The comparison has revealed that some elements of Williams's 1960s scores already placed the composer closer to the classical style than to the modern style. The undeniable evidence would appear in the 1970s with *Star Wars*. Yet a fundamental milestone in the development of the neoclassical trend was *Jaws* (Steven Spielberg, 1975). The film bridged the two periods of Williams's work: the emerging composer's multifaceted modern-style first period and the following stardom as the *Star Wars* composer who revived the Hollywood music tradition.

6

Jaws

Williams's Neoclassicism Floats Up to the Surface

John Williams reached stardom in the mid-1970s, a period in which Hollywood cinema was recovering from the previous decade's debacles. In those years, a new generation of filmmakers and screenwriters—among them George Lucas and Steven Spielberg—was building their reputation, launching the so-called New Hollywood. It has been claimed that "music, and specifically the orchestral scores of John Williams, has become an important part of the New Hollywood."[1] So, Williams is said to be the New Hollywood composer par excellence. To fully understand the meaning of this, it is necessary to understand first what is meant by New Hollywood.

The New Hollywood Cinema

The term "New Hollywood" is somewhat equivocal. It is often applied to films that are very different from each other: on the one hand, *Bonnie and Clyde* (Arthur Penn, 1967) and *Easy Rider* (Dennis Hopper, 1969); on the other hand, *Star Wars* (George Lucas, 1977) and *Superman: The Movie* (Richard Donner, 1978).[2] The period between approximately 1967 and 1975, often called "Hollywood Renaissance" or "American New Wave" and including the first two films, is generally confused or at least fused with the subsequent period, in which the Hollywood film industry regained its international predominance. In this book "New

Hollywood" refers only to this second period, to indicate Hollywood's reorganization around new distribution practices and horizontal integration. Film companies became merely a portion — often of minor importance — of the network of business of larger corporations operating in the multimedia market, and Hollywood studios were at this point taken over by multinational entertainment companies. Although there seems to be a general consensus on using the term "New Hollywood" in this sense,[3] when it comes to defining the period in terms of aesthetics and form, things get more controversial.

Some contrast the New Hollywood style with the classical one and equate New Hollywood either with "postclassical"[4] or with "postmodern cinema."[5] According to these positions, contemporary Hollywood cinema, compared to classical cinema, has a very different form and style, characterized by fragmented and superficial narratives, and an emphatic style that largely displays bombastic visual and sound effects to induce visceral sensations and intense emotions. According to the postclassical theorists, this style is the direct consequence of the New Hollywood's market fragmentation and the reduction of films to mere commodities to an unprecedented extent.[6] According to postmodern theorists, style mirrors the very fragmented and superficial identity of contemporary man and the society in which he lives.[7] Other scholars argue against this sharp break between the classical period and the so-called postclassical period claiming that regardless of market fragmentation and pervasive commercial practices, the form and style in most films are not that different from those of the classical cinema.[8] Film style has simply updated itself and has incorporated new stylistic options from modern cinema and video clip aesthetics, following a longtime enduring "cannibalistic" practice, as in the incorporation in the Hollywood paradigm, during the 1920s and 1930s, of the Soviet montage or the high-contrast cinematography of German Expressionism. The continuity theorists use two different approaches. David Bordwell calls "hyperclassical" those films that emphasize their affiliation with the classical form: for example, the narration of *Jerry Maguire* (Cameron Crowe, 1996) is so attentive to classical procedures as to be called "hyperclassical."[9] Other authors contrast the term "postclassical" with the term "neoclassical"; the latter term is used to indicate those films that are overt remakes and tributes to traditional genres and to the classical style in an almost philological spirit.[10] In this sense, a "post-*noir*" like *Mulholland Drive* (David Lynch, 2001) — which is set in the present day and modernizes themes and narrative topics of the classical genre — can be distinguished from a "neo-*noir*" like *Chinatown* (Roman Polanski, 1974) or *L.A. Confidential* (Curtis Hanson, 1997), both of which are set in the past and re-create accurately the costumes, locales, and moods of the original 1940s films.[11]

A recurring term in contemporary film studies is "postmodern." Postmodern films are said to be those with anticlassical, nonlinear, less causally tight narrative forms, and these characteristics may derive from the postmodern idea that all-embracing Grand Narratives no longer exist.[12] The style of postmodern films is flamboyant, showy, and based on pastiche, parody, and stylistic patchwork. The life of the postmodern man is characterized by a tourist-like superficiality, a ludic attitude, a decontextualized use of history. Typical postmodern themes are simulacra and virtual reality, in such films as *Blade Runner* (Ridley Scott, 1982); *SimOne* (Andrew Niccol, 2002), or *The Matrix* (Andy Wachowski, Lana Wachowski, 1999): in the postmodern society, images are worth more than reality. Yet postmodern scholars seem to dwell on a handful of outstanding suitable examples and selected characteristics in order to validate their theoretical framework; at the same time they seem to carefully omit most of the average productions that escape their classification, or those formal traits that may confute their argument.[13] For example, Laurent Jullier identifies *Star Wars* as the inaugural film of the postmodern cinema because it is the first remarkable product of the new spectacle-based aesthetics.[14] *Star Wars* can surely be seen as the film that established the New Hollywood in the sense that it was the first global manifestation of the new horizontally integrated distribution based on merchandising and on the exploitation of every possible corner of the world market; indeed, *Star Wars* was the first film associated with a wide selection of tie-in gadgets, and it has grossed more from merchandising than from the box-office revenues.[15] However, it is debatable that *Star Wars* was also a turning point in terms of "postmodern" style and form. A close formal analysis of the film tends to show the contrary. Stylistically, *Star Wars* is based on traditional editing techniques and classical shot/reverse shot alternation to make the narrative flow linearly, not to mention its inclusion of classical-style music. The narrative form is extremely classical too: there is a hero with a clear-cut personality, a precise goal, strong motivations, and the narrative is built around causality and "stairstep construction," as in the "canonical story format."[16] Finally, its themes are anything but postmodern: the film is about one of the most classical themes of all, the archetypal hero's journey.[17] *Star Wars* seems to lack any postmodern characteristics, apart from those pointed out by Jullier: the film leans on prominent spectacular moments; it indulges in playful quotations, patent intertextuality, and metalanguage; it boasts striking special effects. These allegedly postmodern characteristics, however, were already present in some classical Hollywood films like *Hell's Angels* (Howard Hughes, 1930) and *King Kong* (Merian C. Cooper and Ernest B. Schoedsack, 1933) with their striking special effects; *The Adventures of Robin Hood* (Michael Curtiz, William Keighley, 1938) and *The Wizard of Oz* (Victor Fleming, 1939) with spectacular key moments; *Three Ages* (Edward F. Cline, Buster Keaton, 1923) and *A Night in Casablanca* (Archie Mayo, 1946), using playful quotations and intertextuality; *Show People* (King Vidor, 1928) and *Hellzapoppin* (H. C. Potter, 1941), employing meta-language. If so-called postmodern films are actually only partially postmodern, it is even more difficult to convincingly apply this label to embrace indiscriminately an entire period of the whole film industry. A film like *Back to the Future* (Robert Zemeckis, 1985) is a typical product of the New Hollywood cinema, but it can hardly be called postmodern.[18] The main problem with postmodern arises from the number of areas in which the term itself is controversially used: there is one postmodern in economy, one in philosophy, and one in sociology;[19] it seems that theorists of the various disciplines cannot agree on a shared definition.[20] Since the term lacks a clear-cut stable meaning, although topical and widely diffused it might be, it will not be used herein, in order to avoid confusion.[21] Indeed, if we thought of *Star Wars* as a postmodern film and of New Hollywood as a postmodern aesthetic trend, consequently John Williams—who became famous thanks to *Star Wars* and is considered the most important New Hollywood composer—would be a postmodern composer. The problem is that the postmodern label has been applied to composers like Ennio Morricone, Hans Zimmer, and, in art music, Luciano Berio.[22] It is obvious that Williams's idiom is very different from Morricone's and Zimmer's, not to mention Berio's.

In this book we consider New Hollywood not as a new style but as a period in Hollywood history characterized by a transformation of its industrial, commercial, and distribution practices and structures. In this period, a number of films were produced that overtly paid homage to the classical Hollywood tradition and imitated that style, and these can be tagged as "neoclassical." One of such neoclassical films is *Star Wars*, a revival of classical genres, with some emphasis on spectacular elements that can be called at most "hyperclassical." Likewise, John Williams acted in these films as a *neoclassical composer*, since he has paid homage to the classical Hollywood music and revived that style.[23]

Neoclassicism Takes Form

Williams's neoclassicism can be spotted particularly in his collaborations with neoclassical filmmakers like George Lucas and Steven Spielberg, and became a dominant trend from 1975 to 1983.[24] However, a previous artistic relationship must be mentioned because it produced two remarkable early examples of neoclassicism. Between the late 1960s and early 1970s Williams started a four-film collaboration with the director Mark Rydell: "Mark Rydell is very comfortable with music. He is a pianist himself, he loves music, it's very good to work with him on a certain kind of scene in a movie," says Williams.[25] The collaboration resulted in *The Reivers* (1969), *The Cowboys* (1972), *Cinderella Liberty* (1973), and the later *The River* (1984). *Cinderella Liberty* is the story of a sailor who, during a leave, falls in love with a prostitute and acts as a surrogate father to her son; its score is modern in style, featuring jazz dialect, harmonica solos by Toots Thielemans, and two theme songs— "Nice To Be Around" and "Wednesday Special," lyrics by Paul Williams. *The River* involves a rural family fighting against floods and banks to keep their farm; its music is a product of the eclectic style, blending symphonic Americana strings, pensive jazz trumpet solos, country-ballad instrumentation, synthesizers, and 1980s pop rhythm sections. The remaining two, *The Reivers* and *The Cowboys*, stand out in Williams's early canon as the first two neoclassical scores, both having been instrumental in signaling the composer to a wider attention and producing seminal consequences for Williams's career.

The Americana symphonic score for *The Reivers* earned Williams his first Oscar nomination for "Best Original Score." *The Cowboys* was one of John Wayne's last Westerns, and carried on the Hollywood Western music tradition, employing a full symphony orchestra, galloping rhythms, syncopations, and pentatonic scales in the manner of Jerome Moross's *The Big Country* (William Wyler, 1958) and Elmer Bernstein's *The Magnificent Seven* (John Sturges, 1960). Attesting to the importance and musical quality of *The Reivers* and *The Cowboys* is the fact that the composer has adapted concert pieces from both scores.[26] More important, then-emerging filmmaker Steven Spielberg approached Williams in 1972 and later hired him on his first feature-length film— *The Sugarland Express* (1974),[27] featuring a blues-inspired score with harmonica solos—because he was a huge fan of both *The Reivers* and *The Cowboys* and had listened to the LPs so many times he wore them out.[28] Spielberg recalls:

> I'm a soundtrack collector and I collected scores of great composers. . . .
> I had a huge collection. And for many years there was like a drought. A
> lot of the great old composers like Dimitri Tiomkin and Max Steiner
> were no longer writing music anymore. . . . There was just a real loss
> of pure symphonic film music. And then when I heard *The Reivers* and
> *The Cowboys* I said, "My God, this guy must be eighty years old!" . . . I
> really thought, "Maybe he's some guy who's eighty years old, who
> maybe wrote the greatest scores of his life." And I wanted to know who

this guy was and I met this young man named John Williams. . . . I
was amazed! You know, "It's a rebirth, film music is back. It's alive!
Hallelujah!"[29]

Yet, though important they might have been, the scores to *The Reivers* and *The
Cowboys* cannot be said to have been groundbreaking for the neoclassical trend.
Both are period films in which a more classical-style score would have hardly
been an unexpected event. The score that really launched Williams's neoclassicism was *Jaws* (Steven Spielberg, 1975), the second entry of his collaboration
with Steven Spielberg. It was the first instance in which a fully neoclassical
score was applied to a dramatic contemporary story.

Here Comes "Bruce"

Jaws was somehow in the "disaster movies" category that was fashionable at
that time. In this case, the deadly threat is not determined by a lightning-stricken,
about-to-crash plane, a transatlantic cruise-liner turning upside-down, an
earthquake hitting Los Angeles, or a skyscraper on fire, but by a great white shark
eating islanders. *Jaws* indeed has some narrative conventions of the disaster-
movie genre: a threat by an irrational and unstoppable natural element—fire,
water, earthquakes, a dangerous predator in this case—looms on a large group
of people; the protagonist warns the local authorities in due time, who nevertheless do not listen to him and take action only when it is too late.[30] Williams
was the ideal and obvious choice to score *Jaws*: not only did he have a good
relationship with Spielberg but at that time he was also *the* disaster-movie
composer.

The making of *Jaws* was particularly troubled, and the project was even on
the verge of being aborted and never reaching the theaters.[31] The estimated
budget of $8.5 million quickly climbed to $11 million. The fifty-five-day production schedule ended up exceeding 150 days.[32] There were many technical
and logistical problems, mainly due to the choice of shooting as many scenes as
possible out to sea on location, for realism's sake, rather than in a studio tank.
The biggest hitch and a major cause in slowing down the pace of shooting was
"Bruce," the mechanical shark named after Spielberg's lawyer.[33] A pneumati-
cally operated puppet, Bruce cost $750,000 and sank like a stone as soon as it
was put into the ocean for the first time.[34] Its mechanics jammed continuously,
and the shark—when not sinking—was unreliable and mostly unusable. In
order to keep up with the schedule despite the absence of the leading character,
Spielberg resorted to various vicarious elements to signal its presence: piers

torn and dragged away; air barrels previously fixed to the beast's back that emerge on the surface to indicate the presence of the shark underneath, and so on. These solutions were complemented with point-of-view shots: the camera substituted for the monster's eyes and consequently the monster's body could be kept conveniently off-screen. In the film's 119-minute running time, the shark can be just glimpsed at 60 minutes and finally shows up only at 78 minutes.[35] A crucial doubt now haunted the director and producers: in the few shots in which it appeared, would the fiberglass-and-rubber puppet really be credible and therefore perceived as a menacing shark?[36]

As admitted by Spielberg himself, it was Williams's score that made the puppet credible and truly frightening: "I think that his score was clearly responsible for half the success of the film."[37] This is the first element that links the *Jaws* score with the classical period: the same thing had happened with the score for *King Kong* (Merian C. Cooper and Ernest B. Schoedsack, 1933). The producers of *King Kong* similarly feared that the stop-motion-animated puppet would cause laughter instead of fear. And similarly, it was Max Steiner's score that saved the day. And, incidentally, as *King Kong* had been the opening score of the classical style, so *Jaws* is the opening score of the neoclassical trend. Besides these historical parallels, what makes *Jaws* a neoclassical score?

Let's start from the beginning, with Williams watching the film for the first time in the "spotting session," when the composer is shown a rough cut of the film as a basis for discussion about which scenes need music and what kind of music. Williams recalls the first time he watched *Jaws*:

> I knew about the novel. . . . I don't think I read it, but Peter Benchley's book was very, very popular. I remember seeing the movie in a projection room here at Universal. I was alone; Steven was in Japan at the time. I came out of the screening so excited. I had been working for nearly 25 years in Hollywood but had never had an opportunity to do a film that was absolutely brilliant. I had already conducted *Fiddler on the Roof*, and I had worked with directors like William Wyler and Robert Altman and others. But *Jaws* just floored me.[38]

After "spotting" the film, Williams began to plan his work: "Most of the discussions I had with Steven at that point were about the shark. The challenge was to find a way to characterize something that's underwater with music rather than with sound effects."[39] Unlike *Piranha* (Joe Dante, 1978), where the voracious fish are characterized by a sort of excited high-frequency buzz, Spielberg wanted a musical identifier and looked for a musical idea that could be the aural equivalent of the predator.

What Does a Shark Sound Like?

Some time later, Williams invited the director to his studio and played the main theme at the piano. This is Spielberg's recollection:

> I had actually cut in one of John's own pieces of music for the opening titles. That was John's title theme from Robert Altman's film *Images*. So I cut in a section that was a lovely piano solo with some very ominous strings in the background that would probably have been wonderful for a movie about a hunting. And I thought it was playing against the obvious primal feelings that run very deep through *Jaws*. When Johnny heard it, though, he just didn't go for it at all.[40] . . . I expected to hear something weird yet still melodic. But what he played instead, with two fingers on the lower keys, was *dun, dun, dun-dun, dun-dun, dun-dun*. At first I began to laugh, and I thought "John has a great sense of humor!" But he was serious—that was the theme for *Jaws*. So he played it again and again, and suddenly it seemed right. Sometimes the best ideas are the most simple ones and John had found a signature for the entire score.[41]

Unlike the "weird melody" in line with the tradition of horror music that Spielberg expected—dissonant and harmonically eerie, as the more tonal passages of the score for *Images* are—Williams opted for a closer musical equivalent of the shark, a primitive pulsation with no melody at all. Indeed, melody is a product of artistic civilization, which by its nature brings traces of history and culture:

> I fiddled around with the idea of creating something that was very . . . brainless, . . . like the shark. All instinct . . . Meaning something [that] could be very repetitive, very visceral, and grab you in your gut, not in your brain. Remember, Steven didn't have the computer shark. He only had his rubber ducky, so the simple idea of that bass ostinato, just repeating those two notes and introduce a third note when you don't expect it and so on. It could be something you could play very softly, which would indicate that the shark is far away when all you see is water. Brainless music that gets louder and gets closer to you, something is gonna swallow you up.[42]

Williams came up with the primitive rhythmic simplicity of an *ostinato*, that is, a brief repeating and hammering fragment, more rhythmic than melodic:

Transcription of John Williams, "The Shark Theme" (mm. 12–14), from *Suite from Jaws* (© 1975 BMI), published by USI B Music Publishing, administered by Songs of Universal, Inc., printed by Hal Leonard, "John Williams Signature Edition," 04490414 [Used in compliance with the U.S. Copyright Act, Section 107].

Those three repeated bass notes recall the heartbeat, the primordial rhythm of life.[43] Their seemingly unstoppable constant and mechanical repetition effectively represents the shark: a primitive yet proficient killing machine, moved only by the instinct for eating.

In addition to characterizing the nature of the monster, the shark's motif performs another important function within the film, a function that Spielberg's "weird melody" could hardly have carried out. Being an *ostinato*, the shark motif can be more easily shortened, prolonged, or repeated in loops as required by visuals, so to become the aural equivalent of the shark's *movement through space*. Williams commented, "I thought that altering the speed and volume of the theme, from very slow to very fast, from very soft to very loud, would indicate the mindless attacks of the shark. Steven was a bit skeptical, but when the orchestra performed the piece, it worked better than we had anticipated."[44] Music is often the only sign of the presence of the monster that can be perceived, since the monster itself is off-screen for most of the time. Williams plays fair with the audience, since the shark motif is not used to cheat when the shark is not around but is played only when it is present. For example, in the fake-fin prank scene, visually we can be led to take it as a real fin, but there is no music accompanying it, thus signaling that the shark is not there. On the contrary, in the same sequence, the music anticipates the real shark being spotted in the estuary. The shark's motif does not just perform the function of classical leitmotiv but is also a peculiar type of Mickey-Mousing: the music adheres perfectly to the spatial movements of the beast. But, unlike the classical Mickey-Mousing that replicated the on-screen movements, in this case it mostly indicates *off-screen* movements.

Consider Chrissie's death scene at the beginning of the film: it is the music that conveys the "obscene" violence and horror of the underwater off-screen attack—*ob scene* being Latin for "off-stage." Chrissie undresses and decides to take a nude night swim in the sea. A point-of-view shot looking up from the abyss shows us the body of the girl on the surface—as in the opening titles, we are seeing through the eyes of a mysterious sea creature. We hear a harp *arpeggio* evoking the waves, then two of those ominous low notes, which we have previously identified with the sea creature. The notes become louder and repeat faster and faster as the creature approaches the girl and points at its prey. Then, the narration reverses the perspective and cuts to Chrissie on the sea surface. Suddenly, something we cannot see starts pulling her down: the action is marked with a violently *sforzando* horns rip, a kind of *rrrrrruhah!* That is the shark's bite; the music conveys both the shark's fury and Chrissie's pain. She screams while she is tossed around. We do not see what is happening beneath the surface, but we can easily imagine the horrible scene of the shark tearing its victim. Frantic shrill violin writing, violent percussion, and repeated horns "bites" depict the off-screen violence. The scene takes shape in our imagination through music, which fulfills both a spatial perceptive and an emotive function.

The shark motif replicates the shark's movements on both the horizontal and the vertical axes. Horizontal trajectories are rendered through variations of dynamics and tempo: when the music slows down and the volume decreases, we know that the shark is slowing its pace; when the music speeds up or the volume increases we know that the shark is attacking. Movements on the vertical axis are rendered through variations of orchestral texture: when the writing gets thicker, we know that the shark is coming to the surface; when the writing thins down to dark timbres only (contrabasses, cellos, bassoons) we know that the beast is plunging into the dark abyss. For example, consider the pier scene in which two islanders try to hook the shark, with the only result of having the pier torn away, falling into the water, and thus risking being eaten up. When the shark bites the bait and points offshore, dragging along the torn pier to which the bait was fastened, the shark *ostinato* starts, played by contrabasses and cellos. The *ostinato* keeps playing at the same level and speed during the tearing off of the pier and the falling into the water of the two men, one of which is pulled offshore along with the pier. At one point, the pier stops and suddenly reverses, indicating that the shark is now pointing to the swimming islander. Violins and violas abruptly join the cellos and contrabasses in playing the *ostinato*, followed by the horns menacingly presenting the second shark motif (see 115–16). The music's speed and volume increase as the shark chases the man who is frantically trying to reach the shore and come out of the water. The man succeeds, and the shark has to retreat. The music deflates, gradually decelerating and turning into a single sustained bass note that closes the scene.

Another function of the score is to further separate the two worlds—the shark below and the humans above—and this is accomplished by using the timbres of the orchestra. The monster shark lives down, below the water surface; humans live above the surface. The difference between the humans' world—lit by the sun—and the shark's world—the abyss in which darkness reigns—is marked by the contrast between the shark music—mechanical, low pitched, with dark timbre—and the human music—melodic, higher pitched, and with the bright timbres of violins, flutes, and trumpets.

The *Jaws* score has the important emotive function of creating suspense, anxiety, fear. Yet its most successful contribution consists in its embodying the shark and skillfully tracing its movements both on-screen and off-screen. The score is particularly outstanding for its spatial perceptive function.

Jaws's Neoclassicism

The first neoclassical element of the *Jaws* score is the recovery of classical techniques like Mickey-Mousing and leitmotivs. *Jaws* has also many explicit synch-points embedded in the overall orchestral writing. Here are a few examples. In the beach scene when the young Alex Kintner is cut to ribbons along with his yellow Lilo, a shrieking violins upward glissando strengthens the zoom-in/track-out *Vertigo*-like shot that captures Brody's horrified reaction. In the pond scene, a low flutter by the brass replicates the victim's blood coming to the surface. When the shark passes by Brody's son—in a point-of-view shot of the beast—music underlines its swimming toward and then away from the boy respectively with an upward and then a downward harp *glissando*. During the barrel chase out to the sea, music marks the actions with accents when the shark is harpooned, with a perfectly synchronized cymbal clash when one of the barrels hits the water surface, and with descending scales when the barrels are dragged down. In one scene, Quint is gathering up one of the barrel's lines. The shark abruptly emerges, and out of the silence the music punctuates the scaring surprise with a violent horns rip. Quint gets his hands cut by the rope, the painful scratch being stressed by a rapid and biting piccolo upward scale. When the shark submerges again, this is marked by a downward contrabasses scale, followed by an acute upward scale mirroring the shark's fin splashing water over the boat.

As for leitmotivs, they are employed throughout the score, with particular variety in the second half of the film, whereas the first half is dominated by the shark motif and violent or eerie music passages. One theme is a broad melody, which can be heard when the shark hunters' boat *Orca* is seen leaving the harbor, then across the whole second half of the film, and over the end credits in a serene rendition for strings. This is the principal "human" melody that contrasts the primitive pulse of the shark motif. It can be associated with the man-versus-the-beast struggle. Another theme is a buoyant hornpipe-like tune, which can be heard again when the *Orca* leaves. It is associated with sea life and punctuates the humorous and bright moments of the shark hunt. Another recurring theme that can be heard during the shark hunt is a heroic fanfare, which conveys the excitement and adventurousness of the deed.

There is also a second leitmotiv associated with the shark. One is the *ostinato* indicating the movements of the beast and heard only when the monster is around; the second one is the horn-and-tuba motif associated with the shark when someone talks about it or just thinks of its menacing presence, as in the scene in which Brody reads a book on shark attacks. The central musical interval of the motif—the second and third notes, from G to C-sharp—is the tritone or augmented fourth, a dissonant interval traditionally associated with evil, the *diabolus in musica* (see also chap. 9).

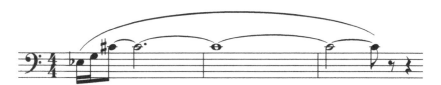

Transcription of John Williams, "The Shark Theme" (mm. 16–18), from *Suite from Jaws* (© 1975 BMI), published by USI B Music Publishing, administered by Songs of Universal, Inc., printed by Hal Leonard, "John Williams Signature Edition," 04490414 [Used in compliance with the U.S. Copyright Act, Section 107].

The second shark motif is also subtly used during the *Indianapolis* story sequence, which is a good example of proficient dialogue (monologue, actually) underscoring. Quint starts recounting his dreadful experience as a survivor of the USS *Indianapolis*, sunk during World War II. (The crew floated around in the ocean for four days. Only 317 men survived, out of 1,196, many having been eaten by sharks.) Quint's tale of the sinking begins without music, the serious faces of the listeners conveying the mood for the dramatic shipwreck being told. Then Quint's tale focuses on an inside tragedy within the shipwreck: the shark attacks that the survivors had to sustain in the following days. On the words "Very first light, sharks come cruising . . ." an ominous bass pedal point sneaks in from the silence, followed by a *piano* grating layer of dissonant high strings. During the monologue, low harp tones and watery arpeggios reverberate within the music texture, as to depict something moving in the abyss, below the surface. Strings writing provides more chilling effects through sinister gliding motions. Then Quint tells that at a certain point he saw a friend of his floating nearby and, thinking he was asleep, he reached him to shake him awake. "He bobbed up and down in the water just like a kind of top. Upended. Well . . . He'd been bitten in half, below the waist." At the beginning of this line, the second shark motif can be heard, to anticipate Quint's macabre discovery and its cause.

Another neoclassical trait is the revival of the dialect used in the classical period, that is, the late-romantic symphonic dialect. One of Williams's felicitous intuitions was that of emphasizing the adventurous spirit of the film. Spielberg reports: "When I first showed *Jaws* to John, I remember he said: 'This is like a pirate movie! I think we need pirate music for this, because there's something primal about it—but it's also fun and entertaining!'"[45] What did Williams mean when he spoke of "pirate music?" Here are Williams's words: "When I first saw *Jaws*, it was clear to me that it would require an action/adventure score. . . . For *Jaws*, I imagined something big and operatic, something very theatrical."[46] Evidently, the action/adventure score that Williams had in mind referred to the old Warner Bros. pirate films boasting Erich Wolfgang Korngold's operatic scores. The barrel chase sequence in the open sea, for example, is scored with lush symphonic music and heroic fanfares: "It suddenly becomes very Korngoldian, . . . you expect to see Errol Flynn at the helm of this thing. It gave us a laugh." says Williams.[47] As a sign of the composer's neoclassical tastes, this is indeed Williams's favorite part of the film: "But my own favorite cue in *Jaws* has always been the barrel chase sequence, where the shark approaches the boat and the three heroes think they have captured it. The music accelerates and becomes very exciting and heroic. Suddenly, as the shark overpowers them and eventually escapes, the music deflates and ends with a little sea-chant called 'Spanish Lady.' The score musically illustrates and punctuates all of this dramatic outline."[48]

And yet another neoclassical trait is the use of the symphony orchestra as a musical means. Among the early 1970s films set in the present time and designed to hopefully become box-office hits, *Jaws* was the first one employing a symphonic score and having no theme song. A significant example is the montage sequence showing the flocking of tourists to the island to celebrate the Fourth of July. This ninety-second sequence would have been the ideal showcase for a marketable song, perhaps in the style of The Beach Boys' surf music—a choice that would have been clever from a commercial point of view and would have also been interestingly motivated by the contrast between the cheerful tone of the music and the deadly danger looming over the tourists. Instead, the montage is accompanied by a baroque-dialect piece for strings, solo trumpet, and harpsichord. From under the serene and formal surface of the piece, the shark *ostinato* emerges played by cellos and contrabasses, offering a kind of black-humored comment on the impending menace. This choice also cleverly expresses in music one of the narrative themes: the city council refuses to close the beaches, preferring to ignore the menace rather than risk jeopardizing the Fourth of July tourism revenues. As in the music, a formal and pompous surface states that everything is fine so as to conceal the pending danger. Moreover, the music also carefully underscores the dialogue lines interwoven to the montage—by sustaining them with a thinner texture—and lets the trumpets play in full stride over the dialogue-free segments. A second very "non-pop" choice is the use of *fugato* writing for the sequence in which the hunters' trio sets up the shark cage.[49] The relentless complexity of the *fugato* provides the right compelling drive and anxious excitement for the elaborate and risky trap that the shark hunters are preparing.

Jaws was the first commercial film since the end of classical music style to discard pop music and modern style, and opt for a revival of past models. Eventually, this choice proved to be a good one. It was the first film that grossed more than $100,000,000, and Williams won his second Oscar, his first one for original music.[50] Moreover, as *King Kong* did, *Jaws* demonstrated once again the important contribution that non-diegetic orchestral music could give to film narration. Critics acknowledged the fact and, even before *Star Wars*, praised Williams's symphonic restoration: "Williams has been highly instrumental in trying to bring back to the movies the full symphonic score, with all its potential for pleasurable manipulation and its intimations of life larger than life. This was an important part of what we got from the movies once, and there are many signs that many [of] us want it back again."[51]

Williams expanded his canvas with *Jaws 2* (Jeannot Szwarc, 1978) and produced another neoclassical work, cleverly avoiding a copycat score. Only the shark *ostinato* survives from the 1975 film score; the second shark motif is not used. The shark ostinato is less present and less manipulated than in the first installment, probably because the shark is much more visible, the director being more interested in on-screen horror than in off-screen menace. On the other hand, Williams provided new symphonic set pieces for the montage sequences, this time sounding like Prokofiev in the spirited and youthful music for the catamaran race, or in the sardonic and angular trumpet melody played during the crowded beach sequence, named "The Menu" on the LP album.[52] The film has two scuba-diving sequences. The opening one is accompanied by watery harp arpeggios and impressionistic harmonies. When the two scuba divers find the wreck of the *Orca*, Williams quotes the "Man-versus-the-Beast Theme" from the previous film, confirming musically that what we are seeing is that very boat. The other sequence has the weightless moves of the scuba divers scored with a graceful waltz-like harp piece, titled "Ballet for Divers" on the LP album. The score features heroic fanfares again, during the catamaran race and, more prominently, during the end credits to appropriately mark the successful outcome of another man-versus-the-beast heroic deed. Williams comments again about the importance of *Jaws* for his career: "*Jaws* was the first major film opportunity that I had. . . . With Spielberg, it was the beginnings of our relationship really, and a lot of opportunity came my way as a result of it, including the *Star Wars* films. Spielberg introduced me to George Lucas and he was directly responsible for that relationship developing. The success of the *Star Wars* films brought unbelievable opportunities. I went to Boston and conducted the orchestra there for 15 years as a direct result of that."[53]

The wide success of *Jaws* not only launched the neoclassical trend but also established Williams as a neoclassical composer.

7

Williams's Neoclassicism

Style and Habits

What is musical neoclassicism? In art-music historiography, neoclassicism was a trend that brought back the clarity of past forms as opposed to the excesses of contemporary music:

> [It is a] musical trend that arose in the second half of the nineteenth century (with the Bach revival promoted by such composers as Brahms and Max Reger) and gained full visibility in the 1920s as a reaction against post-Wagnerian thematicism and chromaticism and with the purpose of the stylistic re-creation of clear-cut pre-Romantic forms. Neoclassicism can be placed within those twentieth-century artistic movements inspired by the ideals of objectivity, rationality and concreteness, as opposed to those of subjectivity and irrationality typical of Romanticism and in large part inherited by Impressionism and Expressionism.[1]

For example, the musicologist Guido Salvetti writes the following about Igor Stravinsky's neoclassicism in *Pulcinella* (1920):

> The modifications of the original music were not aimed at the deformation of the model: Stravinsky just added some canon-like dissonant passages, major seconds to some perfect chords, in a cadence he placed

119

the chords built on the V and I degrees simultaneously, shifted a bar's accent on the weak beat, and of course, invented a personal orchestral color. . . . This Stravinskyan "neoclassicism" was characterized, even in its early days, by the dual aspect of both the respectful reconstruction and the irreverent parody. . . . The Stravinskyan neoclassicism reached its peak in *The Rake's Progress* (1951). . . . The huge variety of cultural references resulted in a huge number of musical "tips of the hat" where once again the whole history of music is leveled on a ground where everything can be reused and enjoyed anew.[2]

What Salvetti says about *Oedipus Rex* (1927) in the following passage seems to apply to the neoclassical nature of the *Star Wars* score too: "Neoclassicism is even better understood in this sense: it is the escape from the present and the plunging into the eternal dimension of Myth, where Time and History lose any perspective."[3] The decision to choose this kind of music for *Star Wars*—very unusual for a sci-fi film—also followed the desire to evoke a common musical heritage that would reinforce the mythic dimension of the narrative. These neoclassical traits are also acknowledged by the musicologist Sergio Miceli:

> [T]here are some characteristics that distinguish Williams from everyone else. . . . Williams has proved to be able to take on the most representative stylistic traits of his generation while smoothing their excesses by drawing inspiration from the second and even first genera-tion of Hollywood film composers. To put it another way, in a work of synthesis rather than innovation, Williams has skillfully recovered leitmotivic functions, more extensive and complex thematicism, together with thematic interplay and implicit symbolism. The most significant difference if we compare his work to that of his predecessors consists in the complete absorption of blues and jazz influences, which causes his scores to sound much more up-to-date. As for the direct borrowing from the art music repertoire (the other side of the coin) they are numerous but very blurred and well integrated, which is precisely due to Williams's extraordinary skillfulness in music assimilation. . . . In short, the fusion of different stylistic traits, from both art and popular music, had already been accomplished . . . but nobody had ever weighed and mixed the ingredients so carefully. To all of this, Williams has also added an ironic and playful spirit which was undoubtedly favored by the narrative nature of the films.[4]

Neoclassicism in art music is the revival of past forms and styles updated through the hybridization with twentieth-century harmonic progressions and dissonances, and reworked through an ironic mannerist exaggeration of certain traits. Similarly, in film music John Williams has revived and updated the classical Hollywood music style, starting a neoclassical trend within the broader eclectic style of the New Hollywood. Williams recalls:

> Way back, I used to go to the movies on Saturday with my sister. . . . I loved several things, but mainly I loved the music I could hear in films, which one couldn't hear anywhere else. I loved certain kinds of scenes. Obviously the love scenes, where you have a very expressive, lyrical and melodic piece of music. I also loved action-adventure scenes. I was talking the other night about this, particularly sword fight scenes. First off, no one ever got hurt. They were choreographically expert. And the sword fights always had great music. Swashbuckling stuff! You could see Errol Flynn and Basil Rathbone doing their great turns. The other thing I loved was the cartoons, with all that quick music.[5]

What Is Neoclassicism in Film Music?

As with the classical style, neoclassicism in film music is not just a matter of reviving the old-fashioned symphonic language. As this book has maintained throughout, the concept of style as applied to film music should be a broader one, a combination of language, techniques, musical means, and functions. The more a score revives as many as possible of these four classical stylistic elements, the more it can be called neoclassical. For clarity's sake, consider three almost coeval pirate films, all clearly looking back on the 1930s swash-buckler models: *Pirates* (Roman Polanski, 1986, music by Philippe Sarde); *Hook* (Steven Spielberg, 1991, music by John Williams); and *Cutthroat Island* (Renny Harlin, 1995, music by John Debney). Each film has a full-blown symphonic score that harks back to the classical Hollywood scores. In *Pirates* and *Cutthroat Island*, music is also given a prestige symphonic treatment: Sarde's score is performed by the Orchestre de Paris, while Debney's is performed by the neoclassical-trend signature orchestra itself, the London Symphony. However, upon watching the films, listening to their scores, and comparing them, it is clear that the most neoclassical one is Williams's. His score has a number of clear-cut and very recognizable leitmotivs each appearing as its related character appears on-screen, features decidedly Korngoldian fanfares, and, above all, displays an overtly higher classical adherence to the visuals—a prominent spatial perceptive function. This is evident if we pay particular attention to the sword-fight scenes, a trademark of the swashbuckler genre. Sarde's score displays a refined writing that convincingly refers to the Golden Age models, but the composer's techniques are decidedly more steeped in the European tradition. His treatment of the sword-fight scenes consists of music having its own flow, without the classical "catching the action"—no musical accents or gestures hits the many clashes of the blades, lunges, and stunts. Also, there is not a strong network of leitmotivs. Debney's score is more action-oriented, but it is also more similar to the heavy action music in the eclectic style (à la Hans Zimmer) than to the classical-style balletic scoring. Its perceptive function is more temporal than spatial. We hear a lot of pounding rhythms to sustain the pace of the scenes, overwhelming bass tones that act as a background for the sound effects, while explicit synch-points between the music and the visuals are mostly underlined with emphatic cymbal clashes and loud, isolated stingers. On the contrary, in the sword-fight scenes in *Hook*, the score is closely tailored on the visuals in a balletic way. Consider the final assault on Captain Hook's ship and the following denouement duel between Peter Pan and the pirate leader. Somersaults are replicated with woodwinds whirls, whip pans are accompanied by harp *glissandos*, lunges are stressed by woodwinds runs, and musical accents precisely hit the moves and gyrations of the duelists. Both Sarde's and Debney's score have neoclassical traits, but only Williams's score is outright neoclassical.

Williams's old-fashioned style is acknowledged by a direct witness of the Golden Age, Lionel Newman (Alfred's brother): "Now he writes for films the way one would write an opera; he develops the characters dramatically through the music he writes. What he does enhances the film; he doesn't just write musical sequences, the way so many others do."[6] However, these classical stylistic traits are handled in a neoclassical way: "The nineteenth-century symphonic model is still present but now it is more credible and appropriate to the times since it has been revised to become more flexible, efficient but also more ironic and metalinguistic. . . . Unlike the previous 1930s and '40s musical themes, Williams's themes are designed to showcase the devices and techniques of musical rhetoric through the playful use of quotations, which are not taken literally but in their spirit."[7]

Williams's Neoclassical Style

The basic dialect employed in these neoclassical scores is late romanticism, but compared with those of Steiner and Korngold, Williams's idiom is more influenced by the twentieth-century dialects. For example, episodes of poly-tonality and atonality are frequently found, and jazz chords color the symphonic texture, for example, the frequent use of thirteenth chords or syncopated rhythms—think of the march for *1941* (Steven Spielberg, 1979). Williams was also influenced by Copland's Americana dialect—pandiatonicism and quartal harmony—especially in his American themes, for example John Quincy Adams's trumpet theme in *Amistad* (Steven Spielberg, 1997).[8]

Pandiatonicism typically employs the notes of the diatonic scale freely without conventional resolutions and without the standard chord progressions; unlike the traditional functional tonality, the chords built on the scale grades are not assigned fixed functions and different degrees of importance. "Hedwig's Theme" and "Fawkes the Phoenix," respectively from *Harry Potter and the Sorcerer's Stone* (Chris Columbus, 2001) and *Harry Potter and the Chamber of Secrets* (Chris Columbus, 2002), are two examples of themes with pandiatonic passages, as well as the "Journey to the Island" theme from *Jurassic Park* (Steven Spielberg, 1993). Pandiatonicism allows instantaneous key changes, and the frequent shifts and unexpected modulations from one tonality to others in Williams's music are powerful attention-catchers, like sudden color changes in the lighting of a room. Musically, they are very useful in keeping the interest level high; cine-matically, they are very effective in stressing noteworthy twists in the narrative or events in the visuals. When analyzing the "Indiana Jones Theme" in chapter 8, one can see how strikingly the sudden use of a D-flat-major chord within a C-major key gives a bright refreshing twist to the tune.

Quartal harmony, on the other hand, builds chords not as juxtaposed thirds—as traditional harmony does—but as juxtaposed fourths. For exam-ple, the model of the "Main Title" from *Star Wars* is Korngold—namely *Kings Row* (Sam Wood, 1942). Williams, however, "Americanizes" Korngold, employing quartal chords and choosing to close the musical phrase with a chord progression typical of the Americana dialect used in Westerns—the major triad built on the flattened seventh degree resolves to the dominant chord.[9]

Williams has also blended the idioms of Hollywood's first generation with those of the second generation. Parts of *Jaws* have timbres, motifs, and *ostinatos* that recall Herrmann's concise writing: the effective simplicity of the shark's motif and the violent string writing of Chrissie's death evoke *Psycho* (Alfred Hitchcock, 1960). This Herrmannesque modernist influence coexists in those works of Williams with extended themes, richly orchestrated textures, and solid musical structure à la Korngold, and also with Steiner's precisely descriptive Mickey-Mousing. Harmonically, Aaron Copland is again a major influence as for harmonic choices, and the IV–I progression and plagal cadence frequently used by Williams—for example, in the main theme from *Jurassic Park*—are also typical of Copland's Americana modal sound.

As for the influences from art music, Williams is often linked to Richard Wagner, especially for his penchant for using leitmotivs extensively. Nonetheless, besides leitmotivs and continuous musical accompaniment, *Star Wars* does not sound very Wagnerian in terms of melodies and harmonies—and it is not Wagnerian in Williams's intention.[10] Perhaps the most Wagnerian Williams piece is the sentimental music for the farewell scene in *E.T. the Extra-Terrestrial* (Steven Spielberg, 1982), which is reminiscent of the longing "unending melody" technique used in *Tristan und Isolde* (1865). More than Wagner's chromaticism, Williams uses pandiatonicism. Definitely more influential than Wagner in linguistic terms have been such Russian composers as Sergei Prokofiev and Dmitri Shostakovitch—think of "The March of the Villains" for *Superman: The Movie* (Richard Donner, 1978), or the "Parade of the Ewoks" from *Return of the Jedi* (Richard Marquand, 1983); or the music of the British twentieth-century school such as Ralph Vaughan Williams, William Walton, Benjamin Britten, and, above all, Edward Elgar. The most prominent examples are *Jane Eyre* (Delbert Mann, 1970); more recently *War Horse* (Steven Spielberg, 2011); and the "Throne Room" music for the epilogue of *Star Wars*, which owes much to Walton's coronation march *Orb and Sceptre* (1953). Claude Debussy's ethereal impressionism has also been an influence: think of the mermaid music for *Hook* (Steven Spielberg, 1991); the séance scene music for *Family Plot* (Alfred Hitchcock, 1976); and the "Fortress of Solitude" sequence in *Superman: The Movie*. Richard Strauss's extroverted orchestral grandiosity is the model, for example, of the end credits music for *Close Encounters of the Third Kind* (Steven Spielberg, 1977), or of the "Planet Krypton" heraldic music for *Superman: The Movie*; while there are traces of Gustav Mahler's tragic, monumental romanticism in the elegy written for the Jedi immolation sequence in *Star Wars: Episode III—Revenge of the Sith* (George Lucas, 2005); or in the melancholic final music for *Minority Report* (Steven Spielberg, 2002).[11] In general, Russian impressionism—Nicolai Rimsky-Korsakov and Igor Stravinsky's first works—seems to be a primary model for Williams's use of the orchestra. In his scores there is a keen attention for a coloristic and inventive use of timbres, and such recurring traits as high-pitched woodwind runs, prominent harp *glissandos*, glistening touches of the celesta, and the constant presence of the piano used either for adding color to a melody or to reinforce the percussion section.

As for techniques, one of the most prominent traits of Williams's writing is, again, the extensive use of leitmotivs. Williams is a great melodist; he has an instinct for finding just the right musical equivalent for a film or a character and a knack for writing clear-cut themes with a strong identity that get instantly fixed to the listener's memory. "So much of successful film scoring relies on a gratifying melodic identification for the characters. . . . I try to draw on something that marries very well with what I'm seeing."[12] For instance, on the "Indiana Jones Theme" Williams comments: "A piece like that is deceptively simple to try to find the few notes that will make a right leitmotivic identification for a character like Indiana Jones. I remember working on that thing for days and days, changing notes, changing this, inverting that, trying to get something that seemed to me to be just right. I can't speak for my colleagues but for me things which appear to be very simple are not at all, they're only simple after the fact. The manufacture of those things which seem inevitable is a process that can be laborious and difficult."[13] The creation of recognizable melodies and their skillful combination into a leitmotivic network allows Williams's scores to be a proficient musical retelling of the film's narrative. Themes and musical motifs associated with characters or concepts and their manipulation for narrative purposes are consistently present in virtually all his work, even in more experimental scores like *Close Encounters of the Third Kind*. The six scores for the *Star Wars* saga are exemplarily built with dozens of leitmotivs.

The musical manipulation of leitmotivs also implies good skills in the theme-and-variation technique. Says a reviewer: "Even more impressive, though, are the myriad ways in which he transforms the arching lines of that main melody, fragmenting and poisoning them as the mood turns from triumphant to ominous. The terse, tense music in "Jurassic Park" isn't fundamentally different from the soaring stuff. Mr. Williams, for all his lyrical lavishness, is an expert at recycling, at making a given theme do many different things in the course of a film."[14]

For example, "Darth Vader's Theme" is widely used as the militaristic and threatening "Imperial March" in *The Empire Strikes Back* (Irvin Kershner, 1980). When Darth Vader, in *Return of the Jedi*, eventually repents and gives his life to save his son, Williams sensitively penned a benign variation of Vader's theme gently played by a solo harp. A striking instance, again from the *Star Wars* catalogue, is "Augie's Great Municipal Band," a joyful piece for chorus and orchestra that accompanies the celebration in the closing scene of *Star Wars: Episode I—The Phantom Menace* (George Lucas, 1999). A close listening reveals that the cheerful major-mode theme is, meaningfully, a variation of the minor-mode sinister Emperor's theme already featured in *Return of the Jedi*, as if to say that the victory of Good versus Evil being celebrated here is deceitful and tragically ephemeral[15]—indeed, Senator Palpatine (the future evil Emperor) can be spotted among the onlookers. Williams also masters the Mickey-Mousing technique, which in Williams's case is usually not pushed to the extremes as in Steiner's, but when needed, Williams can be very Steineresque: in the opening train-chase sequence of *Indiana Jones and the Last Crusade* (Steven Spielberg, 1989) there is, on average, one explicit synch-point every six seconds.[16] Another classical technique that Williams can handle proficiently is the dialogue underscoring (see especially chaps. 2 and 5).

A typical Williams technique that is connected with the macro-emotive function is what can be called "gradual disclosure of the main theme." The main theme is presented gradually across the film, in the form of progressively longer melodic fragments, and the final exposition of the theme in its entirety comes only at a strategic point in the narrative. Typically such a strategic point is a scene requiring a strong emotional response from the viewers. Williams explains: "What is so important is an hour and a half or ten reels of preparation to that moment. . . . [I]n the first reel we only heard two notes, in the third reel we heard four, in the fifth reel we heard six manipulated, in the tenth . . . and so on. But in the twelfth you hear all twelve coming. So, to the audience, you've created an expectancy to deliver something that's not only very emotional but is also inevitable. It's a moment that had to happen."[17]

Having being prepared throughout the previous part of the film, the viewers can easily recognize the theme when it is presented in its entirety and be gratified by the long-awaited full statement of the familiar theme. Perhaps the best instance can be found in *E.T. the Extra-Terrestrial*, whose main theme—fragments of which are presented throughout the first half of the film—is completely stated by the full orchestra only in the spectacular and emotionally uplifting sequence of the bicycle flight over the moon. Locally, the gratification produced in the viewers by recognizing and finally hearing the long-delayed presentation of the full melody is projected onto the images, thus amplifying their emotional impact and performing a micro-emotive function.[18] This "gradual disclosure of the main theme" technique also works globally, performing a macro-emotive function on the whole film's form: it casts onto the entire film the sense of cohesion and unity given to the score by the recurrent thematic reprises and their development and formal closure. In *Jaws*, the technique circumscribes the whole shark-hunt final act: what we have called the "Man-versus-the-Beast" theme is heard for the first time when the *Orca* leaves the harbor; it is presented in fragmentary ways throughout the sea hunt; and appears in its complete form only after the shark is killed, over the end credits, enhancing the sense of fulfillment for the man having defeated the beast.

Last, as for the musical means, Williams is evidently fond of the symphony orchestra: "The symphony orchestra itself is one of the greatest inventions of our artistic culture. Fabulous sounds it can produce and a great range of emotional capabilities."[19] From *Star Wars* on, Williams's orchestra has been much bigger than the classical studio orchestras. This is another trait that can be called neoclassical—or "hyperclassical," in Bordwell's words[20]—being an exaggeration of classical traits.

Williams's Neoclassical Attitude

Besides stylistic traits, there are also a number of habits and practices that link Williams with the classical Hollywood music.[21] Williams commented, "My own preference is not to read scripts. It's like when you read a novel: you envisage the locales, you cast the players in your mind. That's the reason, I think, why people are so often disappointed by film versions of novels they have read—they don't conform to their preconceptions. So I'd rather not read scripts, and I tell producers that I'd rather go into a projection room and react to the people and places and events—and particularly the rhythm—of the film itself."[22] Compare Williams's words to Max Steiner's:

> I write what I see and what I hear and the way the character affects me. That is why I have a rule I have had all my life. I never . . . I never but never read a script. I have had one or two bad experiences. I read a script and I think this is the greatest script I ever read and I see the picture and it is the most horrible thing you ever saw. The characters are changing and you build up an image of characters when you read a script. On the other hand I have read scripts that were so terrible I wouldn't touch them. But when the picture came out, I loved it. So I decided I'd wait until I see the picture. I would never write . . . most producers never understand it. They say to me, "Shall I send you the script?" and I say, "Hell no, I don't want to read it," because I know it will steer me all wrong . . . good or bad.[23]

Besides the fact that written pages can evoke images that can be disappointingly different from the film version, this choice can be explained in stylistic terms too. Says Williams, "You really can't get that off the page of script, . . . there may be one page of script that could be five minutes of film, or five pages of script that's 30 seconds of film. We need to see it."[24] Composing music from a screenplay is possible in those cases in which the music is written prior to the film, as in the Leone/ Morricone collaboration[25] or when explicit synch-points between music and visuals are not required, as in the modern style—for example, in Nino Rota's scores. If, on the one hand, the music has to fulfill only a cognitive or emotive function, the composer can acquire the needed informa-tion by reading the script and discussing it with the director. On the other hand, if the score is also supposed to follow the image tightly and perform a significant spatial perceptive function, the composer must necessarily work from a film's cut in order to conform the music to the visuals second by second. Williams explains, "In the film work I look at the film a lot. There is a cutting room, a viewing room so to speak, within the building I work in, and I can look at a scene I am working on for two or three days and see it as often as I need to see it. I can write a few bars, then go look at it."[26]

Williams has stated: "The test of a good score . . . is that you hardly even notice it. It's like a good tailor. You don't want to know how he sewed it, you just want to know that it holds."[27] And this statement, again, sounds much like Steiner's "[Music should fit] a picture like a glove."[28] Williams's typical work routine is reported in a 1984 article:

> Williams—along with the producer, the director, the film editor, and the music editor—"spots" the film, that is, they decide when the music should start and stop. The exact spot, precise to one-third of a second, is marked on the film. Then the music editor writes out a detailed cue sheet—a chronological listing of every event and sound effect that happens during the parts of the film that will be accompanied by music. With the cue sheet as his guide, Williams composes about two minutes of music each day. He is allowed four weeks to write the music for an average feature film which requires about 60 minutes of music. . . . Most film cues are from a few seconds to two or three minutes long, so the film composer often adopts a piecemeal approach, concentrating on two minutes of film at a time. "When I come in in the morning, I like to look at the sequence that I'm going to work on that day, so it's fresh in my mind. . . . I look at my assignment for the day on the Moviola (a machine that reduces the movie to a four-inch wide viewing screen), mark up the cues sheet, restudy just that bit of film, and then work on it. I may check the clip again later in the afternoon. . . . There are many extra-musical problems. The biggest one is having the music co-exist with a lot of noises. It should be conceived orchestrally with these things in mind. You not only need to study the film, you need to study the

sounds associated with the film in these areas and try to create a
marriage between the orchestra and those sounds."[29]

As for the writing itself, Williams still uses an old-school modus operandi.
Unlike the next-generation composers and some same-age composers—Jerry
Goldsmith, for example—Williams does not use synthesizers, MIDI, or any
other technological tool to compose his music. In his words: "I don't use synthesizers or electronic equipment and all that stuff. My musical education is such
that it pre-dates all of that and although I know a little bit about it, I haven't
developed the skills. I use the piano, that's my old friend in music."[30] And
"Antique tools. Not even a pen these days. Pencil and paper. . . . And I find that
at least for me pencil and paper introduces a process of working that's as much
part of it, it becomes part of the conceptual routine or process of working. It's
tangible. It feels good to hold a pen or pencil in your hand and dirty up paper.
I suppose it must seem to young composers a completely antediluvian or old-
fashioned way of doing it."[31] "It's an influence that would be hard to quantify,
but I think methodology is intimately connected to result. . . . It's something
you do with your hands, so there's an aspect of craftsmanship involved, even
penmanship."[32]

On the recording stage, Williams, unlike the majority of contemporary film
conductors, does not use too constrictive technical aids: "Williams conducts
with the film projected on a screen behind the orchestra and a clock in front of
the podium. Timings are marked in the score at least every other bar. Other
mechanical aids, like a "streamer" which shows up on the screen as a band
of light followed by a bright flash at the crucial moment help maintain stop-
watch precision. Many composers rely on click tracks (a variation on the metro-
nome) that let the conductor and the orchestra members hear a beat that has
already been synchronized with the movie. But Williams finds the unrelenting
beat coming through the headphones too confining for musical expression.
With the clock to mark off the moments that must be matched exactly, he prefers
to allow his musicians some flexibility in between those key points."[33] In the old
days, the click track was employed by Max Steiner to allow his very tightly
synchronized scores to be recorded in less time and as precisely as possible.
Williams, on the contrary, conducts freestyle as Korngold did, which is a more
complex method to achieve the perfect synchronization but allows the music to
flow more freely and to sound less mechanical.[34]

In chapter 6, we underlined the importance of Williams's apprenticeship
during the last years of the studio system and his training in the fast-paced
television production. His work habits seem to have been influenced by those

past experiences as it seems that he prefers to compose in a work environment somewhat reminiscent of the old music departments. Being no more in-house employees but freelancers, most of Hollywood composers have their studios at home (e.g., Danny Elfman, but Jerry Goldsmith also used to compose at home)[35] or at their own musical company (e.g., Hans Zimmer). Howard Shore's studio is located in New York, far away from the Hollywood studios. On the contrary, Williams has routinely worked in an office located in some film studio or production company throughout his career. He had had an office in the 20th Century Fox studios for twenty-five years, until he moved to Spielberg's Amblin compound at Universal Studios in 1987 (Amblin is now within the DreamWorks SKG facilities). However anecdotally this might sound, it somewhat attests to Williams's fondness for the old days:

> We knew it was, say, Warner Bros Orchestra, because unlike now, where you have one or two honored freelance groups recording everything, it wasn't the same people playing on every film. . . . In the isolation of a few miles across Los Angeles you had inspirational individuality coming out of these studio systems.[36] We had a music department table where we all went every day for lunch. We'd sit around and between ordering sandwiches, we'd talk about your problems and my problems, this dreadful director and that hateful producer, and we'd got a better cellist here than they have across the street—the kind of inside stuff that really puts you in touch with how things work. Every studio had that, but it's all gone now. Every composer works at home. We don't even know each other any more. We're not connected.[37]

Another similarity with classical Hollywood composers is Williams's parallel career in concert music both as a composer and as a conductor, whereas modern-style film composers typically have a parallel career in songwriting or pop music—apart from some exceptions like Rota and Morricone. Among the film composers who have also produced a considerable amount of concert music are Korngold, Waxman, Rózsa, Moross, and Herrmann. Williams's concert pieces are unusually numerous for a film composer of his generation: twelve concertos, one symphony, somewhere around thirty other works comprising celebratory fanfares, orchestral miniatures, and solo or chamber pieces. Williams also has a parallel career as a concert conductor, as did Alfred Newman, who used to conduct the Hollywood Bowl Orchestra; Franz Waxman, who founded and was musical director of the Los Angeles International Music Festival; and

Bernard Herrmann, who spent his last decade mostly as a conductor in London.[38] Newman, in particular, seems to have been a role model for Williams: "[As for conducting skills], of film composers, though, Alfred Newman was the best I've ever seen or heard: he was a magician with an orchestra, could get amazing effects. And such a disciplinarian, in the most natural and simple way."[39]

Even more unusual is Williams's care in adapting concert suites from his film scores. This is another element linking him to the classical period, whose film composers mostly came from theater or concert music and were used to that medium, whereas modern-style composers had radio stations and the record market as the primary target for their film music outside of the films. Even Steiner, noted for the fragmentary structure and highly functional nature of his film works, showed some concern for the structural solidity of the music: "Even though the themes [of *Gone with the Wind*] are popular it's written in symphonic style. I tried to be as musical as possible. It's in itself a serious work, in itself. The score is symphonic, even if it is in a popular vein here and there. [Of course it can be played in concert halls,] sure. It has been. It has been played everywhere. I played it with the New York Philharmonic. There was just another one with the London Symphony, and now they are going to do it in Tokyo. . . . I have made a suite out of it."[40]

On arranging film music for concerts, Williams has stated: "If I can take the music out of the sound track and have it almost resemble music, this is a minor miracle, and a double asset. . . . If I write a 100-minute score, there may be 20 minutes that could be extracted and played. The other 80 minutes is functional accompaniment that could never stand on its own and was never intended to."[41] Although Williams underplays it, his particular care for concert versions is proved by the fact that he is the only film composer whose numerous concert suites can easily be found for sale in authoritative full scores.[42]

Like his colleagues of the past—particularly Rózsa, Waxman, and Herrmann—Williams often uses musical forms similar to those of art music: the *scherzo* in *Jane Eyre*, *Dracula* (John Badham, 1979), and *Indiana Jones and the Last Crusade*; the *fugato* in *Jaws*, *Black Sunday* (John Frankenheimer, 1977), and *Harry Potter and the Prisoner of Azkaban* (Alfonso Cuaron, 2004); set-pieces for chorus and orchestra like the carols in *Home Alone* (Chris Columbus, 1990), "Gloria" in *Monsignor* (Frank Perry, 1982) and "Exsultate justi" in *Empire of the Sun* (Steven Spielberg, 1987); and quasi-ballet music for action scenes, for example in *Jurassic Park*, of which the composer says, "[It is] a massive job of symphonic cartooning. You have to match the rhythmic gyrations of the dinosaurs and create these kind of funny ballets."[43] In the classical period, this attention to the solidity of the musical form on the part of classically trained composers can be explained by the hope that the best bits of a film score might be extracted and thus have a life outside of the films.[44] Likewise, from the outset Williams inserts traditional forms when writing his film scores, so that he can obtain—with a minimum of changes—stand-alone pieces for concert presentations. For example, he might add a coda to close a passage left open in the film score, as in the case of "The Asteroid Field" from *The Empire Strikes Back* or "The Lost Boys Ballet" from *Hook*.[45] From the score for *Harry Potter and the Sorcerer's Stone*, Williams adapted an eight-movement children's suite in the spirit of Benjamin Britten's *The Young Person's Guide to the Orchestra*, op. 34 (1946).[46] An example of the musical solidity of Williams's compositions is the finale of *E.T. the Extra-Terrestrial*, which was adapted with the mere removal of a few central measures into the symphonic poem *Adventures on Earth*:[47] "Thanks to its thematic concatenations, the piece alludes convincingly to the musical macro-forms of the nineteenth and early twentieth centuries . . . showing a musical legitimacy rarely to be found in film-music adaptations . . . These same forms were also able to cope with and satisfy each narrative need in their natural place—that is, the film—and this is a proof of the overall quality of the composer."[48]

Moreover, Williams has often employed famous or well-known concert soloists to play on his film scores: the violinist Isaac Stern in *Fiddler on the Roof* (Norman Jewison, 1971); the violinist Itzhak Perlman in *Schindler's List* (Steven Spielberg, 1994); and the cellist Yo-Yo Ma in *Seven Years in Tibet* (Jean-Jacques Annaud, 1997).[49] The involvement of these illustrious guest stars, mostly planned at the beginning of the compositional process, has led to a conspicuous quantity of film-music pieces for solo and orchestra, all of which are practically ready for concert presentation as well.

Besides concerts but still outside the cinema, Williams has accomplished another fusion between classical and modern practices. He carefully supervises the creation of the film-music album to be marketed—which is typical of the modern-style composers—while also striving to have a musical form as solid as possible—which is characteristic of classical-style composers. Following Mancini's example, Williams records selections from the film score expressly rearranged for the albums in order to have a better musical solidity and closure. The track list of the album does not reflect the order in which the pieces were presented in the film, but here the list meets criteria of musical variety and balance aimed at an autonomous music experience.[50] The LP album of *Star Wars* is a clear example: the "The Little People Work" track follows "Ben's Death/TIE Fighter Attack," in a reverse order compared to the film. The "Main Title" of *Star Wars* on the album is different from that in the film: "I combined part of the end title with the opening music to give the beginning of the record the feeling of an overture."[51] If we compare the 1982 LP album of *E.T. the Extra-Terrestrial* (40', MCA Records 1982, CD, MCLD 19021), which has pieces expressly re-recorded for the album, with the 1996 CD containing the music used in the film's sound track (78', MCA Records 1996, CD, MCAD-11494), we notice that the pieces in the 1982 LP albums were considerably adapted and expanded for a better listening experience. For example, on the CD with the original music track the music for the Halloween sequence and the following bicycle flight over the moon (titled "The Magic of Halloween") lasts 2' 53" while on the album the corresponding track "E.T.'s Halloween" lasts 4' 07". Williams added additional phrases to get a more extended musical development that closed the piece more formally, while the film version stops abruptly with the bicycle landing. Similarly, the music in the montage sequence of *Jaws* lasts 1' 30" in the film—and on the original music track CD (Decca 2000, CD, 467045-2)—while in the album (MCA Records 1975, CD, MCD01660-MCAD1660) the piece is humorously named "Promenade (Tourists on the Menu)" and was expanded to 2' 46".[52]

Besides inheriting stylistic traits and habits from the past, Williams as a neoclassical composer has also become the target of the same old prejudices that used to surround classical Hollywood composers, along with new prejudices against the very idea of neoclassicism.

8

Williams's Naysayers

A Deconstruction of Classical and New Criticisms

lassical Hollywood composers were typical targets of highbrow critics. For example, Miklós Rózsa saw his credibility as an art composer prejudicially questioned: "Only a light-headed critic would suggest that Rózsa's chamber music and his symphonic works sound like 'movie music,' although there have been critics who have not been able to avoid this fatuous view. After a performance in England of his *Theme, Variations and Finale*, op. 13, a critic commented that it showed unmistakable signs of the composer's involvement in films. It was written in 1933, four years before Rózsa began his association with motion pictures!"[1]

Hollywood composers were often attacked and blamed for their lack of originality and for over-popularizing art music in their compositions.[2] They were accused of unoriginally borrowing from past composers, even sometimes of shamelessly stealing. In this light, Dimitri Tiomkin delivered this self-ironic acceptance speech in his trademark "Russian-English" upon receiving an Oscar in 1955 for *The High and the Mighty* (William A. Wellman, 1954): "Ladies and gentlemen . . . I like to make some kind of appreciation to very important factor which makes me successful and adds to quality of this town. I like to thank Johannes Brahms, Johann Strauss, Richard Strauss, Richard Wagner . . ."[3] Like the classical Hollywood composers, Williams is the polemic idol of a conspicuous number of particularly vehement detractors. Oddly enough, such a thing does not happen to such an extent with other equally popular composers, like Ennio Morricone.

Williams, in particular, has been accused of being too commercial, of stealing from the past masters, and of resorting to mere musical clichés. Some statements are overtly subjective and peremptory, like the following comment to a recent Williams interview, which appeared on the *New York Times* website: "Williams is sort of like the Andrew Lloyd Webber of film music. Lots of pretty melodies but (the "Jaws" music aside) nothing that really supports the tone or mood of the film. The only great composer of film music who's still working is Ennio Morricone."[4] The statement has the visceral nature of the disputes between sport supporters—"Williams versus Morricone," not too different from "Boston Red Sox versus New York Yankees." If the commentator had taken into consideration Williams's *Close Encounters of the Third Kind*, just to name one, his assertion might have been different. But besides amateurs, some practitioners, critics, and scholars with more credibility and competence also show a biased view.

Ennio Morricone once called the "Main Title" from *Star Wars* a "marcetta [cheap march]," stating that he would have rather composed an eight-voice fugue.[5] This claim—besides sounding slightly arrogant—is surprising for the alternate solution proposed. It is clear that an eight-voice fugue would be out of place in the opening titles of *Star Wars*. Morricone does not lack narrative sensitivity or experience in the film-music business: this controversial assertion cannot be due to incompetence but to a haughty attitude.

The "Morriconian" composer Marco Frisina once stated: "[Williams] uses trumpets very well. But always with a taste and in a way that are typically American: the fifths, for instance. The fifths are typical of a characteristically American 'bad taste.'"[6] In this case, saying that open fifths, which are indeed typical of the quartal harmony and pandiatonicism of American music—think of Aaron Copland's *Fanfare for the Common Man* (1942)—are American bad taste is like saying that the Neapolitan chord is Italian bad taste and the augmented-sixth chord is German bad taste!

The film director Dario Argento, speaking of film music during a conference at the University of Genoa, Italy, praised musicians like Morricone, Pino Donaggio, Bernard Herrmann, and the Goblin—the Italian progressive-rock band known for the main theme of Argento's *Profondo Rosso* (1975).[7] When asked about the not-mentioned Williams, Argento replied, "Oh, that's a commercial composer." What does "commercial" mean? Is Williams "commercial" because he sells many records and is widely popular? If yes, is not Morricone as commercial as Williams?

The Orchestrators, Again

Russell Lack, in his book on film music, drags up the old bromide stating that using an orchestrator is a symptom of artistic incompetence: "In foregrounding the symphonic score, Williams is siding with tradition, but his very tight working schedules mean that he works extensively with orchestrators. . . . One might argue that his celebrity is due more to the films he has scored rather than the scores themselves, which whilst stirring enough are hard to single out as distinctively his own since they are so varied, due in part to Williams' frequent use of a variety of different orchestrators and arrangers."[8]

Working under "very tight working schedules" is something that any composer in Hollywood is used to, Williams being not an exception: "A standard contract for his movie compositions gives him three months to create a score. A Lucas or Spielberg epic might require 120 minutes of music. A little calculating and presto. Williams must compose forty minutes of original score a month, or 10 minutes a week, or two minutes every day (assuming he rests on the weekend, which he often does not)."[9]

The use of orchestrators is indeed a traditional aspect of the Hollywood practice aimed to optimize labor time, and I have also argued against the necessary equation of orchestrators with ghostwriters. In Lack's statement, though, he seems to ignore both the Hollywood tradition and Williams's specific work method. Had Lack dug a little deeper under the surface, he might have easily found out that Williams had not used "a variety of different orchestrators" but collaborated for more than twenty years with Herbert W. Spencer (1905–92)—from *A Guide for the Married Man* (1967) to *Home Alone* (1990). Williams commented:

> [Spencer's] been my first choice for a very long time. He's an expert orchestrator but he's also a guy I can live with for the length of time it takes to do a picture. It's more of a personal thing. . . . We know each other very well, so I suppose we do [create a form of shorthand]. He knows my idiosyncrasies. In doubling, for example, you may want to lean on something, to be à "2" or à "3" or whatever, and sometimes Herb will be in the next room and pound on the piano and say, "How

much do you want that B flat? Three or four horns, or six?" And I may remember there's a great sword whack on the soundtrack, so I say, "Six!" That sort of thing. We have a great relationship.[10]

Williams had with Spencer a long and trusting collaboration—recalling that between Korngold and his orchestrator Hugo Friedhofer—which guaranteed an even and stylistically homogeneous output.[11] After Spencer's death, Williams began consistent collaborations with a few recurring names: John Neufeld, Alexander Courage, Conrad Pope, Eddie Karam, many of whom had served as Spencer's associates and assistants in the past. Williams, like most Hollywood composers of the past, needs the help of orchestrators to meet deadlines: "Without the orchestrator's help, Williams estimates that his daily output would be cut in half."[12] Nonetheless, his sketches are so detailed that using a different orchestrator would not affect the results in terms of idiom and orchestral texture:

> I don't want to minimize the contribution of orchestrators but, on the other hand, I try to be *very* careful about my sketches so that I get just what I want: winds on two or three staves, horns, brass, low brass, piano, percussion, etc., in the middle, and then three or four staves for strings, so that on eight or ten staves you can get almost a note-perfect accurate score. But the sheer labor of laying it out in full score for symphony orchestra would greatly slow me up, so here orchestrators help. When you consider that *Star Wars* had some 90 minutes of orchestral music and had to be written in some six-plus weeks . . . about half the length of an opera. Well, to do that without even stenographic help from an orchestrator would be physically impossible. On *Star Wars* I used four: Herb [Spencer] was contracted to do it and he receives the credit (he must have done about 500 of the 800-or-so pages of score), but Arthur Morton, Angela Morley and Al Woodbury also helped a lot. I even did some sequences myself, so I hope that it's a compliment to my sketches that you can't tell who did what![13]

The Boston Pops percussionist Patrick Hollenbeck debuted as an orchestrator after Williams had asked for his help on *Indiana Jones and the Last Crusade*: "When I got out there I heard these horror stories of orchestrators being handed a page with a title, a key signature and a number of bars and nothing else on it; so orchestrators have developed a mystique as, allegedly, 'the secret composers,' and in many cases it may be true—but not with John Williams. With him, orchestrating means taking his notes from the little green paper and putting them in the big yellow paper."[14]

Evidence proves that Williams is fully capable of orchestrating his works, schedule permitting: he personally orchestrated the scores for *Fiddler on the Roof* (Norman Jewison, 1971); *Jane Eyre* (Delbert Mann, 1970); *Cinderella Liberty* (Mark Rydell, 1973); *The Missouri Breaks* (Arthur Penn, 1976); and *Images* (Robert Altman, 1972).[15] Williams's works are consistent with his overall idiom and orchestral sound, as Kathryn Kalinak points out: "Such detailed sketches and long-term collaborations leave little room for deviation and insure a consistency in terms of the Williams sound."[16] In short, Lack's statements sound as if they are the result of either incompetence or prejudice, insinuating that ghostwriters are employed so as to downplay Williams's skills.

The Aesthetic Prejudice

In 2002 the music critic Norman Lebrecht penned a fierce article, eloquently titled "The Magpie Maestro." This article appears to be an emblematic reservoir of prejudices sustained by weak points and masked with sensationalistic rhetoric but illustrates what are the typical arguments used to attack Williams. "John Williams has cornered the film-score market. But his patchwork soundtracks that borrow from the classics are an offence to the ear . . . Williams has, for three decades, been Hollywood's composer of choice. Hitting the jackpot with Jaws and Star Wars, he added a gloss of culture (known as 'class') to harum-scarum adventure movies."[17] The article opens assertively with a rhetorical statement based on Lebrecht's personal taste, and later somewhat contemptuously links the composer's work to "harum-scarum adventure movies," which serves to downplay Williams's importance to that of a merely commercial artisan. The statement also suggests Lebrecht's dislike for Hollywood cinema, and a formal analysis of *Jaws* carried out with competence (and without prejudice) would demonstrate that the film is anything but "harum-scarum."

Lebrecht continues: "He is, beyond question, the most famous living orchestral composer. Posterity, however, is not so slickly secured. The word in Hollywood is that Williams is on the wane . . . He has not won an Oscar since *Schindler's List* in 1993."[18] Again, here Williams's importance is downplayed by conceding that his merit is only that of being famous. Yet such fame is questioned as for its longevity, thus implying that Williams is nothing but a fad. What is the exact source of this "word in Hollywood"? How can an informed (and unbiased) critic speak of decline in 2002, a year in which Williams composed as many as three films: *Star Wars: Episode II—Attack of the Clones*; *Harry Potter and the Chamber of Secrets*; and *Catch Me If You Can*? Moreover, these scores are very different from each other in their "intra-opus" style: they reflect not only the quantity of Williams's 2002 output but also its variety and inventiveness. Significantly, in the same year, another critic declared: "[T]he indefatigable composer shows no signs of slowing down."[19] As for the Oscars, Williams had already won five as of 2002, and in the next decade he became the most-nominated living person and the second most-nominated in Academy Award history. Undeniably, Oscars have always been questionable as a criterion for gauging success. Many times they are awarded to a certain film because of the producers' and voting colleagues' lobbying—just think that Kubrick, Hitchcock, Chaplin, and Morricone never won an Oscar or won only the Honorary Lifetime Achievement Awards.

After stating, "What John Williams did to the modern movie score was to reduce it to a string of clichés and strip it of musical character," Lebrecht praises the old Hollywood composers: "His themes [Korngold's] would run for 30 minutes continuously and while traces of Strauss and Mahler are often audible, the music has an unmistakable signature. Korngold, once heard, is not readily forgotten. His Hollywood followers, emigrants all, included Max Steiner (Casablanca), Franz Waxman (Sunset Boulevard), Dmitri Tiomkin (High Noon) and Mikos [*sic*] Rózsa (Spellbound). Each had his own sound, each added melodic and harmonic novelty."[20] The accusation against Williams's music of being merely a string of clichés sounds exactly like the 1947 Adorno and Eisler accusation against classical Hollywood film music. Proverbially, the good old days are always better than the present day, and indeed Lebrecht now takes the much-blamed classical Hollywood music as an example of personal originality and music solidity if compared to Williams. As for the alleged novelty added by each old Hollywood composer, this may be true for Waxman, Rózsa, and Korngold, but talking of melodic and harmonic novelty for Steiner and Tiomkin's traditional idioms is exaggeration.

Lebrecht then compares Hollywood composers with European art-film composers:

> Some are remembered merely for an effect—Bernard Herrmann, for instance, for the mass-stringed chills he applied to Alfred Hitchcock's thrillers. Others, like Nino Rota, co-created with Federico Fellini the essential ambience of cinematic legend. Late in life, Rota plundered his own score to 8 ½ for a theme that became The Godfather's. . . . Just how much a composer brings to a movie is heard in Hiroshima mon

Amour (1959), where Alain Resnais' somnolent pace and flimsy plot are
sustained by Georges Delerue's compelling soundtrack. . . . Delerue,
who died in 1992, wrote 294 film scores but never collected the million-
dollar fee that is the Williams benchmark. . . . More's the pity, since
there are still musicians producing fine work for the screen—Gabriel
Yared, Jocelyn Pook, Wojciech Kilar—to name three of the best. But
theirs is an uphill battle against the Williams method of plastering
movies with bits of what we know, rather than revealing an unseen
dimension.[21]

Bernard Herrmann, universally acknowledged as one of the most inventive
and outstanding composers having worked in Hollywood, is dismissed here as a
merely sensationalist composer for one Hitchcock thriller. What about *Citizen
Kane* (Orson Welles, 1941), just to name one of Herrmann's landmark works?
More important to our deconstruction of the article's argument, Lebrecht's
positive examples are films completely different from those made in Hollywood, and composers whose style is consequently very different. Since the aim
is to criticize Williams, a Hollywood composer, examples of good film music
and valuable composers should be taken from the same stylistic group, that of
the Hollywood repertoire. By sticking to European art-film examples and commenting that Williams's music simply restates in films what the viewers already
know, Lebrecht unveils his preference for modern style, his scant understanding of the Hollywood music style, and his biased view of Hollywood cinema.
An analysis of films like *Close Encounters of the Third Kind* and *Jaws* would reveal
that music does much more than simply say what we already know. And so it
seems that what Lebrecht wants to demolish is not just Williams but the kind
of commercial cinema he supposedly represents, defined by the generic term
"harum-scarum." Williams is chastised because he is a symbol of Hollywood
cinema and because he is financially very successful. Indeed, the money argument is brought forward when Lebrecht reports that Delerue earned less money
than Williams, which should imply that Delerue was a better composer. This is
based on an old idea that can be traced back to the nineteenth-century romantic
view of Art (with capital letter) as a quasi-religion exercised for Art's sake, as
opposed to craft, whose aim is to make money. The same equation was revived
by Adorno and Eisler, who also used to chastise the commercialism of Hollywood film music of the 1930s and 1940s: the conclusion is that true art cannot
be commercial. This old split between Art and commodity emerges again in
Lebrecht's closing: "There is no denying the success of John Williams, any
more than one can ignore that of Bill Gates. We may have to live with it, but
there is no law yet that says we must like it."[22]

This fierce attitude of classical music critics against film music is a consequence of the nineteenth-century distinction between "absolute music"—music that is *ab soluta* (untied), composed for a stand-alone listening experience freed from any external influences and extramusical references—and "applied/functional music"—a musical rendition of a literary text, like a symphonic poem, or a musical accompaniment to an extramusical event, such as a ballet, an opera, or a film. The idea that the former is intrinsically and necessarily better music than the latter and that the two types must be kept distinct and neatly separated harks back to the nineteenth-century dictum.[23] Connected to this is the presence of a "Beethoven-centered" criterion that has had a consistent influence on musicology and has determined a bias against what deviates from the canonical models. In David Neumeyer's words: "A distinction between 'popular' and 'academic' canons is certainly present in music as well, but the situation is considerably more complex [than in film studies] due to institutional factors, especially the oppressive presence of the Beethoven-Centered canon, oriented toward instrumental rather than vocal or dramatic music."[24]

A textbook example of this "canonical prejudice" is an article printed in the *Los Angeles Times* in 1983, when the Hollywood composer and Boston Pops conductor had "dared" to conduct a "serious" concert program:

> This week's concerts by the Los Angeles Philharmonic at the Dorothy Chandler Pavilion raise only one essential question: Why? Why would Carlo Maria Giulini, a man of lofty principles and impeccable taste, entrust a presumably serious winter-season program to John Williams, an amiable musician whose claim to fame and fortune are predicated on movie-score bombast and Boston Pops bagatelles? . . . Why would our cultural guardians want to devote an entire evening's diet to such junk food as Samuel Barber's crunchy "School for Scandal" overture . . . the aforementioned Williams [Violin] Concerto and— horror of horrors—Gustav Holst's "The Planets," a banal thumpety- thump 1916 ooze orgy now prized by some observers as a preview of spacey "Star Wars" attractions? . . . Since Williams did not venture into anything like Mozart or Beethoven or Brahms or even Tchaikovsky, it is impossible to gauge his skill as an interpreter of great music. He did reveal himself, however, as an efficient musical traffic cop, despite a disconcerting tendency to gild the expressive lily with excessive facial choreography.[25]

Here we can clearly discern the critic's prejudice against the music not included in the revered canon of the deities of absolute art music. Mozart, Beethoven, and Brahms are authors of "great music." Along with Bach, they are the indisputable masters of a German-centric, stiff, and academic set of values—the wording "*even* Tchaikovsky" implies that the Russian composer is somewhat considered a lesser master than the great Germans. What is not in the Canon is automatically not worthy of even being taken into consideration: it is "junk food" and the protection of "cultural guardians" is invoked against those who, like Williams, attempt to trespass from the "applied music/popular music" realm onto that of "absolute/art music."

The Ideological Prejudice

Neil Lerner, in an analysis of *Star Wars* and *Close Encounters of the Third Kind*, while praising the effectiveness of Williams's music also accuses it of authoritarianism: "What is so remarkable about Williams' scores . . . is the way that they so effectively limit any oppositional readings of the films they accompany. In *Star Wars*, the music makes it difficult to identify any other character besides Luke as the central hero . . . Williams' sweepingly nostalgic music reassures, persuades, and above all else, lulls us into being uncritical."[26] A concise explanation for this interpretation is that it descends from those film theories—mostly based on semiotics, (Lacanian) psychoanalysis, and Marxism—that see films as ideological vehicles to be unmasked or as texts to be deciphered, rather than as artifacts to be approached in aesthetic terms.[27] Such an approach runs throughout the film studies of the last decades, in the works of Jean-Louis Comolli and Jean Narboni, Jean-Louis Baudry, Marie-Claire Ropars, in feminist film theory, and in deconstructionism, which seems to be Lerner's framework because he uses the characteristic term "oppositional readings."[28] From a (neo) formalist point of view, *Star Wars* is a well-constructed film: the scope of the narration is to present Luke as the protagonist of *Star Wars*, and the music is asked to help viewers to connect empathetically with him. The final result—viewers do identify with Luke—shows that the narration fulfilled its scope and the music accomplished its duties effectively.

On the music for *Jaws*, for example, Williams says: "So we can play the shark music even if he wasn't present, . . . and suggest that he's coming, and by getting louder and louder and louder—even if the camera doesn't move—you get a sense that he is getting closer to you because music is getting faster or louder or both. So in that way, I don't use the word manipulate, because it's become an ugly word, but it's actually a good word, because you can manage and choreograph these emotions we talk about."[29] The word "manipulate" here means that the music cooperates with the other formal devices to assist the narration in obtaining certain aesthetic effects and emotive reactions in the viewers. In Lerner's contra view, manipulation is an ideological deceit. From a deconstructionist perspective, music is seen as an authoritarian imposition by a director who is slyly trying to manipulate the viewers ideologically. Similarly, the term "nostalgia" (in Lerner's article "nostalgic music") is used with reaction-ary/regressive connotations, implying that music insidiously "anaesthetizes" the viewers' critical conscience.[30] As the leading exponent of neoclassicism—a trend that restored a past style and can be easily labeled as nostalgic—Williams is automatically seen as an ideologically reactionary composer.

Besides matters of personal taste, which are difficult to take into considera-tion, the aesthetic and ideological prejudices so far analyzed can explain why Williams is more vehemently attacked than other equally popular and successful composers. Being neoclassical and past-oriented, he is seen—either consciously or unconsciously—as regressive and conservative. Inversely, Morricone and other modern-style, future-oriented composers who challenged traditional rules are seen as progressive and revolutionary—hence necessarily better, when ideology is confused with style.

This same prejudice may also explain the *damnatio memoriae* against the Spielberg/Williams duo as well. One must remember that this is one of the most outstanding director/composer collaborations in history. Begun in 1973 and entering its fortieth year of continuous partnership in 2013, it has produced twenty-six films so far, the majority of which are remarkable case studies of perfect film and music integration.[31] Sergio Miceli says that "[Williams's] collaboration with Spielberg is a partnership among the most solid and fruitful ones in the history of film music and has undoubtedly produced works which are above the average."[32] Similarly, Mervyn Cooke writes: "The longstanding collaboration between Spielberg and Williams is universally regarded as em-blematic of the perfect marriage of audio-visual creative imagination, technical accomplishment, solid narrative and commercial savviness that distinguished the finest Hollywood blockbusters of the modern age."[33]

Despite the evidence, there is a film-music historical "negationism," which tries either to downplay or to ignore the duo's contributions, and it has a num-ber of adepts. In his 1994 book *Overtones and Undertones: Reading Film Music*, the film-music scholar Royal S. Brown did not even mention the duo but included Hitchcock/Herrmann, Leone/Morricone, and Eisenstein/Prokofiev. He de-fined the collaboration between Claude Chabrol and Pierre Jansen as "the most fruitful director/composer collaboration in the history of cinema."[34]

The Italian musicologist Roberto Calabretto's *damnatio memoriae* is even more disconcerting: "[In film history] the relationships between director and musician are very varied. Sometimes in fortunate but rare cases, although they may come from different backgrounds, the two move together successfully on the same artistic path. Therefore, we have felicitous collaborations like those between Federico Fellini and Nino Rota, Sergio Leone and Ennio Morricone, Alfred Hitchcock and Bernard Herrmann, Sergei Eisenstein and Sergei Proko-fiev, the Taviani brothers and Nicola Piovani."[35] Calabretto lists other "felicitous collaborations," a list in which everyone but Spielberg and Williams is men-tioned: "In film history there have been very happy collaborations, in which the composer and the director worked in perfect harmony and with common goals and which produced very beautiful scores. Among the many examples, we can report Erik Satie and René Clair; Zbigniew Preisner and Krzysztof Kieslowski . . . ; Joe Hisaishi and Takeshi Kitano . . . ; Marco Bellocchio and Carlo Crivelli; Alfred Hitchcock and Bernard Herrmann; Hiroshi Teshigahara and Toru Takemitsu . . . Ennio Morricone and Sergio Leone . . . One of the best duos in film history is that between Michael Nyman and Peter Greenaway."[36] Evidently, this omission cannot be due to ignorance but simply to ideological prejudice or idiosyncratic dislike.

As a neoclassical film composer Williams, on the one hand, inherited the aesthetic prejudices typically attached to the classical Hollywood composers; on the other hand, he is also the target of new ideological prejudices precisely due to his being neoclassical.

9

Raiders of the Lost Ark

Background

A Neoclassical Film

May 1977. Mauna Kea Hotel, Hawaii. Steven Spielberg and George Lucas are on vacation together. *Star Wars* is just coming out in theaters. Lucas, thinking it would be a commercial flop, decided to flee California, away from the expected box-office disaster—which, on the contrary, would soon turn into the biggest success of all time. The two filmmakers and close friends are on the beach, working on a gigantic sand castle, and George tells Steven an old idea of his: a story, or rather a series of adventures, whose protagonist is a fearless archaeologist who travels the world in search of treasures.[1] This was the quasi-legendary moment in which *Raiders of the Lost Ark* and the Indiana Jones saga were born, a saga that would develop over the next twenty-seven years into four feature films—*Raiders of the Lost Ark* (1981), *Indiana Jones and the Temple of Doom* (1984), *Indiana Jones and the Last Crusade* (1989), *Indiana Jones and the Kingdom of the Crystal Skull* (2008), and a TV series, *The Young Indiana Jones Chronicles* (1992–93). Lucas, story author and executive producer with his film company Lucasfilm Ltd., relied on his friend Steven Spielberg to direct all the films of the series. Spielberg accepted the task enthusiastically as he saw in it the chance to somewhat fulfill one of his long-standing desires: to direct a James Bond film.[2]

Actually, the two series are very different. The James Bond films are firmly set in the contemporary world and, since the first films and up to those realized in the twenty-first century, they have always been a showcase for the trends and habits of the society of the time. They flaunt the fads of the day in terms of cars, clothing, men's and women's hair styles, technology, musical tastes, and the state of the art in current film style. Armed with the futuristic gadgets of Dr. Q, Bond is committed to protecting Western civilization; Bond lives in the present day and is concerned in the future of his society. Indiana Jones, armed with his PhD in archaeology, is committed to retrieving ancient relics and is interested in past societies, not merely because he is an archaeologist—the past is his job—but because his adventures are set in the 1930s. Rather than being immersed in a contemporary and up-to-date context like Bond, Indiana lives in a "vintage" past.[3] Said Spielberg: "[That was a] period where adventures could happen, a romantic time when it took a little longer to get around the world by air than it does today, a period without advanced technology, where the cleverness of the individual against the enemy was what mattered. So it wouldn't use laser guns and light sabers and James Bond weaponry."[4]

As had happened before with *Star Wars*, the idea was to pay homage to the classical Hollywood genre films. Particularly, inspiration was drawn from B-movies like *The Masked Marvel* (Spencer Gordon Bennet, 1943) and serials like *Don Winslow of the Navy* (Ford Beebe, Ray Taylor, 1942) and *Blackhawk: Fearless Champion of Freedom* (Spencer Gordon Bennet, Fred F. Sears, 1952). Even more than in the *Star Wars* case, all those involved in the film seemed to have the nostalgic wish of recovering not only those past genres but also their old-fashioned style.[5] When the film came out, the catchphrase on the posters and billboards was: "The return of the great adventure." A reporter from the set noted: "For all of us, it became a great experience, something we could all remember from our childhood—a full-color adventure tale, the manifestation of the battle between good and evil, a handsome hero and beautiful heroine, an ugly and horrible villain and a handsome and not-so-horrible villain, the pursuit of a desired object that in good hands will be a beautiful and respected thing, but that in the wrong hands will destroy the world. . . . It became clear that the majority of people making *Raiders* . . . had a core of romanticism several inches in diameter."[6]

George Lucas described the idea behind the film: "The essence of *Raiders* is that it's a throwback to an older kind of film. It's a high-adventure film vaguely in the mode of the old Saturday afternoon serials. Actually the serials were C-movies and I would say that *Raiders* is an old-fashioned B-movie. . . . What inspired me to make *Raiders* was a desire to see this kind of movie. You sit back and say, 'Why don't they make this kind of movie anymore?' And I'm in a position to do it. So I'm really doing it more than anything else so that *I* can enjoy it—I just want to see this movie."[7]

Steven Spielberg directly declared his love for classical films: "I went back and looked at my favorite films from the 1930s and 1940s and thought how quickly and cheaply they were made. I think I'm basically a reincarnated director from the 1930s."[8] Compared to *Jaws* and *Close Encounters of the Third Kind*, Spielberg's style for *Raiders* was more direct and strictly functional, "a model of stylish economy."[9] Even the screenwriter Lawrence Kasdan expressed his fondness for old adventure films: "Adventure films were absolutely at the heart of my love of movies. . . . Everything in the movie resonates from other movies. That's the feeling we were after. It doesn't take itself too seriously."[10] In the same spirit, Harrison Ford gave life to the main character: "[The film is] really about movies more than it's about anything else. It's intrinsically designed as a real tribute to the craft."[11]

Drawing from the Oldies

Throughout *Raiders* it is no surprise to find not only a number of influences but also outright quotations from B-movies and serials.[12] For example, the hero pursued by an indigenous tribe comes from *Too Hot to Handle* (Jack Conway, 1938); the fight against the Nazis comes from *Spy Smasher* (William Witney, 1942); the hero using a whip comes from *Man with the Steel Whip* (Adreon Franklin, 1954); the Arab disguise used by Indiana when he infiltrates the archaeological site comes from *Lawrence of Arabia* (David Lean, 1962); the animated map showing the route of the journeys is from *Casablanca* (Michael Curtiz, 1942), which also inspired the sequences set in Cairo and Indiana getting drunk à la Bogart after losing Marion; and the finale with the crate containing the Ark stocked in a huge warehouse reminds us of *Citizen Kane* (Orson Welles, 1941). As for the main character's look and nature, Spielberg said: "He's a remarkable combination of Errol Flynn from *The Adventures of Don Juan* [Vincent Sherman, 1948] and Humphrey Bogart as Fred C. Dobbs in *The Treasure of the Sierra Madre* [John Huston, 1948] . . . villainous and romantic all at once."[13] Two other films also seem to have had more than a little influence on the character and look of Indiana Jones: *King Solomon's Mines* (Compton Bennett, Andrew Marton, 1950) and *Secret of the Incas* (Jerry Hopper, 1954). As in *Raiders*, the male leads—Allan Quartermain and Harry Steele, respectively—are rugged adventurers who initially are quite rough with and definitely impolite to the woman with whom they are forced to travel but end up falling in love with her. In *King Solomon's Mines*, when the female lead's elegant dress proves to be totally inadequate for a trip into the jungle, Quartermain ungracefully tears it off, as Indiana will do with Willie's in *Indiana Jones and the Temple of Doom*. In *King Solomon's Mines* there is also a capuchin monkey called Lulu, which is very similar to the monkey that Jones meets in Cairo. Also the huge rolling boulder that traps Quartermain and his fellows in a mine cave resembles the one we see in *Raiders*—though another rolling-boulder line of ancestry can be traced back to *Journey to the Center of the Earth* (Henry Levin, 1959), in which Professor Lindenbrook and his team narrowly escape from being crushed by a gigantic rock. In *Secret of the Incas* the river escape on a yellow dinghy is similar to that of *Indiana Jones and the Temple of Doom*. Moreover, the precise spot where the Inca treasure is hidden is indicated by a ray of sunlight reflected from a mirror placed in a precise position at a precise moment of the day, a trick that will be reprised for the Ra medallion and the map room in *Raiders*. Above all, in *Secret of the Incas* the protagonist's look is very similar to Jones's: dark brown leather bomber jacket, wide-brimmed fedora hat, a revolver in his belt, and his name *Harry* (Steele) sounds very akin to *Henry* (Jones.)

Raiders of the Lost Ark can be defined as a neoclassical film because of its many explicit and ironic quotations of past works and its retrieval and update of previous stylistic options. For example, the film mocks the time-honored cliché of the hero knocking out an enemy to steal his uniform so as to inconspicuously mingle with the crowd. In this case, Indiana punches a Nazi soldier but when putting the stolen uniform on, he realizes that it is so small that he cannot even button it up.

Unlike the low-budget films by which it was inspired, *Raiders* is intentionally naive and flimsy-looking. It is well-grounded in a deep appreciation and knowledge of classical cinema to the extent that sometimes it even borders on a philological approach. In line with this, the protagonist here is not just the explorer/adventurer type like Quartermain, Steele, and Dobbs but is also a scholar, a professor of archaeology passionately splitting his life between the study of the past and the recovery of its relics. The same happens for Lucas and Spielberg. As cinephiles they know and admire the classical Hollywood films; as "archaeologists/directors" they attempt to recover that style. Lucas and Spielberg are correctly regarded as two of the main promoters of the recovery of classical narration based on linearity and causality in the New Hollywood cinema.[14]

The Film's Synopsis and Form and the Scope of the Analysis

Professor Henry "Indiana" Jones has just come back to the college where he teaches archaeology, after a daring adventure in South

America, during which he had recovered a golden idol, immediately stolen from him by his rival Belloq. Some representatives of the U.S. government come to inform Jones that Hitler is on the trail of important archaeological artifacts near Cairo and they ask for Jones's help. Interpreting the information, Jones realizes that Hitler is looking for the Ark of the Covenant, whose immense power would be a massive threat in the hands of the dictator. The archaeologist then accepts the task and leaves. The first step is to retrieve the headpiece of the Staff of Ra, a medallion capable of indicating on a three-dimensional map the place where the Ark is buried. However, the medallion belongs to Abner Ravenwood, Jones's old mentor, who is now in Nepal. There, Jones meets Abner's daughter, Marion, who runs a tavern in the Himalayas and has inherited the medallion upon her father's death. Since Jones and Marion had previously been involved in a love affair gone awry, she is only willing to swap the headpiece for a large sum of money. Meanwhile, the Nazis reach the bar, led by the unctuous and vicious Toht. Jones saves Marion and succeeds in retrieving the medallion. The tavern is destroyed by a fire, and Marion has to reluctantly follow Jones, hoping to gain a reward for her loss. The next stop is Cairo, where the Nazis have already found the room with the three-dimensional map of the ancient city of Tanis—Belloq is the head of the excavation site. Since they do not have the medallion, they cannot locate the spot where the Ark is buried. In Cairo, Jones is welcomed by his friend Sallah, one of the excavators hired to search for the Ark. In order to get the medallion, the Nazis kidnap Marion and attempt to kill Jones. With the help of Sallah, Jones manages to sneak into the excavation site. He enters the map room and, thanks to the medallion, identifies the exact point where the Ark is buried—the Nazis have a partial copy of the headpiece and are digging in the wrong spot. That night, Jones and Sallah find the "Well of Souls," a large tomb that houses the Ark and is crammed with poisonous snakes. However, the Nazis discover the clandestine operation and steal the Ark, encapsulating Jones and Marion in the tomb to a certain death. The two manage to escape; Jones, after chasing the truck carrying the Ark, succeeds in stealing it from the Nazis. Jones and Marion board Capt. Katanga's ship with the Ark, but the Nazis find them, take the Ark, and kidnap Marion, giving her to Belloq, who has fallen in love with her. Jones has managed to avoid being captured and sneaks into the Nazi submarine. The U-boat emerges on an island in the Aegean Sea, and the Ark is carried through a gorge to be opened during an ancient Hebrew ritual. Threatening to destroy the Ark with a bazooka, Jones blocks the convoy and calls for the release of Marion. Belloq knows that Jones is bluffing and does not comply with him. Indeed, Jones is reluctant to blow up the Ark and eventually surrenders. Together with Marion, Jones is taken to the site of the opening rite. The rite begins and when the lid is removed, the Ark is revealed to contain nothing but sand. Belloq's disappointment soon turns into surprise when light and smoke start pouring out of the Ark. Jones warns Marion to keep her eyes shut: fire leaps out from the Ark and strikes down the Nazi soldiers, while some Death Angels kill Toht, Belloq and the Wehrmacht colonel. Jones and Marion, who kept their eyes closed, are the only survivors. The Ark is handed over to officials in Washington, who exclude Jones from any research on it and even refuse to reveal the place where it is kept. Jones leaves the building in bitter disappointment, complaining about the bureaucrats' obtuseness. He finds Marion waiting for him outside the building, and she tries to cheer him up. Meanwhile, the Ark is locked in an anonymous wooden crate and stored in a vast warehouse full of hundreds of identical crates, probably to be lost again.

The most interesting formal characteristic of *Raiders* is the way in which the classical narration merges with episodic and freer modalities typical of serials and B-movies:

> It is also clear that *Raiders* itself tells a story, a story which is structured according to the principles of the serial format that operated in B-movie adventure films in the 1930s and 1940s. . . . It can thus be divided into six distinct episodes, each of which is relatively self-contained, and each of which ends in a series of rapid dramatic actions and/or in an unresolved cliff-hanging sequence . . . As is the case in most serial narratives, causal motivations appear at times to be suspended; it is unclear, for instance, precisely how Jones escapes from the Nazi Submarine. . . . However, a single plot-line linked to the search for the ark of the covenant, and an antagonistic relationship between the hero, Jones, and the villain, Belloq, link each of these sequences together.[15]

Under the episodic and spectacular appearance of the film's surface, in its deeper structure we recognize the solid pillars of classical narration. Each character unambiguously shows his psychological traits; his actions are and remain consistent with his psychology and are motivated by clear reasons. Each action is oriented to the achievement of a known scope/object, and this pursuit linearly guides the chain of actions to the end of the story. Actions, typically, are ordered along a well-constructed progression and linked by cause-and-effect relations. For example, in order to find the Ark, Jones needs the medallion of Ra, and in order to find it he has to ask Marion's help. Marion hates Jones and will give him the medallion only in return for a significant amount of money. When the Nazis attack, Jones manages to save her but not her tavern, which ends up being destroyed. Therefore, Marion, though detesting Jones, cannot do anything else but follow him in the quest, demanding a part of the reward as compensation for the loss of her tavern.

Marion's character is introduced according to the classical standards. Her character traits are straightforwardly defined from the very first moments of her first appearance, and they remain unchanged throughout the story. Marion is introduced in her tavern in the Himalayas while she is challenging a burly Nepalese to a drinking contest. From the beginning, the narration shows Marion as a tough, tenacious Katharine Hepburn–like woman. The narrative device of the drinking contest is not only functional to introduce the character but also has a compositional motivation, which will be revealed later when Belloq tries to get Marion drunk in the hope that she will inadvertently give away some information about the medallion. Unlike the viewers, Belloq does not know that Marion is used to drinking hard liquor, and his scheme will be thwarted, ending up with him getting drunk. We are not just informed that Marion is a tough woman but we are also given a piece of information that we use later in the story: this is the classical device of planting a "set-up," which later blossoms into a "pay-off."[16]

The same dual function is found in the episode in which Toht the Nazi—moments after having threatened Marion with a red-hot poker—brands the palm of his hand in grabbing the red-hot medallion. Apparently, the motivation for this action could be seen as a "karmic" balance punishing the evil Nazi, which also serves as comic relief, with Toht screaming hysterically and frantically running out of the tavern to shove his hand into the snow. Later, we discover that this comic gag was also a set-up motivated compositionally. Why do the Nazis have the medallion of Ra if it is in Jones's possession? They had a copy made from the firebrand on Toht's hand, as the narration reveals when Toht displays it during an open-palm Nazi salute: here is the pay-off.

There are also some dialogue hooks typical of classical narration where a line of dialogue anticipates what will happen in the next scene, serving as a bridge to smooth the transition.[17] For example, after the escape from the Well of Souls, Sallah informs Jones that the Ark has just been loaded onto a truck. Jones looks at his Egyptian friend and asks: "What truck?" Immediately after, we see the truck leaving the excavation site and Jones chasing it on horseback.

We have seen that *Raiders* is a neoclassical film resorting to some staples of the classical narration form. In the following pages, the film is analyzed as to the way John Williams's neoclassical score supports such narration and as to the way it fulfills, through an extensive use of leitmotiv and Mickey-Mousing, the typical function of the classical music style: the spatial perceptive function.

Since the analysis centers on the formal functions of film music, interpretive readings seeking to unearth the "symptomatic meanings" of the film—frequently indicated as an early case of right-wing "Reaganite entertainment"—is not the main concern here.[18] Undeniably, *Raiders* flaunts many racial and quasi-racist stereotypes: South Americans as cowards, lazy, and petty; Arabs as untrustworthy, threatening, and deceitful; along with some overt celebrations of American superiority, as in the famous scene in which Jones looks down on an imposing Arab showing off his scimitar and simply shoots him down with his stars-and-stripes revolver. However, discussing the ideology behind these stereotypes is also not the focus of this analysis.[19] Here, these stereotypes are seen as classical conventions imported in the film's neoclassical "package" along with the fake exoticism of the scenery. Such rough-cut stereotypical characters were copiously present in the genre cinema and B-movies that inspired *Raiders*, for example, the Mexicans in *Treasure of the Sierra Madre* or the Indians in *The Naked Jungle* (Byron Haskin, 1954). They are not so much full-bodied characters as immediately recognizable one-dimensional figures representing a specific ethnic or social group—something similar to the Soviet cinema *typage*.

The Score:
Its Main Themes and Motifs

In 1981, after having composed the music for the film, Williams described his work: "It is a wonderful adventure film in the style of the '30s—like a Bogart-Bacall film set in the Middle East. It has an 80-minute score which I wrote in December and January and which I recorded with the London Symphony Orchestra in February. It's all in the manner of Max Steiner . . . things like the hero's theme and the big love theme."[20]

Like the two biggest neoclassical examples that preceded *Raiders*— *Star Wars* and *Superman: The Movie*—the music plays a major role. And the distinguishing features of the classical style are similarly recovered: leitmotiv, Mickey-Mousing, thematic development, use of the large symphony orchestra, and late-romantic dialect. However, compared to the other two films, the score for *Raiders* stands out for its more frequent and emphasized use of Mickey-Mousing and for its meticulous reenactment of classical music clichés. Williams recalled, "The Indiana Jones movies were great fun. There was nothing I had to take too seriously musically. They were theatrical and over-the-top.[21] . . . I mean, we have the Nazis, you know, and the orchestra hits these 1940s dramatic chords, you know, seventh degree of the scale on the bottom, which is a kind of an old signal of some evil, militaristic doer. We just unabashedly did that just for the fun of it. I mean, for the camp fun of it. It's admissible, it seems, in the style of a picture like this."[22]

The intra-opus style is more straightforward and simpler in terms of harmony than those of *Star Wars* and *Superman*. The references for those scores were Wagner's operatic thematicism, Richard Strauss's rich orchestral palette, and Korngold's balance between cinematic functionality and musical form. For *Raiders* the model was Max Steiner and his highly functional idiom aiming to illustrate each image and catch each action musically. It was not a "space opera," but a homage to the low-cost adventure B-movies. Williams conse-quently made his writing more direct and essential in order to mirror in music that straightforward and stripped-down film style. Not that the *Raiders* score is stripped-down in the sense that it sounds like a Giovanni Fusco score for an Antonioni film, of course. On the contrary, the music is emphatic and heroic and—like *Star Wars* and *Superman*—Williams recorded it with the London Symphony Orchestra, again showcasing the brilliant sound of its principal trumpet Maurice Murphy.[23] The point is that from a harmonic point of view, the writing is simpler, and from a melodic point of view the themes have a more hummable quality—compare "Princess Leia's Theme" from *Star Wars* to "Marion's Theme" from *Raiders*.

The first Indiana Jones theme is the famous one featured in the concert version called *Raiders March*.[24] From here on, it will be called "Indy 1" because this is the principal leitmotiv associated with the Indiana Jones character. From a harmonic point of view, it is built on the simple alternation of I and V degrees—tonic and dominant. It features such Williams idiomatic traits as the added fourth and the omitted leading tone coloring the harmonic pattern, which has a twist in the eighth bar with a chord built on the flattened second degree—a sort of Neapolitan chord in major mode. If compared to the I–IV–I harmonic progression that characterizes *Star Wars* and *Superman*, this I–V–I progression sounds less modal and more diatonic—that is, more popular. As for the melodic component, it is clear that a good leitmotiv is one capable of revealing musically many traits of a character. Sticking to our previous comparison between the two heroes, it is interesting to compare the Indiana Jones theme with the James Bond theme.[25] The following is Sergio Miceli's insightful analysis:

> The "James Bond Theme" stands out in the collective imagination as an icon of "Bondism," that is, supermanhood. . . . [It has] a dynamic component, intrinsically capable of expressing an unstoppable energy and determination (the analogy with Bond requires no comment). . . . The rhythmic pattern sounds like a martial formula: a simple trumpet signal similar to a "call to arms" or "charge!" At the same time, the electric guitar gives a modern urban mood to it and an insolent tone to the overall pattern. Indeed, there is the coexistence of a conformist, strict side with an unconventional, unpredictable one (as the protagonist is.) [There is also] a sense of self-satisfaction deriving from his own omnipotence, which can be heard both in the contrapuntal writing . . . —which is like an irrepressible extroversion of different components—and in the harmonic structure . . . whose chords sound like a celebratory chorus (Bond's prerogatives seem to be out of control but they are nevertheless the expression and the product of a complex and multiform government apparatus).[26]

Another comparison can be made with Luke's theme ("Main Title") from *Star Wars*. The theme opens with the perfect-fifth upward leap played by the trumpets—the perfect-fifth upward leap being another of Williams's idiomatic traits typically employed to depict heroism, as in *Superman*. The following downward triplet of contiguous notes is like a run before the minor-seventh jump to the high B-flat. The high B-flat is sustained for two beats across two measures— as to depict a sustained heroic effort—and the minor-seventh introducing it is a larger interval than the fifth.[27] Thus such a combination—minor-seventh jump and sustained high B-flat—signifies a victorious achievement. From B-flat, the melodic line goes down to F—a perfect-fourth downward leap—which is the inversion of the upward perfect fifth. The triplet and the minor-seventh leap are restated, and the theme closes with a triplet that brings the music to rest on the second degree (C). Luke's theme speaks of heroism and victorious high achievements, which are confirmed twice by the repetition of the minor-seventh jump. Not a single note descends below the starting point (B-flat above the middle C) from which the heroic melodic journey has begun.

Transcription of John Williams, "Main Title" (mm. 3–10), from *Star Wars: Suite for Orchestra* (© 1977 BMI), published by Bantha Music and Warner-Tamerlane Publishing Corp., administered by Warner-Tamerlane Publishing Corp., printed by Hal Leonard, "John Williams Signature Edition," 044900057 [Used in compliance with the U.S. Copyright Act, Section 107].

In the Indiana Jones theme, the heroic traits are also present, but their nature is more uncertain and ironic, and the overall tone is less idealized and a little more braggart. Here, the theme does not open with a perfect-fifth upward leap—Williams's trademark for "pure heroism." It opens with a cheeky dotted rhythm followed by a perfect-fourth leap to the tonic. The perfect-fourth leap, unlike the perfect-fifth leap (from the tonic to the dominant), sounds like a closure (the return to the tonic) rather than a start (separation from the tonic.) The music seems to be saying: "Here it is, I have heroically completed my mission." However, as the film repeatedly demonstrates, Jones is not at all infallible and indestructible. In a scene where Marion starts kissing and cuddling Jones on the bed—after a day of jeopardy faced together—rather than seeing a passionate love scene, we see Jones falling asleep, aching and exhausted. The narration is sharply ironic in showing us not a hero that is always elegant and well-groomed as Bond, but a man covered in mud, scratches, and bruises who typically manages to get himself out of trouble quite clumsily. At the beginning of *Raiders*, when Jones puts a bag of sand on the security mechanism on which the idol is placed in order to block the trigger, he smiles proudly for having shrewdly avoided the ancient alarm system. "I made it," his smile seems to say. His self-satisfaction soon turns into fear when he realizes that he has miscalculated, and the bag is not heavy enough to stop the device. He cannot but fall back on a hasty and rather unheroic flight. Similarly, in the leitmotiv, after the first perfect-fourth leap ("I made it!") the melodic line contradicts it by going down a minor seventh, even below the starting note. Then the opening dotted rhythm is repeated but stops after a minor second (the minor second being the smallest move in the scale). As with the film narration, the music also takes Jones's heroism ironically down a peg or two. Nonetheless, Jones is stubborn and not inclined to giving up altogether: we expect him to win in the end. Indeed, the melody goes on, repeating the dotted rhythm starting from a higher note (G) and jumping up to the high F. It is a better result, but still not enough: this jump to the high F is a *diminished*-fifth leap, that is "incomplete heroism," if we take the *perfect*-fifth leap as the musical equivalent of heroism. The next musical gesture restates the dotted rhythm, starting from A—a position higher than the previous G starting point—followed by three contiguous notes on the scale, played well-marked, as to suggest Jones's determination to achieve his goal. The melody reprises from the initial position (E), repeating the dotted rhythm and the fourth leap. This time, however, the line continues its rise through contiguous notes, replicating an octave higher the same notes previously heard as an ironic gesture of defeat, now transformed into a successful progression, which stops on the high F that had been previously reached "imperfectly" through the diminished-fifth leap. At the moment in which the high F is finally achieved, the harmony presents a bright chord on the flattened-second degree: this has the function of stressing in an emphatic way the conquest of that position. Then, there are two bars in which the trumpets do not play in unison as they have done so far but in vigorous chords and performing four leaps covering a major sixth, sounding even more heroic than the heroic perfect fifth. It is a tongue-in-cheek depiction of the heroic gesture, a swaggering celebration of victory after many defeats. "You know the kind of thing . . . a heroic theme that swells when things are going well for our hero, the kind of music that makes the audience want to cheer," said Williams.[28]

Transcription of John Williams, "Indiana Jones's A Theme" (mm. 3–12), from *Raiders March* (© 1981 BMI), published by Bantha Music and Ensign Music Corp., administered by Ensign Music Corp., printed by Hal Leonard, "John Williams Signature Edition," 044900015 [Used in compliance with the U.S. Copyright Act, Section 107].

That this leitmotiv is in the march form, as in *Superman* and *Star Wars*, is a further neoclassical element because, as Williams comments, it evokes memories of and feelings for the past:

> [T]his isn't a period of time many people associate with march music. That seems to belong to Sousa's period, but I must enjoy writing marches. One friend I have worked with for years has said, "John's happy to write a march at the drop of the foot." Of course each of my marches was written to meet some musical film requirements. . . . A good march does get the blood up, and it might take a clever musicologist or sociologist or combination of the two to explain why this is true. . . . One of the most significant aspects of a march is the nostalgia involved. In a way it might be similar to baseball in that everyone who goes to a game surrenders a part of contemporary life. . . . The ballpark takes us back to the eras of our parents, grandparents, and great-grandparents, who had a very different sense of time. I believe the days seemed to be longer because the pace was slower. If people had three hours to kill, they went to a ballpark, ate hot dogs, and waited for somebody to hit the ball, knowing it might never happen. Today people go to the ballpark and surrender to a kind of regression that leads back to an earlier time in this country. I think that the Sousa march and the swingy march—the kind of marches the Bill Finegan and Glenn Miller bands played—go to some place in the American soul and are part of what defines us as a nation.[29]

A further note on the Indiana Jones theme: Following the aesthetics of the serials, when the main theme is introduced for the first time (at the end of the opening South American Jungle sequence) it is immediately presented in its outright nature of heroic theme, without following the classical tradition requiring a gradual introduction of the protagonist and his evolution over the course of the narrative. A comparison with *Star Wars* and *Superman* can make the point clearer. In both cases the main theme is presented in the opening credits as an anticipation of the musical goal to be reached; we hear it again much later but only when the protagonist has attained a certain degree of evolution on the "heroism scale." In *Star Wars*, after the opening title sequence, we hear the main theme again when we see Luke on Tatooine for the first time. The narration tells us here that the "Main Title" theme is Luke's leitmotiv, but it is played as a horn solo, and then reprised by the woodwinds in a light orchestration— still an "immature" version. Only when Luke rescues Princess Leia from the prison and, pursued by the imperial guards, crosses a chasm with her in his arms, we now hear his leitmotiv played heroically by the trumpets: Luke has taken the first step toward his heroic maturity. Similarly, we hear the *Superman* theme again, played by the trumpets, when Clark Kent emerges from the spiritual retreat of the "Fortress of Solitude," no longer a youngster and ready to be a superhero. As for Indiana Jones, the narration does not show the evolution he has made to become what he is now but introduces him directly as he already is: a shrewd hero (see chap. 10). Moreover, Luke's and Superman's leitmotivs are presented in the opening credits and only later associated with a particular character. Therefore, they are also perceived as the signature musical theme of the film in a more pronounced way and as musical equivalents of the idea of the Hero in general, besides the particular heroes featured in those films.[30] On the contrary, in *Raiders* the main theme is not presented in the opening title sequence, but it always appears when Indiana Jones shows up. Undoubtedly, it has ended up with being associated with the film in the minds of the viewers, but it is primarily Indiana Jones's "personal" leitmotiv. Again, *Raiders* is not about *the* Hero's journey but about *a* hero's journeys; the music has to represent not Heroism but one type of heroism. This may also explain why the Williams-trademark heroic perfect-fifth upward leap, which is the basis of Luke's and Superman's leitmotivs, is not used for Indiana Jones.

Indiana Jones also has another theme (featured in the *Raiders March* as the "B Theme"), which is linked not so much to the main character as to his reckless stunts. The Indiana Jones leitmotiv previously discussed appears in the films orchestrated in more subtle ways as well—for instance, for woodwinds with an emotive function. The best example is perhaps the warm cello rendition that can be heard at the end of *Indiana Jones and the Last Crusade* when Jones's father holds out his hand to pull his son out of the rift into which he is about to fall. On the contrary, the second theme, usually played by brass, is employed in action scenes—"Indy 2." It is akin to "Indy 1" as it opens with the same dotted rhythm and has the same alternation of upward heroic leaps and downward retreats.

Transcription of John Williams, "Indiana Jones's B Theme" (mm. 28–32), from *Raiders March* (© 1981 BMI), published by Bantha Music and Ensign Music Corp., administered by Ensign Music Corp., printed by Hal Leonard, "John Williams Signature Edition," 044900015 [Used in compliance with the U.S. Copyright Act, Section 107].

"Marion's Theme" acts as the film's love theme and recalls those of the classical Hollywood. It is played by violins or flutes ("female" instruments) and sounds outright "romantic" thanks to the opening major-sixth emotional leap to the whole note, the languishing rhythmic dilatation given by a triplet of quarter notes—three notes played on two beats—and the stretching of the melodic line creating an effect of longing, which is typical of the romantic dialect.[31] Williams commented, "I used to love those old romantic themes in Warner Bros. films like *Now, Voyager*. For the love story between Indiana Jones and Marion I thought that the music could be like one of those '30s themes and that would contrast well with the humor and silliness, even if it is inappropriate emotionally."[32] The harmony is chromatic and more complex if compared to the leitmotiv of Indiana Jones, and serves to add to the tough Marion character a gloss of feminine charm, which she may lack: here the Hollywood musical clichés of feminine strings and sentimental music are projected onto the character in order to make her appear more feminine. It also creates a musical contrast with Jones's "masculine" theme and gives body to that sense of nostalgia for their lost love that is barely mentioned by the film narration.

Upward major-sixth leap   Languishing triplet

Transcription of John Williams, "Marion's Theme" (mm. 64–71), from *The Adventures of Indiana Jones* (© 1981 BMI), published by Bantha Music, administered by Warner-Tamerlane Publishing Corp., printed by Hal Leonard, "John Williams Signature Edition," 04490826 [Used in compliance with the U.S. Copyright Act, Section 107].

Finally, the last major leitmotiv is the one associated with the Ark.[33] It is a brief motif whose dynamic range and color goes from the muted trumpets in low register backed by *tremolo* violins when the Ark is mentioned for the first time to the brass *fortissimo* with chorus when the Ark is opened. The mysterious and ominous tone of the Ark leitmotiv is given by both the minor-mode harmonic instability between distant keys (B-flat minor and E minor, in the transcription reproduced below) and the nature of the melodic intervals. The motif moves downward within a perfect fifth from F to B-flat, within which can be found the "dreaded" augmented-fourth interval—the tritone. Once considered a "forbidden" dissonant interval called *diabolus in musica* (the devil in music), typically it has been associated with disturbing, ominous events.[34] The Ark is a magnificent and powerful object, but it is also a treacherous and deadly one, and the leitmotiv is built in such a way as to prefigure this doubly, dangerous nature.

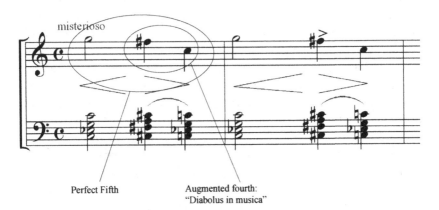

Transcription of John Williams, "The Ark's Motif [tentative title]," from the *Raiders of the Lost Ark* film score (© 1981 BMI), published by Bantha Music (ear transcription from the film's soundtrack) [Used in compliance with the U.S. Copyright Act, Section 107].

In the next chapter we will take a thorough look at how Williams's score operates within the film.

10

Raiders of the Lost Ark
Analysis

The Return of Max Steiner

Opening:
A South American Jungle

Like all the chapters of the series, the film opens with the Paramount logo, a mountain, which dissolves onto a visually similar form.[1] In this case, the Paramount mountain becomes a real mountain, the profile of which is then blocked off by the entrance of a character donning a fedora hat and coming into the frame facing away from the camera. We find out later that the man with the hat is the protagonist. At the moment, we can only recognize in him the typical "explorer type." Viewers in 1981 were familiar neither with Indiana Jones nor with Harrison Ford, who at that time was not as well known as he is today. The man is leading an expedition in the jungle; with a superimposed title, the narration informs us that we are in "South America, 1936." We know the time, the place, and we are already in the midst of an adventure.

This opening is striking for one element that differentiates it from classical films and from the other two neoclassical models, *Star Wars* and *Superman*. In the classical period, the opening title sequence was a fixed presence and had some recurring features.[2] The names of the cast and crew were shown on a background and with graphics that anticipated some narrative themes or visual motifs of the film—like the falcon's image in *The Maltese Falcon* (John Huston, 1941). Moreover, there used to be a little musical overture presenting the main musical themes of the score: sticking to our *Maltese Falcon* example, the opening titles are accompanied by Adolph Deutsch's mysterious and menacing music. Neoclassical films like *Star Wars* and *Superman* begin with a memorable extradiegetic title sequence that serves as a frame to the film narrative. *Superman* even has a metalinguistic prologue that bares its comic-book origin. *Star Wars* does not have classical opening titles—cast, crew, and so on—but has an opening sequence anyway, telling the backstory through crawling titles of a striking visual impact. Even *Jaws*, which is the least overtly neoclassical of these three films, has a memorable opening title sequence. In all these cases, the music brings the viewer into the film, starting its overall macro-emotive function of unifying the narrative. Oddly enough, a neoclassical film like *Raiders* has no extradiegetic opening title sequence and no musical overture. George Lucas explained: "The idea was that instead of starting off the film slow, we would start off fast. The whole thing in serials is that they always recapped what happened before. I didn't wanna make it that much of a serial. So I said, 'The fun part is if we take the last episode or last film, and start at the climax.' You take that—the best part of a movie you haven't seen—then stop, then you start a new movie 15 to 20 minutes in. It was kind of an outrageous idea at the time."[3]

Following the aesthetics of serials, *Raiders* was not designed as a single, stand-alone film but as a portion of a larger series of adventures, not only open to more episodes to come featuring Indiana Jones,[4] but also in continuity with the past films with Harry Steele, Alan Quartermain, Tarzan, and others. So, we are deliberately thrown into the middle of the action. As soon as the Paramount logo dissolves onto the real mountain, the music starts to accompany the expedition. First of all, it denotes the exotic location, using clichéd percussion instruments typically associated with the idea of wilderness and uncivilized locales. The suspense builds through a very slow barely tonal melody for flute in low register and sustained high-pitched dissonant notes of the strings, creating a sense of anxiety due to the music stasis.[5]

Next, a native who is taking part in the expedition finds an effigy of a threatening deity behind the vegetation and flees in terror, causing the desertion of the other natives as well. The music emphasizes the frightening discovery with a startling dissonant trumpets stinger in perfect synchronization. It is already clear that we should expect from the score a prominent use of the old-fashioned Mickey-Mousing technique. Indeed, shortly after that, another explicit synch-point—a muted trumpets *sforzando* and a tam-tam rub—directs our attention to a poisoned dart stuck in a nearby tree. When Satipo, one of the guides, says concernedly that the Hovitos (a dangerous local tribe, we infer) are probably on their trail, the dialogue underscoring presents menacing, low-pitched trombones minor chords. The association between low-pitched trombones minor chords and "villains" will be a recurring idea throughout the film. This association of the minor mode with dramatic events and the low register with darkness and menace are old musical conventions.[6] It is also a well-established cliché in film music, already used in the silent era.[7] For brevity, henceforth these chords will be called "villains' chords."

The expedition party arrives at a river, and the other guide treacherously tries to shoot the man with the hat: a low-pitched turn of the contrabasses is brought out to anticipate the man's criminal intent. The man with the hat hears the gun hammer clicking and with a rapid whip crack—highlighted by a trumpets burst of repeating notes—he disarms him and makes him flee. Then, the man with the hat emerges from the shadows with a menacing look in his eyes; here we see his face for the first time. When he comes out of the shadows, a marked downward scale of trombones minor chords is heard, which increases the menacing nature of his look. Interestingly, the villains' chords are used here for the man with the hat. We do not know anything yet about his intentions and nature, and the music plays on this ambiguity, choosing to use those chords instead of the character's leitmotiv.

The two remaining members of the expedition—Satipo and the man with the hat—arrive at the treasure cave. The music texture gets thinner to make room for the dialogue between the two men. They enter the cave, the music becoming almost a background noise–like atmospheric patina: low-pitched piano notes, soft tam-tam roll, and high-pitched cluster effects of the violins creating a reverberating "cavernous" sound.[8] The musical texture presents sparse *pianissimo* movements by the strings: low-pitched *tremolo* chromatic scales, contrabasses and violins *pizzicato*. They do not correspond to any visible movement *yet* but seem to suggest the presence of an unknown something, moving off-screen. As anticipated by the music, a horrified Satipo points at something on the shoulders of the man with the hat. A *fortissimo* bow slap by the contrabasses is heard in synchronism with the cut to the man with the hat, revealing that he is covered in tarantulas. This musical gesture is followed by a creeping, almost aleatory high-pitched violins *pizzicato*, which mimics the movement of the legs of the spiders and emotionally heightens the viewer's shudder of revulsion at the sight of the spiders on the protagonist's neck. Soon, Satipo realizes that many more tarantulas are on his shoulders too. The emotive function of music here is to depict Satipo's repulsion, which is accomplished through an upward violins *glissando* of high-pitched dissonant chords, a musical equivalent of a "shiver running down the spine."

Once they get rid of the spiders, the two move on to the treasure room. The music—with a prevalent spatial perceptive function—plays throughout the whole sequence, catching each action.[9] The music also has an emotive function: a strings *tremolo* creates tension over the fate of Satipo being on the verge of the bottomless pit and a slow atonal strings arpeggio projects its tonal uncertainty onto the images, making the success of the expedition feel uncertain.[10]

In order to take the golden idol away from its pedestal, the man with the hat has to remove it without triggering the weight-activated security mechanism, and to do so he has devised a plan to swiftly substitute it with an equally heavy bag of sand. The atonal arpeggios are superseded by equally uncertain harmonic progressions, a dynamic *crescendo* and a thickening of instrumentation. Music is now gaining momentum and building the cinematic suspense. When the man quickly replaces the idol with the bag, the musical progression stops with a rapid upward scale duplicating the movement of his hand. Everything seems to have gone fine. However, a sustained high-pitched strings note can still be heard—not a good omen. Indeed, in spite of the sand bag the pedestal of the idol lowers—wrong weight!—and the cave begins to collapse. The man with the hat is forced to make a hasty retreat, accompanied by hectic music characterized by rapid high-pitched repeating notes of the trumpets when a rolling boulder chases the man with the hat. Here, the main function is temporal perceptive: the music emphasizes the pace of the frenzied escape and supports the speedy rhythm of the editing. The man with the hat manages to escape and jumps out of the cave at the very last minute, the disloyal and greedy Satipo having found a deserved death. The music accompanies the hasty, final rush of the retreat with a *crescendo* chord played *fortissimo* by the whole orchestra. The chord stops abruptly and makes way for a contrasting silence when we unexpectedly see the menacing Hovitos waiting outside and surrounding the man with the hat.[11]

The Hovitos are led by Belloq, a treasure hunter and archenemy of the man with the hat, whose name is finally revealed: "Dr. Jones," as Belloq calls him. Belloq takes the idol away from Jones and incites the Hovitos to kill him. The music, which has been silent for only fifty-nine seconds, resumes to provide accompaniment to Jones's escape. The musical piece opens with a sinister horn motif played as Belloq laughs wickedly. So far, the music has maintained a sort of ambiguity about the nature of the man with the hat. The narration has now revealed his name and in the previous scenes has shown that he is not only a grave robber but also a man of principles: after all, he saved Satipo from falling into the bottomless pit. Moreover, now we know that Belloq is the real villain.

According to the black/white Manichaeism of the popular Hollywood cinema, if Belloq is the villain, then Jones must be the hero. The music confirms this inference, emphasizing Belloq's laugh with a dark horn motif. Jones is revealed as the hero of the narrative, but what kind of hero is he?

The music does not accompany his escape from the Hovitos with a powerful rhythmic section or vigorous action music, but with a bumbling strings *pizzicato*, awkward *staccato* accents by muted trombones, and funny gestures of the piccolo clarinet. The music casts a comic emotional overtone onto the chase, giving an ironic image of Jones, a resourceful and brave adventurer but quite far from being the traditional infallible hero. When Jones swings on a vine to reach the seaplane that is waiting for him but instead plunges into the river, we hear the main Jones leitmotiv ("Indy 1") for the first time, played by the trumpets, with only its first four bars repeated twice; the full theme will be stated only much later. An upward high-pitched trumpets gesture celebrates the success of the daredevil retreat.

Jones's plane finally flies away from the hostile Hovitos. The narration taunts him again, downplaying his heroic status: Jones is rumpled, soaked through, and his fedora now resembles a bowl-shaped wet rag. Then he realizes with horror that a python is crawling on his legs and shouts to the pilot, almost whimpering, that he hates snakes. (Jones's reptile phobia is introduced as a gag, but once again it is also a set up that will have its pay off later in the sequence of the Well of Souls.) The pilot reassures him by telling him that it is Reggie, his pet python, and invites Jones to be a man: "Come on, show a little backbone! Will ya?" The music accompanies the scene presenting for the first time the secondary Indiana Jones leitmotiv ("Indy 2") during the python gag. As we have seen, "Indy 2" will be used throughout the film to underline the heroism of Jones's feats. Here the musical irony is given by the presentation of the heroic motif over a gag unveiling one of Jones's weak spots, thus stressing once again his fallible, comically human side. Then, "Indy 1" is taken up by the trumpets when we see the plane flying into the sunset, and the episode set in the South American jungle is over. A diminished coda for strings with a cadence resolving to the tonic reinforces the closure effect and bridges the cut to the establishing shot that opens the next scene: the austere exterior of a college.

At Home:
Getting Ready for a New Mission

We soon discover another facet of Dr. Jones: his second life as an archaeology professor. Two government officers come to see Dr. Jones: they inform him and Brody, the dean of the college, that the Nazis are on the trail of the Ark of the Covenant. Jones opens a bulky book to show the officers what the artifact is expected to look like. As soon as the book is opened, we hear a "pedal point," a sustained low-pitched note of the contrabasses that conveys a sense of threat and uneasiness to the scene. This is another classical musical cliché: the low-pitched pedal point denotes a pending threat and as such it is employed throughout the film. When Jones shows an illustration of the Ark with lightning bolts coming out of it to exterminate the enemy armies, we hear for the first time the Ark motif, emerging over the pedal point. In film music, orchestration is as important and significant as the melody and harmony. The Ark motif is played by muted trumpets, backed by a vocalizing female choir and *tremolo* violins: the *tremolo* gives a shivering sense of threat to the melody indicating that the Ark is a powerful and dangerous object indeed. The use of the mute in the trumpets aptly represents the latent power of the Ark. In the scene in which the Ark is finally found, its leitmotiv will be played without any mute: from that moment on the menace will be a real one and the power of the Ark liable to be unleashed at any moment. As for the vocalizing female choir, it is an interesting musical choice that foretells what will be found inside the Ark. The scene closes with "Indy 1" played interrogatively by a clarinet backed by a low-pitched pedal point: Jones is going to be involved in a dangerous new quest.

The next scene moves to Jones's house and shows him packing for the expedition, with Brody paying a visit. The first thing to do is retrieve the Ra medallion, the key to the exact location of the Ark. This means that Jones has to get in touch with Marion. Just before Jones mentions her name to Brody, the music introduces Marion's theme, played by the flute. The narration anticipates that we will soon meet the heroine. Brody reminds Jones that Marion will be the smallest of his problems and advises him to be careful when dealing with the Ark. Here, the music—following the classical dialogue underscoring technique—moves from Marion's leitmotiv to the Ark's, played again by ominous muted trumpets. This further presentation of the Ark motif is not only functional in emphasizing the danger mentioned by Brody but is also useful to strengthen the identification of this musical motif with the Ark and fix it in the viewers' memory.

Jones embarks on a plane, accompanied by "Indy 1" in a minor mode: a new risky adventure is about to begin. Then, the music points our attention to a black-clad passenger who spies on Jones from behind a magazine: the use of the villains' chords immediately identifies the nature of the character. In the following air-travel montage, the music gives cohesion and links the unfolding images, until the animated line on the map (as in *Casablanca*) reaches a red dot:

Nepal. Immediately, ethnic colors and mannered orientalism are added to the music: bells, gongs, and a hint of pentatonic scales, following a classical and typically Steineresque use of ethnic musical clichés or quotes of national anthems to set the locale.

Nepal:
Meeting Marion and Retrieving the Medallion

Jones meets a resentful Marion in her tavern. It is interesting to note that Marion is presented without her theme; we shall discover why later. When Jones states that he will come again the next day and leaves the tavern, Marion pulls the medallion out of her neckline. We hear a sinuous theme: the melody is chromatic and is played by a solo English horn—both of these choices give the melody a Middle Eastern flavor consistent with the medallion's Egyptian origin. Furthermore, some traits in the melody are akin to the Ark motif, and in this way the music reminds us of the connection between the two artifacts.

After Marion has put the medallion away, the door opens and some not-very-friendly-looking thugs led by a sinister black-clad man—reminiscent of the slimy criminals played by Peter Lorre—enter the tavern. The music accompanies this entrance with the villains' chords, strongly marking their downward move and accentuating the dissonant seventh at the bottom of the chord in the manner of Steiner. The downward move of the musical line emphatically ends on the close-up of Toht, the black-clad Nazi—"He is the worst of all," the music seems to be saying. This downward trombones progression is followed by a low-pitched pedal point supporting a snare drum rhythmic pattern and martial repeating notes played *piano* by the trumpets. Toht is not wearing a Nazi uniform, but we can readily imagine that he is one of them; yet the music, in accordance with the "excessively obvious" classical style, makes sure that we understand Toht's nature. Toht mellifluously asks Marion about the medallion. Marion, in response, puffs the smoke of her cigarette into Toht's face. The cigarette puff is duplicated by a high-pitched upward scale by the harp and the celesta. Here Williams is overtly quoting a famous episode of Steiner's Mickey-Mousing. In *The Informer* (John Ford, 1935), Katie, the reluctant prostitute, is puffed some smoke into her face by a potential customer, the action being scored by Steiner with the very same musical gesture. Toht opts for strong-arm tactics and threatens Marion with a red-hot poker: a piercing chromatic upward movement by the trumpets marks the entrance of the firebrand into the frame from the lower off-screen zone. The trumpets *crescendo*, rising proportionally with the approach of the firebrand toward Marion's face, is suddenly interrupted by Jones's whip crack that disarms Toht. The musical Mickey-Mousing closely follows the action and culminates in an upward scale by the trumpets duplicating the visual upward movement of the flames propagating from a curtain ignited by the firebrand that has been tossed away, here reprising the association of the bright sound of the trumpets with fire. A *crescendo* with strings tremolo and triangle trill announces the battle. When we hear the first gunshot, the music stops and the sequence proceeds without music. When the fight is over and the villains momentarily defeated, the music resumes on Marion telling Jones that he will have the medallion provided she becomes his business partner, and now we hear the opening bar of the medallion's theme. During the following travel montage, "Indy 1" is presented in major mode — the first stage of the adventure has been successfully completed, Jones has the medallion — and is followed by Marion's theme — Marion has joined him in the adventure.

(Mis)Adventures in Cairo

Arabic-like chromatic music accompanies the visit to Sallah's house and the introduction of the capuchin monkey that will accompany Marion and Jones on the streets of Cairo. Then Jones sets eyes on Marion — she has dismissed her masculine clothes and is now wearing more feminine apparel — and we hear Marion's theme. On closer observation, "Marion's Theme" is not actually her leitmotiv but Jones's love theme for her. As we have seen, the theme is not played when Marion is introduced — she is alone in that scene — but only in the scenes in which she is with Jones, or in those in which Jones is thinking of her.

In the next sequence, Jones and Marion are taking a stroll in the streets of Cairo — instrumental Arabic-sounding diegetic music can be heard.[12] Besides setting the "local color," the diegetic music serves here to define the position of the characters in space. The point of highest volume is the square, but the same music can be heard also from the room in which the villains are preparing to attack: thus the music locates the room in the environs of the square. A different vocal diegetic music is present in the scene under the arcade between the thug with the monkey and the Nazis, separating the indoor arcade space from the outdoor square space.

The non-diegetic music resumes; we hear the villains' chords when one of the Nazis appears under an arch, and the diegetic music gradually tails out. A suspended dissonant harmony increases the suspense: unlike the viewers, Jones and Marion are unaware that they are about to be assaulted. When two local killers — announced by a timpani roll *crescendo* — start the attack, a balletic musical sequence begins. Williams explains: "I look at it as a kind of musical number that has a beginning, a middle and an end, and try to calculate a series of tempos, and a series of changing tempos. I will try to design it almost in the same way as you would a balletic number, which may contribute a certain aspect of fun and adventurousness in this Harrison Ford character. The music may sound serious but it's not really, it's more theatrically conceived and hopefully always has an aspect of fun or even camp about it."[13]

The music keeps up the fight pace (temporal perceptive function), punctuates each action and piece of narrative information (spatial perceptive function), and gives the sequence a comic overtone through the use of humorous Prokofiev-like melodies (micro-emotive function). Mickey-Mousing is glaring: when the narration cuts on the villains, trombones minor chords are played; when Marion stuns a killer with a frying pan, a downward scale by strings and piano comically underlines his fall; when the monkey searches for Marion, comedic *pizzicato* violins punctuate the action; when the villains abruptly stop and turn back because they have located Marion's hiding place, a theatrical trombones *sforzando* acts as a stinger to mark their reaction; when an Arab intimidatingly brandishes a scimitar, his appearance is dramatically stressed by brass minor chords, while an oriental motif for horn—punctuated by exhibition-istic repeating chords—accompanies his spinning the scimitar with threatening skill; when Jones in turn looks at him unimpressedly and quite condescendingly, strings *pizzicato* accentuates the comical effect of Jones's unexpected reaction; the musical phrase closes resolving to the tonic when Jones simply shoots him down with his gun.

Marion is trapped into a big basket, abducted, and loaded onto a truck. Jones shoots down the truck driver to rescue Marion: an exuberant trumpet fanfare stresses the heroic act. Unfortunately, the death of the driver causes the overturning of the truck and its explosion: Jones's heroic act has (supposedly) killed Marion. This is what Jones believes and what the narration tries to make us believe as well. Dramatic chords and the desperate minor-mode rendition of Marion's theme by strings topped by a piercing *sforzando* final note by the horns "manipulate" our emotion and belief about what we have just watched.

The music calms down and leads us into the next scene, in which Jones sits alone at a bar table while trying to soothe his grief with alcohol, like Rick in *Casablanca*. Marion's theme is played mournfully by the woodwinds. When two Nazis arrive—we recognize them as the people behind the assault—to take Jones with them, the villains' chords are played softly by the bassoons and not by the more menacing trombones. In terms of musical form, this makes the music more homogeneous, since all the instruments used here are woodwinds.

From a narrative point of view, music may imply that Jones's grief makes every-thing else of no importance to him, as his suicidal attitude seems to confirm in the next dialogue scene: "Do you want to talk to God? Let's go see Him together. I've got nothing better to do."

Later, Sallah takes Jones to visit an old sage, to decipher the inscription on the medallion. The scene begins with a muezzin chant heard in the distance, then enters a low-pitched pedal point by the contrabasses, indicating that a threat is looming. Indeed, we see the thug with the monkey sneaking into the room, accompanied by an Arabic motif for English horn. A turn by the flutes points our attention to the appearance of a red bottle from his sleeve and a high-pitched violin trill marks the man pouring a poison over some dates in a bowl. In the meanwhile, Jones and Sallah are engaged in a conversation with their host.

When the old sage mentions "The Hebrew God," wind suddenly begins to blow through the open window, swinging the lamps in the room. Beneath the sound of the wind, "noise-like" music can be perceived: violins playing artificial harmonics in super-acute register and tam-tam rolling *pianissimo*. One of the themes of the film is the loss of faith, archaeological in a narrow sense, and religious in a broader one. In the conversation scene after Marion's "death," Belloq tells Jones that they are not so different from each other: "Archaeology is our religion, yet we have both fallen from the purer faith." In the first act of the film, Jones tells Brody, who has just warned him to beware of the powers of the Ark, "I don't believe in magic or superstitious hocus pocus. I'm after a find of incredible historical significance and you're talking about the boogeyman!" At the beginning of the film, we see Jones as a grave robber, plundering a temple whose finds will be sold to Brody's museum. Jones's archaeological faith is in-deed similar to Belloq's: it is just an exciting search of objects having historical and economic value; objects that have been deprived of their original, deepest cultural/religious significance. Jones equals religion and faith to magic and superstition. For him, the Ark is just an object of inestimable value and a de-sirable prey. The mysterious Ark motif has already suggested that the Ark does possess some kind of supernatural power. Here, the sudden wind blowing when the Hebrew God is named is a further signal in this sense. The mysteri-ous music hidden beneath the sound of the wind suggests the presence of God: as the Bible says, "a sound of a gentle blowing."[14] In this scene the music, besides having the emotive function of increasing the concern for this strange phenomenon, also has the cognitive function of providing a clue as to how the faith theme will be an important one in the development of the narrative.

After the wind episode, still in the old sage's house, we see Sallah sing a Gilbert and Sullivan song to celebrate the successful deciphering of the medallion, while Jones takes a date from the bowl and throws it in the air to swallow it up.[15] We see a slow-motion detail of the date floating in the air. Sallah's song stops abruptly, and a timpani roll amplifies the perception of time dilation given by the slow motion. The timpani roll ends with a sharp hit perfectly in synch with Sallah's hand catching the date in midair, instants before it falls into Jones's mouth. Piercing chords by the violins accompany Sallah turning his head to point at something on the floor. The chords continue on the cut to the monkey lying dead—we have seen it eating a date earlier in the scene. The scene ends with a high-angled full shot showing a ceiling fan rotating in the foreground and the monkey corpse on the carpet in the background. The music duplicates the movement of the fan blades with fast circular turns by the celesta.

Digging Up the Ark

Once the precise height of the staff on which the medallion must be inserted has been obtained, Jones can finally sneak into the excavation site and enter the map room, which houses a miniature replica of the ancient town of Tanis. When sun enters the map room, the medallion is supposed to channel its rays onto the replica to indicate the spot in which the Ark is buried. As soon as Jones goes down into the room, a long musical sequence begins. It starts with the Ark motif, played by flutes in the lower register and muted trumpets, backed by the harp and a low-pitched pedal point by the contrabasses. The score closely follows the cross-cutting upon which the sequence is built, alternating between the inside of the map room (where the Ark motif is heard) and the outside where Sallah keeps watch over the entrance: here the music is militaristic, with rhythmic snare-drum patterns and minor-mode trombones fanfares. The cross-cutting music helps to further separate and make a comparison between the two sets: the inner Egyptian room, where a supernatural power is hidden, and the outside Nazi camp, where a worldly power is flaunted. Jones deciphers the inscriptions over the replica to find out where the pole must be inserted. The music reprises those atonal arpeggios that we have already heard when Jones was trying to bypass the traps in the South American temple at the beginning of the film. When Jones finally finds out which is the right hole, an upward chord progression follows Jones turning his head toward the entrance of the room. The narration cuts to the detail of the bright sunlight starting to filter through and the progression resolves to a piercing brass chord played right on the editing cut. When Jones inserts the pole, the Ark motif starts over, played *forte* by the full orchestra, with a vocalizing female choir rising from the orchestral texture and coming to the fore in the second reprise of the theme. (Notice that here, again, female voices *emerge* from the instrumental texture of the Ark motif.) An orchestral *crescendo* of harmonic progressions resolves to the tonic when the sun hits the medallion and a beam illuminates the burial spot. Sallah helps Jones climb out of the room.

Jones wanders around the camp disguised as an Arab—coherently, we hear a "disguised" Arabic-like version of "Indy 1" played in minor mode by the English horn—and enters a tent. Inside he finds Marion alive, and a stinger followed by a Steiner-like musical pause underlines his surprise. Jones is dressed in an Arab outfit and his face is covered: for this reason the music presents ominous low-pitched notes. The music here is focusing our emotion on Marion, who has not recognized him and fears that the stranger may have evil designs on her. When Jones uncovers his face, Marion's theme is played liberatingly. However, the musical phrase is soon suspended by an interrogative modulation: Jones has just realized that freeing Marion means disclosing his presence in the camp and jeopardizing the recovery of the Ark. Between Marion and the Ark, Jones chooses the Ark and, after trying to explain his motive, he leaves her inside the tent.

With the help of Sallah and a group of diggers, Jones starts working on the site indicated on the replica. When the upper trapdoor opens, Sallah and Jones look down into the dark pit—the "Well of Souls." The score presents a high-pitched chromatic scale by *tremolo* violins, a "creeping" music gesture, quite fitting, as we are about to see. Indeed, Sallah asks Jones why the floor is moving. They throw a torch down to bottom of the well—the fall is duplicated by a downward flute scale—and realize that the chamber is crammed with poisonous snakes. The music presents slow *glissando* clusters by the violins with the emotive function of heightening the repulsive images of the reptiles. We hear high-pitched circular woodwinds scales, mimicking the snakes coiling up. The narration cuts back to Jones, who pulls his head out of the trapdoor and lies down, depressed: "Snakes. Why did it have to be snakes?" The music once again mocks the hero, with a comical downward trombones *glissando*. Here is the pay-off of the gag of Weggie the python in the first act: that episode was not only a comic relief but also served to inform us of Jones's phobia.

The narration cuts to the tent where Marion is imprisoned. Belloq enters and unbinds her. He soon proves to be well-behaved and friendly. We understand that he wants to flatter and seduce her in order to obtain information on the medallion . . . and maybe something else—after all, Belloq is French and, as we have seen, stereotypes abound in the film. Belloq offers her a tray with food and water. Marion glances at a knife among the cutlery on the tray: the music points our attention to the potential weapon with a bright triangle tinkle, suggesting Marion's scheming thoughts. A low-pitched pedal point plays under the whole scene and increases the suspense over Marion's fate and the success of her escape, despite the tone of the conversation being friendly and relaxed. When Belloq presents her with a white dress and asks her to wear it, a romantic gesture of the violins underlines the gift. Marion goes behind the room divider and Belloq peeps at her reflection in a mirror while she is taking off her brassiere. The music repeats the romantic gesture of the strings, with an added upward woodwinds trill to mark the growing excitement of the man. A stronger trill accompanies Marion coming out from behind the screen and displaying herself wearing the dress. The scene closes with Marion putting her old dress on the table to hide the knife: the music switches to low register again. As previously happened, Marion's theme never appears in this scene—and similarly will not in the next two—confirming that it is the love theme between Jones and Marion, rather than Marion's own leitmotiv.

The entire night sequence is based on a cross-cutting between the Well of Souls and Belloq's tent. In the Well of the Souls the music continues to enhance the sense of disgust for the reptiles and to duplicate their creeping, coiling movements. A few examples: when Jones lands in front of a cobra, muted trombones increase the comical effect of Jones's disgusted grimace with a slow upward *glissando*. When we see a close-up of the cobra, we hear an upward arpeggio, which recalls that of the shark motif in *Jaws*—not for tuba and horns but for flute and oboe, reminding us of snake charmers.

In the tent, the seduction goes on, and Belloq fills two glasses with a strong liquor. He wants to get Marion drunk in order to obtain the information he needs. The suspenseful low-pitched pedal point is still there. Unlike Belloq, we know that Marion is an experienced drinker. A light violins *pizzicato* accompanies the toast, and a bold turn of the clarinets underlines Belloq swallowing his glass with a smirk on his face. Marion answers by emptying her glass at a single stroke, and a turn of the flutes answers to the clarinets. A *pizzicato* comically emphasizes Belloq's surprise. This time it is Marion's turn to fill the glasses, and we realize that she is already leading the game. The score closes the scene with the low-pitched pedal point, still reminding us that, although partly comic, Marion's plan is a risky one. In the following tent scene, the low-pitched pedal point is gone. The two contestants are both drunk, apparently. Marion goes on pouring the liquor. Funny gestures by the clarinets and trombones mimic the uncoordinated movements of the drunks. Suddenly, Marion grabs the knife from the table and points it at Belloq: a low-pitched stinger stresses the surprising twist. Belloq's reaction is a fit of laughter, and Marion does the same while she backs away toward the exit. We hear again comical gestures in the score, but the low-pitched pedal point reemerges so as to warn us of an impending danger. A close-up shows Belloq looking at the entrance to the tent: his smile fades from his face. Marion bangs against Toht, blocking the exit behind her, and the villains' chords mark his appearance. When Toht picks up his bag and pulls out a menacing black object with chain inserts, a dramatic brass low-pitched *crescendo* heightens the suspense and seems to confirm our impression that we are about to see a torture scene. When the object is revealed to be simply a hanger for Toht's coat, the comic effect given by the sudden contradiction of our expectations is enhanced by the deflating of the musical *crescendo*. Proverbially, the mountain has brought forth a mouse.

In the meantime, Sallah has joined Jones, and the two lift the Ark out of a large stone sarcophagus. As soon as the profile of the object emerges, the Ark motif is stated by the horns, to which unmuted trumpets playing *forte* are added when the Ark comes completely out of the sarcophagus. Earlier, the Ark was hidden—muted trumpets—and now the object has been brought to light and its power is a real threat. When the Ark is placed into a wooden crate, we hear a disturbing atonal vocalizing female choir.

Losing the Ark/Getting the Ark/ Losing the Ark Again

A new day has come and Belloq, out of the tent, notices the clandestine excavation and summons all the soldiers. In the Well of Souls, Sallah is climbing to the exit accompanied by a spirited version of the Ark motif. When it is Jones's turn to grasp the rope, the rope falls back into the Well—a dynamic *crescendo* by the trumpets duplicates the falling movement. When the rope touches the ground, the *crescendo* stops and leaves room to a low-pitched pedal point. Another *crescendo* accompanies the upward whip-pan to the top, which stops on the image of Belloq tauntingly greeting from above: "Hello!" A *piano* note by the trombones serves as a coda for the tailing-out of the music to make room for the unaccompanied dialogue. The music starts again dramatically when Toht arrives and throws Marion into the Well. Mickey-Mousing closely duplicates the following events, such as Marion's fall; Marion clinging to the teeth of an Anubis; a tooth of the statue cracking; a snake coiling up inside the shoe that Marion has lost during the fall; the tooth finally breaking apart; Marion's falling into Jones's arms; and her landing in front of the cobra. The Nazis take the Ark, and the two are locked into the Well, apparently sentenced to death.

To flee the place, Jones understands that he has to tear down one of the walls. The music starts with a rhythmic pattern expressing Jones's determination and Mickey-Mousing marks the action. Jones climbs onto one of the huge Anubis statues, makes the statue swing, and manages to detach it from its base, causing it to fall and land on the wall, demolishing it—the trumpets play "Indy 1" while Jones "rides" the falling statue.

In the following scene, Jones tries to get hold of an airplane and engages in a fistfight with a mechanic. Again the music treats the action as a ballet. The fists are emphasized by trumpets stingers and woodwinds runs, while a brass *ostinato* serves as rhythmic drive across the action—the brass *ostinato* also recalls the rotating propellers of the plane, which are an extra pending danger that will play a key role in the outcome of the fight. Jones has knocked down the mechanic and is now climbing on the wing to get rid of the pilot. Unfortunately, he is stopped by another, much more robust mechanic who insists that he step down from the wing and have a fist fight. The rhythmic *ostinato* stops and gives way to a middle-register pedal point by the horns, on which the oboe and clarinet play a weary minor-mode version of "Indy 1." This reinforces the ironical image of the hero reluctantly giving the brawny mechanic a tired nod, as if to ask him to be allowed some time to climb down from the wing. Once on the ground, the musical *ostinato* suddenly resumes when Jones, with a trick, distracts the man and unfairly kicks the rival between the legs. The mechanic takes the blow—and the others to follow—as if he were indestructible. Meanwhile, Marion knocks out the pilot, who collapses onto the control stick, thus making the plane move in circles. When the control stick lowers, a new musical section begins, serving as a frame for the subepisode of the sequence. Now Jones must not only get rid of the burly mechanic but also pay attention to not being crushed by the wheels of the aircraft or being cut to ribbons by its rotating propellers. There is more: a wing strikes a tanker truck causing a leak from which fuel begins to spill out onto the tarmac; a high-pitched flute trill focuses our attention on this narrative event that will trigger a chain reaction. Jones sees a gun on the ground and runs toward it; we hear the trumpets starting to play "Indy 1." When the mechanic blocks his way to the gun, the melodic line of "Indy 1" is suddenly diverted by an abrupt modulation. When Marion sees a military truck passing by, we hear for the first time a minor-mode march, which will be henceforth associated with the Nazis. If Jones had to deal with single enemies like Belloq, Toht, or some Nazis in civilian clothes generically marked by the villains' chords, now he has to steal the Ark from the Wehrmacht itself. Marion uses the aircraft machine gun to shoot the truck and other approaching enemies. However, in the shooting some fuel cans explode, causing a fire. A shot of the fuel flowing onto the runway is highlighted by fast and flowing strings scales. Jones realizes that Marion is locked in the cockpit and that the airplane could explode at any minute. He climbs onto the fuselage, accompanied by a heroic version of "Indy 1" played by the trumpets. However, the melody stops again after four bars: the mechanic has climbed on the plane and diverts Jones from rescuing Marion. The fistfight continues on the plane, backed by dramatic Mickey-Mousing. The fuel is now about to reach the fire, and the music emphasizes the danger with an alarming high-pitched trill of the woodwinds. The seemingly invincible mechanic gets accidentally killed by the airplane propellers—a convenient narrative turn to eliminate the mighty opponent. Jones is now free to save Marion, a last-minute rescue before the plane explodes. "Indy 1" played by horns accompanies the rescue, stopping at the fourth bar and repeating the same half phrase twice.

Jones and Marion meet Sallah, surprised and happy to see them alive. Sallah informs Jones that the Ark was loaded onto a truck to be taken away. The next sequence shows Jones chasing the truck on horseback. Once again, the long musical sequence (7'44") treats the chase like a ballet. The uninterrupted musical accompaniment, besides creating a unified perception of the frenzied editing of the sequence, supports the action with extensive Mickey-Mousing embedded in a relentless *ostinato*. During the sequence the score also develops and weaves cells of the various leitmotivs, and switches from one to the other, directing our attention to the various related characters—for example, the "Nazi march" when we see the convoy escorting the Ark, and "Indy 1" over the shots of Jones riding his horse. In this sequence we hear "Indy 2" for the second time in the film, after its ironical use in the initial python-on-the-airplane gag. This time, "Indy 2" accompanies an episode in which Jones does "show a little backbone": the theme is used when Jones takes possession of the truck and rams the Nazi car; when Jones—after having being thrown in front of the moving truck and dragged under the vehicle—skillfully succeeds in climbing back on board; when Jones takes back control of the truck and pushes the Nazi car off the road. Arriving in Cairo, Jones hides the truck in a safe place. The success of the mission is celebrated by the horns playing "Indy 1," but still limited to the half phrase: the battle is won, the war not yet.

Jones, Marion, and the Ark embark on Captain Katanga's ship. After having been buried alive, almost beaten to death by a stout mechanic and thrown out of a speeding truck, Jones—covered in bruises and scratches—can finally lie down and take some rest. Marion takes care of him; from dressing his wounds, the action soon progresses to kissing. We first hear Marion's theme for solo flutes when she offers to take care of the beaten man. Then, the theme is repeated by the flutes backed by the strings. A cell of Marion's theme warmly played by cellos is heard when it is clear that the nurse is about to become the lover. When Marion kisses Jones on the lips, the theme is restated by the violins, and then the full orchestra soars with a passionate *crescendo* leading to a repeated sweeping arpeggio in triplet rhythm. Suddenly, the crescendo stops and the music deflates: Jones has fallen asleep. The score has created a sort of musical *coitus interruptus*. The comic effect of this scene is obtained by firstly building expectations—through the use of romantic, passionate musical clichés like the love theme by strings, the thickening of the instrumentation, the yearning effect of the triplet rhythm—and then frustrating those expectations, which provokes laughter serving as an emotional outlet.[16] The image of the sleeping Jones is not only accompanied by a musical deflation but also by a delicate motif played *piano* by the celesta, imitating a music box that winds down, as the final notes of a lullaby.

The narration takes us to the cargo hold in the ship's hull, where the Ark is stowed. A slow tracking shot moves forward to the wooden crate, marked with a Nazi swastika. An insert shot shows a mouse behaving oddly, as if affected by an invisible force. The tracking shot completes its movement and stops on the detail of the swastika, which is suddenly burned out by some heat emanating from the inside. As in the scene in which a mysterious wind blew through the house of the Arab sage, here we perceive again some musical presence beneath the low-frequency noise of the ship engines.

The next morning, the ship is seized by a Nazi U-boat; they retrieve the Ark and kidnap Marion. Jones has managed to hide, and Katanga justifies his absence by telling the Nazis that he killed him to keep Marion for himself. The Nazis search the ship without finding Jones, so they believe Katanga's story and go back to their submarine. Indeed, even Katanga and his men have no idea where Jones might be. Then the music presents "Indy 2" played by the strings, as to anticipate that a feat of heroism is about to take place. Indeed, one of Katanga's men looks overboard and says, "I found him," pointing at something off-screen. The music duplicates his pointing gesture with a woodwinds run, which leads to a cut to Jones climbing onto the U-boat. Reaching the upper deck, Jones salutes Katanga and his men, accompanied for the first time by the complete phrase of "Indy 1"—including the "show-off modulation"[17]—in the form of an exuberant march, with its bold major-sixth leaps emphasizing the cheers of Katanga and his crew. Here, the music celebrates the hero and distracts us from thinking about the implausibility of Jones swimming toward and climbing onto a U-boat. In such moments, the music has the scope of diverting our attention from the narrative logic and directing it to the spectacular and emotional qualities of the scene. The effect is achieved by Williams's typical technique of "gradual disclosure of the main theme" discussed in chapter 7.[18] After recurrent presentations of the first semiphrase only, "Indy 1" is heard here in its entirety for the first time. The recognition of a familiar melody finally heard in its full form has a resulting effect of gratification that attaches to the visual, and the music also projects onto the scene a sense of coherence deriving from the cohesion of the score—thus masking the weakness of the narrative logic.

Opening the Ark

The U-boat arrives at some Mediterranean island and docks in a hidden military base. Jones disembarks and spies on Marion and Belloq from behind some crates. We hear "Indy 1" played by the clarinets and flutes in low register, backed by the low-pitched pedal point by the contrabasses. Two *pizzicato* notes by the contrabasses pinpoint a soldier in a long shot being suddenly pulled away behind some crates. Having knocked him out, Jones steals his uniform. During the gag in which Jones discovers that the uniform is too tight for him, the comic effect is strengthened by "Indy 1" played by the clarinet and reprised in canon-like imitation by ironic contrabasses *pizzicato*. "Indy 1" is then interrupted when a soldier arrives. His legs threateningly enter the on-screen space and create a frame-in-the-frame of Jones's face. A minor-mode trombones chord and martial repeating notes by the trumpets accompany his unexpected arrival. The soldier does not recognize the impostor and believes he is just a shabby recruit. He yells in German, evidently ordering Jones to tidy up. Jones plays along, smiling embarrassedly and proving his compliance by combing his hair. The music presents a comic version of "Indy 1" backed by violins *pizzicato*. The gag ends when Jones suddenly kicks the soldier down, catches his hat in midair, and dons it: an upward run by the clarinets comically duplicates his catch. Then, Jones mingles effortlessly with other soldiers, and—in case viewers might have missed something—the music draws our attention to his presence among the Nazis by presenting a cell of "Indy 1" played by a solo clarinet as he passes by.

In the next sequence, the Ark is brought into a gorge. The Ark motif arranged as a minor-mode march accompanies the soldiers on the trek. Jones is at the tail of the line of soldiers: the music indicates his presence with "Indy 1" played by the horns. Jones breaks away from the convoy and hides behind some crates: a harp *glissando* reinforces our perception of his abrupt movement and also serves as a musical bridge to the reprise of the Ark motif when the narration cuts to the next shot. Jones appears on an upper ridge saying "Hello!" and threatens the soldiers below with a bazooka. His elevated position mirrors the previous scene with Belloq looking down from the trapdoor of the Well of Souls and similarly saying "Hello." A telling *crescendo* precedes Jones's appearance, and a thinning of the music makes room for Jones's cue, while a stinger emphasizes the surprise of the soldiers. The music inconspicuously tails out under the dialogue.

In a gorge, the Ark is placed on a stone altar, around which we see Toht, the Wehrmacht colonel, and Belloq, who is dressed as an ancient Hebrew priest. Before them, soldiers are filming the event with swastika-branded cameras. Jones and Marion are on the side of the gorge opposite the altar, tied to a pole. At the beginning of the scene, wind blowing through the gorge can be detected: we can hear the wind's whisper and see Belloq's clothes move. The score does not present the Ark motif but instead a high-pitched pedal point by the strings and some chromatic oriental-flavored gestures by the woodwinds. After Belloq has uttered some ritual formulas, the Ark is opened. Disappointingly, instead of wonderful treasures and the Tablets of Law, the Ark contains nothing but sand. The colonel raises a handful of sand, which begins to slide through his fingers. The music emphasizes the sand sliding with silvery high-pitched notes by the piano, harp, and the cascading sound of the Mark Tree.[19] This musical choice recalls a scene in *The Treasure of the Sierra Madre* (John Huston, 1948) in which Steiner's music stresses the pouring of gold dust into scale pans in the same way: for that gold dust Dobbs (Humphrey Bogart) will lose his life. Here, there seems to be not only a tribute to Steiner but also an anticipation of what will soon happen to Belloq and his comrades: like Dobbs, they will lose their lives because of an ineffable treasure.

Suddenly, the electrical equipment mysteriously begins to break down: the Ark motif enters played by the trumpets. A weird light appears from the bottom of the Ark; fog starts to billow out of it and envelop the area. Jones looks at the ominous phenomena in astonishment and urges Marion to keep her eyes squeezed shut. Spirits with beautiful feminine faces come out of the Ark and start to float around, with fast-flowing strings runs duplicating the spirits' flight. The musical choice of the angelic vocalizing female choir often heard under the Ark motif is now clear: the music was anticipating what would emanate from the Ark. The Nazis stare at the fascinating spirits that suddenly turn into Death Angels. Bolts of lightning spring out from the Ark and strike each soldier to the ground. Belloq, the colonel, and Toht scream in terror and explode, implode, and liquefy, respectively. Flames envelop the entire gorge, destroying everything in it. A column of fire rises up to the sky and then returns into the

Ark, on which the lid finally falls. The only survivors are Jones and Marion: God's Fire has spared their lives as it happened to Lot during the destruction of Sodom and Gomorrah.[20]

Once again, the music in this scene represents the presence of God. While previously it was an almost unnoticeable presence hidden beneath the wind sound and the ship's engine, now God's power is unleashed and his presence evident. Williams said: "For the opening of the Ark, I wanted to try and evoke a biblical atmosphere."[21] He certainly succeeded. During the terrible demise of Belloq, the colonel, and Toht, the score states a peremptory horn motif, which may be called "The Wrath of God Motif":

Transcription of John Williams, "The Wrath of God Motif [tentative title]," from the *Raiders of the Lost Ark* film score (© 1981 BMI), published by Bantha Music (ear transcription from the film's soundtrack) [Used in compliance with the U.S. Copyright Act, Section 107].

This horn motif has an ancient flavor given by musical intervals that can be played using the natural harmonics of the instruments.[22] Moreover, the *Shofar*—one type of ancient horn—is the ram's horn used in Jewish liturgy and mentioned several times in the Bible. In the book of Exodus the very sound of the horn indicates the presence of God: "There was thunder, lightning and a thick cloud on the mountain. Then a *shofar* blast sounded so loudly that all the people in the camp trembled. . . . Mount Sinai was enveloped in smoke, because *Adonai* descended onto it in fire—its smoke went up like the smoke from a furnace, and the whole mountain shook violently. As the sound of the *shofar* grew louder and louder . . ."[23] Jones, who previously professed not to believe in superstition and magic, discovers a supernatural facet of life that he had never considered. The themes of (archaeological) faith and (religious) Faith, introduced since the first act as an open question, find here a possible answer. Maybe this experience has taught Jones that the archaeological finds are not just trophies to win and sell, but are symbols that must be respected. In life there is much more than what one can see, feel, and touch.

Set free by the Divine Fire, Jones and Marion embrace each other, and we hear Marion's theme, which closes the scene and the adventure with an authentic cadence (V–I) and a slow upward harp arpeggio. All ended well . . . but maybe not. On the cut leading to the epilogue, the musical line goes up a half step, contradicting the closure effect of the authentic cadence.

Epilogue

There is still something pending: What will become of the Ark? In Washington, Jones is informed by some bureaucrats that the relic is being kept in a safe place and studied by their qualified "top men," which excludes him.

Outside the building, Marion asks him the reason for his disappointment. Jones insults the bureaucrats: "They don't know what they've got there." Marion tries to cheer him up: "But I know what I've got here." She invites him to go for a drink together. Again, we hear Marion's theme. Jones offers his arm to her, and Marion's theme is reprised by the strings—violins and cellos, female and male. The lost Ark has been found and lost again, but during this adventure Jones has retrieved something else: a lost love. This scene confirms our previous claim that Marion does not have her "own" theme. Marion's theme is actually the projection onto her of Jones's love for her—the romantic idealization of the beloved woman.[24] From this perspective, the music can also prompt a feminist interpretation: in the patriarchal Hollywood cinema the woman is only a passive object of desire and "gaze" for the male protagonists, in this case Jones and Belloq.[25] Therefore, even if she is the film's co-protagonist, she does not have an identity of her own—that is, her own musical theme—as the male lead has.[26]

What has happened to the Ark? This is the last narrative question still left open. While Jones will probably never know, the omniscient narration provides the viewers with the answer, as in *Citizen Kane* (Orson Welles, 1941). We are shown that the Ark is locked in an anonymous crate and stored in a huge warehouse full of identical crates. Probably the Ark will eventually get lost again. The Ark motif accompanies the Ark being pushed on a trolley through the stacks of crates. Interestingly, in the CD album this final track closes with a *crescendo* leading to a *forte* authentic cadence by the full orchestra: thus, the piece closes sharply. In the film, on the contrary, the closing tonic chord is cut and the crescendo is overlapped by a suite starting exactly at the beginning of the end credits and accompanying their crawl.[27] The cut of the closing tonic chord and the sudden shift to "Indy 1," the "signature tune" of the series, seems to avoid a sharp closure of the film narrative, which is in line with the lack of opening titles in this film—the opening titles being the other strong element that typically frames a film narrative. Following the aesthetics of serials once again, the narration seems to reject a sharp closure effect as if it were telling us that the adventures of Indiana Jones are not over.

Ian Freer commented: "[F]ew concerns are closer to Spielberg than film lore, and it is this respect and passion for the craft that gives *Raiders* its soul. Indeed, what ultimately separates *Raiders* from the action pack is affection, not only for the genres and staples it is parodying but for the sheer delight in yarn spinning. The mark of all great cinema, *Raiders* joyously reaffirms why we love movies in the first place."[28]

The score is a fundamental element of the vintage quality of this film.[29] The use of clichés, techniques, and dialects from the past is dealt with by Williams with similar respect and passion for the film music craft and with an equal fondness for the past masterpieces. "To discern a '30s mood and express it isn't like doing a pastiche. A pastiche is not that difficult. What is not easy is taking it a stage further and doing the real thing, with some sincerity," says Williams.[30] The *Raiders* score manipulates the perception of cinematic time by supporting the rhythm of cutting and heightening the pace of the staged actions. It fulfills a micro-emotive function not only giving the proper romance to love scenes but also stressing the sense of revulsion for snakes and other unpleasant images, or adding further comedy and irony to the gags. It also performs a macro-emotive function, since it makes the narrative seem more cohesive and its episodic nature more unified. In a careful analysis, this extroverted and illustrative score reveals to fulfill an important cognitive function as well: it suggests the presence of God and outlines the stages of development of the theme of Faith. A good classical-style score is not merely "plastering movies with bits of what we know, rather than revealing an unseen dimension," as many critics of Williams and Hollywood music in general claim.

Above all, the *Raiders* score is "an object lesson in how to mirror screen action in memorable music."[31] Its core is precisely the classical spatial perceptive function—Mickey-Mousing, stingers, and leitmotivs—fulfilled at many different levels and with such a virtuosity and inventiveness that *Raiders of the Lost Ark* can be said to be one of the finest examples of neoclassical film scores, as John Williams can be said to be the greatest heir to Max Steiner.

11

Beyond the Films

Conductor John Williams

Each year in spring, Boston's Symphony Hall undergoes a major transformation. The rows of seats on the main floor are replaced with tables; the walls are decked with flowers and lit in cheerful colors. The orchestra plays light symphonic pieces spanning from famous opera overtures to selections from operettas, ballet suites, American marches, standard songs, concert extracts, and symphonic arrangements from the latest Broadway hits. Concerts take place in an easygoing, informal atmosphere: one can listen to the music while sipping a glass of wine, drinking a pint of beer, or enjoying one of the many sandwiches and plates offered on the menu. It is the annual Pops season in Boston. The concert programs may be light in content, but they are solid with respect to performance quality. Indeed, the members of the Boston Pops Orchestra come from the roster of the Boston Symphony, one of America's top orchestras. The Boston Pops plays in Boston each year from May through June and again in December for the "Holiday Pops" season.[1]

The Boston Pops Orchestra

The orchestra's mission is to bridge the gap between the classical and the popular repertoires, and to introduce the concertgoing custom and the sound of a symphony orchestra to wide audiences. Founded in 1885, the Boston Pops has become one of America's most important musical institutions, a world ambassador of American culture, and perhaps one of the most widely known orchestras because of its extensive presence on television, radio, and in the record market.

In 1929, after seventeen Europeans holding the title, for the first time an American-born orchestra member was appointed conductor-in-residence: the Bostonian thirty-five-year-old violinist Arthur Fiedler (1894–1979). He would bring widespread fame to the orchestra and forge its unmistakable identity; he had leadership, enthusiasm for popular music making, and an open, unprejudiced mind interested in the potential value of every kind of music: "There's nothing wrong with playing light music. You don't always read Milton, Shakespeare, and Schopenhauer. You can enjoy Mark Twain."[2] During his almost fifty-year tenure from 1930 to his death in 1979, he reinvented and transformed the Boston Pops into what they are now: an American institution and perhaps the most famous orchestra in the world.

During its first five decades, the orchestra was simply known as "the orchestra of the pops concerts," that is, the Boston Symphony playing popular programs, and the orchestra was mostly a local institution. In 1935 Fiedler signed a contract with RCA Victor and ushered the orchestra into the record market, launching a long series of successful releases. For the occasion the orchestra was christened "Boston Pops Orchestra."[3] During the years, Fiedler's Boston Pops albums would sell a total of close to fifty million copies. Fiedler also pioneered the multimedia expansion. He launched local live radio broadcasts in 1952, which expanded to reach national diffusion in 1962. In 1967 the Pops moved to television, and from 1969 to 2004 it was featured in a regular, nationally aired TV program, *Evening at Pops*; with about 250 episodes in those thirty-five years, it made the Boston Pops the only orchestra in the world with such a visibility.[4] On 4 July 1929 Fiedler had launched the free outdoor *Esplanade Concerts* on Boston's Charles River Esplanade, a tradition he carried on annually with increasing success. The 4th of July 1976 concert—celebrating the bicentennial of the Declaration of Independence—had an attendance of more than four hundred thousand people, marking the record for the largest audience for a symphonic concert at that time.[5]

Fiedler took over the traditional Pops three-part program and refurbished it by assigning, as in a well-balanced menu, precise musical characters, and "nutritional factors" to each section. The first part included the classics of the symphonic repertoire: overtures, ballet suites, symphonic poems, and the like. The central part featured a soloist from either classical music (performing parts of some concerto with the orchestra) or from popular music (presenting some songs accompanied by the orchestra). The third part was the site of the truly popular repertoire, which would close the program with bright marches or vaudeville and Broadway songs in orchestral arrangements.

Fiedler expanded the classical European repertoire to include much more American music. Besides presenting the then brand-new compositions of George Gershwin and adding more pieces by America's "March King" John Philip Sousa, Fiedler also commissioned new pieces from compatriot composers, such as Leroy Anderson (1908–75). In the third part of the programs, Fiedler showcased the most popular and up-to-date music. He opened the door of symphonic concerts to the Broadway musical repertoire, which increasingly took the place of traditional selections from operas and operettas, and to jazz, featuring such artists as Ella Fitzgerald, Dizzy Gillespie, Benny Goodman, and Lionel Hampton, all of whom performed on the Symphony Hall stage during the Fiedler years. In the last two decades of his tenure, Fiedler also ventured into the field of the younger generation's pop music, presenting orchestral arrangements of the Beatles' current songs and even of disco-music hits. His success had become an indispensable asset for the finances of the Boston Symphony Orchestra (BSO): in Fiedler's reign, the Pops season—lasting two/three months—brought in one-third of the total revenues of the Boston Symphony Orchestra Inc.[6]

On 10 July 1979, Fiedler died at the age of eighty-five, having conducted his beloved Pops for a staggering fifty years, until two months before his death. The BSO management had to face a daunting, almost impossible task: to find a successor to this iconic figure.

John Williams from Hollywood

After a lengthy search for candidates and a painstaking short listing, on 9 January 1980 the Hollywood composer John Williams was appointed as the nineteenth conductor-in-residence of the Boston Pops Orchestra. Williams was the least experienced in concert conducting among the frontrunners, having led only a few concerts at that time and being mostly a recording-stage conductor. According to Williams, this might have been one of the reasons why he was eventually chosen: "I started conducting only out of self-defense. . . . I felt I could get what I wanted [with my music] more quickly than some conductors working in the film studios. I certainly never had an ambition or studied to be a public performer as a conductor. . . . [N]obody could successfully succeed Arthur Fiedler, and some professional conductors might actually damage his or her own career by trying. . . . I had nothing to lose, and I could gain the joy of experiencing a live audience, which we don't have in the studio."[7] Modesty aside, this was hardly the main reason. Although little experienced, Williams scored the highest grade among the short-listed conductors in the assessment questionnaires filled in by the orchestra's members.[8] In May 1979 Williams had performed twice with the Boston Pops as one of the season's guest conductors, and those two concert appearances had probably been quite impressive to the musicians. One of the major issues of complaints among the orchestra members in Fiedler's last years was the declining musical quality of his arrangements of pop material. In his appearances as guest conductor, Williams showed his command of both the classical and the popular repertoire (the canonic Mozart Horn Concerto No. 2 in E Flat, K. 417 and the traditional Irish "Londonderry Air"); the higher quality of his own arrangements (his own *Excerpts from Fiddler on the Roof* displayed a virtuoso violin part); and, of course, the enormous potential that his famous film music had in attracting a wider and younger audience (excerpts from *Superman*, *Star Wars*, and *Close Encounters of the Third Kind*).[9]

In the peak of the neoclassical trend that he launched, Williams's success in bringing back the old-fashioned symphonic sound to mass audiences was a major factor in signing him for the Boston post. One commentator observed: "Perhaps the most fortunate result of Williams' later movie scores is the way in which they exposed the general movie audience to the symphonic sound. In this way, he is similar to Fiedler, whose televised performances with the Boston Pops brought symphonic sound to the TV masses."[10]

This was the first time in which a prominent and highly successful Hollywood composer was given the leadership of such an important musical institution.[11] The initial reactions to Williams's appointment were generally positive, some even enthusiastic. For instance, this was the reaction of André Previn, then conductor-in-residence of the London Symphony:

> Anybody who thinks John Williams is just a Hollywood musician is completely wrong. He is such a good musician, so thorough, so completely schooled. John is damned fortunate at this stage of his career that the job at the Pops should open. . . . At the same time, the Pops is lucky that John is available. He is a first-class pianist, and he knows a terrific amount of music. . . . He can make superlative arrangements of pop materials, and he can edit, fix, handle anything that comes up in someone else's arrangement, make it better, and all in a matter of minutes. . . . He is also a very efficient conductor; the players of the London Symphony Orchestra, who have recorded several film scores with him, are full of admiration. They say there's no nonsense about him, that he knows what he wants and he knows how to get it.[12]

Jaws producer David Brown commented upon Williams's election: "His appointment to the Pops lends great prestige to the entire movie industry."[13] Similarly, the reviews of his inaugural Boston concert on 29 April 1980 were largely favorable: "A new era began tonight for the Boston Pops Orchestra as John Williams, the award-winning film composer who was named the Pops conductor three months ago to succeed the late Arthur Fiedler, put down his baton at the end of his first public performance and was greeted with a sustained roar of applause. . . . 'People wanted to love him,' Patricia Kavanaugh, an artist from nearby Gloucester, said. . . . 'They couldn't dislike him if they had tried. He was fantastic.'"[14] However, this trespassing from the commercial film music into the "sacred" concert hall territories did not pass unnoticed by some "cultural guardians" who chastised the outrageous affront. The most bitter reaction came from Jordan N. Whitelaw, producer of the TV series *Evening at Symphony*, who commented: "Williams made no impression on me whatsoever. His music shouldn't happen to a dog."[15]

The Boston Pops post was a unique chance for Williams to advance a further step in his effort to revive the classical Hollywood music. From such a prestigious podium, he could contribute in creating a canon of Hollywood music and disseminate the best pieces in live concerts, radio and TV broadcasts, and orchestral albums. Williams had the occasion to crack the "iron curtain" that had been keeping film music out of concert programs on the grounds of prejudicial points. Film music can be a source of legitimate music and an important repertoire from which symphonic pieces can be drawn for symphonic popular programs as those of the Boston Pops.

In the first press conference, Williams described his plans for the Pops and the goals that he wanted to achieve, one of which was that "It is possible that I can bring prestige to the best film music by presenting it in a concert format. Only one half of one percent of the music written in the nineteenth century is anything we ever hear today; surely there must be at least that percentage of good music written for films."[16] To give film music a better recognition did not simply mean to increase the amount of film music in concert programs—Fiedler programmed film music too—but it meant to have a more attentive care for quality.

Fiedler used to choose film music written in a pop language, something akin to the pop song repertoire. He looked for something accessible that could fit the third part of the programs, reserved for what he called "gumdrops."[17] Fiedler preferred new pieces with a recent successful performance in the easy-listening record charts such as "Lara's Theme" from *Dr. Zhivago* (David Lean, 1965, music by Maurice Jarre); the theme from *Love Story* (Arthur Hiller,

1970, music by Francis Lai); "Gonna Fly Now" from *Rocky* (John G. Avildsen, 1976, music by Bill Conti); the sirtaki from *Zorba the Greek* (Mihalis Kakogiannis, 1964, music by Mikis Theodorakis)—or marketable songs featured in a film's sound track—"The Way We Were" (lyrics by Alan and Marilyn Bergman, music by Marvin Hamlisch, from *The Way We Were*, Sidney Pollack, 1973) and "Raindrops Keep Fallin' on My Head," (lyrics by Hal David, music by Burt Bacharach, from *Butch Cassidy*, George Roy Hill, 1969) for two prominent occurrences. After the unprecedented sales of the *Star Wars* symphonic album, from 1978 on, there was an obvious increase in the quantity of film music presented in the Fiedler programs. There was a slight change in preference for pieces that were notable for being prominent examples of film music, rather than for being prominent hits in the pop charts. Concerts featuring film-music selections were held in both the 1978 and the 1979 seasons. From a *quantitative* perspective, in those seasons Fiedler did give more importance to film music. However, from a *qualitative* perspective, things remained unchanged: Fiedler's preference was again for pop language and easy-listening sounds. Regardless of the origin of the music, whether from Broadway, Hollywood, or pop music top-ten charts, Fiedler would have all the new pieces arranged according to his idea of popular music and conformed to the standard Pops sound, which in his last years consisted of a thick sound either loudly showy and band-like or old-fashioned and sentimentally bel canto–like. In 1978, for example, Fiedler programmed the main theme from *Star Wars* not in its original orchestration but in an arrangement titled "Theme and Dance [!] from Star Wars"—incidentally, anyone familiar with *Star Wars* probably wondered where this "dance" mentioned in the title could be found in the film. The arrangement starts with a band-like rendition of the main theme in which the canon-like structure of the opening fanfare was elided, as well as every sign of contrapuntal writing, and spurious, showy cymbal clashes were generously added. Then, an incongruous Spanish-sounding bridge is introduced, leading to a Charleston-like version of "Cantina Band," the diegetic piece that can be heard in the background during the Mos Eisley scene in the film.[18] In a nutshell, when Fiedler chose to play film music, he chose it not as film music but as a subgenre of the up-to-date pop genre fitting for the third part of the program.

On the contrary, Williams's approach to film music was quality-driven. He would search the film-music repertoire not merely to find trendy pop pieces but to find musically interesting pieces. Film music is seen as an art to be taken more seriously and as a repertoire that could provide musically legitimate material. The first sign of this different view was the placement of film music entries in Williams's programs. He began to include film-music pieces in the first part, which was traditionally reserved for the art-music classics. This apparently inconspicuous change actually had a groundbreaking meaning: now film music was put on the same level with concert music. The 7 May 1980 concert did not open with music from the opera or ballet repertoire but with Erich Wolfgang Korngold's overture to *The Sea Hawk* from his film score for the 1940 Michael Curtiz swashbuckler. Williams also approached film music with an unprecedented philological care. Unlike previous cases like "Theme and Dance from *Star Wars*," Williams presented only the original versions—not only for film-music classics like Korngold's but also for contemporary works like those by Jerry Goldsmith.[19] If the originals were not available, Williams would commission new arrangements based on the author's original orchestration reconstructed from surviving orchestral parts and from the film's music track. For example, Williams commissioned Alexander Courage to reconstruct Conrad Salinger's original orchestration of "Singin' in the Rain" and premiered the piece on 12 May 1981. Courage was one of the top orchestrators and arrangers that Williams brought along from Hollywood, the others being Angela Morley, Morton Stevens, Sid Ramin, Eddie Karam, and Herbert Spencer.

"Artistic and Creative Differences"

Williams's tenure with the Boston Pops came—apparently—to an abrupt end after only four years, perhaps because of a prejudicial attitude of a few high-brow musicians in the orchestra. In a brief press statement on 13 June 1984 Williams announced his resignation due to "artistic and creative differences between myself and the orchestra."[20] What were the reasons behind the drastic decision? A widely spread rumor had it that during the rehearsal of Tuesday, 12 June, some players in the orchestra had hissed at Williams's new piece *America, the Dream Goes On*.[21] In the following days, more reports were published in the newspapers, adding details about the notorious demotivated and careless attitude of the orchestra members during Pops rehearsals. It emerged that such low morale and bad attitudes were inherited from and had been constant since the last decade of the Fiedler era.[22] Fiedler was used to his musicians' uncooperative attitude and managed to stoically live with it and to get things done anyway.[23] Williams, with a different personality and sensitiveness and with different aims, was no longer willing to tolerate such unprofessional manners.

After apologies from and meeting with the musicians, on 3 August it was announced that Williams had withdrawn his resignation and had given an explanation of the reasons for his protest. His concern, he stated, was not so much the orchestra discipline as their low morale, and the "artistic and creative differences" were over the status of popular music: "The high point of my music year is coming to Boston. . . . To them, it's playtime, but to me it's serious. I wanted to express my musical goals pretty high. It was kind of an attitudinal disagreement."[24] Williams then called a number of assemblies with the orchestra members. Many confessed that they hated Fiedler and despised the poor quality of his music.[25] Many were worried and thought that playing the light repertoire could weaken their technique and affect their skills. As an answer to the complaints and concerns, Williams launched a series of changes to make the orchestra members feel more gratified when playing in the Pops. Some of the changes were dimming the hall's lights and making the table service during the concerts less noisy and disturbing by providing waiters with rubber-soled shoes and the tables with soft tops.[26] The biggest innovation was a new clause, which would allow BSO players to opt not to play in the Pops, thus transforming the orchestra into a more motivated and cooperative group.[27] Williams also carried on with his policy of featuring musically interesting, high quality arrangements, with reciprocally satisfying results: "The biggest thrill I've gotten out of Boston is when some players have come to me after the season and said, 'That was great, we had a real stretch, and the brass players had a wonderful blow, and we got to Tanglewood [BSO's Summer season] in better shape than ever before, because of what the Pops repertoire was able to do for us.' That is the biggest praise I could get."[28] Musicians welcomed Williams's reconsideration and were particularly pleased with his involvement in listening to their complaints and proposals, and in trying to accommodate their needs.[29]

After the 1984 crisis, Williams led the Pops for another nine seasons, in which he disseminated the classical film-music canon through the PBS TV show *Evening at Pops*, dozens of best-selling orchestral albums, tours around the United States, and three trips to Japan (1987, 1990, 1993). At the end of the 1993 season, though, Williams left the very demanding job to concentrate more on composition and private life.[30] The *Boston Globe* music critic Richard Dyer described Williams's overall contribution: "The statistics on his tenure are pretty staggering: 13 seasons [*sic* 14], more than 300 concerts [ca. 600 in fact], six national or international tours, 24 premières and commissions, 28 CDs and nearly 50 television shows. Along the way, Williams has brought some of the leading artists of several musical worlds to the Pops. . . . Williams took from Fiedler what worked: the shape of the program, the mix of music, putting the spotlight not only on celebrities but on members of the orchestra and young musicians. Williams improved discipline and morale and raised the standard of performance."[31]

Seiji Ozawa, at that time the artistic director and conductor-in-residence of the Boston Symphony, later admitted that he had been wrong on Williams:

"Many people—I was one of them—misjudged him as a composer. . . . But I found out when I studied his pieces. His knowledge and background and training, how he does his music [demonstrates] a very high standard and deep musicianship."[32] In the 1994 season Williams agreed to lead the Pops during the transition period as its conductor emeritus, leading most of the concerts and helping the committee as a musical consultant in their search for a successor.[33] In 1995 Keith Lockhart was named twentieth conductor-in-residence of the Boston Pops, while Williams has since maintained a steady relationship with the institution, appearing several times each year with the title of "Boston Pops Laureate Conductor."

Williams's Multimedia Experiments

Since his retirement, Williams has specialized in multimedia forms of concert presentation, which has become the trademark of his concerts. Film clips are projected onto a big screen above the stage as the orchestra plays the related music live. The resulting experience is one that combines the live music performance with the visual or audio-visual pre-recorded medium; in these concerts the sound track is generally completely discarded from the projected clips, but sometimes parts of the dialogue or sound effects are kept and played through the hall's sound system. Williams has since become perhaps the most accomplished conductor of multimedia film-music presentations.

Film music, performed as concert piece, progresses from an ancillary to a leading role, allowing the listeners to concentrate on the music without the distractions from the images and the other elements of the sound track. On the other hand, in such a setting film music loses part of its essence. When film music is separated from its visual counterpart, one cannot fully appreciate the specific work beyond the strictly musical one. A good film composer has to be not only a good musician but also as precise as the finest tailor while "measuring" and "cutting" the music onto the film, and as acute and visual-sensitive as a portraitist while he "paints" on the musical canvas what he sees on the screen. Restoring this audiovisual coupling in the concert halls may prove a good way to enhance the experience and provide a truly "specific" concert presentation of film music.

Although cases of audio-visual film concerts have been occurring since the early nineties (e.g., the 1992 *David Lean Tribute* at the Royal Albert Hall in London conducted by Maurice Jarre), Williams and the Boston Pops have been regularly performing such "multimedia film music" since 1993 with unmatched synch-precision, variety, and flair. On 12 May 1993 in "A Gala Celebration for John Williams," the farewell concert for his last season as conductor of the Pops, Williams launched his experiments and surpassed in quality and virtuosity the previous attempts. During the event, he and the Hollywood actor Richard Dreyfuss teamed up to treat the audience with a special surprise: a demonstration of how film music works. After a few introductory words by Dreyfuss, the barrel chase sequence from *Jaws* was screened without music. The same footage was then screened again, but this time with music, performed live and in perfect synch. Following this, a spectacular eight-minute medley of Williams's most famous themes from *Star Wars* to *Superman* to *Indiana Jones* to *E.T.* was played, accompanied by clips from the related films.

Particularly spectacular are those cases, like the barrel chase sequence, in which an entire scene or sequence from a film is presented with its original score played live. The re-creation of the audiovisual coupling that once happened in the controlled and secluded setting of the recording stage—where retakes are possible and frequent in case of lost synchronization—is now reenacted in the "unsafe" setting of the concert stage, before an audience, without the possibility of adjusting a bad synchronization. Apart from the music, the evocative images, and the consistent audio-visual blend, much of the spectacular experience is given by the high-wire-stunt quality of such virtuoso synch-playing. Examples from the Boston Pops's programs are the *Finale from E.T.*, the *Flying Sequence from Superman*, and a series of dance pieces—the "Singin' in the Rain" scene, the "I Like Myself" roller-skating dance from *It's Always Fair Weather* (Stanley Donen, Gene Kelly, 1955), the Gene Kelly–Jerry Mouse dance from *Anchors Aweigh* (George Sidney, 1945), the "Barnyard Dance" from *Seven Brides for Seven Brothers* (Stanley Donen, 1954), Fred Astaire's ceiling dance to the notes of "You're All the World to Me" from *Royal Wedding* (Stanley Donen, 1951), the Nicholas Brothers's tap dance numbers from *Orchestra Wives* (Archie Mayo, 1942), *Sun Valley Serenade* (H. Bruce Humberstone, 1941), and *Down Argentine Way* (Irving Cummings, 1940). During these multimedia concert presentations, the orchestra accompanies seamlessly the dancers' moves and hits flawlessly each synch-point and music-visual twist: generally the dancers dance to the music, but here the music plays to the dancers.

On 16 March 2002, on the occasion of the twentieth anniversary of *E.T. the Extra-Terrestrial*, Williams extended this extraordinary multimedia presentation to an entire film. With the Recording Arts Orchestra of Los Angeles, he conducted the full score live throughout the film, something often performed with silent films but unheard of with such a complex and musically rich sound film. Another offspring of Williams's duodecennial experiments in multimedia is the *Star Wars in Concert*, a multimedia road show similar in size to big rock-music tours. It features music from the double trilogy performed by the Royal Philharmonic Orchestra and Chorus conducted by Dirk Brossé. The package is complemented by *Star Wars*'s C3-PO Antony Daniels as narrator, projected clips from the films, smoke and laser-light effects, and a coherently spaceship-shaped stage. Since its debut on 1 October 2009, the show has been successfully touring throughout America and Europe.[34]

Williams's Legacy

After his retirement, Williams's innovations and the repertoire he built during his tenure are still part of the Boston Pops concerts. Film music remains a staple of the Pops programs, as well as multimedia presentations. In 2006 a fixed panoramic screen—covering all the length of the stage—was installed in Boston Symphony Hall, replacing the temporary "Film Night" setting. Now an integral "multimedia" part of the Pops stage, the screen is also used by the present Pops conductor Keith Lockhart for multimedia performance of non-film-music too, in order to enhance the experience.[35]

John Williams's conductorship of the Boston Pops and his commitment to legitimize film music in concerts have had a large influence on other orchestras as well. As for other Pops orchestras in the United States, an evident increase in their number and activities during and particularly following Williams's tenure is evident.[36] In particular, the Cincinnati Pops and the Hollywood Bowl Orchestra—the former launched during the last years of Fiedler's tenure and the latter established in the last years of Williams's—are both very active in the promotion and live presentations of film music.

The Cincinnati Pops (founded in 1977) is second only to the Boston Pops as far as television and record-market exposure and international reputation. Its founder, Erich Kunzel, appeared thirty-seven times as a guest conductor of the Boston Pops between 1977 and 2009, and followed the Bostonian model closely in his establishment of the Cincinnati Pops. A candidate for the Boston Pops conductorship after Fiedler's death, Kunzel was considered as a successor to John Williams in 1994.[37] In 1984 he recorded his first film-music album *Star Tracks*, devoted to Williams's music for *Star Wars*, *Superman*, *Close Encounters of the Third Kind*, *Raiders of the Lost Ark*, and *E.T.*, all in the wake of the commercial success of Williams and the Pops's 1980 space-music album *Pops in Space*.[38] In 2005, on the release of the last episode of the second *Star Wars* trilogy, Kunzel conducted a series of concerts centered on Williams's scores for the six films.[39]

The Hollywood Bowl Orchestra was founded in 1991, and its conductor-ship given to John Mauceri, who had regularly appeared as a guest conductor of the Boston Pops (twenty-six times between 1979 and 1994). The main mission of the Hollywood Bowl Orchestra was to perform Pops concerts at the Hollywood Bowl and to record albums with Philips Classics. Mauceri soon proved to be in line with Williams's belief that each genre of music requires respect and care, and that film music is a legitimate repertoire for concerts. In Mauceri's first album with the orchestra (*Hollywood Dreams*), pieces from the art-music repertoire are presented side by side with film music, with composers spanning from Arnold Schoenberg, Igor Stravinsky, and Sergei Prokofiev to Williams, Max Steiner, Alfred Newman, Erich Wolfgang Korngold, John Barry, Franz Waxman, Leonard Bernstein, and even selections from *The Wizard of Oz* (Victor Fleming, 1939, music by Harold Arlen and Herbert Stothart). Mauceri also shares with Williams the same philological accuracy and search for the originals when dealing with film music.[40]

As for minor orchestras, film music has increasingly become a frequent feature in their programs. Beginning in November 1991, *Film Score Monthly* has had a column listing all the concerts featuring film music all around the world.[41] The variety that can be perceived reading through the issues of the magazine is far too wide to be reported here, although a few cases may be enough to attest to the better acceptance of film music in concert after Williams's example: A film-music concert was held during the Atlanta Olympics in 1996, on 26 July;[42] a prestigious tribute to the classical Hollywood composers was paid by the U.S. Postal Service with the issue of six commemorative stamps portraying Max Steiner, Erich Wolfgang Korngold, Alfred Newman, Franz Waxman, Bernard Herrmann, and Dimitri Tiomkin in the Legends of American Music series, thus acknowledging Hollywood film music as an important part of the American heritage;[43] on 11 September 2004 Michael Tilson Thomas opened the symphonic season of the San Francisco Symphony Orchestra with a program featuring Bernard Herrmann's suite from *Vertigo* (Alfred Hitchcock, 1958) along with Debussy's *La Mer* (1905), Copland's *Danzón Cubano* (1942), and Gershwin's *An American in Paris* (1928).[44]

Abroad as well, one can observe many signs of a "détente" in the so-called cold war between applied film music and absolute art music. In 1992 Zubin Mehta and the Israel Philharmonic recorded Franz Waxman's *Carmen Fantasy* from his film score for *Humoresque* (Jean Negulesco, 1946); in London, the Royal Academy of Music in collaboration with the British Film Institute dedicated the eleventh edition of the "International Composers Festival" to film music (16–22 June 1996);[45] in 2004 the London Symphony Orchestra celebrated the first centennial of the "powerful relationship between music and the movies" with an American tour presenting film music concerts;[46] in Italy, on 10 October

2004, Leonard Rosenman conducted the Roma Sinfonietta at the "Parco della Musica" in Rome in a program of his own film works; in Leipzig, Germany, the prestigious Gewandhausorchester played Bernard Herrmann's film works on 23 January 1998;[47] in Spain, on 4 and 7 November 1998, Jerry Goldsmith was invited to conduct two concerts in Seville with the Real Orquesta Sinfónica.[48] In Warsaw, Poland, Elmer Bernstein was invited to conduct a concert on 25 May 2000 within the "Viva Arts Festival";[49] and on 8 June 2010 the Wiener Philharmoniker played a suite from *Star Wars* along with music by Josef Strauss, Liszt, and Holst during their annual "Sommernachtskonzert" outdoor concert in the park of the Schönbrunn castle. If one reads through the archives of the London's famous BBC Proms, he will notice an increasing presence of film music alongside concert pieces from the canonical repertoire.[50]

As for Williams, after his retirement from the Pops he has remained an active conductor and an indefatigable advocate of film music in concert programs. He is a regular guest conductor for the major American orchestras, and in addition to his longtime annual appearances at the Hollywood Bowl with the Los Angeles Philharmonic, Williams has enjoyed steadfast collaborations with the New York Philharmonic and the Chicago Symphony, bringing film music to those prestigious concert stages too. In particular, beginning with the 2003/2004 season (curiously enough, the same season of Williams's debut at the Symphony Center in Chicago) the Chicago Symphony started a series of recurring events devoted to film music: "Friday Night at the Movies."[51] In 1996 Williams was invited to conduct a concert at the Royal Academy of Music in London; in 1998 he held a film-music composition seminar at the revered Tanglewood Music Center;[52] in 2003 he collaborated with Leonard Slatkin, the conductor of the National Symphony Orchestra in Washington at that time, in the organization of a film music festival in Washington, DC, titled "Soundtrack: Music and Film." The festival ran from 21 January to 1 February and consisted of six film-music concerts, conferences, and panel discussions moderated and animated by Slatkin and Williams themselves and by the film-music historian Jon Burlingame and the famed film director Stanley Donen.[53] Two concerts in the series were centered on and conducted by Williams. Others concerts were titled "Music and Film: Made in Hollywood, USA," which focused on the Hollywood classical composers, and "Music and Film: The European Aesthetic," which dealt with European film composers like Dmitri Shostakovich, William Walton, Sergei Prokofiev, and Camille Saint-Saëns, this last represented by his 1908 score for *L'Assassinat du duc de Guise*. One evening offered the projection of *Metropolis* (Fritz Lang, 1927) accompanied live with a compilation score from the classical repertoire. Of particular interest was the program "In Synch: How Do They Do It?," a sort of concert/conference on the specificities of composing for films and on the technicalities of the music/images synchronization, with Williams and Slatkin giving practical demonstrations.[54] In 2009 Gustavo Dudamel, the newly appointed artistic director of the Los Angeles Philharmonic, invited Williams to conduct three film-music concerts, in the first part of the symphonic season, titled "Music from the City of Angels," acknowledging Hollywood film music as a major Los Angeles contribution to the music repertoire.

In 1993 the *Boston Globe* music critic Richard Dyer noted: "The main reason Williams took the job in 1980 was to win greater recognition for the artistic legitimacy of his life work in film and the life work of many of his colleagues. Whether he succeeded in that aim (it's too early to tell), he certainly brought film music out of the background and into the limelight. Now people can judge for themselves. And other pops concerts all across the country have followed his example."[55] Twenty years later, it is safe to say that Williams did indeed succeed in his aim.

John Williams's conductorship of the Boston Pops has been widely influential in bringing the film-music repertoire to the fore in concert programs. As an integral part of Williams's commitment to revive the classical Hollywood music, this facet of his double life as a composer/conductor has also been seminal in the creation and acknowledgment of a canon of the Hollywood music classics. What the conductor Charles Gerhardt had done in the 1970s in the record market, promoting the Hollywood classics as a legitimate repertoire for symphonic albums in his successful RCA series *Classic Film Scores*, Williams did in the 1980s in the concert programs. Probably no one else has done more to legitimize and give film music a better recognition in concert halls than John Williams.

Conclusion

I t seems appropriate at this point to offer some concise reflections on and questions about present Hollywood film scores.

How Has Neoclassicism Influenced the Music Style in Contemporary Cinema?

As previously explained, the impact of neoclassicism was quite limited. Jeff Smith stated: "And despite a major revival in the Korngold-styled scores of John Williams, Romanticism's hold on film scoring was further weakened by the incorporation of rock, folk, and soul elements in the 1960s and 1970s, and electronics, minimalism, and even New Age elements in the 1980s. By the 1990s, Romantic-styled film music was still being composed, but it was merely one stylistic option among many."[1]

Laurent Jullier identifies in what he calls "film-concert" a predominant characteristic of contemporary cinema, which consists in "the prevailing of the sound dimension over the visual one: the sound track embraces the viewer and occupies the frequency spectrum almost entirely; coming out from loudspeakers, the sound track plunges the audience into a sound atmosphere from which it is impossible to escape."[2] Contrary to what could be expected, though, the role of music in the contemporary Hollywood "film-concert" is anything but dominant. Music is undoubtedly found in large quantities, but it is given a minor role, mostly used as a mere kind of binder of or supplement to the sound-effect track.

During the classical period, the sound-effect track was the third element of the sound track, less important than dialogue and music, since monaural technology and analogical systems made it infeasible to have many tracks simultaneously in the sound mix.[3] In contemporary cinema, however, the sound-effect track holds a prominent position in the sound design. This supremacy is encouraged by the huge potential of digital processing and the many technologies of sound diffusion that can create a surrounding and hyper-realistic aural "super-field" not only in theaters but also in home theaters.[4] Therefore, music itself has mostly been pushed down to the third, lowest position in the sound track. The composer Danny Elfman, whose scores for *Batman* (Tim Burton, 1989) and *Dick Tracy* (Warren Beatty, 1990) follow a neoclassical approach, is one of those who have complained about this phenomenon: "Contemporary dubs to my ears are getting busier and more shrill every year. The dubbers actually think they're doing a great job for the music if a crescendo or a horn blast occasionally pops through the wall of sound."[5]

What Are the Consequences of Music Being Placed Lower Down on the Agenda in Terms of Film Music Style?

Contemporary film music is typically lacking in hues and details; its form has become less structurally solid and less musically interesting, and has lost some of the formal functions of the previous styles. In uneven competition with the sound-effect track and struggling to resist its hegemony, now music concentrates on the micro-emotive function (e.g., creating sentimentalism in love scenes or anxiety in horror films) and on the temporal perceptive function (e.g., increasing the perception of fast pace in action scenes through the use of loud percussions and sharp rhythmic *ostinatos*). The cognitive function, which requires moments of acoustic foregrounding of the music in order to suggest thematic connotations or narrative implications, is barely possible with the contemporary sound mix in which music is, for the most part, drowned out. Even the classical macro-emotive function, in which music as a frame signals the boundaries of the narrative, seems to have disappeared. This is due to the obsolescence of opening-title sequences and their musical "overtures" that used to set up the narrative frame: in contemporary cinema, all the titles and credits tend to be concentrated at the end of the film. In addition, the leitmotiv technique, which used to build a thematic network throughout the film and bind the overall musical structure, has been mostly discarded.[6] Finally, the use of non-diegetic songs both within the narrative and over the end-titles sequence for sheer economic motivations—an element of the modern style adopted by the eclectic style—is certainly a good way to promote records but a poor one to give the film's musical structure a congruent closing frame.

As to techniques and dialect, the sound-effect track rarely gives enough aural room for leitmotivic development or theme-and-variation treatment. In terms of musical writing, in contemporary film music melodies are essentially homophonic, counterpoint is almost extinct (there is no need to use such refined a technique if music is bound to get covered by a noisy flood of sound effects), and music is often a formless and superficial color varnish or a mere rhythmic pattern that backs the sound-effect track. The symphony orchestra as a musical means seems to be the only neoclassical element that has really had some influence on contemporary Hollywood film music. Nonetheless, the musical language is often anything but symphonic. Rather, it sounds more like a kind of orchestral arrangement of techno/rock music. Padded with synthesizers and boosted with an enlarged percussion section, the symphony orchestra is still in use because it can produce a loud and massive sound, which can compete with the sound-effects volume and thus contribute to the characteristic aural saturation of the "film-concert."

The weakening of the musical language is also a consequence of the technological progress of synthesizers and music software. MIDI technology allows a keyboard to be connected to a computer, which directly transcribes the music as one plays. Moreover, computer-composed music can be cut, pasted, transposed, and transformed with great rapidity and less effort. Therefore, the whole process of composition is enormously quickened. Warner Bros.'s cofounder Jack Warner's motto "I don't want it good. I want it Tuesday" is proverbial as to the producers' typical preference for efficiency over quality. Under Jack Warner, in the classical studio system, composers were generally required to write a score in eight to ten weeks;[7] these days, two-hour-long scores can be commissioned within a three- to four-week deadline.[8]

Apart from the tightest deadlines, the use of computers has had a negative influence on the quality of composition, because it allows poorly trained or completely untrained musicians, often with the most diverse and unorthodox backgrounds, to write music. With the help of computers, many orchestrators and arrangers (who can definitely be called ghostwriters in these cases), musicians who would not be able to write music in the traditional way, become composers of "symphonic" music. Hans Zimmer, a self-taught keyboardist with a background in rock music and whose specialty is scoring action films, can be considered the epitome of contemporary eclecticism. His music is a kind of rock/techno arranged for symphony orchestra by a team of collaborators, arrangers, and orchestrators. Zimmer is famous for having founded Media Ventures, later renamed Remote Control Productions, a firm specializing in film scores co-written by a pool of musicians, a sort of factory where Zimmer seems to act more as an executive producer and coordinator than as a composer.[9] His idiom can be recognized by simple motifs characterized by homophony, basic chord progressions, no contrapuntal writing or use of inner voices, synthesizer pads as harmonic backing for the acoustical instruments, a pounding rhythmic section, and overwhelming low frequencies. Like techno music, all these elements have a strong, visceral, and immediate impact on the listener. The results are effective but are all quite similar to each other, regardless of whether the narrative is set in San Francisco in the late twentieth century: *The Rock* (Michael Bay, 1996); during World War II: *Pearl Harbor* (Michael Bay, 2001); in the Caribbean of the eighteenth century: *Pirates of the Caribbean: Dead Man's Chest* (Gore Verbinsky, 2006); or in ancient Rome: *Gladiator* (Ridley Scott, 2000). In *Pirates of the Caribbean: On Stranger Tides* (Rob Marshall, 2011) Hans Zimmer is credited as the film's composer, but if we read through the end credits, we can spot as many as seven "additional music" composers. Another sign of the state of the art of contemporary Hollywood music can be noticed in Zimmer's score for *Sherlock Holmes: A Game of Shadows* (Guy Ritchie, 2011). The single music piece that stands out for having a superior musical quality and harmonic richness can be heard in the wedding scene: if one reads the end credits, he will found out that the piece is drawn from Ennio Morricone's score for *Two Mules for Sister Sara* (Don Siegel, 1970). Moreover, in the sequence at the Opéra de Paris, the diegetic performance of Mozart's *Don Giovanni* is also "Zimmerized," Mozart's original score having being given a thicker and louder reorchestration. Today, Zimmer is one the most successful and sought-after Hollywood composers. His music is very direct and has no virtuoso-writing pretensions that would require aural foregrounding; he employs instead visceral and pulsating rhythms along with basic melodies with uncomplicated textures that act as a background to the sound effects' starring role. Zimmer's music blends perfectly with the aggressive sound design of contemporary cinema.

In the 1980s James Horner was an emerging classically trained composer, showing neoclassical traits and being one of those practitioners who did not compose with the help of computers. He distinguished himself with such outstanding scores as *Star Trek: The Wrath of Khan* (Nicholas Meyer, 1982); *Krull* (Peter Yates, 1983); *Aliens* (James Cameron, 1986); and *Willow* (Ron Howard, 1988). In the 1990s, he wrote a subtle cool jazz-like score featuring Branford Marsalis's saxophone for the comedy/thriller *Sneakers* (Phil Alden Robinson, 1992); he provided a richly melodic score for the ghost comedy *Casper* (Brad Silberling, 1995), which presents touching piano solos, comical Prokofiev-like marches, atmospheric ghost music, and heroic Korngoldian fanfares; he penned the epic, Scottish-flavored score for *Braveheart* (Mel Gibson, 1995, performed by the London Symphony Orchestra). However, after the success of *Titanic* (James

Cameron, 1997) and the song "My Heart Will Go On," Horner appears to have retreated from his neoclassical outpost and opted for the secure shelter of "modern-style" commercial songs as pièce de résistance of the music track, as in *The Mask of Zorro* (Martin Campbell, 1998); *A Beautiful Mind* (Ron Howard, 2001); *Troy* (Wolfgang Petersen, 2004); and *Avatar* (James Cameron, 2009). Lately, Horner seems to be specializing in spectacular but mostly repetitious and often self-plagiarized lengthy scores delivered upon incredibly short notice, as for *Troy*, which he composed in less than a month after Gabriel Yared's dismissal.[10] At the same time, his recent interviews reveal a resigned disillusionment toward his own job.[11]

The weakness of the neoclassical trend can also be seen in the fact that even George Lucas and Steven Spielberg, whose films marked the birth of this movement, partially conformed to the poetics of contemporary cinema. Despite their continuing to work with Williams, both Lucas and Spielberg followed the musical trend of the moment. Spielberg appointed Hans Zimmer as head of the film-music department of his film studio, DreamWorks SKG, a choice that hardly seems to promote neoclassicism.[12] In the new *Star Wars* trilogy, particularly in *Star Wars: Episode III—Revenge of the Sith* (George Lucas, 2005), music has been given less importance in the new audio mix than in the previous trilogy. In action scenes the music is drowned out by the overwhelming flood of sound effects: two hundred audio tracks constitute the starting point for the final mix.[13] During a lecture at the Thornton School of Music of the University of Southern California, Williams talked about the musical difficulties in coping with the seventeen-minute-long noisy battle at the beginning of that film.[14] Moreover, the making-of documentary on *Star Wars: Episode III* shows Kenneth Wannberg—Williams's longtime music editor—at the mixing console complaining about the excessive volume of the sound-effect track and trying to advocate a more relevant role for music: "It's noisy. I think the music should live a little bit more than it does. I mean, it just gets wiped out. The music is kind of a thread through that whole montage of cutting back and forth. . . . And it just gets lost."[15]

Lucas not only followed the new trend but also altered the sound balance of the classic trilogy. He tinkered with the first three films of the *Star Wars* saga in order to re-release them in theaters in 1997 and on DVD in 2004. These versions, characterized by new CGI shots and various digital corrections, have received many complaints from the fans and caused the general perplexity of critics.[16] John Williams's score was severely compromised, marginalized by a new audio mix, which gave such a predominant role to the new sound effects that the original music track is muffled in many points. One reviewer writes that "John

Williams' awe-inspiring *Star Wars* score has been severely mishandled on the new DVD,"[17] and a brief research on the Internet shows how fans and critics are generally baffled and discontented:

> While you're at it, find the original six-channel soundtrack released in theaters (or the two channel . . . how about both?) and properly remaster it into a loss-less surround format without "enhancing" it. I want to feel that magnificent brass theme rip my face off at the opening moment of the first film and hear the perfectly transparent string section soar during the beautiful final scene of Empire.[18]

> There is, however, one change I can't stomach, and it has to do with the music. During the first part of the Death Star battle at the end of the film, John Williams' score has been reduced in prominence in the sound mix. This is particularly obvious right as the X-Wings make their dive down to the surface to begin the attack—the familiar "Force Theme" trumpet fanfare is now almost inaudible. Lucasfilm says this was a deliberate creative decision and I absolutely hate it.[19]

> The familiar Force theme trumpet fanfare that used to play right after Red Leader says: "This is it!" and just as the X-wings start diving towards the Death Star's surface has been dialed back in volume so that it's almost inaudible—it's almost completely buried in the surround mix. . . . Possibly most critically, John Williams' entire score for the film has been flipped in the rear channels, so that what should be the left rear channel is playing from the right rear channel (and vice versa). . . . The sound effects definitely sound like they've been ratcheted up a LOT, to the point that they now overwhelm the dialogue and the music in a lot of scenes.[20]

There have been so many protests that in 2006 Lucas decided to release a two-disc DVD set including both the 2004 "enhanced" version and the 1977 original one.[21] A comparison between the two versions does indeed show Lucas's choice to follow the contemporary trend, that is, giving more importance to the sound-effect track than to the music track.

Neoclassical scores in contemporary cinema are few.[22] The most recent examples are both Williams's: *Indiana Jones and the Kingdom of the Crystal Skull* (Steven Spielberg, 2008) and *The Adventures of Tintin* (Steven Spielberg, 2011). Even if it has a leitmotivic network, Howard Shore's majestic symphonic tapestry for *The Lord of the Rings* trilogy (Peter Jackson, 2001/2002/2003) does not perform a spatial perceptive function to such an extent as to be defined neoclassical. Moreover, it is simply an exception for a composer that is otherwise not famous for being neoclassical, as his scores for David Cronenberg's films clearly show.

What Is the Importance of This Neoclassical Trend Initiated and Led by Williams?

If the influence on contemporary musical style has been limited and circumscribed to the most superficial traits of Williams's work, such as the use of the symphony orchestra and the thickness of the orchestral sound, the importance of neoclassicism consists in having drawn attention to the classical Hollywood musical heritage. Apart from his commercial success and artistic achievements, John Williams is a key figure in cinema and film-music history for his seminal role in bringing the classic Hollywood music style and its canon into the limelight, to the attention and consideration of both the audience and the scholars. The growing rediscovery of Korngold, Steiner, and Rózsa in the last three decades is also due to the fact that Williams, as a composer, revived some elements of their works in a period in which they were considered outdated; at the same time, as a conductor, he programmed the best of the film-music repertoire in a time when it was still strongly out of favor in concert halls. The importance of John Williams's contribution has been perhaps more historical than stylistic. He has restored dignity to a neglected facet of the Hollywood tradition. Scholars and critics should put aside individual tastes and ideological biases and acknowledge John Williams's fundamental contribution to film-music history. As Lionel Newman—Alfred Newman's brother and a film composer of the classical period in his own right—once stated: "But his biggest contribution may have been to make people aware of the importance of music to films."[23]

The contemporary French composer Bruno Coulais wrote: "John Williams is the last survivor of Hollywood music," which might be true indeed.[24] Without any successor to follow in his footsteps, John Williams seems to be the only heir of the classical style of Korngold and Steiner, the very last survivor of the Hollywood music tradition. At least, until another skilled and trained enough "neo-neoclassical" composer appears on Hollywood's horizon.

Appendix 1: Completing the Picture

Williams's Versatility for Spielberg (and Others)

Neoclassicism is the style mostly associated with John Williams. However, he also possesses a chameleon-like ability to write in a number of diverse musical dialects and to adjust his personal idiom to the requirements of the film at hand:

> When I do a film . . . I'm not thinking about stylistic purity; I'm not thinking about anything but, "Okay, here's a film and my musical job is to construct something that will live within it and seem to be part of it and will sound like the picture looks." If I have to write a scene from

Jane Eyre for instance, I write something that sounds like Yorkshire in the eighteen-sixties. Why? Not because I'm trying to write original music, but because I'm trying to get something behind the picture that smells like Yorkshire. You don't think about that when you watch the movie, but somehow you're very comfortable because it's *right*. . . . If you have only one style of music and do only one thing . . . you're in trouble in the film business. If you want to have a career in films, and do a hundred films, you need to be very versatile.[1]

For example, Williams employed contemporary dialects and musical means in *Heartbeeps* (Allan Arkush, 1981) and *Space Camp* (Harry Winer, 1986). In the former, he used synthesizers and mixed them with his trademark orchestral sound; in the latter, he adopted both synthesizers and 1980s pop-music dialects. Later, he also ventured into Asian dialects for *Seven Years in Tibet* (Jean-Jacques Annaud, 1997), for which he blended a Tibetan chorus and Eastern scales with a Western romantic main theme featuring Yo-Yo Ma's lyrical cello solos. Williams would explore Asian dialects again—this time more deeply and substantially—for *Memoirs of a Geisha* (Rob Marshall, 2005). *Variety* reporter Jon Burlingame described the process: "The challenge of *Geisha* . . . was 'to incorporate the grammar of Japanese music with what we recognize as Western harmonic and melodic idioms—to bring those two things together to create a third element that would seem at home in the film.' Throughout, the score is flavored with traditional Japanese instruments: the 13-stringed koto, or Japanese zither; the shakuhachi, an end-blown bamboo flute; the shamisen, a three-stringed plucked lute; taiko drums; plus other wind and percussion instruments appropriate to the setting."[2]

That same year, Williams also worked on a completely different score for *Munich* (Steven Spielberg, 2005), switching to Middle Eastern timbres and scales. Williams told *Variety*:

"It couldn't be more different from *Geisha* in ambiance and texture." For it, he created "a kind of prayer for peace, a lyrical composition associated with Avner (Eric Bana) and the home he leaves behind in Israel," and another theme for solo voice and orchestra "that accompanies one of several flashbacks to the tarmac at Munich, and also one of several scenes that recall the abduction of the Olympic athletes from their rooms at the Olympic Village" in 1972. Lisbeth Scott, the vocalist on *The Passion of the Christ*, is the soloist. Searching for an authentic Palestinian sound, Williams employed the oud, a Middle Eastern lute, and added the cimbalom, a Hungarian zither, as well as clarinet and strings for "an almost fantastically Oriental quality," he says.[3]

The Spielberg/Williams Collaboration

In tracing the main trajectories of Williams's career, an appropriate starting point is certainly his collaboration with Steven Spielberg, surely the longest lasting, and perhaps also the most prominent, successful, artistically homogeneous and harmonious relationship between a director and a composer. Says Spielberg:

> I usually try to give him the book or the script to go on. Sometimes he reads it and sometimes he doesn't, depending on how busy he is. What John prefers to do is just talk a lot with me, before I even make the movie—about what the picture's about and how I see it. Then after I'm finished with the picture, I show John a very rough assembly. And then John, without really needing to hear any more from me because the film pretty much says it all, goes off and writes his themes. Then he performs sketches of the themes for me on the piano. I usually fall in love with all of his themes. I've often made a fool of myself sitting there weeping, hanging over the piano after he's played me something, either from *E.T.* or *Schindler's List.* Or I just admire what he's done. More often than not, the first thing he plays me is what goes into the movie. . . . I don't think there's been a single moment where we've had a disagreement about music. We certainly have a high regard for each other, but I just think that's about Johnny hitting the target in an uncanny way. . . . I call him Max. As a matter of fact, when I named my first child Max, that came from a nickname that I gave Johnny from the first time we met. It's a joke that sometimes his music reminded me of Max Steiner. And he would always laugh, so I got to calling him Max.[4]

Spielberg also remarked, "Without question, John Williams has been the single most significant contributor to my success as a film-maker."[5]

Williams, in turn, speaks in these terms of his longtime associate: "I've been lucky to work with Steven because he loves music. Some directors feel as though they've failed if they need lots of music. It's cosmetic, even unwanted. Spielberg's aesthetic is a very fanciful one and is comfortable in the presence of music, so his pictures always offer the opportunity for lots of music."[6]

Close Encounters of the Third Kind
(1977)

The duo's third project, this is one of the most outstanding examples of combination and interplay of film and music in film history, and one of their finest achievements. The screenplay required that humans and aliens communicate through musical signals, in particular, through a five-note pattern, which served as the musical identification of the mostly unseen aliens—as the *ostinato* did for the rubber shark in *Jaws*. Since the five-note signal was so central to the narrative and had to be ready before the shooting phase, Williams and Spielberg began working on the music long before the production started—something uncommon in Hollywood practice. In a 2009 interview, Williams said:

> Well, *Close Encounters* is, in my experience at least, unique. The five-note motif that you mentioned was the result of a lot of experimentation, meeting with my friend Steven Spielberg. I think I wrote about 300-plus examples of five notes starting with all on one note and with no rhythmic variation, just intervallic, that is to say pitch differences. And we settled on this one [five-note motif from the film] for whatever reasons. . . . It wasn't even a theme. It was more like a signal to incorporate in the orchestral material. . . . And I kept trying to say to Mr. Spielberg, "I need more than five notes to make this point. It isn't enough." And his point to me was, "It should not be a melody. It should be a signal." . . . So it was an interesting exercise for me in getting to the point, absolute minimal number of syllables, words, to use a literary analogy, perhaps, of saying it all in three words instead of allowing yourself five.[7]

Although completed in the same year, the score for *Close Encounters of the Third Kind* is diametrically opposite to that for *Star Wars*. As the latter is overtly romantic and exuberantly melodic, so the former is dissonant and avant-gardist. Its structure is an inventive musical journey from atonality to tonality. It begins with Pendereckian avant-garde tone-clusters, then moves to Schönberg's expressionist atonalism, then to Debussy's impressionism, and finally reaches a late-romantic tonal grand finale à la Richard Strauss. The score closely follows the gradual evolution of how earthlings perceive the arrival of the extraterrestrial visitors. At the beginning, the extraterrestrials are perceived as an unknown threat, then they are recognized as friendly messengers: "It starts really when the extra-terrestrials appear from the mother-ship: here the tone-clusters involve all the twelve notes of the chromatic scale. Then you take one strand away, then another, so the music grows more and more consonant, until you end up with a pure, liturgical E major."[8]

1941
(1979)

This film is a parody of war films and deals with the fear of a possible Japanese invasion spreading hysterically in Los Angeles after the Pearl Harbor attack. In this zany film, music itself is zany and excessive, flaunting a parodic tongue-in-cheek spirit, which helps the narration mock many targets. The heroic machismo of the war genre is spoofed with the bombastic march associated with Wild Bill Kelso, the deranged pilot played by John Belushi. Williams stated, "I felt, and Steven did also, that certain characters, I think especially John Belushi, should be characterized by a typical World War II American march, of the kind that I grew up with as a child and played with even in school. And that march has a kind of jazzy, almost southern swagger to it . . . and the accents are tilted and the synch-ups are a little bit off, and it's a little bit impertinent in its character."[9] The 1940s dance music, particularly Benny Goodman's "Sing, Sing, Sing" became "Swing, Swing, Swing" in Williams's piece for the jitterbug contest scene at the USO.[10]

Old Hollywood romantic music is also given a memorable parodic treatment. In the first act, a Japanese sailor sees a naked blonde girl clinging to the periscope of his submarine; when he excitedly points at her, screaming "Hollywood!" we hear an old-fashioned passionate melody for strings and horns that mocks Steiner's melodramatic music. Steiner is again the target of more tributes and parodies. When Wild Bill Kelso puffs his cigar, a synchronized upward harp glissando replicates the rising smoke just like Steiner's score does for an identical action in *The Informer* (John Ford, 1935). Another tribute to Steiner is the use of the German anthem *Das Deutschlandlied* to characterize the Nazi captain von Kleinschmidt, as Steiner did in *Casablanca* (Michael Curtiz, 1942) for Major Strasser. Like the film itself, the score also has a number of nods to other films. The traditional Irish polka "The Rakes of Mallow" is the basis for the music accompanying the fight at the USO, and it was similarly used by Victor Young for the fight scenes in *The Quiet Man* (John Ford, 1952). Moreover, the beginning of the film includes a self-quotation of *Jaws* on the part of both the director and the composer. When a blonde girl removes her clothes and takes a night swim in the sea, we hear the famous low-pitched *ostinato* emerging from the silence, this time to surprisingly announce the arrival of a Japanese submarine.[11]

E.T. the Extra-Terrestrial
(1982)

This film concerns the friendship between a boy and an extra-terrestrial, and is another masterpiece of Williams and Spielberg. The music is sentimental, tender, and emotional; harp, strings, and woodwinds are the prevailing orchestral colors. Music is the major force in turning what could have been a teenage sentimental film set in the Los Angeles suburbs into a poignant and universally affecting love story, as Williams explains: "In *E.T.* . . . there's a theme for the little alien creature and for the little boy, Elliott, who finds and hides him, and that theme is kind of like a love theme. It's not sensual in the way a love theme would be, but it develops as their relationship develops."[12] The "Flying Theme" from *E.T. the Extra-Terrestrial* is one of Williams's most famous creations. It perfectly captures the miraculous power of friendship and love, and tangibly conveys the feeling of flying:

> What do we have to do musically to accompany a thing like that? I looked for the melody [*he sings the melody*] . . . all these intervals reach up, up, up all the time, to stretch the musical grammar, to give this kind of feeling. And then in performance, [it's] the same thing. . . . [It requires] a kind of energy [to] make a hundred-piece symphonic orchestra feel like it's gonna come right off the floor, and not be all these heavy people playing violins. . . . You have a creature that you can fly with, that's not of our own species, but of our own spiritual oneness, that we'd come together in joy and we'd go over the moon. Fantastic idea! It needs great sweep in the music and great feeling of freedom. Freedom being in this case the loss of gravity. We speed up, speed up . . . , we will lose gravity, we're now in space, and we are finally free. And that's what the orchestra has to give us . . . [What] the composer has to give us.[13]

Following his "gradual disclosure of the main theme" technique, Williams carefully develops and gradually unveils the main theme across the first half of the film, finally presenting it in full form and in perfect timing at the moment in which Elliott and E.T.'s bicycle takes off in the night sky and flies over the moon—an iconic film/music moment—and again in the film's grand finale. "[The love theme] starts with a few notes, they look at each other—a little bit uncertain. And it grows and becomes more confident, and more lyrical as E.T. begins to communicate with the boy. At the end it's kind of a full-blown sort of operatic aria when E.T. goes away. . . . In that scene their theme or love theme . . . comes back. It's like, in a way, a moment in opera when two lovers are being separated. I build to that kind of musical denouement."[14]

The film's finale consists of fifteen minutes with continuous symphonic accompaniment, a memorable set piece that is one of the highest achievements of the art of composing for films:

> That sequence involved a lot of specific musical cues. . . . So you can imagine in the space of that 15 minutes of film how many precise musical accents are needed and how each one has to be exactly in the right place. I wrote the music mathematically to configure with each of those occurrences and worked it all out. Then when the orchestra assembled and I had the film in front of me, I made attempt after attempt to record the music to exactly all those arithmetic parameters. But I was never able to get a perfect recording that felt right musically and emotionally. I kept trying over and over again and finally, I said to Steven, "I don't think I can get this right. Maybe I need to do something else." And he said, "Why don't you take the movie off? Don't look at it. Forget the movie and conduct the orchestra the way you would want to conduct it in a concert so that the performance is just completely uninhibited by any considerations of mathematics and measurement." And I did that and all of us agreed that the music felt better. Then Steven re-edited slightly the last part of the film to configure with the musical performance that I felt was more powerful emotionally.[15]

In this case again, Spielberg reversed the standard practice and cut the film to the music, so as to achieve a perfect fusion of image and music. Williams explains, "[There is] an intimate connection between picture and music that I don't think the greatest expert in film synchronization could quite achieve. There is an ebb and flow, where the music speeds up for a few bars, then relents, the way you would conduct for a singer in an opera house. There is something visceral, organic, about the phrasing. That last 10 minutes deliver something, emotionally, that is the result of the film fitting the music, and not the other way around, I am delighted to say."[16] Williams also quoted Victor Young's love theme from *The Quiet Man*. Elliott is in telepathic connection with E.T., who is at home watching *The Quiet Man* on TV. The boy feels the urge to kiss his blonde classmate at the exact time when E.T. is watching John Wayne kiss Maureen O'Hara. The kiss is scored by quoting Young's theme, followed by an arrangement of the E.T. main theme in the manner of the old Hollywood love themes—a brief neoclassical Williams moment.

Indiana Jones and the Temple of Doom
(1984)

The second Indiana Jones film is set in India; this time Dr. Jones is not fighting the Nazis but Khali's Thuggees. The film opens with a musical extravaganza: a flamboyant dance number on Cole Porter's "Anything Goes" arranged by Williams in a full-blown MGM-like sound, and with lyrics sung in Mandarin. The score is generously tinged with exotic touches, such as the Eastern pentatonic scales in the opening Shanghai sequence, the ethnic instrumentation for the jungle and village sequences, and the Asian-flavored march associated with the slave children. The film's tone is darker than that of the first Indiana Jones film, and the music provides appropriate atonal chilling effects, as in the temple sequence, in which there is also a satanical, unremitting piece for choir and orchestra to accompany the Thuggee human sacrifice. A new heroine sides with Dr. Jones in this second adventure, and Williams consequently wrote a new love theme, similarly old-fashioned and Warner Bros.-like, but more tongue-in-cheek in its soaring sentimentalism than Marion's theme in *Raiders*.

Empire of the Sun
(1987)

After taking a break with *The Color Purple* (1985)—as producer Quincy Jones also provided the score[17]—Williams reunited with Spielberg for this World War II drama about a British boy separated from his family and interned in a prison camp after the Japanese invasion of Shanghai. Strings and wordless chorus are the predominant features of a score with a dual nature. On the one hand, Jim's drama, the separation from his parents and the harsh life in the Japanese prison camp, is scored with dissonant and "anti-emotional" music. On the other hand, Jim's dreams of flight and his contemplation of the airplanes taking off from the nearby military airport—the only bright moments in his life of incarceration—are scored with uplifting tonal music for soaring strings and celestial voices. The liberation is scored with a baroque-like piece for orchestra and chorus singing in Latin: "Exsultate justi," from Psalm 33—the piece is reprised in the end credits. The use of a hymn when Jim is finally set free is an interesting choice on Williams's part. It may fulfill a cognitive function: in earlier scenes Jim had repeatedly proclaimed his agnosticism. This particular musical choice might suggest that now he has finally found an answer to his religious search—to strengthen the point, during "Exsultate justi," food capsules are dropped by American airplanes: like manna from Heaven.

Indiana Jones and the Last Crusade
(1989)

In the third installment of the saga, Dr. Jones manages to unearth the Holy Grail and prevent the Nazis from seizing it, while also reuniting with his estranged father—brilliantly played by Sean Connery. Williams reprises the series' signature march, but the overall tone of the score is less bombastic and histrionic and more mature and restrained. One of the main points of interests is the father/son relationship, and a somewhat melancholic mood about the passing of time can be felt throughout the film. Aptly, Williams's score features a tender theme for the father/son relationship and a solemn, pastoral theme for the Grail, with touches of religious transcendence reminiscent of Wagner's "Good Friday Spell" music from *Parsifal* (1882). However, the film certainly does not lack adventure sequences scored with thrilling music. The opening circus train chase is a virtuoso Mickey-Mousing effort, having around fifty synch-points precisely hit by music within the piece's five minutes; the boat chase in Venice is sustained musically both for the action pace and for the locale, featuring picturesque Italianate mandolin solos; the motorcycle chase is scored with a driving scherzo, humorously titled "Scherzo for Motorcycle and Orchestra" in the concert version.

Always
(1989)

Concurrently, Williams provided the appropriate romantic overtones for Spielberg's remake of *A Guy Named Joe* (Victor Fleming, 1943). Anticipating *Ghost* (Jerry Zucker, 1990), *Always* is similarly about a man's untimely dying and coming back in spiritual form to console his fiancée's grief and help her to recover from the loss. Like *Ghost*, the key diegetic musical element is the two lovers' heart song, which here is Jerome Kern's "Smoke Gets in Your Eyes." Williams provides the non-diegetic music, sentimental for the romance, poignant for the two lovers' parting, and soaring/dramatic for the firefighters' daredevil flights.

Hook
(1991)

This film's idea was to pick up the story from the point in which James M. Barrie's *Peter Pan* (1911) ended, thus involving a grown-up Peter Pan (now Peter

Banning) who has repressed the memories of his past and makes a living as a dull, workaholic lawyer. When Capt. James Hook kidnaps his children, Peter has to cope with his past and travel to Neverland to rescue them. The film was originally conceived as a musical to be shot in 1985 and indeed has kept some characteristics typical of the genre: eye-catching scenery, quasi dance numbers, and a foregrounded position for the music.[18] The score covers almost the entire film. Lush and imaginative, it is one of the best examples of Williams's neoclassicism and of his fondness for the music of Erich Wolfgang Korngold. Leitmotiv and Mickey-Mousing abound, and Korngold's idiom is a constant reference for the pirate scenes, especially in the big sword fight in the final act, which is probably the best homage to Korngold's pirate music ever done. *Hook* was not as financially successful as expected and received mostly negative reviews. The overall film has formal unevenness, some occurrences of wrong casting (Rufio, for instance), and for all its scope and budget it indulges too much in childish moments. Consequently, Williams's score has not received the attention it should deserve. However, there are a few outstanding film/music moments that stand out: the flight to Neverland—featuring early Stravinskyan writing and kaleidoscopic orchestration; the arrival in the pirate town and the presenting of the hook—opening with folk fiddles, moving to Smee's comical march, and closing with Capt. Hook's pompous entrance, accompanied by his *Flying Dutchman*-like theme and Korngoldian fanfares; Peter's recollection of his childhood and the recovery of his ability to fly—a ten-minute music piece starting from Peter's frustration for not remembering his past and not being able to fly, moving through melancholia and nostalgia as Tinkerbell helps him remember his childhood, and finally bursting into a joyful celebration as Peter finds his "happy thought" and takes off.

Jurassic Park
(1993);
The Lost World: Jurassic Park
(1997)

Jurassic Park, based on Michael Crichton's 1990 best seller, made up for *Hook*'s disappointing performance by breaking all the box-office records. It concerns the inauguration of an amusement park on a tropical island whose draw is live dinosaurs, re-created though DNA engineering. For this adventure/thriller, Williams composed a multifaceted score: a jubilant fanfare is heard on the arrival to the island, as if to symbolize the victory of science over nature; majestic and almost reverent music is associated with the leviathans of ancient history—the main theme recalls a hymn, the harmony continuously alternating between the first and fourth degree of the scale, the plagal ("amen") cadence; South American percussions set the right locale for the jungle sequences—as when Dennis steals the embryos; *Rite of Spring*-like music is used for the action scenes. The score for the sequel, *The Lost World: Jurassic Park*, is decidedly more action oriented. The previous film's soaring main themes are reprised minimally—in the finale—and the score is less melodic and uplifting, and more rhythmically driving and pounding—as in the hunt sequence, or when the T-Rex visits San Diego.

Schindler's List
(1994)

Right after *Jurassic Park*, Williams and Spielberg embarked on an ambitious and completely different project. For this austere black-and-white drama about the Holocaust, Williams was assigned a demanding task: "I felt writing this film was a particularly daunting challenge; nothing could be good enough to meet a story like this. What I was most conscious of was a desire not to melodramatize . . . I felt this story required music that was gentle and loving. The orchestra of Richard Strauss, which was the orchestra of the period, would have been the wrong noise for a film like this. The main theme, I felt, should be something like a Hebraic lullaby heard at your mother's knee—not actually a lullaby, but something original, created for the film."[19] The main theme is a minor-mode piece for violin and orchestra full of dignified poignancy and sweet melancholy. Williams resorted to the Hebrew liturgy for one of the most devastating scenes, the corpses of the Jews gathered and burned over a huge pyre by Nazis: "Williams asked Rabbi [Bernard] Mehlman for a selection of appropriate texts from the Hebrew liturgy. 'He very generously made a collection for me, with translations; I chose one of them because I loved the thought it expressed: "With our lives, we give life." From this kind of horror, this kind of sacrifice, life can come. I set the words for chorus, and we recorded that in Toronto and in California.'"[20]

Amistad
(1997)

This film is set in Connecticut in the first half of the nineteenth century and concerns the issue of slavery. A court has to decide whether some Africans who mutinied their traders are indeed slaves—thus guilty of mutiny—or free men—thus perfectly entitled to mutiny as self-defense. The overall design of the score replicates the encounter between the African and the Quaker American culture presented in the film. Two pieces stand out as representative of these two cultures: a noble piece for solo trumpet and orchestra—in Americana dialect—is the theme of the elderly president emeritus John Quincy Adams; while a cheerful piece for children's chorus singing in an African dialect celebrates the final liberation of the slaves:

> For some of the scenes requiring an African texture, I felt that the use of children's voices would be particularly effective. . . . As I searched for a text of what the children might sing, I discovered in a volume of West African poetry, a poem by Bernard Dadié written decades ago, which was entitled *Dry Your Tears, Africa, Your Children Are Coming Home.* I was thrilled to discover this, however accidentally, as it seemed ideal for the final scene of this film. . . . The words of the song that I wanted to write would, of course, have to be sung in Mende, the native tongue of the Africans associated with this true story, and so with the help of a translator at the Sierra Leone embassy in Washington, D.C., I arranged to have the poem translated from English to Mende. After slightly adjusting the text to fit the musical phrases, and with Mr. Dadié's permission, and adding some generic phrases such as "sing a song of joy . . . hush child don't cry," it only remained to teach our children's choir to phonetically sing the song.[21]

A typical Spielberg/Williams moment is the trial sequence when, in a claustrophobic courtroom, Cinque—the leader of the African slaves—is anxiously trying to understand what the many witnesses for both the prosecution and the defense are saying about the "middle passage." Music emphasizes the distressful state of Cinque, with atonal writing, echoing effects, and occasional distant and muffled ethnic percussions and vocalises, as if to symbolize Cinque's thinking of the far homeland from which he has been abducted. At one point, music freezes on a suspenseful sustained note by the strings as we hear Cinque trying to say something. Everyone in the courtroom stops and looks at him. Cinque stands up and, pointing his chained hands at the court, he screams repeatedly: "Give us free!" Williams music uplifts the moment by building a moving musical crescendo, starting with a vocalizing chorus singing *mezzo forte* the theme of "Dry Your Tears, Afrika" and then, with an arresting modulation, reprising the theme *fortissimo* with the full chorus and orchestra. Using his customary technique of gradual disclosure of the main theme, Williams introduces here only the melody of "Dry Your Tears, Afrika," while the full version with lyrics will be foregrounded during the final liberation sequence of the Lomboko slave prison.

Saving Private Ryan
(1998)

This war drama focuses on D-Day and the Allied invasion of Normandy in 1944. The musical choices are characterized by sobriety: only one hour of music for more than two hours of running time. The music is absent in action scenes—as in the opening landing on Omaha Beach and in all the following battle scenes—and enters only in the pauses between one action sequence and another, having the function of framing those moments of reflection. Says Spielberg: "Restraint was John Williams' primary objective. He did not want to sentimentalize or create emotion from what already existed in raw form. *Saving Private Ryan* is furious and relentless, as are all wars, but where there is music, it is exactly where John Williams intends for us the chance to breathe and remember."[22] The score has warm lyrical episodes for strings—especially for basses and cellos—and solemn parts for brass in which the trumpet and horn solos stand out for their intense pensive tone. Unlike Williams's usual practice, the score is composed of a dozen long pieces lasting eight to ten minutes, and the music has no perceptive, but mainly emotive, function. Although there are a few recurring themes, the closed musical number technique is used instead of leitmotivs. The end titles are accompanied by the poignant "Hymn to the Fallen" for vocalizing chorus and orchestra, not present elsewhere in the film. It is a concert piece in its own right, dedicated to the memory of the fallen. The score was performed by the Boston Symphony Orchestra and the Tanglewood Festival Chorus, and recorded at Boston's Symphony Hall.

A.I. Artificial Intelligence
(2001)

This sci-fi tale is based on a Stanley Kubrick project, which Spielberg inherited upon Kubrick's death. The score has one part featuring atonal dialect and a sort of futuristic minimalism—with coloring touches of synthesizers and electric guitars—which is the musical equivalent of the "outside": the chillingly techno-logical future world. The other part is based on a sweet lullaby for soprano and orchestra, which represents the "inside" of robot-boy David: his feelings, fond memories, and his yearning love for his lost human mother. The score pre-sents a quotation of Richard Strauss's *Der Rosenkavalier* (1911), reportedly a homage to Kubrick, as he had planned to use the piece in the film, following his repertoire-compilation approach to film music.[23] Particularly memorable is the finale, in which David's deceased mother is temporarily resurrected and the robot-boy is given one last day to spend in her company. Williams's music employs the lullaby to score the sequence poignantly by maintaining the tone in an aching equilibrium between David's happiness for having his mother back and his painful awareness that their time together is mercilessly ticking away.

Minority Report
(2003)

For this thriller set in a future hyper-technological society, Williams composed a homage to the noir genre and shows many references to Bernard Herrmann's idiom: "'I wanted to do this in a film noir kind of way; the grandparent of the score is the work of my old mentor and friend, Bernard Hermann, who scored so many films for Alfred Hitchcock,' says Williams. The story takes place in 2054, 'but Steven Spielberg and I wanted the musical atmosphere of an old Bogart film like *The Maltese Falcon*. Some elements of the music are not tonal and depict the futuristic aspect of the film, but the movie is also about nostalgia and memory, and that's where the film noir element comes in.'"[24]

Catch Me If You Can
(2002)

For this con-artist comedy/drama, Williams jumped back to the 1960s comedies of the first period of his career, and thus revisited his jazz background. The furtive main theme for alto saxophone is reminiscent of Henry Mancini's famous theme for *The Pink Panther* (Blake Edward, 1963) and is presented over a 1960s-like opening title sequence, which pays homage to the graphic designer Saul Bass:

> The title sequence of the film was an opportunity to create something with finger-snapping, 1960s swagger, and I thought a jazz saxophone solo in the style of Art Pepper or Stan Getz would be perfect. . . . In a film setting, such as the title sequence, the musical events have to happen exactly in synch with the visual events. If someone were truly improvising, the music might not ascend or quicken exactly when it should. . . . This music is a two-part invention for bass and alto saxophone. The

advantage of traditional notation is that there can be more tightly constructed counterpoint than when people improvise. If the players were
improvising, the bass player wouldn't really know what the saxophonist
was going to do until it happened, but through traditional notation the
piece sounds improvised even though it has carefully controlled
counterpoint.[25]

The Terminal
(2004)

A Frank Capra–like comedy, this film centers on Viktor Navorsky, an Eastern
European, trapped in New York's JFK airport because his country's government
has just been overturned, and Viktor's visa and passport have suddenly ceased
to be valid. While living in the terminal and waiting for a solution to his case
from the U.S. authorities, Viktor meets Amelia, a beautiful stewardess with a
very complicated sentimental life. We later discover that Viktor had traveled to
New York to complete his late father's collection of jazz musician autographs.
Viktor's Eastern European heritage, his encounter with American culture, and
the jazz subplot made it possible for Williams to express this multicultural nexus
musically. The score's intra-opus style ranges from klezmer to jazz to contemporary American minimalism; Williams also created a diegetic Slavonic anthem
for Viktor's fictitious homeland, Krakozhia. "I featured the clarinet, which is in
the idiom of so many groups of Eastern and Southeastern Europe, but also the
cimbalom, an instrument, I think, indigenous to Hungary, and it is played with
hammers, and it would be part of the orchestral texture to suggest latitude and
culture, and so on. And also the very subtle use of an accordion. . . . It is a nice
point about the jazz being a subplot of the film. . . . And the only music that is
somewhat related to that idiom is the music that I have written for Amelia, who
in my mind is so American. There is something I and Steven would call a "love
theme," and that is the theme that springs off in my mind—Amelia—in the
texture of what it is. Which is a very kind of American-sounding piece, in
contrast to Viktor's music."[26]

War of the Worlds
(2005)

This remake of the 1953 classic by Byron Haskin is a contrasting item in the
Spielberg extraterrestrial-related filmography. After *Close Encounters'* childlike
aliens and the amiable E.T., for the first time Spielberg chose to portray vicious

extraterrestrials, probably as a consequence of the 9/11 events.[27] Accordingly, Williams's score is rather poor in melodies: "*War of the Worlds*, where we have this machine coming to bring aliens here that are so destructive, [is] an interesting deviation for Steven. It creates a different musical opportunity and a different role for the orchestra and for the music. And there are a few sections in there, a few cuts to the alien machine, where the orchestra does a grand gesture of a classic monster film."[28] Piercing dissonance, disorienting atonality, stalking rhythms, and frenetic percussions are the score's pillars, with the moments of respite making room for brooding trumpet solos.

Indiana Jones and the Kingdom of the Crystal Skull
(2008)

In the series' fourth chapter, Williams—besides using the "Indiana Jones Theme" and "Marion's Theme" taken from the previous films—has composed new melodies that represent three decades of Hollywood music history. "Mutt's Theme" is a bright symphonic piece, which recalls Korngold's scores for Michael Curtiz's 1930s swashbuckling films;[29] "Irina's Theme," for the ruthless female KGB agent, is a seductive and tortuous saxophone melody reminiscent of the old femmes fatales themes of the 1940s noir films; the "Skull Theme" is a nod to the sci-fi music of the 1950s, with the synthesizer reproducing the trembling timbre of the theremin.

The Adventures of Tintin
(2011)

Part of the fascinating nature of this computer-generated-imagery (CGI) animation film, based on the comic books by the Belgian author Hergé, is its vintage flavor. *Tintin* is vintage not just because its tales and adventures are old-fashioned treasure hunts and puzzling mysteries; the vintage quality is also given by the detailed historical locales in which the stories are set and the characters move. In Steven Spielberg's film, one of the main "vintage-making" factors is the music. The score for *Tintin*—Williams's first animation film—has such a strong leitmotivic structure and use of Mickey-Mousing that it reminds us of *Raiders of the Lost Ark* and can be highlighted as an excellent recent example of neoclassicism. If the Korngoldian references can be spotted in the pirate scenes and duels between Capt. Haddock and Rackham the Red, Max Steiner's Mickey-Mousing technique is scattered all over the score, accompanying each jump, fall, and run of the characters—particularly those of Snowy, Tintin's white dog.

Williams's score is also based on a network of interwoven and developed leitmotivs—one for Tintin; one for Snowy; one for the Thompsons, the detective twins; one for Capt. Haddock, the alcoholic sea wolf. Haddock's theme, for example, is presented as a faltering piece in minor mode comically played by bassoons when the captain is drunk; later in the film, when Haddock reforms and regains his dignity, his theme is rendered in major mode and played nobly by the horns. Moreover, Williams reinforces the film's vintage backgrounds by musically evoking the bygone days: in the main title sequence Tintin's theme is presented in an early 1930s European jazz arrangement; the Thompsons' theme is played by the euphonium—very fashionable at the times and now a "vintage-sounding" instrument; and the accordion is used extensively to give a French nostalgia color all over the score.

War Horse
(2011)

This drama set in World War I concerns the friendship of a young man, Albert, and his horse, Joey. Joey is sold to the British cavalry, employed in war actions, and switched to a number of diverse owners, to finally survive the war and be reunited with Albert. Williams's score is richly melodic, combining noble tones and foregrounded flute solos with strong hints of the British music dialect—for example, Ralph Vaughan Williams and Edward Elgar. The film's beginning has a continuous musical flow introducing us in Dartmoor in 1912, and then accompanying the newborn horse in his first shaky gait through the British moors—a galloping string writing tracks the horse's moves. Atonal passages provide the tense atmosphere for the battle scenes, while a noble and poignant horns theme uplifts the moment when Albert and Joey reunite and go back home—in a *Gone with the Wind*-like sunset.

Lincoln
(2012)

Spielberg and Williams's latest collaboration is a biopic about America's sixteenth president, who had the Thirteenth Amendment passed, thus outlawing slavery. The nearly three-hour film depicts with serene pace and a realistic attention to details an intimate, anti-triumphalist portrait of Abraham Lincoln. Williams delivered a restrained score that covers only about one-third of the film's length. Dialogue is mostly not underscored and, contrary to other Williams presidential themes—such as John Kennedy's in *JFK* and Quincy Adams's for

Amistad—the leading solo instrument is not a celebrative trumpet but a pensive, intimate piano. Noble Americana dialect, nineteenth-century hymnal music, and spiritual-song inflections are the linguistic basis of the score—with a humorous episode featuring a spirited country fiddle in the searching-for-the-votes sequence. The Unionist song "Battle Cry of Freedom" is jubilantly arranged for chorus and orchestra and featured when the Amendment is finally approved.[30] It must be noted that the score is performed by the Chicago Symphony Orchestra, which marks the famed orchestra's debut in film music.

Williams's Eclecticism Besides Spielberg (and Lucas)

Williams has lent his versatile skills to other directors as well, of course. Here are some notable outcomes. *Black Sunday* (John Frankenheimer, 1977) is a thriller about terrorist attacks, in which a montage sequence—the inspection of the stadium in search of a bomb—stands out for a fugato, which reworks the previously introduced leitmotivs. *Midway* (Jack Smight, 1976) is a World War II drama about the famous battle in the Pacific Ocean and features the "Midway March"—a staple of the Williams march repertoire—in the style of John Philip Sousa, and the inspiring "Men of Yorktown March."

Family Plot (1976)—Alfred Hitchcock's last film—is a suspense/comedy about a couple of swindlers who get involuntarily involved in a kidnapping. The film features baroque fugato for suspense sequences, Debussy-like impressionist harmonies for the séances, and a lively main theme colored by a brisk harpsichord reminiscent of some of Williams's 1960s comedies like *Fitzwilly* or *How to Steal a Million*. Says Williams about his collaboration with the director:

> [Hitchcock] had had a long relationship with Bernard Herrmann, who was a great friend of mine at the time. The first conversation I had with Hitchcock, I was a bit sheepish because of my closeness to Herrmann. I didn't feel I could accept the assignment without either talking to Herrmann or understanding why it was that Hitchcock had broken off with him, which was one of those relationships in film that we all were hoping would continue. Hitchcock said to me, "No, no need to be sensitive about that because Mr. Herrmann and I have agreed not to work together again. I'm sure he'll be very happy if it's you, if it's not going to be him." I did ring up Herrmann and he said about the same thing. He said, "No, no, Hitch and I will not work together any longer but I am delighted that you will be doing this." . . . [A]t one of our

lunches, Hitchcock was describing a composer he'd hired to write a score for a film about a murder. He said he went to a scoring session and the composer had every double bassoon and tympani that was capable of making an ominous sound for the score. I said, "Well, Mr. Hitchcock, that sounds as if it was close to the mark," and he said, "No, you don't understand, murder can be fun."[31]

Dracula (John Badham, 1979) is a retelling of Bram Stoker's book as a doomed love story. John Badham states:

> As we were about to begin [and watch the film for the first time] he [Williams] confessed that he had never seen a vampire movie of any sort before. Somehow he had managed to stumble upon full adulthood without having been exposed to the veritable gauntlet of Dracula films produced in the last fifty years. Not a frame. . . . How fortunate to have the pre-eminent film composer of the day arrive with no advance notion of the kind of ketchup and thunder music that prevails in the horror film genre. . . . When the London Symphony Orchestra got its collective teeth on the music in May they played a score that is wildly romantic, shamelessly so. . . . Operatic in scale, it surrounds and elevates this often told tale of the Vampire King who takes a Queen for himself.[32] . . . When I first showed the movie to John [Williams], his initial fix on it after looking at it and thinking about it for a while was *Tristan and Iseult*, a great love story, a great tragic love story. That was his sort of inspiration at the starting point.[33]

The score is darkly romantic, with a Slavic tragic flavor, which—unlike James Bernard's thunderous scores for the Hammer films—emphasizes the character's Byronic charm rather than his monstrous nature, and the eroticism rather than the horror of the story.[34] Says Williams: "I've always felt that Dracula was a very erotic story. . . . It's a wonderful subject for music, really, for the sweep of the kind of romance and areas that we are uncertain about, an odd world that we're attracted to but we're a bit afraid of at the same time. The magnetism of the unknown, mixed with the erotic aspects of the story made it for me a very romantic piece in many ways."[35]

The Fury (Brian De Palma, 1978) has perhaps the most Herrmann-like score, with dissonant motivic writing and the eerie sound of the theremin. The "Main Title Theme" has a hypnotizing spiral quality, which resembles Herrmann's *Vertigo* (Alfred Hitchcock, 1958): "I'd admired *Obsession*, which had a Herrmann score I liked very much, and I thought Brian [De Palma] had served Herrmann's music better than anyone in so many years. I wrote him and thanked him for that. Later I met Brian and it turned out he was a close friend of Steven Spielberg. One day he burst into my office at Fox and said, 'Look, we're doing this picture called *The Fury* and, alas, poor Benny isn't with us and Amy [Irving— Spielberg's girlfriend] is the star—would you do the score?'—and I said, 'With great pleasure.'"[36]

In 1982 Williams composed the music for *Monsignor* (Frank Perry), a drama set in Italy during and after World War II and concerning a Catholic priest who makes black-market business with the Sicilian Mafia and has a love affair with a nun. This film—decidedly not well received—is worth mentioning for its score (brilliantly performed by the London Symphony Orchestra), which features at least three noteworthy set-pieces. The first one (the main theme) is a minor-mode slow waltz for trumpet tinged with a sense of doom and written in an Italianate dialect reminiscent of Nino Rota's music for *The Godfather* films (Francis Ford Coppola, 1972–74). "The Meeting in Sicily" (thus titled in the LP album) is a sunny, lively orchestral showpiece that contrasts the prevalently darker mood of the score—in the following year Williams reworked it into a concert piece (*Esplanade Overture*). Finally, "Gloria" is a powerful piece for chorus, orchestra, and pipe organ written as a background for a solemn-Mass sequence: the tonal church music is occasionally punctuated by strident dissonant chords— for example, in the organ introduction—so as to depict musically the priest's discordant morals behind the pious facade.

The Faustian comedy *The Witches of Eastwick* (George Miller, 1987) has a sardonically "satanic" score boasting a grotesque tarantella as the devil's leit-motiv. It is also memorable for a classy scherzo written for the tennis-match scene, and a lavish love theme for the balloon scene, which can be heard only partially in the film, since its first part was replaced by Puccini's "Nessun Dorma."

Williams has also composed very intimate and restrained scores, which are often ignored by his detractors who strategically focus on his allegedly "pompous" and "bombastic" scores of major "commercial" successes. Examples of what could be called "chamber-music Williams" show up in *The Accidental Tourist* (Lawrence Kasdan, 1988) and *Stanley & Iris* (Martin Ritt, 1990), both of which feature lyrical piano solos, and the thriller *Presumed Innocent* (Alan Pakula, 1990), again with prominent piano solos, atonal passages, and synthesizer touches.

Williams's collaboration with Oliver Stone for the controversial American trilogy formed by *Born on the Fourth of July* (1989), *JFK* (1991), and *Nixon* (1995) deserves a niche of its own. The core of the score for *Born on the Fourth of July* is an elegiac trumpet solo backed by poignant string writing: "I knew immediately I would want a string orchestra to sing in opposition to all the realism on the screen, and then the idea came to have a solo trumpet—not a military trumpet, but an American trumpet, to recall the happy youth of this boy."[37] As for *JFK*, the composer was involved in the project before shooting, and his music was later used to edit the film. Williams explains: "Actually what drove the idea was the fact that *JFK* had been made like a documentary film. . . . [It] was going to be edited more in terms of a documentary film than a live action drama, accompanied by a lot of narration, voice-overs, that had to be edited or cut. Oliver Stone and I thought that it might be a good idea to have set pieces of music, on which to build these segments of the film."[38]

In the blockbuster-film department, Williams also contributed to the success of the slapstick children's comedy *Home Alone* (Chris Columbus, 1990) and its sequel *Home Alone 2: Lost in New York* (Chris Columbus, 1992). He composed comedic cartoon-like scores with extensive Tom and Jerry–like Mickey-Mousing, enriched with original Christmas carols—"Star of Bethlehem," "Somewhere in My Memory," "Christmas Star," "Merry Christmas, Merry Christmas." In *Home Alone 2*, in particular, a tip of the hat to the music of Max Steiner must be pointed out. For the fake *noir* film *Angels with Filthy Souls II*—watched on TV by little Kevin—Williams penned a parody of Steiner's music for *The Big Sleep* (Howard Hawks, 1946).

In 1992 Williams worked on Ron Howard's *Far and Away*, a nineteenth-century migration epic about a young Irish couple moving to America. He adopted the Irish musical dialect and colored the score with the sound of ethnic instruments performed by the Irish group The Chieftains: "I liked the movie very much when I saw it and I also loved the subject. One of the films I admired the most when I was a very young person was a John Ford picture *The Quiet Man*. . . . I always felt that I would love to write the score, and this opportunity came along through Ron Howard. . . . I also had worked with the Chieftains in Boston about a year before this, when they came as guests and they played with the [Boston Pops] orchestra. There were Uilleann pipes, bagpipes, these Irish things, penny whistles, fiddle. So I looked at Ron Howard's movie and thought it was a wonderful opportunity to bring in Paddy [Maloney]'s group, to give that particular flavor to the orchestration."[39]

Williams returned to an Irish setting with *Angela's Ashes* (Alan Parker, 1999). However, for this story of poverty and immigration, Williams did not resort to ethnic music but to a more universal dialect. The overall score—with prominent solo parts for piano and harp—is austere, alternating between restrained episodes and more expansive, hopeful impulses, with some humorous touches as well—for instance, the pizzicato writing for the telegram delivering scene: "Parker said he didn't feel that the music should be in the Irish idiom particularly, that it should be broader, more universal—an emotionally direct score. I thought that probably was a right decision. I found the film to be a kind of chamber piece in the sense that you had the father and the mother and the children—four or five principal parts. Obviously, the music shouldn't be scaled on a Strauss opera; it would have been too big for the film. So I felt that a chamber music approach with musical protagonists that would more or less match the acting ones might work. I wrote a score that featured the piano, harp, oboe and cello set in front of a string orchestra."[40]

A few words should also be said for *Rosewood* (John Singleton, 1997)—a drama set in the early nineteenth-century southern United States—with consistent solo parts for guitar, bass guitar, harmonica, piano, and featuring three *a cappella* spirituals: "Look Down, Lord," "Light My Way," and "The Freedom Train," a further demonstration of the composer's versatility.

At seventy, Williams opened the new millennium with another box-office hit: the Harry Potter trilogy (*Harry Potter and the Sorcerer's Stone*, Chris Columbus, 2001; *Harry Potter and the Chamber of Secrets*, Chris Columbus, 2002; *Harry Potter and the Prisoner of Azkaban*, Alfonso Cuarón, 2004). "I wanted to capture the world of weightlessness and flight and sleight of hand and happy surprise. This caused the music to be a little more theatrical than most film scores would be. It sounds like music that you would hear in the theater rather than in the film."[41] Williams's musical tapestry for the trilogy is a very rich one, and only a few examples can be given here. The series' signature tune is "Hedwig's Theme," Hedwig being Harry's white owl. It can be heard at the beginning of each film—it is also retained in the subsequent five film chapters not scored by Williams. In the narrative it is associated with the magical world of Harry and his friends. It is a music box–like ethereal melody, backed by kaleidoscopic harmonies, and played with silvery timbre by the celesta—a carillon-like sounding instrument notably used in Tchaikovsky's "Sugar Plum Fairy Dance" from *The Nutcracker* (1892). Indeed, the scores for the first two films hark back to the Russian school, with Tchaikovskyan melodies, Rimsky-Korsakov–like orchestrations, and timbres and colors reminiscent of Stravinsky's *The Firebird* (1910). Expansive and soaring Williamsesque flying themes abound—for the broomstick rides and the magical bird Fawkes the Phoenix. A lively staccato woodwinds theme—"Nimbus 2000"—is associated with Harry's flying broomstick and with spells in general. A dark, satanic, slithery motif is the trademark for Voldemort and black magic—featuring the tritone, the *diabolus in musica*. An odd duet, harp and contrabassoon, accompanies the heavy snoring of Fluffy, a two-headed monster dog. A noble, British-sounding brass theme acts as a musical signature for the "Hogwarts School of Witchcraft and Wizardry," while the Quidditch matches are scored with heraldic fanfares, kinetic action music, and a tight network of snippets from the various leitmotivs. The overall tone of the music changes radically in the third film, where only a couple of the old themes are kept—"Hedwig's theme" and "Nimbus 2000." The tone of the film is less childlike as Harry and his friends approach adolescence. The music accordingly becomes more experimental and varied. There are fugato episodes—in the Quidditch match; virtuoso solos—as the exhilarating flute solo in the butterfly flight scene; archaic instrumentation—crumhorns, recorders, fiddles—and medieval modal dialect—as in the music accompanying Hagrid's lessons. There is a "Greensleeves"-like theme for Harry and his memories of the past; chilling atonal writing for the Dementors—ghosts who feed on people's happiness, driving them desperate and mad; an oddball Leonard Bernstein-like symphonic jazz piece accompanying the reckless trip of a magical "knight" bus; when Harry takes a long-awaited revenge by casting a spell on the nasty Aunt Marge, a Rossini-like waltz humorously accompanies her with appropriate *crescendo* as she inflates like a balloon, rises in the air, and floats over the rooftops of London. There is even a diegetic choral piece—"Double Trouble"—based on William Shakespeare's witch-spell scene from *Macbeth* and played on ancient instruments by the Dufay Collective.

This overview, which has no pretense of being a thorough account of Williams's production, has hopefully traced a fly-over trip on the remaining part of his major films in order to show that besides his neoclassical scores, Williams is also a resourceful, versatile composer who has ventured in the most diverse territories.

Appendix 2: Film and TV Scores, Concert Pieces, and Arrangements

Scores for Feature Films

*The Book Thief,** 2013, Brian Percival
*Lincoln,** 2012, Steven Spielberg
*War Horse,** 2011, Steven Spielberg
*The Adventures of Tintin,** 2011, Steven Spielberg
Indiana Jones and the Kingdom of the Crystal Skull, 2008, Steven Spielberg
*Memoirs of a Geisha,** 2005, Rob Marshall
*Munich,** 2005, Steven Spielberg
War of the Worlds, 2005, Steven Spielberg
Star Wars: Episode III—Revenge of the Sith, 2005, George Lucas
The Terminal, 2004, Steven Spielberg
*Harry Potter and the Prisoner of Azkaban,** 2004, Alfonso Cuarón
*Catch Me If You Can,** 2002, Steven Spielberg
Harry Potter and the Chamber of Secrets, 2002, Chris Columbus (Music arranged by William Ross)

Note: Film titles followed by an asterisk (*) were nominated for an Academy Award (for Best Original Score unless noted otherwise). Film titles followed by a dagger (†) won an Academy Award.

Minority Report, 2002, Steven Spielberg

Star Wars: Episode II—Attack of the Clones, 2002, George Lucas

Harry Potter and the Sorcerer's Stone,* 2001, Chris Columbus

A.I. Artificial Intelligence,* 2001, Steven Spielberg

The Patriot,* 2000, Roland Emmerich

Angela's Ashes,* 1999, Alan Parker

Star Wars: Episode I—The Phantom Menace, 1999, George Lucas

Stepmom, 1998, Chris Columbus

Saving Private Ryan,* 1998, Steven Spielberg

Amistad,* 1997, Steven Spielberg

Seven Years in Tibet, 1997, Jean-Jacques Annaud

The Lost World: Jurassic Park, 1997, Steven Spielberg

Rosewood, 1997, John Singleton

Sleepers,* 1996, Barry Levinson

Nixon,* 1995, Oliver Stone

Sabrina,* 1995, Sidney Pollack (nominated for Best Original Comedy Score and
    Best Original Song)

Schindler's List,† 1993, Steven Spielberg

Jurassic Park, 1993, Steven Spielberg

Home Alone 2: Lost in New York, 1992, Chris Columbus

Far and Away, 1992, Ron Howard

JFK,* 1991, Oliver Stone

Hook,* 1991, Steven Spielberg (nominated for Best Original Song)

Home Alone,* 1990, Chris Columbus (nominated for Best Original Score and
    Best Original Song)

Presumed Innocent, 1990, Alan Pakula

Stanley & Iris, 1990, Martin Ritt

Always, 1989, Steven Spielberg

Born on the Fourth of July,* 1989, Oliver Stone

Indiana Jones and the Last Crusade,* 1989, Steven Spielberg

The Accidental Tourist,* 1988, Lawrence Kasdan

Empire of the Sun,* 1987, Steven Spielberg

The Witches of Eastwick,* 1987, George Miller

Space Camp, 1986, Harry Winer

The River,* 1984, Mark Rydell

Indiana Jones and the Temple of Doom,* 1984, Steven Spielberg

Star Wars: Episode VI—Return of the Jedi,* 1983, Richard Marquand

Monsignor, 1982, Frank Perry

E.T. the Extra-Terrestrial,† 1982, Steven Spielberg

*Yes, Giorgio,** 1982, Franklin J. Schaffner (nominated for Best Original Song) (Main theme and song "If We Were In Love"—Additional music by Michael J. Lewis)

Heartbeeps, 1981, Allan Arkush

*Raiders of the Lost Ark,** 1981, Steven Spielberg

*Star Wars: Episode V—The Empire Strikes Back,** 1980, Irvin Kershner

1941, 1979, Steven Spielberg

Dracula, 1979, John Badham

*Superman: The Movie,** 1978, Richard Donner

Jaws 2, 1978, Jeannot Szwarc

The Fury, 1978, Brian De Palma

*Close Encounters of the Third Kind,** 1977, Steven Spielberg

Star Wars: Episode IV—A New Hope,† 1977, George Lucas

Black Sunday, 1977, John Frankenheimer

Midway, 1976, Jack Smight

The Missouri Breaks, 1976, Arthur Penn

Family Plot, 1976, Alfred Hitchcock

Jaws,† 1975, Steven Spielberg

The Eiger Sanction, 1975, Clint Eastwood

*The Towering Inferno,** 1974, John Guillermin

Earthquake, 1974, Mark Robson

The Sugarland Express, 1974, Steven Spielberg

Conrack, 1974, Martin Ritt

*Cinderella Liberty,** 1973, Mark Rydell (nominated for Best Original Score and Best Original Song)

The Long Goodbye, 1973, Robert Altman

The Paper Chase, 1973, James Bridges

The Man Who Loved Cat Dancing, 1973, Richard C. Sarafian

*Tom Sawyer,** 1973, Don Taylor (nominated for Best Score Adaptation) (Arrangement of Richard M. Sherman and Robert B. Sherman's original songs and additional background music)

*Images,** 1972, Robert Altman

The Screaming Woman (TV Film), 1972, Jack Smight

Pete 'n' Tillie, 1972, Martin Ritt

*The Poseidon Adventure,** 1972, Ronald Neame

The Cowboys, 1972, Mark Rydell

Fiddler on the Roof,† 1971, Norman Jewison (Arrangement of Jerry Bock and Sheldon Harnick's original songs and additional background music)

Jane Eyre (TV Film), 1971, Delbert Mann

Storia di una Donna, 1970, Leonardo Bercovici

The Reivers,* 1969, Mark Rydell

Goodbye, Mr. Chips,* 1969, Herbert Ross (nominated for Best Score Adaptation) (Arrangement of Leslie Bricusse's original songs and additional background music)

Daddy's Gone A-Hunting, 1969, Mark Robson

Heidi (TV Film), 1968, Delbert Mann

Sergeant Ryker, 1968, Buzz Kulik

Valley of the Dolls,* 1967, Mark Robson (nominated for Best Score Adaptation) (Arrangement of André Previn and Dory Previn's original songs and additional background music)

Fitzwilly, 1967, Delbert Mann

A Guide for the Married Man, 1967, Gene Kelly

The Plainsman, 1966, David Lowell Rich

Penelope, 1966, Arthur Hiller

Not with My Wife, You Don't!, 1966, Norman Panama

How to Steal a Million, 1966, William Wyler

The Rare Breed, 1966, Andrew V. McLaglen

John Goldfarb, Please Come Home, 1965, J. Lee Thompson

None But the Brave, 1965, Frank Sinatra

The Killers, 1964, Don Siegel

Nightmare in Chicago (TV Film), 1964, Robert Altman

Gidget Goes to Rome, 1963, Paul Wendkos

Diamond Head, 1963, Guy Green

Bachelor Flat, 1962, Frank Tashlin

Stark Fear, 1962, Ned Hockman (Composer of diegetic music; non-diegetic music by Ned Hockman)

The Secret Ways, 1961, Phil Karlson

Because They're Young, 1960, Paul Wendkos

I Passed for White, 1960, Fred M. Wilcox (Music co-written with Jerry Irvin)

Daddy-O, 1958, Lou Place

TV Scores

Masterpiece Theater, 2000 (Main Theme)

Amazing Stories, 1985 (Main Theme and episodes "The Mission" and "Ghost Train")

The Virginian, 1970 (Main Theme, last season)

Land of the Giants, 1968 (Main Theme and scores, 1968–70)
The Ghostbreaker, 1967 (Score for the pilot episode)
The Time Tunnel, 1966 (Main Theme and score for the pilot episode)
The Tammy Grimes Show, 1966
The Kraft Summer Music Hall, 1966
Lost in Space, 1965 (Main Theme and scores, 1965–68)
Voyage to the Bottom of the Sea, 1964
Gilligan's Island, 1964
Bob Hope Presents the Chrysler Theater, 1963 (Main Theme and scores)
Kraft Suspense Theater, 1963 (Main Theme and scores, 1963–64)
Kraft Mystery Theater, 1963 (Main Theme, third season)
Big G, 1962
Flashing Spikes, 1962
The Wide Country, 1962
Alcoa Premiere Theater, 1961 (Main Theme and scores, 1961–63)
Checkmate, 1960 (Main Theme and scores, 1960–62)
M-Squad, 1957
Wagon Train, 1957
Bachelor Father, 1957
Tales of Wells Fargo, 1957
Playhouse 90, 1956
You Are Welcome (Documentary), 1954

Principal
Early-Year Collaborations

The Pink Panther, 1964, Blake Edwards (Pianist, music by Henry Mancini)
To Kill a Mockingbird, 1962, Robert Mulligan (Pianist, music by Elmer Bernstein)
Hemingway's Adventures of a Young Man, 1962, Martin Ritt (Pianist, music by Franz Waxman)
The Guns of Navarone, 1961, J. Lee Thompson (Orchestrator, music by Dimitri Tiomkin)
West Side Story, 1961, Robert Wise (Pianist, music by Leonard Bernstein, arrangement and musical direction by Johnny Green)
Breakfast at Tiffany's, 1961, Blake Edwards (Pianist, music by Henry Mancini)
Studs Lonigan, 1960, Irvin Lerner (Pianist, music by Jerry Goldsmith)
The Apartment, 1960, Billy Wilder (Pianist and Orchestrator, music by Adolph Deutsch)

The Magnificent Seven, 1960, John Sturges (Pianist, music by Elmer Bernstein)

Mr. Lucky (TV series), 1959 (Pianist, music by Henry Mancini)

Twilight Zone (TV series), 1959 (Pianist, music by Bernard Herrmann)

Johnny Staccato (TV series), 1959 (Pianist, music by Elmer Bernstein)

Some Like It Hot, 1959, Billy Wilder (Pianist, music by Adolph Deutsch)

City of Fear, 1959, Irving Lerner (Pianist, music by Jerry Goldsmith)

Bell, Book, and Candle, 1958, Richard Quine (Pianist, music by George Duning)

The Big Country, 1958, William Wyler (Pianist, music by Jerome Moross)

Porgy and Bess, 1958, Otto Preminger (Pianist, music by George Gershwin, arrangement and musical direction by André Previn)

Peter Gunn (TV series), 1958 (Pianist, music by Henry Mancini)

South Pacific, 1958, Joshua Logan (Pianist, music by Richard Rodgers, arrangement and musical direction by Alfred Newman)

God's Little Acre, 1958, Anthony Mann (Pianist, music by Elmer Bernstein)

Funny Face, 1957, Stanley Donen (Pianist, music by Adolph Deutsch)

Sweet Smell of Success, 1957, Alexander Mackendrick (Pianist, music by Elmer Bernstein)

Carousel, 1956, Henry King (Pianist, music by Richard Rodgers, arrangement and musical direction by Alfred Newman)

Fanfares, Orchestral Miniatures, and Concert Pieces

Conversations, 2013 (Four pieces for solo piano)
    "I. Phineas and Mumbett"
    "II. Claude and Monk"
    "III. Chet and Miles"
    "IV. Strays, Duke . . . and Blind Tom"

For "The President's Own," 2013 (Fanfare for the 250th Anniversary of the President's Own United States Marine Band)

Rounds, 2012 (For solo guitar)

Song for World Peace, 2012 (Revised version—with extended violin and cello solos)

Fanfare for Fenway, 2012 (For the centennial of Boston's Fenway Park)

La Jolla Quartet, 2011 (Quartet for violin, harp, clarinet, and cello commissioned by La Jolla Quartet)

Concerto for Oboe and Orchestra, 2011

A Young Person's Guide to the Cello, 2011 (For solo cello)

"On Willow and Birches"—Concerto for Harp and Orchestra, 2009 (Commissioned

by the Boston Symphony Orchestra upon the retirement of harpist Ann Hobson Pilot)

Concerto for Viola and Orchestra, 2009

Air and Simple Gift, 2008 (Quartet for violin, cello, clarinet, piano. Commissioned for President Barak Obama's first inauguration. Also arranged for string orchestra)

Duo Concertante for Violin and Viola, 2007

Star-Spangled Banner, 2004 (Arrangement for wind band written for the Rose Bowl Ceremonies in Pasadena, CA)

Concerto for Horn and Orchestra, 2003 (Commissioned by the Chicago Symphony Orchestra)

Soundings, 2003 (Commissioned for the inauguration of the Walt Disney Concert Hall in Los Angeles)

The Silent Era, 2003 (Piano duet composed to accompany a silent-film anthology at the "Soundtrack: Music and Film" festival in Washington, DC)

Heartwood: Lyric Sketches for Cello and Orchestra, 2002

Call of the Champions, 2002 (Commissioned for the 2002 Winter Olympics in Salt Lake City, UT)

Elegy for Cello and Orchestra, 2002 (Orchestral version of the 1997 piece for cello and piano)

Three Pieces for Solo Cello, 2000

TreeSong, Concerto for Violin and Orchestra, 2000

American Journey (aka *The Unfinished Journey—Celebration 2000*), 1999 (Commissioned by President Bill Clinton for the Millennium Celebrations in Washington, DC)

For Seiji! Concerto for Orchestra, 1999 (Written for the twenty-fifth anniversary of Seiji Ozawa's conductorship of the Boston Symphony Orchestra)

Seven for Luck, 1998 (Song cycle for soprano and orchestra)

Elegy for Cello and Piano, 1997

Concerto for Trumpet and Orchestra, 1996 (Commissioned by the Cleveland Orchestra)

Summon the Heroes, 1996 (Commissioned for the Centennial Olympics in Atlanta, GA)

Variations on Happy Birthday, 1995 (Written for Seiji Ozawa's, Yo-Yo Ma's, Itzhak Perlman's and Leon Fleisher's birthdays)

Song for World Peace (aka *Satellite Celebration*), 1994 (Written for Seiji Ozawa)

Concerto for Cello and Orchestra, 1994 (Commissioned by the Boston Symphony Orchestra)

Sound the Bells! (two versions: for winds and percussion; for symphony orchestra),

1993 (Written for the Royal Wedding of Prince Naruhito and Princess Masako)

Concerto for Bassoon and Orchestra, The Five Sacred Trees, 1993 (Commissioned by the New York Philharmonic Orchestra)

Aloft . . . To the Royal Masthead! (aka *Fanfare for Prince Philip*), 1992 (Written on the occasion of the visit to Boston of Prince Philip, Duke of Edinburgh)

Concerto for Clarinet and Orchestra, 1991 (Commissioned by the Los Angeles Philharmonic Orchestra)

Celebrate Discovery, 1990 (For the 500th anniversary of Christopher Columbus's Discovery)

Winter Games Fanfare, 1989 (Commissioned for the Alpine Ski Championship in Vail, CO)

Fanfare for Ten-Year-Olds, 1988 (Written for the tenth anniversary of the Young Charleston Theater Company)

For New York (aka *To Lenny! To Lenny!*), 1988 (Variations on themes by Leonard Bernstein written for Bernstein's seventieth birthday)

Fanfare for Michael Dukakis, 1988 (Written for the presidential campaign of Senator Michael Dukakis)

The Olympic Spirit, 1988 (Commissioned by NBC in celebration of the 1988 Olympics in Seoul, South Korea)

"We're Lookin' Good!," 1987 (Written for the 1987 Special Olympics)

A Hymn to New England, 1987 (Commissioned by Boston's Museum of Science)

Celebration Fanfare, 1986 (Commissioned by the Houston Symphony Orchestra for the 150th anniversary of Texas's Declaration of Independence)

Liberty Fanfare, 1986 (Commissioned for the celebration of the 100th anniversary of the Statue of Liberty)

The Mission Theme, 1985 (Written for NBC News)

Concerto for Tuba and Orchestra, 1985 (Written for the 100th anniversary of the Boston Pops Orchestra)

Olympic Fanfare and Theme, 1984 (Commissioned for the 1984 Olympics in Los Angeles, CA)

America, the Dream Goes On, 1983

Esplanade Overture, 1983 (Written for the Boston Pops Orchestra)

Pops on the March, 1981 (Written for the Boston Pops Orchestra and dedicated to the memory of Arthur Fiedler, who had commissioned the piece in 1978)

Fanfare for a Festive Occasion, 1980 (Commissioned by the Boston Civic Orchestra)

Jubilee 350 Fanfare, 1980 (Written for the 350th anniversary of the City of Boston)

Concerto for Violin and Orchestra (revised in 1998), 1976 (Dedicated to the memory of Barbara Ruick Williams)

Thomas and the King, 1975 (Musical)
A Nostalgic Jazz Odyssey, 1971 (Commissioned by the Eastman Wind Ensemble)
Concerto for Flute and Orchestra, 1969
Sinfonietta for Wind Ensemble, 1968 (Commissioned by the Eastman Wind Ensemble)
Symphony no. 1, 1966
Essay for Strings, 1965
Prelude and Fugue, 1965 (Commissioned by the Stan Kenton's Los Angeles Neophonic Orchestra)

Catalogue of Film-Music Concert Pieces

The Book Thief, 2013
    Suite from *The Book Thief*
Lincoln, 2012
    Suite from *Lincoln* *
        "The People's House"*
        "Getting Out the Vote"*
        "Elegy"*
        "With Malice Toward None"*
War Horse, 2011
    "Dartmoor, 1912"*
The Adventures of Tintin, 2011
    "The Duel"
    "The Sea Battle"
Indiana Jones and the Kingdom of the Crystal Skull, 2008
    "Swashbuckler (The Adventures of Mutt)"*

Note: Williams is famous for adapting concert versions from most of his film scores. He is also the only film composer whose scores have authoritative concert versions easily available for purchase. In the following catalogue, only the versions prepared by Williams himself have been listed. Namely, they are either the pieces that have been presented by Williams during his Boston Pops concerts—archived at Boston's Symphony Hall in the "John Williams Music Library"—or published in full-orchestra score by Hal Leonard in the John Williams Signature Edition series (http://www.halleonard.com/search/search.do?menuid=1788&seriesfeature=&subsiteid=6). The pieces published in said series are marked with an asterisk (*). Reductions for solo instruments are not listed.

"Irina's Theme"*

"The Crystal Spell"*

"A Whirl through Academe"*

Memoirs of a Geisha, 2005

"Sayuri's Theme"*

"Going to School"

"The Chairman's Waltz"*

"Brush on Silk"

"Chiyo's Prayer"

"Becoming a Geisha"

War of the Worlds, 2005

"Escape from the City"

"Epilogue"

Munich, 2005

"A Prayer for Peace"

Star Wars: Episode III—Revenge of the Sith, 2005

"Battle of the Heroes"*

The Terminal, 2004

"Viktor's Tale"*

Harry Potter and the Prisoner of Azkaban, 2004

"Witches, Wands, and Wizards"*

"Aunt Marge's Waltz"*

"The Knight Bus"*

"A Bridge to the Past"*

"Double Trouble"* (SATB and children chorus and orchestra; lyrics from William Shakespeare's *Macbeth*)

Catch Me If You Can, 2002

*Escapades for Alto Saxophone and Orchestra**

"Closing In"*

"Reflections"*

"Joy Ride"*

Harry Potter and the Chamber of Secrets, 2002

"Fawkes the Phoenix"*

"Dobby the House Elf"*

"Gilderoy Lockhart"*

"The Chamber of Secrets"*

Star Wars: Episode II—Attack of the Clones, 2002

"Across the Stars"*

Harry Potter and the Sorcerer's Stone, 2001

"Hedwig's Theme"*

"The Sorcerer's Stone"*
"Nimbus 2000"*
"Harry's Wondrous World"*
Children's Suite from *Harry Potter and the Sorcerer's Stone**
    "Hedwig's Flight"*
    "Hogwarts Forever"*
    "Voldemort"*
    "Nimbus 2000"*
    "Fluffy and His Harp"*
    "Quidditch"*
    "Family Portrait"*
    "Diagon Alley"*
    "Harry's Wondrous World"*
The Patriot, 2000
    "Theme from *The Patriot*"*
Angela's Ashes, 1999
    "Theme from *Angela's Ashes*"*
    "Angela's Prayer"* (harp and orchestra)
    "The Lanes of Limerick"* (solo harp)
    Suite for Narrator, Piano, Cello, Harp, and Orchestra from *Angela's*
        Ashes (Text by Frank McCourt)
Star Wars: Episode I—The Phantom Menace, 1999
    "The Flag Parade"*
    "Anakin's Theme"*
    "The Adventures of Jar Jar"*
    "Duel of the Fates"* (SATB chorus and orchestra)
Stepmom, 1998
    "The Days Between" (guitar and orchestra)
Saving Private Ryan, 1998
    "Hymn to the Fallen"* (SATB chorus and orchestra)
Amistad, 1997
    "Dry Your Tears, Afrika"* (SATB and children chorus and orchestra)
Seven Years in Tibet, 1997
    "Seven Years in Tibet" (for cello and orchestra)
The Lost World: Jurassic Park, 1997
    "Theme from *The Lost World*"*
Rosewood, 1997
    "Look Down, Lord" (Spiritual for a cappella chorus)
    "Light My Way" (Spiritual for a cappella chorus)
    "The Freedom Train" (Spiritual for a cappella chorus)

Sabrina, 1995
  "Theme from *Sabrina* for Piano and Orchestra"
  "Theme from *Sabrina* for Violin and Orchestra"
Schindler's List, 1993
  Three Pieces from Schindler's List for Solo Violin and Orchestra*
  "Theme from *Schindler's List*"*
  "Jewish Town (Krakow Ghetto—Winter '41)"*
  "Remembrances"*
Jurassic Park, 1993
  "Theme from *Jurassic Park*"*
  "My Friend, the Brachiosaurus"
Home Alone 2: Lost in New York, 1992
  "Christmas Star" (SATB and children chorus and orchestra)
  "Merry Christmas, Merry Christmas"* (SATB and children chorus
    and orchestra)
Far and Away, 1992
  Suite from *Far and Away** [aka Excerpts from *Far and Away*]
  "County Galway, June 1892"*
  "The Fighting Donnellys"*
  "Joseph and Shannon"*
  "Blowin' Off Steam"*
  "Finale"*
  "Theme from *Far and Away* for Violin and Orchestra"
JFK, 1991
  Suite from *JFK**
  "Theme from *JFK*"*
  "Motorcade"*
  "Arlington"*
Hook, 1991
  "The Flight to Neverland"*
  "Smee's Plan"
  "The Face of Pan"
  "The Lost Boys Ballet"
  "The Banquet Scene"
Home Alone, 1990
  "Somewhere in My Memory"* (SATB and children chorus and
    orchestra)
  "Star of Bethlehem"* (SATB and children chorus and orchestra)
  "Holiday Flight"

Always, 1989
  "Theme from *Always*"
Born on the Fourth of July, 1989
  Suite from *Born on the Fourth of July* for Trumpet and Orchestra
  "Theme from *Born on the Fourth of July*"*
  "Cua Viet River, Vietnam 1968"
  "Massapequa . . . the Early Days"
Indiana Jones and the Last Crusade, 1989
  "Scherzo for Motorcycle and Orchestra"
  "The Circus Train Chase"
The Accidental Tourist, 1988
  "Theme from *The Accidental Tourist*"
Empire of the Sun, 1987
  "Cadillac of the Skies"
  "Jim's New Life"
  "Exsultate justi" (SATB and children chorus and orchestra)
The Witches of Eastwick, 1987
  "The Balloon Sequence"
  "The Devil's Dance"
  "The Devil's Dance—For Gil Shaham" (violin and piano)
Indiana Jones and the Temple of Doom, 1984
  "Parade of the Slave Children"
Star Wars: Episode VI—Return of the Jedi, 1983
  "Parade of the Ewoks"*
  "Luke and Leia"*
  "Jabba the Hutt" (for tuba and orchestra)
  "The Forest Battle"*
Monsignor, 1982
  "Gloria" (SATB chorus, organ, and orchestra)
E.T. the Extra-Terrestrial, 1982
  "Three Million Light Years from Home"
  "Flying Theme"*
  "Stargazers" (for harp and orchestra)
  "Over the Moon" (for piano and orchestra)
  "Adventures on Earth"*
Raiders of the Lost Ark, 1981
  "Raiders March"*
  "Marion's Theme"*
  "The Basket Chase"

Star Wars: Episode V—The Empire Strikes Back, 1980
    "The Imperial March" ("Darth Vader's Theme")*
    "Yoda's Theme"*
    "The Asteroid Field"*
1941, 1979
    "The March from 1941"*
    "The Battle of Hollywood"
    "Swing Swing Swing"
Dracula, 1979
    "Night Journeys"
Superman: The Movie, 1978
    "Superman March"*
    "Love Theme"
    "The Flying Sequence"
    "The March of the Villains"
Close Encounters of the Third Kind, 1977
    "Excerpts from Close Encounters of the Third Kind"*
    "The Dialogue" (synthesizer, chorus, oboe, and tuba)
Star Wars: Episode IV—A New Hope, 1977
    "Main Title"*
    "Princess Leia's Theme"*
    "The Little People"
    "Cantina Band"*
    "Here They Come"*
    "The Battle"
    "The Throne Room and End Title"*
Midway, 1976
    "The Midway March"*
    "The Men of Yorktown March"
Jaws, 1975
    Suite from *Jaws*
        "The Shark Theme"*
        "Out to Sea/The Shark Cage Fugue"*
        "The Barrel Chase"
The Sugarland Express, 1974
    "Theme from *The Sugarland Express*" (for flute and orchestra/harmonica
    and orchestra)
Cinderella Liberty, 1973
    "Theme from *Cinderella Liberty*" (for harmonica and orchestra)

The Cowboys, 1972
    "The Cowboys Overture"*
Fiddler on the Roof, 1971
    "Excerpts from Fiddler on the Roof"* (for violin and orchestra)
Jane Eyre, 1971
    Suite from *Jane Eyre**
    "Lowood"*
    "To Thornfield"*
    "Reunion"*
The Reivers, 1969
    The Reivers: Suite for Narrator and Orchestra (Text by William Faulkner
    adapted by Irving and Harriet Ravetch)

Principal Medleys and Arrangements
from Film Scores, Songs, and Popular Music

A Tribute to George Lucas and Steven Spielberg (medley), 2006
    Jaws, 1975, John Williams
    Star Wars, 1977, John Williams
    Raiders of the Lost Ark, 1981, John Williams
    E.T. the Extra-Terrestrial, 1982, John Williams
Monsters, Beauties, and Heroes (medley), 2003
    King Kong, 1933, Max Steiner
    Jaws, 1975, John Williams
    Casablanca, 1942, Herman Hupfeld/Max Steiner
    An Affair to Remember, 1957, Harry Warren/Hugo Friedhofer
    The Adventures of Robin Hood, 1938, Erich Wolfgang Korngold
    Superman: The Movie, 1978, John Williams
A Tribute to the Film Composer (medley), 2002
    Warner Bros. Fanfare, 1937, Max Steiner
    Casablanca, 1942, Herman Hupfeld/Max Steiner
    Citizen Kane, 1941, Bernard Herrmann
    20th Century Fox Fanfare, 1933/1953, Alfred Newman
    Star Wars, 1977, John Williams
    The Sea Hawk, 1940, Erich Wolfgang Korngold
    Spellbound, 1945, Miklós Rózsa
    Titanic, 1997, James Horner
    Psycho, 1960, Bernard Herrmann
    Jaws, 1975, John Williams

The Pink Panther, 1963, Henry Mancini
Exodus, 1960, Ernest Gold
Out of Africa, 1985, John Barry
Doctor Zhivago, 1965, Maurice Jarre
The Bridge on the River Kwai, 1957, Malcolm Arnold/Kenneth Alford
Patton, 1970, Jerry Goldsmith
Rocky, 1976, Bill Conti
The Magnificent Seven, 1960, Elmer Bernstein
The Natural, 1984, Randy Newman
Cinema Paradiso, 1988, Andrea Morricone/Ennio Morricone
The Godfather, 1972, Nino Rota
E.T. the Extra-Terrestrial, 1982, John Williams
Gone with the Wind, 1939, Max Steiner
"Summertime" from *Porgy and Bess* (Symphonic arrangement of George Gershwin's 1935 aria), 2001
"By the Beautiful Sea" (Symphonic arrangement of Harry Carroll and Harold R. Atteridge's 1914 song), 1999
"Theme from *Now, Voyager*" (Symphonic arrangement for violin and orchestra from Max Steiner's 1942 film score), 1998
"Smile" from *Modern Times* (Symphonic arrangement for violin and orchestra from Charlie Chaplin's 1936 film score), 1998
"Love Theme" from *The Lost Weekend* (Symphonic arrangement for violin and orchestra from Miklós Rózsa's 1945 film score), 1998
"Marian and Robin Love Theme" from *The Adventures of Robin Hood* (Symphonic arrangement for violin and orchestra from Erich Wolfgang Korngold's 1938 film score), 1998
"As Time Goes By" from *Casablanca* (Symphonic arrangement for violin and orchestra of Herman Hupfeld's 1931 song featured in the film), 1998
"Stella by Starlight" from *The Uninvited* (Symphonic arrangement for violin and orchestra of Victor Young's song featured in the film), 1998
"Main Title" from *The Color Purple* (Symphonic arrangement for violin and orchestra from Quincy Jones's 1985 film score), 1996
"Papa, Can You Hear Me?" from *Yentl* (Symphonic arrangement for violin and orchestra of Michel Legrand and Alan and Marilyn Bergman's 1983 song featured in the film), 1996
Il Postino (Symphonic arrangement for violin and orchestra from Luis Bacalov's 1994 film score), 1996
Por una Cabeza (Symphonic arrangement for violin and orchestra of Carlos Gardel's 1935 tango featured in such films as *Scent of a Woman* and *True Lies*), 1996

"Manha de Carnaval" from *Black Orpheus* (Symphonic arrangement for violin and orchestra of Luiz Bonfá and Antonio Maria's 1959 song featured in the film), 1996

"Hooray for Hollywood" (Symphonic arrangement of Richard Whiting and Johnny Mercer's 1937 song featured in *Hollywood Hotel*), 1988

"A Sleepin' Bee" (Symphonic arrangement of Harold Arlen and Truman Capote's 1954 song), 1984

My Fair Lady (Arrangement for jazz band of Frederick Loewe and Alan Jay Lerner's 1956 musical), 1964

Glossary

absolute music: Music that is *ab soluta* (untied), that is, composed for a
stand-alone listening experience freed from any external influences and
extramusical references. The term originated in the nineteenth century,
within the philosophical framework of Idealism.

applied/functional music: A musical rendition of a literary text, like a
symphonic poem, or a musical accompaniment to an extramusical event,
such as a ballet, an opera, or a film.

BMI: Broadcast Music, Inc., one of the top music rights management agencies.

CGI: Computer-generated imagery.

cinephile: Film buff.

cognitive function: An instance in which film music serves to clarify explicit
or implicit meanings implied by the film, giving clues to understand denotations and to interpret connotations.

diegetic: Music or sound presented as originated from some source within the
film's world. It can be heard by film viewers and by characters as well.

emotive function (micro/macro): Locally, film music serves to enhance an
emotional tone already present in a scene or to provide one by transferring
to the images its emotional component (micro-emotive function). Globally—
by presenting the theme in the opening titles, then reprising it in variations
throughout the film and finally presenting it again at the end of the film—
film music performs a function similar to that of a frame in a painting and

unifies the aesthetic experience of the film for the viewer (macro-emotive function).

"gradual disclosure of the main theme": A typical John Williams technique that has both a macro- and a micro-emotive function. The main theme is presented gradually across the film, in form of progressively longer melodic fragments. The final exposition of the theme in its entirety comes only at a strategic point in the narrative, typically in a scene requiring a strong emotional response from the viewers. Globally, the gradual and coherent development of the music projects onto the film's form a sense of overall coherence (macro-emotive function). Locally, when the viewers finally hear the familiar theme presented in its entirety, the effect is a strong emotional gratification that attaches to that particular scene (micro-emotive function).

leitmotiv: In music dramas, and later in film music, the association and identification of a character, situation, or idea with a musical motif, which is reprised and developed narratively throughout the work.

MIDI: Musical instrument digital interface. This technology allows a keyboard to be connected to a computer, which directly transcribes the music as one plays.

Mickey-Mousing: A film music technique aimed at adhering closely to the visuals through a tight series of explicit synch-points where musical gestures duplicate visual actions.

montage: A film editing technique that serves to condense time, space, narrative, and conceptual information. It is mostly used to summarize in an emblematic sequence events that would otherwise require a lengthier presentation, or to convey concepts through semantically meaningful juxtapositions of images.

non-diegetic: Music or sound that is not part of the film's world. Film viewers can hear it; characters cannot.

pandiatonicism: An approach to composition that employs the notes of the diatonic scale freely without conventional resolutions. Unlike in traditional diatonic writing, the chords built on the scale grades are not assigned fixed functions and different degrees of importance.

"pay off": The moment in the film where the function of the "set up" (see below) is revealed and fulfilled.

quartal harmony: Chords are built not as juxtaposed thirds but as juxtaposed fourths, creating freer and more dissonant harmonic patterns than traditional tonal harmony.

"set up": The planting of a piece of information in the film whose function will be clear at a later moment—for example, a detail that initially seems to be of no importance is later revealed to be essential for a turning point in the plot.

spatial perceptive function: An instance in which film music serves to guide or modify the perception of the viewer by pointing his attention to a particular element within the framed space.

synch-point: A moment in a film where a visual event and a musical event are precisely synchronized and perfectly matched.

tam tam: A kind of large indefinite-pitched "gong" used in symphony orchestras.

temporal perceptive function: An instance in which film music serves to influence the perception of the pace of the film, by using its own rhythm to speed up or slow down the visual rhythm and the speed of the cutting.

tone clusters: Groups of contiguous notes played simultaneously and therefore sounding highly dissonant and perceived as "fastidiously" grating.

tritone: An augmented-fourth interval, slightly dissonant. It was known as "diabolus in musica" in medieval treatises.

typage: An immediately recognizable one-dimensional figure representing a specific ethnic or social group.

"villains' chords": Low-pitched minor chords played by the brass, mostly with the seventh degree of the scale on the bottom, recurrently used in Hollywood film music of the 1930s and 1940s.

Notes

Preface on Methodology

1. On neoformalism, see David Bordwell and Kristin Thompson, *Film Art: An Introduction*, 9th ed. (New York: McGraw-Hill, 2010); Kristin Thompson, *Eisenstein's "Ivan the Terrible": A Neoformalist Analysis* (Princeton, NJ: Princeton University Press, 1981); David Bordwell, *Narration in the Fiction Film* (London: Routledge, 1988); Kristin Thompson, *Breaking the Glass Armor: Neoformalist Film Analysis* (Princeton, NJ: Princeton University Press, 1988).

2. Leonard B. Meyer, *Emotion and Meaning in Music* (Chicago: University of Chicago Press, 1956); Leonard B. Meyer, *Style and Music: Theory, History, and Ideology* (Chicago: University of Chicago Press, 1989); John Sloboda, *The Musical Mind: The Cognitive Psychology of Music*, new ed. (New York: Oxford University Press, 1999); Robert Jourdain, *Music, the Brain, and Ecstasy: How Music Captures Our Imagination* (New York: HarperCollins, 1997); Annabel Cohen, "Film Music: Perspectives from Cognitive Psychology," in *Music and Cinema*, ed. James Buhler, Caryl Flinn, and David Neumeyer (Middletown, CT: Wesleyan University Press, 2000), 360–77. See also the following articles collected in *Psychomusicology* 13 (Spring/Fall 1994): William Forde Thompson, Frank A. Russo, and Don Sinclair, "Effects of Underscoring on the Perception of Closure in Filmed Events"; Valerie J. Bolivar, Annabel J. Cohen, and John C. Fentress, "Semantic and Formal Congruency in Music and Motion Pictures: Effects on the Interpretation of Visual Action"; Scott D. Lipscomb and Roger A. Kendall, "Perceptual Judgment of the Relationship between Musical and Visual Components in Film"; George Sirius and Eric F. Clarke, "The Perception of Audiovisual Relationships: A Preliminary Study"; Shin-ichiro Iwamiya, "Interactions between Auditory and Visual Processing when Listening to Music in an

Audio Visual Context: 1. Matching 2. Audio Quality"; William H. Rosar, "Film Music and Heinz Werner's Theory of Physiognomic Perception"; Claudia Bullerjahn and Markus Güldering, "An Empirical Investigation of Effects of Film Music Using Qualitative Content Analysis."

3. K. Thompson, *Breaking the Glass Armor*, 10.

4. On cognitivism and narrative frames, see David Bordwell, "A Case for Cognitivism," *Iris* 9 (Spring 1989): 23.

5. On the gratification effect given by the recognition of familiar melodies, following the "law of return" of the Gestalt Theory, see Meyer, *Emotion and Meaning in Music*, 151–52, and the "pleasure of recognition" in Meyer, *Style and Music*, 210n.

6. Fred Karlin, *Listening to Movies: The Film Lover's Guide to Film Music* (Belmont: Schirmer, 1994), 17–18.

7. "Miss Austria" was composed by Korngold in 1929 for his arrangement of Leo Fall's operetta *Rosen Aus Florida*.

8. The terms *intra-diegetic, extra-diegetic*, and *meta-diegetic* are drawn from Gérard Genette, *Figures III* (Paris: Seuil, 1972). The application of Genette's categories to film music is discussed in Claudia Gorbman, *Unheard Melodies: Narrative Film Music* (London and Bloomington: BFI/Indiana University Press, 1987), 20–26. Gorbman named the extra-diegetic level "non-diegetic level" and is credited for having established the terms as canonical tools of film-music analysis. These categories have been renamed *internal level—external level—mediated level* in Sergio Miceli, *La musica nel film: Arte e artigianato* (Fiesole: Discanto, 1982), 223–30. Bordwell and Thompson, *Film Art: An Introduction*, 290, call the meta-diegetic level "internal diegetic sound," while other scholars refrain from taking it into consideration. The remaining categories—diegetic and extra-diegetic—are called *screen music* and *pit music* by Michel Chion, *Audio-Vision: Sound On Screen*, trans. and ed. Claudia Gorbman (New York: Columbia University Press, 1994), 77; *in-music* and *off-music* by Ermanno Comuzio, *Colonna sonora: Dialoghi, musiche rumori dietro lo schermo* (Milan: Il Formichiere, 1980), 4; *source music* and *background music* by Hollywood practitioners, see David Neumeyer, "Introduction," in Buhler et al., *Music and Cinema*, 18.

9. See William H. Rosar, "Film Studies in Musicology: Disciplinarity vs. Interdisciplinarity," *Journal of Film Music* 2, no. 2–4 (Winter 2009): 108–17; Ben Winters, "The Non-Diegetic Fallacy: Film, Music, and Narrative Space," *Music and Letters* 91, no. 2 (2010): 224–44.

10. Theodor W. Adorno and Hanns Eisler, *Composing for the Films* (1947; repr. New York: Continuum, 2007), 2–3.

11. Sergio Miceli, *Musica per film: Storia, Estetica, Analisi, Tipologie* (Lucca: LIM/Ricordi, 2009), 667–70.

12. James Buhler, "*Star Wars*, Music, and Myth," in Buhler et al., *Music and Cinema*, 33–57; Scott D. Paulin, "Richard Wagner and the Fantasy of Cinematic Unity: The Idea of the Gesamtkunstwerk in the History and Theory of Film Music," in Buhler et al., *Music and Cinema*, 58–84; Justin London, "Leitmotifs and Musical Reference in the Classical Film Score," in Buhler et al., *Music and Cinema*, 85–96.

13. For an against-the-tide view of "wallpaper music," see Ben Winters, "Musical Wallpaper? Towards an Appreciation of Non-narrating Music in Film," *Music, Sound, and the Moving Image* 6, no. 1 (Spring 2012): 41–54.

14. Style in the *broader sense* is somewhat similar here to the concept of "paradigm" or "group style" as used in David Bordwell, Janet Staiger, and Kristin Thompson, *The Classical Hollywood Cinema: Film Style and Mode of Production to 1960* (New York: Columbia University Press, 1985), 5.

15. Meyer, *Style and Music*, 23–25.

16. Miceli, *Musica per film*, 616.

17. Bordwell et al., *Classical Hollywood Cinema*, 33–35.

18. Meyer, *Style and Music*, 163, 327.

Introduction

1. Stephen Moss, "The Force Is with Him," *Guardian* (London), 4 February 2002.

2. Geoffrey McNab, "They Shoot, He Scores," *Times* (London), 25 September 2001.

3. Roberto Aschieri, *Over the Moon: La mùsica de John Williams para el cine* (Santiago de Chile: Universidad Diego Portales, 1999); Peter Moormann, *Spielberg-Variationen: Die Filmmusik von John Williams* (Baden-Baden: Nomos, 2010); Alexandre Tylski, ed., *John Williams: Un alchimiste musical à Hollywood* (Paris: L'Harmattan, 2011); Andrés Valverde Amador, *John Williams: Vida y obra* (Seville: Editorial Berenice, 2013).

4. Tom Shone, "How to Score in the Movies," *Sunday Times* (London), 21 June 1998.

Chapter 1
"The Classical Hollywood Music"

1. Rick Altman, *Silent Film Sound* (New York: Columbia University Press, 2004), 199–201.

2. "*Attractions monstratifs*": André Gaudreault and Tom Gunning, "Le cinéma des premieres temps: Un défi à l'histoire du cinéma?," in *Histoire du cinéma: Nouvelles approches*, ed. Jacques Aumont, André Gaudreault, and Michel Marie (Paris: Publications de la Sorbonne, 1989), 49–63.

3. Douglas Gomery, *Shared Pleasures: A History of Movie Presentation in the United States* (London: BFI, 1992), 18–56.

4. Gaudreault and Gunning, "Le cinéma des premieres temps," 49–63.

5. Classical explanations can be found in Kurt London, *Film Music: A Summary of the Characteristic Features of Its History, Aesthetics, Technique; and Possible Developments* (London: Faber and Faber, 1936), 25–46; and Adorno and Eisler, *Composing for the Films*, 50–51. A summary is in Gorbman, *Unheard Melodies*, 53. A more recent summary is in Peter Larsen, *Film Music* (London: Reaktion Books, 2005), 184–201.

6. Altman, *Silent Film Sound*, 231–46.

7. On *The Birth of a Nation*'s score, see Martin Miller Marks, *Music and the Silent Film: Contexts and Case Studies, 1895–1924* (New York: Oxford University Press, 1997), 108–66.

8. Quoted in Caryl Flinn, *Strains of Utopia: Gender, Nostalgia, and Hollywood Music* (Princeton, NJ: Princeton University Press, 1992), 17.

9. Kristin Thompson and David Bordwell, *Film History: An Introduction*, 3rd ed. (New York: McGraw-Hill, 2010), 177.

10. Tony Thomas, *Music for the Movies*, 2nd ed. (1973, repr., Los Angeles: Silman-James, 1997), 139.

11. Michael Slowik, "Hollywood Film Music in the Early Sound Era, 1926–1934" (PhD diss., University of Iowa, 2012). Thanks to Jeff Smith for bringing this to my attention.

12. Roy M. Prendergast, *Film Music: A Neglected Art: A Critical Study of Music in Films* (New York: W. W. Norton, 1977), 23.

13. Barry Salt, *Film Style and Technology: History and Analysis*, 2nd ed. (London: Starword, 1992), 212.

14. In postrecording, the music track originally used on the set as a guide for the actors' singing and dancing is replaced with a definitive new version. See Fred Karlin and Rayburn Wright, *On the Track: A Guide to Contemporary Film Scoring*, 2nd ed. (New York: Routledge, 2004), 441–42. Dubbing is the mixing and balancing of the three separate dialogue, effect, and music tracks into a single, final sound track to be printed on the film's master. See Karlin, *Listening to Movies*, 56–62.

15. Prendergast, *Film Music*, 22–23.

16. Mervyn Cooke, *A History of Film Music* (Cambridge: Cambridge University Press, 2008), 123.

17. Kathryn Kalinak, *Settling the Score: Music and the Classical Hollywood Film* (Madison: University of Wisconsin Press, 1992), 70.

18. Another noteworthy instance is *Mr. Robinson Crusoe* (A. Edward Sutherland, 1932), in which Alfred Newman's score covers virtually each of the film's seventy minutes, not just as a neutral wallpaper but also with moments of functional accompaniment.

19. Tony Thomas, *Film Score: The Art and Craft of Movie Music* (Burbank, CA: Riverwood, 1991), 68.

20. Christopher Palmer, *The Composer in Hollywood* (London: Marion Boyars, 1990), 29.

21. Gorbman, *Unheard Melodies*, 65.

22. In the horror genre, early occurrences of functional non-diegetic music can be spotted in *The Mummy* (Karl Freund, 1932, music by James Dietrich).

23. See Kalinak, *Settling the Score*, xvi; Chion, *Audio-Vision*, 49–50; Gary Marmorstein, *Hollywood Rhapsody: Movie Music and Its Makers, 1900 to 1975* (New York: Schirmer Books, 1997), 71.

24. Music departments are described in Karlin, *Listening to Movies*, 177–95. A typical organization chart can be found in Prendergast, *Film Music*, 37.

25. For further reading on the composers' biographies, see T. Thomas, *Film Score*;

T. Thomas, *Music for the Movies*; Palmer, *Composer in Hollywood*; William Darby and Jack Du Bois, *American Film Music: Major Composers, Techniques, Trends, 1915–1990* (Jefferson, NC: McFarland, 1990); and Marmorstein, *Hollywood Rhapsody*.

26. Copland's most important scores were those for *Of Mice and Men* (Lewis Milestone, 1939); *The Heiress* (William Wyler, 1949); and *The Red Pony* (Lewis Milestone, 1949).

27. On Korngold, see Jessica Duchen, *Erich Wolfgang Korngold* (London: Phaidon, 1996) and Brendan G. Carroll, *The Last Prodigy: A Biography of Erich Wolfgang Korngold* (Cleckheaton: Amadeus Press, 1997).

28. T. Thomas, *Music for the Movies*, 124.

29. See David Bordwell, *On the History of Film Style* (Cambridge, MA: Harvard University Press, 1997), 211–36.

30. Royal S. Brown, *Overtones and Undertones: Reading Film Music* (Berkeley: University of California Press, 1994), 153.

31. Miceli, *Musica per film*, 229.

32. Miklós Rózsa, *A Double Life: The Autobiography of Miklós Rózsa, Composer in the Golden Years of Hollywood* (1982; repr., New York: Wynwood Press, 1989).

33. The theremin is an electronic instrument devised by Lev Theremin in 1928. Electronic oscillators are contained in a wooden box to which are attached a horizontal loop antenna and a vertical upright antenna. The player controls the pitch—with the upright antenna—and the volume—via the loop antenna—by moving his hands around the antennas, thus modifying the electric fields. The Ondes Martenot was invented in 1928 by Maurice Martenot; it is technically similar to the theremin but instead controlled through a keyboard, which makes intonation easier, and it has a sweeter, softer sound.

34. Prendergast, *Film Music*, 64.

35. Salt, *Film Style and Technology*, 245–48.

36. Gomery, *Shared Pleasures*, 226.

37. John Belton, "Il colore: dall'eccezione alla regola," in *Storia del cinema mondiale, Teorie, strumenti, memorie*, vol. 5, ed. Gian Piero Brunetta (Turin: Einaudi, 2001), 801–28.

38. Gomery, *Shared Pleasures*, 239–41.

39. Thompson and Bordwell, *Film History*, 311. The Percepto can be seen at work in *Matinee* (Joe Dante, 1993), in which John Goodman's character is based on the producer/director William Castle.

40. The music sounded so sexually evocative when matched with the visuals that it had to be toned down to comply with the prescriptions of the Production Code. See Cooke, *History of Film Music*, 216.

41. "The New Musical Resources," in Adorno and Eisler, *Composing for the Films*, 21–29.

42. Palmer, *Composer in Hollywood*, 224; and Rózsa, *Double Life*, 192.

43. On "Indian music," see Timothy E. Scheurer, *Music and Mythmaking in Film: Genre and the Role of the Composer* (London: McFarland, 2008), 157–58.

44. Gomery, *Shared Pleasures*, 83–88.

45. Cooke, *History of Film Music*, 185.

46. James Wierzbicki, *Film Music: A History* (New York: Routledge, 2009), 186.

47. Karlin, *Listening to Movies*, 75.

Chapter 2
"The Classical Hollywood Music"

1. Adorno and Eisler, *Composing for the Films*, 21-22.

2. Hugo Friedhofer, quoted in T. Thomas, *Film Score*, 2. See also T. Thomas, *Music for the Movies*, 44-45; and Cooke, *History of Film Music*, 69.

3. Palmer, *Composer in Hollywood*, 19-23.

4. Flinn, *Strains of Utopia*, 13-50. Recent studies even posit that nostalgia is not so much inherently produced by a specific piece of music—let alone by a specific musical dialect—as is the effect of a mental process called "perceptual fluency" of which said piece of music is just an idiosyncratic trigger. "Perceptual fluency" means that recollections stored in the long-term memory are easily retrieved thanks to one particular stimulus, and such ease produces a pleasant nostalgia effect (thanks to Jeff Smith for pointing this out). See, for example, Jason P. Leboe and Tamara L. Ansons, "On Misattributing Good Remembering to a Happy Past: An Investigation into the Cognitive Roots of Nostalgia," *Emotions* 6, no. 4 (2006): 596-610.

5. Flinn, *Strains of Utopia*, 70-90.

6. Ibid., 51-69.

7. Yann Merluzeau, "Hollywood Bowl Conductor John Mauceri," *Film Score Monthly*, August 1996, 9.

8. Scheurer, *Music and Mythmaking in Film*, 14-18.

9. David Bordwell, "The Classical Hollywood Style, 1917-60," in Bordwell et al., *Classical Hollywood Cinema*, 3-84.

10. T. Thomas, *Film Score*, 72, 246; Adorno and Eisler, *Composing for the Films*, 90; George Burt, *The Art of Film Music* (Boston: Northeastern University Press, 1994), 5-6.

11. The composer Hugo Friedhofer gives an explanation in terms of work at subliminal level in T. Thomas, *Film Score*, 214.

12. Gorbman, *Unheard Melodies*, 55. An argument against Gorbman's theory is in Jeff Smith, "Unheard Melodies? A Critique of Psychoanalytic Theories of Film Music," in *Post-Theory: Reconstructing Film Studies*, ed. David Bordwell and Noël Carroll (Madison: University of Wisconsin Press, 1996), 230-47.

13. Stephen Prince, "Psychoanalytic Film Theory and the Problem of the Missing Spectator," in Bordwell and Carroll, *Post-Theory*, 71-86; Bordwell, "A Case for Cognitivism."

14. Cohen, "Film Music," 366-74.

15. The process is described and exemplified with empirical evidence in Sloboda, *Musical Mind*, 166-74 and 264.

16. Meyer, *Emotion and Meaning in Music*, 63; Sloboda, *Musical Mind*, 20; Meyer, *Style and Music*, 201.

17. Bordwell, *Narration in the Fiction Film*, 35 and throughout; Chris Vogler, *The Writer's Journey: Mythic Structures for Writers*, 3rd ed. (Studio City: Michael Wiese Productions, 2007), xiv.

18. Meyer, *Style and Music*, 209, 322.

19. Ibid., 340–42.

20. Meyer, *Emotion and Meaning in Music*, 158–66.

21. Wierzbicki, *Film Music*, 129.

22. Sometimes the clash between traditional associations and contrasting visuals is deliberately sought, most notably by Kubrick—for instance, in *2001: A Space Odyssey* (1968) he accompanied the rotating space station with J. Strauss's waltz *The Blue Danube* (*An der schönen blauen Donau*, 1866, op. 314).

23. Prendergast, *Film Music*, 233.

24. Although in art music "theme and variations" is more properly defined as a form rather than as a technique, here theme and variations is seen as a technique that film music employs to cope with a particular narrative need from the film.

25. Altman, *Silent Film Sound*, 52, 105.

26. On cartoon music, see Scott Bradley, "Evoluzione della musica nei disegni animati," in *Musica e Film*, ed. S. G. Biamonte (Rome: Edizioni dell'Ateneo, 1959), 217–32; Scott Bradley, "Personality on the Soundtrack," in *The Hollywood Film Music Reader*, ed. Mervyn Cooke (New York: Oxford University Press, 2010), 101–6; Ingolf Dahl, "Notes on Cartoon Music," in Cooke, *Hollywood Film Music Reader*, 93–100.

27. For Max Steiner's words on Mickey-Mousing, see Myrl A. Schreibman, "Memories of Max: An Archival Interview with Max Steiner. Part 1," *Film Score Monthly*, January/February 2005, 26.

28. James Buhler, "Analytical and Interpretive Approaches to Film Music (II): Analyzing Interactions of Music and Film," in *Film Music: Critical Approaches*, ed. K. J. Donnelly (New York: Continuum, 2001), 45.

29. Cohen, *Film Music*, 371. The point is also sustained by Kalinak, *Settling the Score*, 86.

30. On Hollywood film orchestras, see Adorno and Eisler, *Composing for the Films*, 70–77; Karlin, *Listening to Movies*, 183–86.

31. Wierzbicki, *Film Music*, 48–49.

32. Altman, *Silent Film Sound*, 308.

33. On orchestral timbres and musical dramaturgy, see Gerard Blanchard, *Images de la musique de cinéma* (Paris: Edilio, 1984).

34. See Mark Evans, *Soundtrack: The Music of the Movies* (New York: Hopkinson and Blake, 1975), 252.

35. On the debate on the use of orchestrators and the different European and American positions, particularly referred to the Seventh International Music Conference held in Florence in 1950, see Wierzbicki, *Film Music*, 169–74. Hollywood practice is described from a European viewpoint in Daniele Amfitheatrof, "La musica per film negli Stati Uniti d'America," in *La musica nel film*, ed. Enzo Masetti (Rome: Bianco e Nero, 1950), 118–28.

36. T. Thomas, *Music for the Movies*, 212–13; David Raksin, "Life with Charlie," in Cooke, *Hollywood Film Music Reader*, 69–81.

37. Cooke, *Hollywood Film Music Reader*, viii.

38. Schreibman, "Memories of Max. Part 1," 27; and Myrl A. Schreibman, "Memories of Max: An Archival Interview with Max Steiner. Part 2," *Film Score Monthly*, March/April 2005, 23.

39. Paul Andrew MacLean, "What Exactly Does an Orchestrator Do?," *Film Score Monthly*, June 1993, 6.

40. Miceli, *La musica nel film*, 327 (my translation).

41. Karlin, *Listening to Movies*, 35.

42. For further reading on orchestration in cinema, see Karlin and Wright, *On the Track*, 320–30; and Richard Davis, *Complete Guide to Film Scoring: The Art and Business of Writing Music for Movies and TV* (Boston: Berklee Press, 1999), 111–16, which compares a composer's sketch and the resultant full score. Hollywood practice is defended in Lawrence Morton, "Composing, Orchestrating, and Criticizing," in Cooke, *Hollywood Music Reader*, 327–40.

43. Prendergast, *Film Music*, 85.

44. Gorbman, *Unheard Melodies*, 88.

45. Larsen, *Film Music*, 89.

46. Cooke, *History of Film Music*, 86.

47. Karlin and Wright, *On the Track*, 157–58.

48. Kalinak, *Settling the Score*, 187.

49. Bordwell et al., *Classical Hollywood Cinema*, 3.

50. A narrative film is made up of a series of events that form the *plot*: what we see in the film in its given order. The viewer is actively engaged in the reconstruction of the correct chronological and causal order of the narrative events presented in the film's plot, and that viewer inferentially fills the gaps when some narrative information is omitted. The result is the mental reconstruction of the *story*, that is, the correct chronological and causal order of all the events concerning the film's narrative, and comprising both those events presented in the plot and those implied by the viewer's inference. On plot/story (*syuzhet/fabula*), see Bordwell, *Narration in the Fiction Film*, 48–62.

51. Chion, *Audio-Vision*, 11 and 122.

Chapter 3
The "Modern" Hollywood Music Style

1. To stick to the "language/techniques/means/function" four-point definition of a film-music style, "modern style" is used instead of "pop score"; see Jeff Smith, *The Sound of Commerce: Marketing Popular Film Music* (New York: Columbia University Press, 1998), 4. A hypothetical atonal score (*language*) with neither leitmotiv nor Mickey-Mousing (*techniques*) but played by a symphony orchestra (*musical means*) cannot be called "classical," but it is not "pop" either. Therefore, the term "modern style" is more precise and flexible a definition here.

2. Bordwell, *Narration in the Fiction Film*, 206–9.

3. Russell Lack, *Twenty Four Frames Under: A Buried History of Film Music* (London: Quartet Books, 1997), 283.

4. Roberto Calabretto, *Lo schermo sonoro: La musica per film* (Venice: Marsilio, 2010), 148n (my translation). On Antonioni's dislike of and uneasiness about film music, see ibid., 170.

5. Calabretto, *Lo schermo sonoro*, 155n (my translation).

6. Comuzio, *Colonna sonora*, 120 (my translation).

7. Lack, *Twenty Four Frames Under*, 161.

8. On European film music, see Miguel Mera and David Burnand, *European Film Music* (London: Ashgate, 2006).

9. Jerrold Levinson, "Film Music and Narrative Agency," in Bordwell and Carroll, *Post-Theory*, 277.

10. J. Smith, *Sound of Commerce*, 131–53; and Charles Leinberger, *Ennio Morricone's "The Good, the Bad and the Ugly": A Film Score Guide* (Lanham, MD: Scarecrow Press, 2004).

11. Stefano Sorice, "Ennio Morricone racconta . . . (parte terza)," *Colonne Sonore*, November/December 2005, 9 (my translation).

12. Miceli, *La musica nel film*, 319 (my translation).

13. Comuzio, *Colonna sonora*, 161 (my translation).

14. Leinberger, *Ennio Morricone's "The Good, the Bad and the Ugly,"* 18.

15. On jazz in films, see Cooke, *History of Film Music*, 222.

16. On the demographical change in audience, see Robert Sklar, *Movie-Made America: A Cultural History of American Movies* (New York: Vintage Books, 1994), 269–304; and Thompson and Bordwell, *Film History*, 472–93.

17. Altman, *Silent Film Sound*, 190.

18. Cooke, *History of Film Music*, 25.

19. Wierzbicki, *Film Music*, 114.

20. On the early attempts to market symphonic film-music albums, see Kyle S. Barnett, "The Selznick Studio, 'Spellbound,' and the Marketing of Film Music," *Music, Sound, and the Moving Image* 4, no. 1 (Spring 2010): 77–98.

21. Laura Mulvey, "Visual Pleasure and Narrative Cinema," *Screen*, Autumn 1975, 6–18.

22. On the aesthetics and functions of pop songs in films, see Cooke, *History of Film Music*, 412–14. On "pop scores" in general, see J. Smith, *Sound of Commerce*, 5–23.

23. J. Smith, *Sound of Commerce*, 32.

24. Marmorstein, *Hollywood Rhapsody*, 387.

25. On the "package-unit system," see Bordwell et al., *Classical Hollywood Cinema*, 330. In the classical period the average annual output was 400 films, while in the 1960s it plummeted to 150 films. See Christopher Wagstaff, "Quasi un'appendice: Alcune cifre sull'industria cinematografica statunitense," in *Storia del cinema mondiale*, vol. 2, *Gli Stati Uniti*, ed. Gian Piero Brunetta (Turin: Einaudi 2000), 1758.

26. J. Smith, *Sound of Commerce*, 146.

27. Ibid., 145.

28. For a musical analysis of *American Graffiti*, see ibid., 172–85.

29. Miceli, *Musica per film*, 679.

30. For a musical analysis of *Goldfinger*, see J. Smith, *Sound of Commerce*, 100–130.

31. Chion, *Audio-Vision*, 8–9.

32. See Larsen, *Film Music*, 155.

33. Prendergast, *Film Music*, 26: "The song was placed in the film in the hopes that it would 'make the charts' and make that much more money for the film." Marmorstein, *Hollywood Rhapsody*, 384: "Utterly incongruous to the action, the song was the equivalent of an early music video."

34. On "compilation scores," see J. Smith, *Sound of Commerce*, 163–72.

35. Ibid., 79. Mancini was the first musician to expressly record new album versions of selected sections of his film scores.

36. Ibid., 78.

37. *Bachelor in Paradise* (Jack Arnold, 1961) is another example of Mancini's ingenuity in displaying and promoting the title song throughout the film. The title song is introduced in the opening titles and then reprised in instrumental form, not only in the nondiegetic score but also as a Muzak-like diegetic wallpaper in the supermarket sequence. It is even evoked through the sound of the protagonist's door bell, whose three tones are the very opening notes of the title song.

38. For a historical overview of the period from a film-music perspective, see L. E. MacDonald, *The Invisible Art of Film Music* (New York: Ardsley House, 1998), 173–333.

39. Jack Sullivan, *Hitchcock's Music* (New Haven, CT: Yale University Press, 2006), 277.

40. Cooke, *History of Film Music*, 396.

41. Sullivan, *Hitchcock's Music*, 288.

42. Ibid., 283.

43. Irwin Bazelon, *Knowing the Score: Notes on Film Music* (New York: Arco, 1975), 190.

44. T. Thomas, *Film Score*, 257.

Chapter 4

Star Wars

1. This was the original working title: J. W. Rinzler, *The Making of Star Wars: The Definitive Story Behind the Original Film* (London: Ebury Publishing, 2007), 8.

2. Ibid., 14–15.

3. Ibid., 48.

4. Ibid., 18–19.

5. Ibid., 31, 37, 178.

6. Ibid., 105.

7. Scheurer, *Music and Mythmaking in Film*, 48–79.

8. Jeff Bond, CD booklet, *Planet of the Apes*, Varése Sarabande, 1997, VSD-5848.

9. James Wierzbicki, *Louis and Bebe Barron's "Forbidden Planet": A Film Score Guide* (Lanham, MD: Scarecrow Press, 2005).

10. Cooke, *History of Film Music*, 442.

11. Ibid., 422.

12. Rinzler, *Making of Star Wars*, 273; and Michael Matessino, "A New Hope for Film Music," CD booklet for *Star Wars: A New Hope*, BMG, 1997, 09026 68772 2, 7.

13. Matessino, "A New Hope for Film Music," 6; Michael Goodson, "Yes, There's Life after Fiedler," *Boston Sunday Herald*, 27 January 1980; John Williams, quoted in T. Thomas, *Film Score*, 334–35; Cooke, *History of Film Music*, 462; Chris Malone, "Recording the Star Wars Saga: A Musical Journey from Scoring Stage to DVD," p. 6, version 1.4, 2012, www.malonedigital.com/starwars.pdf, accessed 2 April 2013; Rinzler, *Making of Star Wars*, 292; John Williams, liner notes for the *Star Wars* LP album, 20th Century Records, 1977, 2T-541 (0898). But on the other hand, when interviewed by Leonard Maltin, Lucas said that he had always had the idea of having an original score—*The Empire Strikes Back*, VHS, Fox, 1995. However, *2001* was an influential model and Lucas had already used a compilation score for *American Graffiti*; in the liner notes for the 1977 album Williams wrote that Lucas originally wanted repertoire music, and Lucas, being the album producer, accepted at that time Williams's statement as true. So, it seems quite probable that Lucas's original idea was to use repertoire music as the film's main themes.

14. George Lucas, video interview with Leonard Maltin, *The Empire Strikes Back*, VHS, Fox, 1995.

15. Rinzler, *Making of Star Wars*, 59.

16. Richard Dyer, "John Williams: New Horizons, Familiar Galaxies," *Boston Globe*, 4 June 1997.

17. As a rule, Williams does not read screenplays. However, Rinzler, *Making of Star Wars*, 60, and Matessino, "A New Hope for Film Music," 6, report that Williams did read the *Star Wars* screenplay. In an interview, Williams stated, "I didn't read the script. I don't like to read scripts. . . . Having said that I don't even remember if George Lucas offered me a script to read." Craig L. Byrd, "The *Star Wars* Interview: John Williams," *Film Score Monthly*, January/February 1997, 18, reprinted in Cooke, *Hollywood Film Music Reader*, 238. Maybe Williams did read the screenplay, his recollections not being clear on the matter. In the same year, when asked about how a director hires, Williams answered by mentioning the sending of a screenplay as a first approach: "Someone like you could send a script to a composer like me and say 'Will you read the script?' But usually I work from a director's cut or a first cut." David Thomas, "Point Blank: The Total Film Interview: John Williams," *Total Film*, September 1997, 79. Therefore, it seems possible that Williams at least glanced at the *Star Wars* screenplay, given the innovative nature of that project.

18. Williams, liner notes for the *Star Wars* LP album.

19. It is customary in contemporary Hollywood that a film's first cut be coupled with a temporary repertoire music track in order to help the editor and the director in

obtaining the required rhythm and mood. Then, the temp-tracked film is shown to the composer, who can gather from the director's musical choices how much music is needed and what kind of approach and language are required.

20. T. Thomas, *Film Score*, 335.

21. Byrd, "The *Star Wars* Interview," 18.

22. *Village Voice* review, quoted in Kalinak, *Settling the Score*, 198.

23. Greg Oatis, "John Williams Strikes Back, Unfortunately," *Cinemafantastique* 10, no. 2 (Fall 1980): 8.

24. Kenneth Terry, "John Williams Encounters the Pops," *Downbeat* 48, March 1981, 20.

25. Timothy Mangan, "Composer for the Stars," *Gramophone* (U.S. Interview), May 2006, A7.

26. Richard Dyer, "Making *Star Wars* Sing Again," *Boston Globe*, 28 March 1999, reissued in *Film Score Monthly*, June 1999, 18–21; Williams, quoted in Richard Dyer, "Q&A with John Williams: Pops' Conductor Talks about His New Beat," *Boston Globe*, 27 April 1980.

27. Among the preeminent film projects were *Things to Come* (William Cameron Menzies, 1936, music by Arthur Bliss); *The Four Feathers* (Zoltan Korda, 1939, music by Miklós Rózsa); *Dangerous Moonlight* (Brian Desmond Hurst, 1941, music by Richard Addinsell, featuring the famous *Warsaw Concerto*); *49th Parallel* (Michael Powell, 1941, music by Ralph Vaughan Williams); *Henry V* (Laurence Olivier, 1944, music by William Walton); *The Man Who Knew Too Much* (Alfred Hitchcock, 1956, music by Bernard Herrmann); and *The Three Worlds of Gulliver* (Jack Sher, 1960, music by Bernard Herrmann). For a list, see http://lso.co.uk/page/3151/LSO-and-Film-Music, accessed 2 April 2013.

28. Malone, "Recording the Star Wars Saga," 11.

29. Ibid., 7. Orchestrated by Herbert W. Spencer, Angela Morley, Alexander Courage, Arthur Morton, Al Woodbury, and Williams himself.

30. Ibid., 11. Using Newman's own 1954 recording dubbed down from the sound track of *River of No Return* (Otto Preminger, 1954).

31. The discarded alternate version can be heard in the CD *Star Wars: A New Hope*, CD 1, track 13, BMG, 1997, 09026 68772 2.

32. Larsen, *Film Music*, 168.

33. Byrd, "The *Star Wars* Interview," 20.

34. For an analysis of the mythopoeic function of the *Star Wars* score, see Buhler, "*Star Wars*, Music, and Myth."

35. Byrd, "The *Star Wars* Interview," 20.

36. Williams, program notes for his *Horn Concerto*, 29 November 2003, concert program, Chicago Symphony Orchestra, Symphony Center, Chicago, IL.

37. Ian Lace, "The Film Music of John Williams," 1998, www.musicweb-international.com/film/lacejw.htm, accessed 2 April 2013.

38. Matt Wolf, "The Olympics Offers John Williams Another Heroic Challenge," *South Coast Today*, 21 July 1996.

39. Norman Lebrecht, "John Williams—The Magpie Maestro," *La Scena Musicale*, 20 November 2002, www.scena.org/columns/lebrecht/021120-NL-williams.html, accessed 2 April 2013.

40. Terry, "John Williams Encounters the Pops."

41. Rinzler, *Making of Star Wars*, 336.

42. Larsen, *Film Music*, 172–73; and "star wars" on www.riaa.com/goldandplatinum .php, accessed 2 April 2013.

43. Rinzler, *Making of Star Wars*, 336. As of 1983, this bonus share reportedly yielded $300,000: David Wessel, "The Force Is with Him . . . 'Rich Is Hard to Define,'" *Boston Globe*, 5 July 1983.

44. "Grammy Rewind: 20th Annual Grammy Awards," 17 January 2012, www .grammy.com/news/grammy-rewind-20th-annual-grammy-awards, accessed 2 April 2013.

45. Richard Dyer, "John Williams Is New Pops Maestro: A Musician's Musician," *Boston Globe*, 11 January 1980.

46. Rinzler, *Making of Star Wars*, 313–14; and Gomery, *Shared Pleasures*, 228.

47. Michael Matessino, "John Williams Strikes Back," CD booklet, *The Empire Strikes Back*, BMG Classics, 1997, 6.

48. Ibid., 12.

49. Transcript from *Star Wars: Episode I—The Phantom Menace: John Williams Interview*, videotape, Sony Classical, 9 April 1999.

50. Bob Thomas, "Williams Looks Backward in Composing Score for New *Star Wars* Movie," *Nevada Daily Mail*, 12 May 1999.

51. Richard Dyer, "An Enduring Love for Music, Movies," *Boston Globe*, 23 June 2002.

52. Josephine Reed, transcript of an interview with John Williams, *Art Works*, produced by the National Endowment for the Arts, 2009, http://arts.gov/audio/johnwilliams, accessed 2 April 2013. It is worth mentioning that a new *Star Wars* trilogy is in pre-production, with the first installment projected for release in 2015, and the eighty-one-year-old John Williams has announced that he does plan to compose the scores: "So, I'm planning my diet very carefully, eating a lot of Wheaties!" (Williams during the Boston Pops concert of 8 June 2013, aired by WGBH Radio on 22 June 2013).

53. J. Smith, *Sound of Commerce*, 217.

54. "Star Wars Tops AFI's List of 25 Greatest Film Scores of All Time," 23 September 2005, http://www.afi.com/100years/scores.aspx, accessed 2 April 2013.

55. Richard Dyer, "John Williams Bows In," *Boston Globe*, 11 January 1980.

56. "Commencement Citation," *Boston University Today*, 29 May 1985.

57. "People," *Time* magazine, 5 December 1977, http://content.time.com/time /magazine/article/0,9171,915779,00.html, accessed 2 April 2013. The program also included Gustav Holst's *The Planets* and Richard Strauss's *Thus Spoke Zarathustra*.

58. William Livingstone, "John Williams and the Boston Pops: An American Institution Enters a New Era," *Stereo Review* 45, no. 6 (December 1980): 76.

264 • Notes to pages 82–86

59. Publicity materials stored in the LucasFilm Archives.

60. Wessel, "The Force Is with Him."

61. Here is a sample list of post–*Star Wars* films featuring symphonic scores: *The Black Hole* (Gary Nelson, 1979, music by John Barry); *Star Trek : The Motion Picture* (Robert Wise, 1979, music by Jerry Goldsmith); *Conan the Barbarian* (John Milius, 1982, music by Basil Poledouris); *The Right Stuff* (Philip Kaufman, 1983, music by Bill Conti); *Out of Africa* (Sidney Pollack, 1985, music by John Barry); *Silverado* (Lawrence Kasdan, 1985, music by Bruce Broughton); *Back to the Future* (Robert Zemeckis, 1985, music by Alan Silvestri); *Lionheart* (Franklin J. Schaffner, 1987, music Jerry Goldsmith); *Willow* (Ron Howard, 1988, music by James Horner); *Who Framed Roger Rabbit* (Robert Zemeckis, 1988, music by Alan Silvestri); *Batman* (Tim Burton, 1989, music by Danny Elfman); in addition to Williams's own scores. One of the most hilarious and touching homages to classical Hollywood music is Miklós Rózsa's last film score, for *Dead Men Don't Wear Plaid* (Carl Reiner, 1982). The film is a parody of the classical *noir* films for which Rózsa composed an affectionate musical parody of his own idiom.

62. Randall D. Larson, *Musique Fantastique: A Survey of Film Music in the Fantastic Cinema* (London: Scarecrow Press, 1985), 293; K. J. Donnelly, "Introduction," in Donnelly, *Film Music*, 13; Kalinak, *Settling the Score*, 188; Larsen, *Film Music*, 166, 173; Marmorstein, *Hollywood Rhapsody*, 401; Miceli, *Musica per film*, 49.

63. Byrd, "The *Star Wars* Interview," 18.

64. Stephen Farber, "Mr. Pops," *Dial—WGBH Boston*, July 1983, 11.

65. Wierzbicki, *Film Music*, 216.

66. Ibid., 209–27.

67. Kalinak, *Settling the Score*, 187.

68. Dyer, "Where Is John Williams Coming From?," *Boston Globe*, 29 June 1980.

69. Malone, *Recording the Star Wars Saga*, 14.

70. Cooke, *History of Film Music*, 469.

Chapter 5
Williams's Early Years

1. See http://raymondscott.com, accessed 3 April 2013. Williams's family was a musical one: his two brothers became percussionists, regularly featured in their brother John's studio orchestras. His sister became a piano teacher. The family tradition has continued, as John Williams's sons Mark and Joseph started their own musical careers— respectively as a percussionist and as a songwriter and singer, most notably for the band Toto. Williams's grandchildren, Barbara and Ethan Gruska, are also musicians, having formed the folk rock duo The Belle Brigade.

2. Williams's biography has been reconstructed from a number of interviews given by the composer. The data of the following pages have been retrieved from Richard Dyer, "John Williams: Bringing Hollywood Magic to the Boston Pops," *Ovation*, June 1983, 14; Michael J. Colburn, "John Williams Returns to Bands Where He Began 50

Years Ago," *Instrumentalist,* June 2004, 13; Gail Jennes, "The Boston Pops Gets a Movie Composer Who Doesn't Chase Fire Engines as Its New Boss," *People Weekly,* 23 June 1980, 51; Dyer, "Where Is John Williams Coming From?," *Boston Globe,* 29 June 1980; John Williams video interview for the TV program *Personal Notes,* produced by Michael Kerr, BBC, 1988; David Thomas, "King of Themes," *Sunday Telegraph,* 13 July 1997, 49.

3. Castelnuovo Tedesco was an Italian Jew émigré who had fled the 1938 racial laws of his country to settle in Hollywood, where he worked as an orchestrator and composer. His most notable contribution was *And Then There Were None* (René Clair, 1945). He was also an in-demand teacher among prospective film composers: other famous pupils were Jerry Goldsmith and Henry Mancini.

4. Colburn, "John Williams Returns to Bands," 13.

5. Paul Galloway, "Airman Composes Way to Movie Career," *Beacon,* 27 August 1954.

6. Dyer, "Where Is John Williams Coming From?"

7. "Rosina Lhévinne," http://www.naxos.com/person/Rosina_Lhevinne/2230.htm, accessed 3 April 2013. See also the documentary *The Legacy of Rosina Lhevinne* by Salome Ramras Arkatov: www.arkatovproductions.com/lhevinne.htm, accessed 3 April 2013.

8. Terry, "John Williams Encounters the Pops," 21.

9. Richard Dyer, "Q&A with John Williams," *Boston Globe,* 27 April 1980.

10. Dyer, "Where Is John Williams Coming From?"

11. Derek Elley, "The Film Composer: 3. John Williams, part 2," *Films and Filming* 24, no. 11 (August 1978): 32.

12. This pigeonholing was typical of Hollywood: Tiomkin, for example, was known as a "Western composer," Rózsa as the "composer for historical epics."

13. Dyer, "John Williams: Bringing Hollywood Magic to the Boston Pops," 14.

14. Private conversation with John Williams, Boston, MA, 21 May 2008.

15. On *Images,* see Williams's interview in Bazelon, *Knowing the Score,* 202–6. The score is discussed further in Brown, *Overtones and Undertones,* 178–79.

16. Bazelon, *Knowing the Score,* 195.

17. *Experiment in Terror* (1962), though excellent both musically and cinematically, has been excluded to avoid having too many Blake Edwards films in the sample, but also to opt for films made in the second half of the 1960s, when the modern style was more steadily established.

18. Altman, *Silent Film Sound,* 52.

19. As confirmed by Blake Edwards himself in his video interview for *Evening at Pops,* WGBH-Boston Symphony Orchestra, episode #2804, taped on 24/05/2004, WGBH Archives, Boston MA.

20. Hawks is one of the founders of the screwball comedy, while Edwards can be said to have updated the slapstick comedy with a touch of Tati's abstractness.

21. "Wait Until Dark," music by Henry Mancini, lyrics by Jay Livingston and Ray Evans, sung by Sue Raney.

22. The tam tam is a kind of large indefinite pitched "gong" used in symphony orchestras. If rubbed with a metal stick instead of being hit by a mallet, it produces a harsh chilling sound largely used for horror effects.

23. T. Thomas, *Music for the Movies*, 270. Mancini had already employed quarter-tone scales to create dizziness in *Wait Until Dark*: see Jeff Smith, "That Money Making 'Moon River' Sound: Thematic Organization and Orchestration in the Film Music of Henry Mancini," in Buhler et al., *Music and Cinema*, 257–58.

24. A good example of Williams's underscoring can be found in *The Reivers*. When Boon pays a visit to Corrie, his favorite mistress at the Memphis brothel, and kisses her, the love theme accompanies the kiss. However, the melodic phrase stops and harmony remains suspended when Corrie moves away from him and tries to say a few words. When Boon hushes the woman by kissing her again, the music resumes and the melodic phrase is completed.

25. Bazelon, *Knowing the Score*, 200–201.

26. Very fast scales in which the individual tones are fused into a single ascending/descending-pitched sound, the glissando is typical of the harp, the strings, the slide trombones (in this case it is called *portamento*), and of any of those instruments that can bend the pitch of the notes.

27. While hitting the drumhead, the timpanist uses a pedal to change the tuning, thus obtaining an ascending or descending effect.

28. Elley, "The Film Composer: 3. John Williams, part 2," 30.

29. Ray Bennett, "John Williams, Composer," *Hollywood Reporter*, 8 March 2000.

Chapter 6
Jaws

1. Neil Lerner, "Nostalgia, Masculinist Discourse and Authoritarianism in John Williams' Scores for "Star Wars" and "Close Encounters of the Third Kind," in *Off the Planet: Music, Sound, and Science Fiction Cinema*, ed. Philip Hayward (Eastleigh, UK: John Libbey Publishing, 2004), 97.

2. Geoff King, *New Hollywood Cinema: An Introduction* (London: I. B. Tauris, 2002), 1.

3. Murray Smith, "Theses on the Philosophy of Hollywood History," in *Contemporary Hollywood Cinema*, ed. Steve Neale and Murray Smith (London: Routledge, 1998), 6–9.

4. King, *New Hollywood Cinema*, 3–5; and Elizabeth Cowie, "Classical Hollywood Cinema and Classical Narrative," in Neale and Smith, *Contemporary Hollywood Cinema*, 178–90.

5. Laurent Jullier, *L'écran post-moderne: Un cinéma de l'allusion et du feu d'artifice* (Paris: L'Harmattan, 1997) [*Il cinema postmoderno*, trans. Carla Capetta (Turin: Kaplan, 2006)].

6. Justin Wyatt, *High Concept: Movies and Marketing in Hollywood* (Austin: University of Texas Press, 1994); and Thomas Schatz, "The New Hollywood," in *Film Theory Goes to the Movies: Cultural Analysis of Contemporary Film*, ed. Jim Collins, Hilary Radner, and Ava Preacher Collins (London: Routledge, 1993), 8–36.

7. Jullier, *Il cinema postmoderno*, 17–35.

8. "Continuity Theories" can be found in Bordwell et al., *Classical Hollywood Cinema*, 367–77; and are also at the basis of Kristin Thompson, *Storytelling in the New Hollywood: Understanding Classical Narrative Cinema* (Cambridge, MA: Harvard University Press, 1999) and David Bordwell, *The Way Hollywood Tells It: Story and Style in Modern Movies* (Berkeley: University of California Press, 2006).

9. Bordwell, *Way Hollywood Tells It*, 63.

10. M. Smith, "Theses on the Philosophy of Hollywood History," 11.

11. Leonardo Gandini, *Il film noir americano* (Turin: Lindau, 2001), 113–30.

12. "Grand Narratives" (or "Meta-narratives") are those overarching explanations of the culture, society, and philosophy of a given period—for example, Enlightenment for the eighteenth century. Postmodernism posits that grand narratives are no longer able to explain the contemporary world (yet postmodernism offers a view of a contemporary world that is itself quite similar to a grand narrative).

13. Bordwell, *Way Hollywood Tells It*, 9; and Thompson, *Storytelling in the New Hollywood*, 8–9.

14. Jullier, *Il cinema postmoderno*, 53.

15. King, *New Hollywood Cinema*, 74.

16. Bordwell, *Narration in the Fiction Film*, 157–62.

17. One of the principal models was Joseph Campbell's comparative mythology essay *The Hero with a Thousand Faces* (Princeton, NJ: Princeton University Press, 1949).

18. An in-depth analysis of the classical narration of *Back to the Future* can be found in Thompson, *Storytelling in the New Hollywood*, 77–102.

19. On the definitions and contexts of "postmodern," see John Hill, "Film and Postmodernism," in *The Oxford Guide to Film Studies*, ed. John Hill and Pamela Church Gibson (Oxford: Oxford University Press, 1998), 96–105, which gives a summary of such canonical texts as Jean-François Lyotard, *La condition postmoderne: Rapport sur le savoir* (Paris: Éditions de Minuit, 1979); Fredric Jameson, *Postmodernism: Of the Cultural Logic of Late Capitalism* (London: Verso, 1991); and Jean Baudrillard, *Simulacres et Simulation* (Paris: Éditions Galilée, 1981).

20. Jullier, *Il cinema postmoderno*, 12; and King, *New Hollywood Cinema*, 139.

21. For the same reason, the term "pastiche" will be avoided here. Defined by the Merriam-Webster Dictionary as "a literary, artistic, musical, or architectural work that imitates the style of previous work," the term is typically used in musicology to indicate those works that revive and update past styles. For example, Sergei Prokofiev's Symphony no. 1, "Classical Symphony" (1917, op. 25) is a pastiche after Haydn. Although appropriate it might have been in *this* sense within this book, the term is a problematic one as it has come to be closely associated with postmodernism and given an ideological connotation: "Pastiche is, like parody, the imitation of a peculiar or unique, idiosyncratic style, the wearing of a linguistic mask, speech in a dead language. But it is a neutral practice of such mimicry, without any of parody's ulterior motives, amputated of the satiric impulse, devoid of laughter. . . . [It is] the cannibalization of all the styles of the past, the play of

random stylistic allusion." Jameson, *Postmodernism*, 17–18. Although more recent studies, such as those by Ingeborg Hoesterey, *Pastiche: Cultural Memory in Art, Film, Literature* (Bloomington: Indiana University Press, 2001) and Richard Dyer, *Pastiche* (New York: Routledge, 2007) have given broader and more dynamic definitions, "pastiche" still sounds too connected to postmodernism to be used here.

22. Respectively in J. Smith, *Sound of Commerce*, 136; Ermanno Comuzio, *Musicisti per lo schermo: Dizionario ragionato dei compositori cinematografici* (Rome: Ente dello Spettacolo, 2004), 2:1051; and Cristina Catherine Losada, "Between Modernism and Postmodernism: Strands of Continuity in Collage Compositions by Rochberg, Berio, and Zimmermann," *Music Theory Spectrum* 31, no. 1 (April 2009): 57–100.

23. Williams is defined as "neoclassical" also in Flinn, *Strains of Utopia*, 152; and K. J. Donnelly, "The Classical Film Score Forever? "Batman," "Batman Returns," and Post-classical Film Music," in Neale and M. Smith, *Contemporary Hollywood Cinema*, 151.

24. Lucas and Spielberg as neoclassical filmmakers are discussed in King, *New Hollywood Cinema*, 106.

25. Yann Merluzeau, "An Interview with John Williams," *Soundtrack!* 12, no. 47 (September 1993): 7.

26. The eight-minute *Cowboys Overture* and the twenty-minute suite for narrator and orchestra *The Reivers: An Old Man Reminisces.*

27. *Duel* (1971) was produced for television and later expanded and reedited for theatrical release. Therefore, Spielberg's first feature film made expressly for the theaters was *The Sugarland Express.*

28. Richard Dyer, "Sounds of Spielberg," *Boston Globe*, 24 February 1998.

29. Steven Spielberg, "Steven Spielberg & John Williams Talk Music," video interview, 1982, www.youtube.com/watch?v=uw4Ngb5F3Hk, accessed 3 October 2013.

30. The success of *Jaws* led to the institution and exploitation of a minor trend, which could be called "zoological disaster movies." Examples are *Piranha* (Joe Dante, 1978), in which genetically modified piranhas invade a lake near a crowded summer camp, and *The Swarm* (Irwin Allen, 1978), in which swarms of vicious killer bees invade the United States.

31. See Carl Gottlieb, *The Jaws Log* (New York: Newmarket Press, 2005), and the documentary *Jaws: The Inside Story*, A&E Television, distributed by Go Entertainment Ltd., 2009, DVD.

32. Gottlieb, *Jaws Log*, 198.

33. Ibid., 89.

34. See *Jaws: The Inside Story.*

35. The analysis was made on the PAL-system DVD *Jaws: 30th Anniversary*, Universal, 2005.

36. See *Jaws: The Inside Story.*

37. Laurent Bouzereau, *Jaws*, CD booklet (Decca 2000, 467 045-2), 8.

38. Jon Burlingame, "John Williams Talks *Jaws*," www.horror-movies.ca/2012/08/john-williams-talks-jaws, accessed 3 April 2013.

39. Bouzereau, *Jaws*, 8.

40. Derek Taylor, *The Making of "Raiders of the Lost Ark"* (New York: Ballantine Books, 1981), 166.

41. Bouzereau, *Jaws*, 7.

42. Rebecca Keegan, "John Williams and Steven Spielberg Mark 40 Years of Collaboration," *Los Angeles Times*, 8 January 2012.

43. On film music resembling heartbeats, see Ben Winters, "Corporeality, Musical Heartbeats, and Cinematic Emotion," *Music, Sound and the Moving Image* 2, no. 1 (Spring 2008): 3–25.

44. Bouzereau, *Jaws*, 8–10.

45. Ibid., 7.

46. Ibid., 8.

47. Burlingame, "John Williams Talks *Jaws*."

48. Bouzereau, *Jaws*, 10–11.

49. The fugue is a revered art-music form that can be traced back to the early baroque period. It is one of the most rigorous compositional patterns, having two or more independent melodic lines (voices) interwoven contrapuntally. A *fugato* is a musical piece that employs the techniques of the fugue, without developing the fugue's entire formal structure.

50. Williams had previously received one Oscar for his arrangements and musical direction of *Fiddler on the Roof* (Norman Jewison, 1971).

51. Tom Shales of the *Washington Post*, quoted in Wierzbicki, *Film Music*, 204.

52. *Jaws 2: Original Motion Picture Soundtrack*, MCA Records, 3045, 1978, reissued in CD by Varèse Sarabande, VSD-5328, 1990.

53. Ray Bennett, "John Williams, Composer," *Hollywood Reporter*, 8 March 2000.

Chapter 7
Williams's Neoclassicism

1. *Enciclopedia della musica*, ed. Andrea Briganti, Giulia Farina, Andrea Lanza (Milano: Garzanti, 1996), 593 (my translation).

2. Guido Salvetti, *La nascita del Novecento*, 2nd ed. (Turin: EDT, 1991), 97–99 (my translation).

3. Ibid., 99.

4. Miceli, *Musica per film*, 248–49 (my translation).

5. Bob Keefer, "Running Up the Score: John Williams Brings His Cinematic Compositions to Eugene," *Register-Guard* (*OR*), 20 September 2012.

6. Dyer, "John Williams Is New Pops Maestro."

7. Miceli, *Musica per film*, 616–18 (my translation).

8. Williams's idiom is analyzed in harmonic terms in Jérôme Rossi, "Le dynamisme harmonique dans l'ecriture filmique de John Williams: Harmonie fonctionnelle versus harmonie non fonctionnelle," in Tylski, *John Williams*, 113–40.

9. Cooke, *History of Film Music*, 129.

10. About Wagner, Williams stated: "The instrumentation of *Star Wars* . . . might sound Wagnerian to some people; it doesn't to me." Keefer, "Running Up the Score."

11. "There are so many [influences]. In the film world, I would have to mention again Alfred Newman and Bernard Herrmann but also Korngold—the great Viennese composer who went to Hollywood in the early years—he was a great hero of mine and Franz Waxman—and many, many others. In the concert field, there were, again, so many. I have to mention William Walton, a great favorite of mine—I admire his film and concert music. Walton was held in very high esteem in Hollywood. I like Elgar too, and all the Russian composers. The twentieth-century Russians: Stravinsky, Shostakovitch, Prokofiev—all were great idols of mine as a youngster." Williams, quoted in Ian Lace, "The Film Music of John Williams," 1998, www.musicweb-international.com /film/lacejw.htm, accessed 3 April 2013.

12. Andy Seiler, "Williams Adds Musical Magic to *Harry Potter*," *USA Today*, 13 November 2001.

13. John Williams, CD booklet, *Raiders of the Lost Ark*, DCC Compact Classic-Silva Screen, 1995, Raiders 001.

14. Zachary Woolfe, "A Summer Blockbuster, Far from the Multiplex," *New York Times*, 19 August 2012.

15. The Emperor's theme is reprised in *Star Wars: Episode III—Revenge of the Sith* (George Lucas, 2005).

16. The sequence under analysis starts at 4' 10" and stops at 9' 34" (running 5' 24") and includes fifty-four explicit synch-points, not counting the starting and closing synch-points. The analysis was made on the DVD included in the box set *The Adventures of Indiana Jones*, Paramount, 2003.

17. Williams, radio interview by Francine Stock, *The Film Programme*, BBC Radio 4, 14 April 2006.

18. On the gratification effect given by the recognition of familiar melodies, following the "law of return" of the Gestalt Theory, see Meyer, *Emotion and Meaning in Music*, 151–52; and the "pleasure of recognition" in Meyer, *Style and Music*, 210n.

19. Byrd, "The *Star Wars* Interview," 18.

20. Bordwell, *Way Hollywood Tells It*, 63.

21. A number of parallels are also pointed out in Kalinak, *Settling the Score*, 190–92.

22. Derek Elley, "The Film Composer: 3. John Williams, part 1," *Films and Filming* 24, no. 10 (July 1978): 23.

23. Max Steiner, quoted in Schreibman, "Memories of Max. Part 2," 25.

24. Wynn Delacoma, "Williams: From Celluloid to CSO," *Chicago Sun-Times*, 28 November 2003.

25. Miceli, *Musica per film*, 641.

26. James C. McKinley Jr., "John Williams Lets His Muses Carry Him Along," *New York Times*, 19 August 2011.

27. McNab, "They Shoot, He Scores."

28. Max Steiner, quoted in Buhler, "Analytical and Interpretive Approaches to Film Music (II)," 45.

29. Bernie Dobroski and Claire Greene, "Pass the Popcorn: An Interview with John Williams," *Instrumentalist*, no. 38, July 1984, 6.

30. T. Thomas, *Film Score*, 334.

31. McKinley Jr., "John Williams Lets His Muses Carry Him Along."

32. Clemency Burton-Hill, "John Williams, the Music Master," *Financial Times*, 17 August 2012.

33. Dobroski and Greene, "Pass the Popcorn," 6.

34. On Korngold's dislike for technical aids, see T. Thomas, *Music for the Movies*, 171–72.

35. See the documentary *Film Music Masters: Jerry Goldsmith*, by Fred Karlin, 1995.

36. Burton-Hill, "John Williams, the Music Master."

37. David Thomas, "King of Themes," *Sunday Telegraph*, 13 July 1997, 50.

38. On Newman and Waxman, see Palmer, *Composer in Hollywood*, 69–70, 95; on Herrmann, see Steven C. Smith, *A Heart at Fire's Center: The Life and Music of Bernard Herrmann*, 2nd ed. (Berkeley: University of California Press, 2002), 81–82, 135–36, 155–56, 187–88, 209–10, 217–18, 262–63, 336–37.

39. Elley, "The Film Composer: 3. John Williams, part 2," 32.

40. Schreibman, "Memories of Max. Part 2," 27.

41. David Patrick Stearns, "2 Emmys, 4 Oscars, 15 Grammys . . . But, Hey, Who's Counting? Not John Williams, Hollywood's Most Honored Composer," Arts & Entertainment, February 1993, 22.

42. See appendix 1 for a catalogue. When planning to perform suites from the film music repertoire, usually one has to contact the composer or the publisher in order to rent the score and orchestral parts. When the original material is not available, one has to resort to more or less faithful arrangements and transcriptions. As for Williams, almost forty orchestral sets (conductor's score plus orchestral parts) are easily available for purchase in the same version that Williams himself conducts in concerts; in addition, each score also has an introductory text by the composer (see John Williams Signature Edition series, published by Hal Leonard).

43. D. Thomas, "Point Blank," 77. Mervyn Cooke pinpoints the balletic nature of Williams's writing and sees it as a tradition that can be traced back to Tiomkin: "Audible links with the Russian ballet tradition prevail to the present day in the music of John Williams and others." Cooke, *History of Film Music*, 120–21.

44. For example, in the score for *The Three Worlds of Gulliver* (Jack Sher, 1960), Herrmann's use of closed forms like minuets and marches made it possible to compile a rich concert suite from the film score (*Bernard Herrmann Great Film Music*, National Philharmonic Orchestra conducted by Bernard Herrmann [1974–75], CD, Decca-London 1996, 443 899-2).

45. Similarly, Korngold's music for the Sherwood ambush sequence in *The Adventures of Robin Hood* (Michael Curtiz, William Keighley, 1938) was transformed with minor modifications into the concert march "Robin Hood and His Merry Men." Compare the forest ambush sequence on the DVD *The Adventures of Robin Hood*, Warner Bros., 2003—in which it is possible to listen to the isolated music track—with the second movement of

the concert suite on the CD *The Film Music of Erich Wolfgang Korngold*, BBC Philharmonic conducted by Rumon Gamba, Chandos, 2005, CHAN 10336.

46. The suite is described in Richard Dyer, "John Williams Casts Spell for 'Potter' Score," *Boston Globe*, 15 November 2001, and is published by Hal Leonard in the John Williams Signature Edition series.

47. Compare the concert piece *Adventures on Earth* ("John Williams Signature Edition," Hal Leonard, 04490009) with the track titled "Adventure on Earth" in the original album of *E.T.* (MCA Records, 1982, CD, MCLD 19021).

48. Miceli, *Musica per film*, 249-50 (my translation).

49. Other notable soloists in Williams's scores: the percussionist Stomu Yamash'ta in *Images* (Robert Altman, 1972); the harmonica virtuoso Toots Thielemans in *The Sugarland Express* (Steven Spielberg 1974) and *Cinderella Liberty* (Mark Rydell, 1973); the trumpet player Tim Morrison in *Born on the Fourth of July* (Oliver Stone, 1989) and *JFK* (Oliver Stone, 1991); the Irish group The Chieftains in *Far and Away* (Ron Howard, 1992); the guitarist Christopher Parkening in *Stepmom* (Chris Columbus, 1998); the saxophonist Dan Higgins in *Catch Me If You Can* (Steven Spielberg, 2002); and both Itzhak Perlman and Yo-Yo Ma in *Memoirs of a Geisha* (Rob Marshall, 2005).

50. A significant example of the difference between an album created according to criteria of listening experience and one created with the aim of following "philologically" the music order in the film is the comparison between the *Star Wars: Episode I: The Phantom Menace* album (Sony Classical 1999, CD, SK 61816)—duration 74'—with the two-disc special edition containing the full music track (Sony Classical 2000, CD, SK2 89460)—duration 124'. In the latter CD, music fragmentation is evident.

51. John Williams, liner notes for the LP album *Star Wars*, 20th Century Records, 1977, 2T-541 (0898).

52. Another example is the collector's edition double CD of *The Fury* (Brian De Palma, 1978): disc 2 contains the original album re-recorded with the London Symphony Orchestra (9 tracks, duration 40') while disc 1 contains the original music track (23 tracks, duration 55') recorded with a freelance orchestra. The comparison between these two discs and the different durations of the pieces is a case study of this process of combining different cues, arranging the forms, and reorganizing their order from the original film score to the album release. "Main Title" lasts 2' 08" on the music track and 3' 08" on the album; "For Gillian" lasts 1' 48" on the music track and 2' 37" on the album; "Vision on the Stairs" lasts 1' 48" on the music track and 4' 03" on the album.

Chapter 8
Williams's Naysayers

1. T. Thomas, *Film Score*, 18.

2. See Wierzbicki, *Film Music*, 150-58; and Adorno and Eisler, *Composing for the Films*.

3. Dimitri Tiomkin, quoted in Flinn, *Strains of Utopia*, 3.

4. See the comments to McKinley Jr., "John Williams Lets His Muses Carry Him Along," http://artsbeat.blogs.nytimes.com/2011/08/19/john-williams-lets-his-muses-carry-him-along, accessed 3 April 2013.

5. Sergio Miceli and Ennio Morricone, *Comporre per il cinema: Teoria e prassi della musica nel film* (Rome: Biblioteca di Bianco e Nero/SNC, 2001), 141.

6. Riccardo Palmieri, "Marco Frisina. Visioni Sinfoniche," *SET*, March 1998, 75 (my translation).

7. Direct testimony, 17 March 2004, DAMS, Imperia, Italy.

8. Lack, *Twenty Four Frames Under*, 329–30.

9. William Booth, "Shark Attack?! John Williams Liked the Sound of That," *Washington Post*, 5 December 2004.

10. Elley, "The Film Composer: 3. John Williams, part 1," 24. Williams and Spencer can be seen at work in the documentary *Star Wars: Music by John Williams*, by David Buckton, BBC, 1980, which is an excellent report on Williams's modus operandi.

11. On Korngold's orchestrators, see Duchen, *Erich Wolfgang Korngold*, 164–65.

12. Dobroski and Greene, "Pass the Popcorn," 6.

13. Elley, "The Film Composer: 3. John Williams, part 1," 24.

14. Fernando Gonzalez, "Orchestrating *Indiana Jones*," *Boston Globe*, 18 June 1989. Herbert Spencer's account on the completeness of Williams's sketches can be found in Karlin, *Listening to Movies*, 37.

15. Elley, "The Film Composer: 3. John Williams, part 1," 24.

16. Kalinak, *Settling the Score*, 191.

17. Lebrecht, "John Williams—The Magpie Maestro."

18. Ibid.

19. Douglas Cannon Hyde, "The Music Man for Jedis and Joneses," http://articles.cnn.com/2003-05-05/entertainment/john.williams, accessed 3 April 2013.

20. Lebrecht, "John Williams—The Magpie Maestro."

21. Ibid. Incidentally, there are also a couple of mistakes in this passage: the theme from *The Godfather* was borrowed from *Fortunella* (Eduardo De Filippo, 1958), not from *8 ½* (Federico Fellini, 1963), with which there is no resemblance at all; and the music for *Hiroshima Mon Amour* is co-composed by Giovanni Fusco.

22. Lebrecht, "John Williams—The Magpie Maestro."

23. On the origins and diffusion of this aesthetic criterion, see Carl Dahlhaus, *Die Idee der absoluten Musik* (Kassel: Bärenreiter-Verlag, 1978), trans. Roger Lustig as *The Idea of Absolute Music* (Chicago: University of Chicago Press, 1991).

24. David Neumeyer, "Introduction," in Buhler et al., *Music and Cinema*, 21.

25. Martin Bernheimer, "Pop! John Williams on Philharmonic Podium," *Los Angeles Times*, 12 November 1983.

26. Lerner, "Nostalgia, Masculinist Discourse and Authoritarianism," 106.

27. On hermeneutics and the methodologies for film interpretation, see David Bordwell, *Making Meaning: Inference and Rhetoric in the Interpretation of Cinema* (Cambridge, MA: Harvard University Press, 1989), esp. 247–74.

28. Jean-Luis Comolli and Jean Narboni, "Cinéma/Idéologie/Critique," *Cahiers du Cinéma*, nos. 216, 217 (1969); Jean-Luis Comolli, "Technique et Idéologie," *Cahiers du Cinéma*, nos. 229, 230, 231, 233, 234, 235, 241 (1971–72); Jean-Louis Baudry, *L'effect cinéma* (Paris: Albatros, 1978); Marie-Claire Ropars, *Le Texte divisé* (Paris: PUF, 1981); Patricia White, "Feminism and Film," in Hill and Gibson, *Oxford Guide to Film Studies*, 117–34; Shohini Chaudhuri, *Feminist Film Theorists: Laura Mulvey, Kaja Silverman, Teresa de Lauretis, Barbara Creed* (New York: Routledge, 2006); and Peter Brunette, "Post-Structuralism and Deconstructionism," in Hill and Gibson, *Oxford Guide to Film Studies*, 91–95.

29. Booth, "Shark Attack?!"

30. On "nostalgia" from a postmodern perspective, see Fredric Jameson, *The Geopolitical Aesthetic: Cinema and Space in the World System* (Bloomington: Indiana University Press, 1992), 118–21.

31. A brief comparison with other famous director/composer duos may be useful: Alfred Hitchcock and Bernard Herrmann worked together for eleven years and produced eight films; Sergio Leone and Ennio Morricone for twenty years and eight films; Federico Fellini and Nino Rota for twenty-six years and sixteen films; François Truffaut and Georges Delerue for twenty-three years and eleven films; Claude Chabrol and Pierre Jansen for twenty years and thirty films; Blake Edwards and Henry Mancini for thirty-five years and twenty-six feature films (not counting the TV shows). The most celebrated team, Sergei Eisenstein and Sergei Prokofiev, lasted for seven years and three films.

32. Miceli, *Musica per film*, 248 (my translation).

33. Cooke, *History of Film Music*, 460.

34. Brown, *Overtones and Undertones*, 187.

35. Calabretto, *Lo schermo sonoro*, 60 (my translation).

36. Ibid., 74–75.

Chapter 9
Raiders of the Lost Ark Background

1. Franco La Polla and Maria Teresa Cavina, eds., *Spielberg su Spielberg* (Turin: Lindau, 1995), 63–65; D. Taylor, *Making of "Raiders of the Lost Ark,"* 12; Ian Freer, *The Complete Spielberg* (London: Virgin Publishing, 2001), 96.

2. D. Taylor, *Making of "Raiders of the Lost Ark,"* 13.

3. Moreover, the Bond character has been played by a number of actors during the last fifty years, thus giving Bond a sort of ageless look and atemporal existence; he belongs to the 1960s as well as to the 1990s and 2000s. Dr. Jones, conversely, is rooted in a defined historical context and has always been played by Harrison Ford and, across the series, we can clearly see the character aging along with the actor (indeed, the fourth installment is set in the late 1950s, not in the 1930s, so as to be congruent with Ford's age). Thanks to Jeff Smith for pointing this out.

4. D. Taylor, *Making of "Raiders of the Lost Ark,"* 13.

5. Ibid.

6. Ibid., 1-2.

7. Ibid., 14.

8. Ibid., 105.

9. Freer, *Complete Spielberg*, 99.

10. "Indiana Jones and the Ultimate Tribute," *Empire*, no. 208, October 2006, 74.

11. Philip Taylor, *Steven Spielberg: The Man, His Movies, and Their Meaning*, 3rd ed. (London: B. T. Batsford, 1999), 107.

12. Freer, *Complete Spielberg*, 97; Omar Calabrese, *Neo-Baroque: A Sign of the Times* (Princeton, NJ: Princeton University Press, 1992), 173; P. Taylor, *Steven Spielberg*, 104.

13. P. Taylor, *Steven Spielberg*, 105.

14. Warren Buckland, "A Close Encounter with *Raiders of the Lost Ark*: Notes on Narrative Aspects of the New Hollywood Blockbuster," in Neale and Smith, *Contemporary Hollywood Cinema*, 170.

15. Buckland, "A Close Encounter," 171-72.

16. Field, *Screenwriter's Problem Solver*, 269-86.

17. Bordwell, *Narration in the Fiction Film*, 158.

18. On "symptomatic meaning," see Bordwell, *Making Meaning*, 9. For *Raiders of the Lost Ark* as an example of Reaganite entertainment, see P. Taylor, *Steven Spielberg*, 107; and Jullier, *L'écran post-moderne*, 30-32. An interpretative analysis of the film can be found in Nigel Morris, *The Cinema of Steven Spielberg: Empire of Light* (London: Wallflower Press, 2007), 78-80. On cinema in the Reagan era, see Sklar, *Movie-Made America*, 339-56.

19. Ideologically, the film does present traits of "Orientalism"—a series of generalized and stereotyped traits created from an Eurocentric perspective to separate Western culture from and define it vis-à-vis Eastern culture(s)—as analyzed by Edward Said in *Orientalism* [1978] (London: Penguin Books, 2003): "a way of coming to terms with the Orient that is based on the Orient's special place in European Western experience. . . . Orientalism is a style of thought based upon an ontological and epistemological distinction made between 'the Orient' and (most of the time) 'the Occident.' . . . In brief, because of Orientalism the Orient was not (and is not) a free subject of thought or action. This is not to say that Orientalism unilaterally determines what can be said about the Orient, but that it is the whole network of interests inevitably brought to bear on (and therefore always involved in) any occasion when that peculiar entity 'the Orient' is in question" (1-3). Likewise, the music resorts to a number of "Orientalist" clichés traditionally employed by Western music, like pentatonic scales for Eastern characters and chromatic scales for Middle Eastern ones.

20. Richard Dyer, "Williams Poised for Pops," *Boston Globe*, 26 April 1981.

21. "Indiana Jones and the Ultimate Tribute," 81.

22. *The Music of Indiana Jones*, video documentary by Laurent Bouzereau, Lucasfilm, 2003, included in *The Adventures of Indiana Jones*, DVD box-set, Paramount Home Video, 2003.

23. Maurice Murphy (1935-2010) was one of the world's best trumpet virtuosi and held the position of LSO's principal trumpet from 1977 to 2007. His debut as LSO principal was the recording of the first *Star Wars* film in 1977. In the following years,

Murphy's unmistakable sound was indelibly linked to such Williams scores as *Superman: The Movie* and *Raiders of the Lost Ark*, not to mention all the subsequent installments of the *Star Wars* saga, which Murphy rendered with a heroic impetus never surpassed and seldom equaled. See the memorial page at the LSO website, http://lso.co.uk/3349, accessed 3 April 2013.

24. *Raiders March*, full orchestral score, "John Williams Signature Edition," Hal Leonard, 04490015.

25. The James Bond theme was composed by Monty Norman and arranged by John Barry, although there has been a long-standing controversy on its authorship: see Geoff Leonard and Pete Walker, "John Barry and James Bond. The Making of the Music," and Lukas Kendall, "Who Wrote the Bond Theme?" *Film Score Monthly*, November 1995, 15–18. Norman eventually won a legal action, being confirmed as the author of the theme: "Norman Wins Bond Libel Suit," *Film Score Monthly*, March 2001, 4.

26. Miceli, *Musica per film*, 463–64 (my translation).

27. Tellingly, this is a major difference with the first draft of the theme: "I went around for weeks with Luke Skywalker's theme slightly different: the top B flat as only *one* beat. Then one day, driving home from the studio (and I'd already scored one sequence with the theme like that), I suddenly thought how much better it would be with *two* beats on the top note." Elley, "The Film Composer: 3. John Williams, part 1," 23.

28. M. R. Montgomery, "John Williams' Quiet Side," *Boston Globe*, 18 March 1981.

29. Colburn, "John Williams Returns to Bands," 16.

30. See chap. 4 for the mythological nature of *Star Wars* and the archetypal heroic journey underlining the narrative. Luke Skywalker is just one of the many incarnations of the Hero archetype as is the leitmotiv, which can certainly be associated with Luke, but above all it comes to represent the film and the archetypes represented in it.

31. On "stretching" as a typically romantic compositional strategy, see Meyer, *Style and Music*, 259–71.

32. "Indiana Jones and the Ultimate Tribute," 82.

33. Since access to the original score is not allowed, for the musical analysis of the main themes we have referred either to transcriptions by ear ("The Ark's Motif" and "The Wrath of God Motif" in chap. 10) or to the philological concert versions published by Hal Leonard in the authoritative series "John Williams Signature Edition."

34. See chap. 6 in this book for its appearance in *Jaws*. The tritone is famously featured in the trombones motif at the beginning of Modest Mussorgsky's fantasy for orchestra, *Night on Bald Mountain*, which musically describes a witches' Sabbath.

Chapter 10
Raiders of the Lost Ark Analysis

1. The film analysis of *Raiders of the Lost Ark* is based on the PAL-system DVD running at twenty-five frames per second, hereafter f/s (Paramount Home Video, 2003). I have also referred to the CDs from the film's original music track (*Raiders of the Lost Ark*,

DCC Compact Classic-Silva Screen, 1995, Raiders 001 and *Raiders of the Lost Ark*, Concord Records, 2008, CRE-31002-02) to better identify the orchestration details in those passages in the film in which the dialogue and sound effects may mask the music.

2. On the characteristics of open-title sequences in the classical Hollywood cinema, see Bordwell et al., *Classical Hollywood Cinema*, 25–29.

3. "Indiana Jones and the Ultimate Tribute," 74.

4. At that time Lucas had already planned at least another two chapters. See D. Taylor, *Making of "Raiders of the Lost Ark,"* 14.

5. On the "Principle of saturation" and the psychological effects caused by ostinatos and music with prolonged tonal uncertainty, see Meyer, *Emotion and Meaning in Music*, 135–38.

6. On the reasons why the minor mode typically sounds either tragic or sad, see Meyer, *Emotion and Meaning in Music*, 222–28. On the connotative mechanisms of music, see ibid., 258–72, and the "metaphoric mimicry" in Meyer, *Style and Music*, 128–31.

7. For example, low-pitched trombones minor chords are used in Gottfried Huppertz's music for the kidnapping of Maria in the catacombs in *Metropolis* (Fritz Lang, 1927). This cliché had also been regularly used by Max Steiner since *The Most Dangerous Game* (Irving Pichel, Ernest B. Schoedsack, 1932).

8. Tone clusters are groups of contiguous notes played simultaneously and therefore sounding highly dissonant and perceived as "fastidiously" grating.

9. Explicit synch-points punctuate the spear trap snapping shut and the gruesome view of the corpse of an unlucky explorer; the snapping of the whip around a beam; the collapsing of the beam while Satipo is crossing over a bottomless pit; and a poisoned arrow hitting the torch held by the man with the hat.

10. On the psychological mechanisms of suspense in music, see Meyer, *Emotion and Meaning in Music*, 163–66.

11. This use of the *crescendo* or the stinger followed by a dramatic musical silence is typical of Steiner and can be found, for example, in *The Informer* (John Ford, 1935).

12. Although the source is not visible, the music volume rises or lowers as the two characters move around, which suggests a diegetic source.

13. CD booklet, *Raiders of the Lost Ark*, DCC Compact Classic-Silva Screen, 1995, Raiders 001.

14. 1 Kings 19:12 (New American Standard Bible).

15. The song is "I Am the Monarch of the Sea" from the operetta *H.M.S. Pinafore* (1878) by Arthur Sullivan and W. S. Gilbert.

16. As in the previous example in which the alleged torture instrument is transformed into a harmless clothes hanger, the music contributes to build a "mountain that has brought forth a mouse."

17. The "show-off modulation" (C major to D-flat major) can be spotted between measures 7–8 in the second musical example in chapter 9, p. 156.

18. Fragments of the main theme are presented in gradually longer configurations throughout the film, until the theme is finally stated in its full form in a topical scene requiring an emotional punch from the music.

19. The Mark Tree is a series of suspended small tubular bells arranged in a line from the shortest (highest pitch) to the longest (lowest pitch). When the bells are rubbed with a stick, they produce an ascending or descending silvery sound. A similarly sounding instrument is the Bell Tree.

20. Genesis 19:15–26. Marion, unlike Lot's wife, did not open her eyes.

21. "Indiana Jones and the Ultimate Tribute," 82.

22. With the ancient natural horns, as well as with the hunting horn, it is possible (unlike the modern valved French horn) to produce only those tones that are within the harmonic series of the instrument's key.

23. Exodus 19:16, 18–19 (Complete Jewish Bible). Most English versions wrongly translate "shofar" as "trumpet" instead of "horn."

24. Marion's theme is indeed far too romantic to express her nature, and probably for this reason Williams said that it is often "inappropriate emotionally." "Indiana Jones and the Ultimate Tribute," 82.

25. On this reading, see the seminal Mulvey, "Visual Pleasure and Narrative Cinema."

26. The analysis was intended to be mainly formalist and not to dwell on ideological readings, but this ambiguous nature of Marion's theme is nevertheless a good example of how a film score—and a classical-style film score in this case—can also have a cognitive function that singles out connotations and paves the way for an interpretative analysis. The sexist or patriarchal ideologies that may certainly be present in *Raiders*—the beautiful damsel in distress and the hero who rushes to rescue her, to later become her partner—are seen, like the ethnic stereotypes, as clichés from the classical popular cinema and as such are revived by this film and by this score, along with other traits of the past films. What is of interest here is their neoclassical style, not their ideological nature.

27. The suite is built with "Indy 1" followed by "Indy 2," then "Marion's Theme" (love theme), and finally again "Indy 1," closing the end credits and the film with a powerful orchestral chord.

28. Freer, *Complete Spielberg*, 106.

29. Part of the neoclassical quality of the score is given indeed by the extensive use of music. The total duration of the narrative from the beginning of the first shot to the beginning of the end credits is 106' 20". The end credits sequence—which is external to the narrative—lasts 3' 50". The film's total running time from the first frame with the Paramount logo to the end of the end credits is 110' 20". On film support at 24 f/s the total running time of the narrative would be 110' 50", the total running time of the film 115'. Music accompanies the narrative for 67' 17", plus 3' 50" of end credit music. Moreover, there are 4' 29" of diegetic music, mostly featured in the Cairo sequences. The non-diegetic score covers 71' 07" of the film, that is, 65 percent of it. However, watching the film the impression is that the percentage of musical presence is higher. This is probably given by the particular exuberance and obtrusiveness of the musical writing, by the primary role that the narration gives it, and by the presence of very long

sequences in which the music never stops—as in the first twelve minutes of the film, where the music is present for 11' 17".

30. D. Taylor, *Making of "Raiders of the Lost Ark,"* 167–68.

31. Freer, *Complete Spielberg*, 101.

Chapter 11
Beyond the Films

1. Launched in 1974, the Christmas season is called "Holiday Pops." *Boston Pops: The Story of America's Orchestra* (Boston: Boston Symphony Orchestra Inc., 2000), 24–25.

2. *Boston Pops*, 37.

3. Despite the new name, the group was and still is a branch of the Boston Symphony, formed by members of the mother orchestra except for its twelve first chairs.

4. Produced by Boston's WGBH Television (William Cosel, producer) and by the Boston Symphony, the series was broadcast nationwide by PBS (Public Broadcasting Service), always ranking in the top positions of the network's viewing reports. On the history of *Evening at Pops* see Ron Bachman, "Behind the Scenes at Evening at Pops," *Nine*, June 1989, 34–46 (clipping in the BSO Archives, Symphony Hall, Boston, MA); and "Evening at Pops: Putting on the Show," *Boston Pops*, 44–47.

5. *Boston Pops*, 13.

6. Goodson, "Yes, There's Life after Fiedler."

7. Tim Smith, "Film Composer John Williams to Make Baltimore Conducting Première," *Baltimore Sun*, 1 June 2013.

8. Richard Dyer, "Williams Is Candidate for Fiedler's Job," *Boston Globe*, 6 January 1980.

9. Concert program, 25–26 May 1979 (BSO Archives, Symphony Hall, Boston, MA).

10. Goodson, "Yes, There's Life after Fiedler."

11. When André Previn, a multifaceted musician, was given the conductorship of the Houston Symphony in 1967 and then the London Symphony in 1968, his Hollywood output had become a minor facet of his musicianship.

12. Dyer, "John Williams Is New Pops Maestro."

13. Margo Miller, "'A Wonderful Choice,'" *Boston Globe*, 11 January 1980.

14. Michael Knight, "John Williams Opens Season with Pops," *New York Times*, 30 April 1980.

15. Ibid.

16. Dyer, "John Williams Bows In."

17. *Boston Pops*, 36.

18. "Theme and Dance from Star Wars" was released for the first time on the CD *The Arthur Fiedler Legacy: From Fabulous Broadway to Hollywood's Reel Thing*, Deutsche Grammophon, 2007, 477 6124, with the deceptive title "Star Wars: Main Title" but without any mention of the arrangers' names, thus passing it off as the original version.

19. Concert program, 21 June 1981 (BSO Archives, Symphony Hall, Boston, MA).

20. Beverly Ford and John Impemba, "John Williams Quits Boston Pops," *Boston Herald*, 14 June 1984.

21. Constance Gorfinkle, "Williams Miffed by Hiss from Pops Orchestra?," *Patriot Ledger*, 14 June 1984. A later source reports that the target of the hisses was *Salute to Fred Astaire* (arranged by Sid Ramin); see Peter Catalano, "John Williams to Leave Boston Pops," *Los Angeles Times*, 21 December 1991. Williams has never confirmed either of the versions. Larry Katz, "Dr. Hollywood & Mr. Pops," *Boston Herald Magazine*, 28 April 1985.

22. Margo Miller, "Williams to Resign as Pops Conductor," *Boston Globe*, 14 June 1984.

23. Richard H. Stewart, "We Didn't Drive Williams Away," *Boston Globe*, 8 July 1984.

24. Peter Goodman, "A Great Little Visiting Band," *New York Newsday*, 11 June 1986.

25. "Boston Pops Members Reveal They Hated Fiedler, His Music," *Journal Inquirer*, 10 August 1984.

26. The idea is credited to Williams himself. Richard Dyer, "The Williams Years: Knowing What Counts," concert program "Opening Night at Pops: A Gala Celebration for John Williams," 12 May 1993 (BSO Archives, Symphony Hall, Boston, MA), 35.

27. In exchange, players not willing to play during the Pops season agreed to have the share covering the period ($7,650) deducted from the annual stipend ($45,000). Constance Gorfinkle, "Why John Williams Changed His Mind," *Patriot Ledger*, 8 August 1984.

28. Katz, "Dr. Hollywood & Mr. Pops."

29. Gorfinkle, "Why John Williams Changed His Mind."

30. Richard Dyer, "Pops' Williams to Retire in '93," *Boston Globe*, 20 December 1991.

31. Richard Dyer, "Pops Star: The Legacy of John Williams," *Boston Globe*, 12 December 1993.

32. Jon Burlingame, "A Career of Epic Proportion," *Los Angeles Times*, 3 February 2002.

33. Richard Dyer, "Williams to Stay on as Pops Adviser," *Boston Globe*, 4 February 1994.

34. An analysis of John Williams's multimedia concert formats (the "multimedia scene/sequence" vis-à-vis the "multimedia concert piece") can be found in Emilio Audissino, "John Williams, the Boston Pops Orchestra and Film Music in Concert," in *Cinema, critique des images*, ed. Claudia D'Alonzo, Ken Slock, and Philippe Dubois (Udine: Campanotto, 2012), 230–35.

35. For one example, Gustav Holst's *The Planets*, op. 32 (1916) was featured in the concert "MIT Giant Leaps," celebrating the fortieth anniversary of the moon landing, with space footage projected on the screen and astronaut Buzz Aldrin as a narrator

(concert program, Boston Pops, 11 June 2009, BSO Archives, Symphony Hall, Boston, MA).

36. David Patrick Stearns, "Music That's Light on the Baton: USA Orchestras Enjoy a Pops Explosion," *USA Today*, 26 April 1985. The principal Pops orchestras in the United States are Austin Pops (est. 2006), Palm Beach Pops (est. 1991), Carolina Pops (est. 2005), Cincinnati Pops (est. 1977), Cleveland Pops (est. 1995), Golden State Pops (est. 2002), Indianapolis Symphonic Pops (est. 1999), Minneapolis Pops (est. 1950), New York Pops (est. 1983), Philly [Philadelphia] Pops (est. 1981), San Francisco Pops Orchestra (est. 1949), St. Louis Pops Orchestra (est. 1976), Tucson Pops (est. 1955).

37. "Cincinnati Pops: Erich Kunzel and his Orchestra Are a Much-loved Cultural Asset," *Cincinnati Enquirer*, 31 December 1991.

38. *Pops in Space* soon became the best seller of the Philips Classics catalogue at the time. Theodore W. Libbey Jr., "Disks Attest to the Versatile Talents of John Williams," *New York Times*, 27 February 1983.

39. See Saul Pincus and Mike Petersen, "Remaking Star Wars," *Film Score Monthly*, September/October 2005, 40-44.

40. David Patrick Stearns, "Hollywood Conductor Taps Studio Talent," *USA Today*, 31 July 1991.

41. *The Soundtrack Club* [*Film Score Monthly*], November 1991, 3.

42. Conducted by Richard Kaufman, *Film Score Monthly*, May 1996, 4.

43. Jeff Bond, "Stamps of Approval," *Film Score Monthly*, November 1999, 24-27.

44. *Film Score Monthly*, March 2004, 8.

45. *Film Score Monthly*, Winter 1996, 2.

46. From 3 to 20 September 2004: *Film Score Monthly*, June 2004, 8.

47. The overture from *The Man Who Knew Too Much*, a suite from *Marnie*, and the prelude from *North by Northwest*. Kyle Renick, "The Halls are Alive," *Film Score Monthly*, May 1998, 13.

48. *Film Score Monthly*, October/November 1998, 8.

49. *Film Score Monthly*, March 2000, 8.

50. Proms archive, www.bbc.co.uk/proms/archive/search, accessed 3 April 2013.

51. In the 2005/6 season (besides Williams on 25, 26, and 29 November), there was "Symphonic Hollywood," conducted by Richard Kaufman and featuring selections from *Psycho*, *Vertigo*, *Forrest Gump*, and *Nuovo Cinema Paradiso* (31 March). In the 2007/8 season Joel McNeely conducted a Bernard Herrmann/Alfred Hitchcock concert (4 April). Concert programs (Chicago Symphony Orchestra, Symphony Center, Chicago, IL).

52. James Miller, "Keeping Time with John: Inside the Tanglewood Film Music Seminar," *Film Score Monthly*, October/November 1998, 20-21; and Richard Dyer, "Composers Learn Film Music from the Master," *Boston Globe*, 20 August 1998.

53. Phil Lehman, "When Capitals Collide: Maestros Slatkin and Williams Join Forces for a Series of Film Music Festivities," *Film Score Monthly*, February 2003, 12, 13, 47.

54. T. Smith, "Maestro and the Movies," *Baltimore Sun*, 19 January 2003.

55. Dyer, "Pops Star: The Legacy of John Williams."

Conclusion

1. J. Smith, *Sound of Commerce*, 7.

2. Jullier, *L'écran post-moderne*, 37 (my translation).

3. On sound effects in the classical era, see Helen Hanson, "Sound Affects: Post-production Sound, Soundscapes and Sound Design in Hollywood's Studio Era," *Music, Sound, and the Moving Image* 1, no. 1 (Spring 2007): 27–49.

4. Chion, *Audio-Vision*, 73.

5. Lukas Kendall, "Danny Elfman: Part 2," *Film Score Monthly*, December 1995, 11.

6. The leitmotiv technique requires that a theme be clearly stated and then reprised a number of times so that it can be recognized by the viewer. If music has not enough aural room in the sound mix, the technique is useless.

7. Karlin, *Listening to Movies*, 200–201.

8. Jeff Bond, "Horner Revealed," *Film Score Monthly*, February 2004, 20.

9. Remote Control Productions, www.remotecontrolproductions.com, accessed 3 April 2013. See Jeff Bond, "Hans Zimmer Takes Aim at . . . FSM!," *Film Score Monthly*, 2 September 1997, 21–24; and Jeff Bond, "The Finale Confrontation: Zimmer vs. FSM," *Film Score Monthly*, October 1997, 17–19; "Media (misad)Ventures," *Film Score Monthly*, December 2003, 4.

10. Jeff Bond, "The Fall of Troy," *Film Score Monthly*, April/May 2004, 18.

11. Bond, "Horner Revealed," 16–20.

12. See *Film Score Monthly*, August 1996, 2.

13. Ben Burtt reports the datum in *Within a Minute: The Making of "Episode III,"* documentary by Tippy Bushkin, Lucasfilm, 2005, in *Star Wars: Episode III—Revenge of the Sith*, DVD, 20th Century Fox Home Entertainment, 2005.

14. Williams, videotaped lecture, 11 January 2006, Thornton School of Music, University of Southern California–Los Angeles.

15. Bushkin, *Within a Minute: The Making of "Episode III."*

16. In the "customer reviews" section of www.amazon.com regarding the 2004 DVD box set, the negative comments number nearly eight hundred. See www.amazon.com/Trilogy-Empire-Strikes-Return-Widescreen/product-reviews/B00003CXCT/ref=pr_all_summary_cm_cr_acr_txt?ie=UTF8&showViewpoints=1, accessed 3 April 2013.

17. Alexandra DuPont, "The Star Wars Trilogy," *The DVD Journal*, 2004, www.dvdjournal.com/reviews/s/starwarstrilogy.shtml, accessed 3 April 2013.

18. See www.amazon.com/Trilogy-Empire-Strikes-Return-Widescreen/product-reviews/B00003CXCT/ref=cm_cr_pr_btm_link_next_3?ie=UTF8&showViewpoints=0&filterby=addOneStar&pageNumber=3, accessed 3 April 2013.

19. Bill Hunt, "The Star Wars Trilogy," *The Digital Bits*, 9 September 2004, http://www.thedigitalbits.com/site_archive/reviews3/starwarstrilogy.html, accessed 3 April 2013.

20. Update to the original review by *The Digital Bits*, reported widely, including at http://forums.audioreview.com/favorite-films/star-wars-dvd-audio-issues-7032.html, accessed 3 April 2013.

21. *Star Wars: Episode IV—A New Hope*, limited edition double DVD, 20th Century Home Entertainment.

22. A further report on contemporary Hollywood film music as opposed to Williams's old-fashioned artistry can be found in John Jurgensen, "The Last Movie Maestro," *Wall Street Journal*, 16 December 2011.

23. Dyer, "John Williams Is New Pops Maestro."

24. Bruno Coulais, "Ce qui reste d'enfance en nous . . . ," in Tylski, *John Williams*, 171 (my translation).

Appendix 1
Completing the Picture

1. David Vernier, "Magnificent Modern Maestro," *Digital Audio*, March 1988.

2. Jon Burlingame, "Master Class: Williams Earns Himself a Spot in Pantheon of Composers," *Variety*, 29 November 2005. The music critic Richard Dyer praised the resulting cross-cultural blend of the score: "Williams' music is transparent, evocative, and subtle, and much of it is colored by authentic Japanese timbres, musical gestures, and instruments. . . . Of course, like everything connected with this venture, beginning with the novel written by an American in Brookline, the score is a Westernized assimilation of and commentary on traditional Japanese music. But it's worth remembering that bridging the gap between Japanese and Western music was a goal of some Japanese musicians even as early as the period of the story (before World War II), and Williams' score to *Memoirs of a Geisha* is more than Hollywood music with a few touches of local color (just as Puccini's *Madama Butterfly* is more than an Italian opera with a few touches of Asian atmosphere)." Richard Dyer, "John Williams Scores Again: 2005 Produces Two More Oscar Nominations," *Boston Globe*, 5 February 2006.

3. Burlingame, "Master Class."

4. Jon Burlingame, "Spielberg and Lucas on Williams: Directors Reminisce about Collaborating with Hollywood's Greatest Composer," *The Film Music Society*, 8 February 2012, www.filmmusicsociety.org/news_events/features/2012/020812.html, accessed 3 April 2013.

5. Steven Spielberg, speech given at "John Williams 80th Birthday Gala," Tanglewood Festival, Lenox, MA, 18 August 2012.

6. Stearns, "2 Emmys, 4 Oscars, 15 Grammys . . . But, Hey, Who's Counting?," 22.

7. Reed, transcript of an interview with John Williams, http://arts.gov/audio/john-williams.

8. Elley, "The Film Composer: 3. John Williams, part 1," 23.

9. John Williams, CD booklet for *1941*, La-La Land Records, 2011, LLLCD 1179, 7–8.

10. Music and lyrics by Louis Prima. "Sing, Sing, Sing" was popularized and most famously covered by Benny Goodman.

11. The girl is again played by Susan Backlinie, who portrayed Chrissie the blonde night-swimmer, the first victim of the shark in *Jaws*.

12. Marian Zailian, "John Williams: Master of Movie Scores," *San Francisco Examiner-Chronicle*, 18 July 1982.

13. Laurent Bouzereau, *The Making of "E.T. the Extra-Terrestrial,"* MCA Home Video, 1996.

14. Ibid.

15. Laurent Bouzereau, "John Williams Interview," CD booklet, *E.T. the Extra-terrestrial*, expanded edition, MCA, 1996, MCAD-11494, 4.

16. Jon Burlingame, "*E.T.* Turns 30 Williams' Score Soars on New Blu-Ray Release," *The Film Music Society*, 10 October 2012, http://www.filmmusicsociety.org/news_events/features/2012/101012.html, accessed 3 April 2013.

17. Merluzeau, "An Interview with John Williams," 9.

18. Freer, *Complete Spielberg*, 199.

19. Richard Dyer, "John Williams: Making Movie-Music History: *Schindler* Composer Is Up for Fifth Oscar," *Boston Globe*, 20 March 1994.

20. Ibid.

21. John Williams, introductory note to *Dry Your Tears, Afrika*, full orchestral score, John Williams Signature Edition series, Hal Leonard, 044900085.

22. Steven Spielberg, CD booklet for *Saving Private Ryan*, DreamWorks Records, 1998, DRD 50046.

23. According to John Williams, in *The Music of "A.I.,"* documentary by Laurent Bouzereau, DreamWorks Home Entertainment, 2002, *Artificial Intelligence*, DVD, Warner Home Video, 2002.

24. Richard Dyer, "An Enduring Love for Music, Movies," *Boston Globe*, 23 June 2002.

25. Williams, quoted in Colburn, "John Williams Returns to Bands," 15.

26. Williams, in *In Flight Service: The Music of "The Terminal,"* documentary by Laurent Bouzereau, DreamWorks Home Entertainment, 2004, *The Terminal*, DVD, DreamWorks Home Entertainment, 2004.

27. See "Spiegel Interview with Tom Cruise and Steven Spielberg," *Der Spiegel*, 27 April 2005, www.spiegel.de/international/spiegel/0,1518,353577,00.html, accessed 3 April 2013; and J. Tirella, "Steven Spielberg 9/11 obsession," 28 December 2005, http://today.msnbc.msn.com/id/10549050, accessed 3 April 2013.

28. Williams, in *Scoring "War of the Worlds,"* documentary by Laurent Bouzereau, DreamWorks Home Entertainment, 2005, *War of the Worlds*, DVD, DreamWorks Home Entertainment, 2005.

29. Tellingly, the concert version is titled "Swashbuckler (The Adventures of Mutt)" (first movement of the suite *The Adventures of Indiana Jones*, full orchestral score, John Williams Signature Edition series, Hal Leonard, 04490826).

30. "Battle Cry of Freedom" was composed in 1862 by George Frederick Root.

31. Ray Bennett, "John Williams, Composer," *Hollywood Reporter*, 8 March 2000.

32. Liner notes for the original LP *Dracula*, MCA Records, 1979.

33. *The Revamping of Dracula*, documentary by Laurent Bouzereau, Universal Studios Home Video, 2004, *Dracula*, DVD, Universal Studios Home Video, 2004.

34. On the music for Hammer films, see Larson, *Musique Fantastique*, 147–53.

35. *The Revamping of Dracula*.

36. Williams, quoted in Elley, "The Film Composer: 3. John Williams, part 1," 24.

37. Williams, quoted in Richard Dyer, "You'll Be Hearing From Him," *Boston Globe*, 31 August 1989.

38. Merluzeau, "An Interview with John Williams," 5.

39. Ibid., 6.

40. Bennett, "John Williams, Composer."

41. Andy Seiler, "Williams Adds Musical Magic to *Harry Potter*," *USA Today*, 13 November 2001.

Bibliography

Cinema History, Theories, and Methodologies

Altman, Rick. *Silent Film Sound*. New York: Columbia University Press, 2004.

Bordwell, David. "A Case for Cognitivism." *Iris* 9 (Spring 1989): 11–40.

————. "A Case for Cognitivism: Further Reflections." *Iris* 11 (Summer 1990): 107–12.

————. "Film Interpretation Revisited." *Film Criticism* 17, nos. 2–3 (Winter/Spring 1993): 93–119.

————. *Making Meaning: Inference and Rhetoric in the Interpretation of Cinema*. Cambridge, MA: Harvard University Press, 1989.

————. *Narration in the Fiction Film*. Madison: University of Wisconsin Press, 1985. Reprint, London: Routledge, 1988.

————. *On the History of Film Style*. Cambridge, MA: Harvard University Press, 1997.

————. *Poetics of Cinema*. New York: Routledge, 2008.

————. *The Way Hollywood Tells It: Story and Style in Modern Movies*. Berkeley: University of California Press, 2006.

Bordwell, David, and Noël Carroll, eds. *Post-Theory: Reconstructing Film Studies*. Madison: University of Wisconsin Press, 1996.

Bordwell, David, and Kristin Thompson. *Film Art: An Introduction*. New York: McGraw-Hill International, 2010.

Bordwell, David, Janet Staiger, and Kristin Thompson. *The Classical Hollywood Cinema: Film Style and Mode of Production to 1960*. New York: Columbia University Press, 1985.

Brunetta, Gian Piero, ed. *Storia del cinema mondiale*. 5 vols. Turin: Einaudi, 1999–2001.

Chion, Michel. *L'audio-vision: Son et image au cinéma.* Paris: Nathan, 1990. Translated and edited by Claudia Gorbman as *Audio-Vision: Sound On Screen* (New York: Columbia University Press, 1994).

Elsaesser, Thomas, and Adam Barker, eds. *Early Cinema: Frame, Space, Narrative.* London: BFI Publishing, 1990.

Field, Syd. *The Screenwriter's Problem Solver: How to Recognize, Identify, and Define Screenwriting Problems.* New York: Dell Publishing, 1998.

Freer, Ian. *The Complete Spielberg.* London: Virgin Publishing, 2001.

Gaudreault, André, and Tom Gunning. "Le cinéma des premieres temps: Un défi à l'histoire du cinéma?" In *Histoire du cinéma: Nouvelles approches,* edited by Jacques Aumont, André Gaudreault, and Michel Marie, 49–63. Paris: Publications de la Sorbonne, 1989.

Gomery, Douglas. *The Coming of Sound.* New York: Routledge, 2005.

———. *The Hollywood Studio System: A History.* Berkeley: University of California Press, 2007.

———. *Shared Pleasures: A History of Movie Presentation in the United States.* London: BFI Publishing, 1992.

Gottlieb, Carl. *The Jaws Log.* New York: Newmarket Press, 2005.

Hill, John, and Pamela Church Gibson, eds. *The Oxford Guide to Film Studies.* New York: Oxford University Press, 1998.

Jullier, Laurent. *L'écran post-moderne: Un cinéma de l'allusion e du feu d'artifice.* Paris: L'Harmattan, 1997. Translated by Carla Capetta as *Il cinema postmoderno* (Turin: Kaplan, 2006).

King, Geoff. *New Hollywood Cinema: An Introduction.* London: I. B. Tauris, 2002.

La Polla, Franco, and Maria Teresa Cavina, eds. *Spielberg su Spielberg.* Turin: Lindau, 1995.

Maltby, Richard. *Hollywood Cinema.* Malden, MA: Wiley-Blackwell Publishing, 2003.

Morris, Nigel. *The Cinema of Steven Spielberg: Empire of Light.* London: Wallflower Press, 2007.

Neale, Steve, and Murray Smith, eds. *Contemporary Hollywood Cinema.* London: Routledge, 1998.

Rinzler, J. W. *The Making of Star Wars: The Definitive Story Behind the Original Film.* London: Ebury Press, 2007.

Salt, Barry. *Film Style and Technology: History and Analysis.* London: Starword, 1992.

Schatz, Thomas. *The Genius of the System: Hollywood Filmmaking in the Studio Era.* Minneapolis: University of Minnesota Press, 2010.

———. *Hollywood Genres: Formulas, Filmmaking, and the Studio System.* New York: McGraw-Hill, 1981.

———. "The New Hollywood." In *Film Theory Goes to the Movies: Cultural Analysis of Contemporary Film,* edited by Jim Collins, Hilary Radner, and Ava Preacher Collins, 8–36. London: Routledge, 1993.

Sklar, Robert. *Movie-Made America: A Cultural History of American Movies.* New York: Vintage Books, 1994.

Spottiswoode, Raymond. *A Grammar of the Film: An Analysis of Film Technique.* 1935. Reprint, Berkeley: University of California Press, 1962.

Taylor, Derek. *The Making of "Raiders of the Lost Ark."* New York: Ballantine, 1981.

Taylor, Philip. *Steven Spielberg: The Man, His Movies, and Their Meaning.* London: B. T. Batsford, 1999.

Thompson, Kristin. *Breaking the Glass Armor: Neoformalist Film Analysis.* Princeton, NJ: Princeton University Press, 1988.

———. *Eisenstein's "Ivan the Terrible": A Neoformalist Analysis.* Princeton, NJ: Princeton University Press, 1981.

———. *Storytelling in the New Hollywood: Understanding Classical Narrative Technique.* Cambridge, MA: Harvard University Press, 1999.

Thompson, Kristin, and David Bordwell. *Film History: An Introduction.* 3rd ed. New York: McGraw-Hill, 2010.

Vogler, Chris. *The Writer's Journey: Mythic Structures for Writers.* 3rd ed. Studio City: Michael Wiese Productions, 2007.

Wyatt, Justin. *High Concept: Movies and Marketing in Hollywood.* Austin: University of Texas Press, 1994.

Music History, Theory, and Aesthetics

Basso, Alberto. *Storia della musica dalle origini al XIX secolo.* Turin: Utet, 2006.

Dahlhaus, Carl. *Die Idee der absoluten Musik.* Kassel: Bärenreiter-Verlag, 1978. Translated by Roger Lustig as *The Idea of Absolute Music* (Chicago: University of Chicago Press, 1991).

Forsyth, Cecil. *Orchestration.* New York: Dover, 1982.

Jourdain, Robert. *Music, the Brain, and Ecstasy: How Music Captures Our Imagination.* New York: HarperCollins, 2002.

Meyer, Leonard B. *Emotion and Meaning in Music.* Chicago: University of Chicago Press, 1956.

———. *Style and Music: Theory, History, and Ideology.* Chicago: University of Chicago Press, 1989.

Seashore, Carl E. *Psychology of Music.* New York: Dover, 1967.

Sloboda, John A. *The Musical Mind: The Cognitive Psychology of Music.* London: Oxford University Press, 1985.

Schönberg, Arnold. *Harmonielehre.* Vienna: Universal, 1922.

Film Music History, Theory, and Aesthetics

Adorno, Theodor W., and Hanns Eisler. *Composing for the Films.* 1947. Reprint, London: Continuum, 2007.

Bassetti, Sergio. *La musica secondo Kubrick.* Turin: Lindau, 2002.

Bazelon, Irwin. *Knowing the Score: Notes on Film Music.* New York: Arco, 1975.

Biamonte, S. G., ed. *Musica e Film*. Rome: Edizioni dell'Ateneo, 1959.

Blanchard, Gerard. *Images de la musique de cinéma*. Paris: Edilio, 1984.

Brown, Royal S. *Overtones and Undertones: Reading Film Music*. Berkeley: University of California Press, 1994.

Buhler, James, Caryl Flinn, and David Neumeyer, eds. *Music and Cinema*. Hanover, NH: Wesleyan University Press, 2000.

Burt, George. *The Art of Film Music*. Boston: Northeastern University Press, 1994.

Calabretto, Roberto. *Lo schermo sonoro: La musica per film*. Venice: Marsilio, 2010.

Cano, Cristina. *La musica nel cinema: Musica, immagine, racconto*. Rome: Gremese, 2002.

Carroll, Brendan G. *The Last Prodigy: A Biography of Erich Wolfgang Korngold*. Portland, OR: Amadeus Press, 1997.

Cohen, Annabel J. "Film Music: Perspectives from Cognitive Psychology." In *Music and Cinema*, edited by James Buhler, Caryl Flinn, and David Neumeyer, 360–77. Hanover, NH: Wesleyan University Press, 2000.

———, ed. *Psychomusicology* 13 (Spring/Fall 1994).

Comuzio, Ermanno. *Colonna sonora: Dialoghi, musiche, rumori dietro lo schermo*. Milan: Il Formichiere, 1980.

———. *Musicisti per lo schermo: Dizionario ragionato dei compositori cinematografici*. 2 vols. Rome: Ente dello Spettacolo, 2004.

Cooke, Mervyn. *A History of Film Music*. Cambridge: Cambridge University Press, 2008.

———, ed. *The Hollywood Film Music Reader*. New York: Oxford University Press, 2010.

Cooper, David. *Bernard Herrmann's "The Ghost and Mrs. Muir": A Film Score Guide*. Lanham, MD: Scarecrow Press, 2005.

Darby, William, and Jack Du Bois. *American Film Music: Major Composers, Techniques, Trends, 1915–1990*. Jefferson, NC: McFarland, 1990.

Davis, Richard. *Complete Guide to Film Scoring*. Boston: Berklee Press, 1999.

Daubney, Kate. *Max Steiner's "Now, Voyager": A Film Score Guide*. Westport, CT: Greenwood, 2000.

De Santi, Pier Marco. *La musica di Nino Rota*. Bari: Laterza, 1983.

Dickinson, Kay, ed. *Movie Music, the Film Reader*. New York: Routledge, 2003.

Donnelly, K. J. "The Classical Film Score Forever? 'Batman,' 'Batman Returns,' and Post-Classical Film Music." In *Contemporary Hollywood Cinema*, edited by Steve Neale and Murray Smith, 143–55. London: Routledge, 1998.

———, ed. *Film Music: Critical Approaches*. New York: Continuum International, 2001.

Duchen, Jessica. *Erich Wolfgang Korngold*. London: Phaidon, 1996.

Duncan, Dean W. *Charms that Soothe: Classical Music and the Narrative Film*. New York: Fordham University Press, 2003.

Evans, Mark. *Soundtrack: The Music of the Movies*. New York: Da Capo Press, 1979.

Flinn, Caryl. *Strains of Utopia: Gender, Nostalgia, and Hollywood Film Music*. Princeton, NJ: Princeton University Press, 1992.

Gorbman, Claudia. "Film Music." In *The Oxford Guide to Film Studies*, edited by John Hill and Pamela Church Gibson, 43–50. New York: Oxford University Press, 1998.

————. *Unheard Melodies: Narrative Film Music*. London: BFI, 1987.

Hagen, Earle. *Advanced Technique for Film Scoring*. Van Nuys, CA: Alfred Publishing, 1990.

Halfyard, Janet K. *Danny Elfman's "Batman": A Film Score Guide*. Lanham, MD: Scarecrow Press, 2004.

Kalinak, Kathryn. *Settling the Score: Music and the Classical Hollywood Film*. Madison: University of Wisconsin Press, 1992.

Karlin, Fred. *Listening to Movies: The Film Lover's Guide to Film Music*. Belmont, CA: Cengage, 1994.

Karlin, Fred, and Rayburn Wright. *On the Track: A Guide to Contemporary Film Scoring*. 2nd ed. New York: Routledge, 2004.

Kendall, Lukas, ed. *Film Score Monthly*. Film music magazine (1990–2005).

Kompanek, Sonny. *From Score to Screen*. New York: Schirmer Trade Books, 2004.

Lack, Russell. *Twenty Four Frames Under: A Buried History of Film Music*. London: Quartet Book, 1999.

Larsen, Peter. *Film Music*. London: Reaktion Books, 2005.

Larson, Randall D. *Musique Fantastique: A Survey of Film Music in the Fantastic Cinema*. London: Scarecrow, 1985.

Lazarou, George A. *Max Steiner and Film Music: An Essay*. Athens: self-published, 1971.

London, Kurt. *Film Music: A Summary of the Characteristic Features of Its History, Aesthetics, Technique; and Possible Developments*. London: Faber and Faber, 1936.

Lustig, Milton. *Music Editing for Motion Pictures*. New York: Hastings House, 1980.

Leinberger, Charles. *Ennio Morricone's "The Good, the Bad and the Ugly": A Film Score Guide*. Lanham, MD: Scarecrow Press, 2004.

Levinson, Jerrold. "Film Music and Narrative Agency." In *Post-Theory: Reconstructing Film Studies*, edited by David Bordwell and Noël Carroll. Madison, 248–82: University of Wisconsin Press, 1996.

Lissa, Zofia. *Ästhetik der Filmmusik*. Berlin: Henschelverlag, 1965.

MacDonald, Laurence E. *The Invisible Art of Film Music: A Comprehensive History*. New York: Ardsley House, 1998.

Manvell, Roger, and John Huntley. *Technique of Film Music*. Waltham: Focal Press, 1957.

Marks, Martin Miller. *Music and the Silent Film: Contexts and Case Studies, 1895–1924*. New York: Oxford University Press, 1997.

Marmorstein, Gary. *Hollywood Rhapsody: Movie Music and Its Makers, 1900 to 1975*. New York: Schmirner, 1997.

Masetti, Enzo, ed. *La musica nel film*. Rome: Bianco e Nero, 1950.

Mera, Miguel, and David Burnand. *European Film Music*. London: Ashgate 2006.

Merluzeau, Yann. "Hollywood Bowl Conductor John Mauceri." *Film Score Monthly*, August 1996, 8–10.

Miceli, Sergio. *Musica e cinema nella cultura del Novecento*. Rome: Bulzoni, 2010.

————. *La musica nel film: Arte e artigianato*. Fiesole: Discanto Edizioni, 1982.

————. *Musica per film: Storia, Estetica, Analisi, Tipologie*. Lucca: LIM, 2009.

Miceli, Sergio, and Ennio Morricone. *Comporre per il cinema: Teoria e prassi della musica nel film.* Rome: Fondazione Scuola nazionale di cinema, 2001.

Palmer, Christopher. *The Composer in Hollywood.* London: Marion Boyars, 2000.

Porcile, François. *Présence de la musique à l'écran.* Paris: Editions du Cerf, 1969.

Prendergast, Roy M. *Film Music: A Neglected Art: A Critical Study of Music in Films.* New York: W. W. Norton, 1977.

Rapée, Erno. *Encyclopedia of Music for Pictures.* 1925. Reprint, New York: Arno Press, 1970.

———. *Motion Picture Moods for Pianists and Organists: A Rapid-Reference Collection of Selected Pieces.* 1924. Reprint, New York: Schirmer, 1974.

Robinson, David. *Music of the Shadows: The Use of Musical Accompaniment with Silent Films.* Pordenone: Giornate del cinema muto, 1990.

Rosar, William H. "Film Studies in Musicology: Disciplinarity vs. Interdisciplinarity." *Journal of Film Music* 2, no. 2–4 (Winter 2009): 108–17.

Rózsa, Miklós. *A Double Life: The Autobiography of Miklós Rózsa, Composer in the Golden Years of Hollywood.* 1982. Reprint, New York: Wynwood Press, 1989.

Scheurer, Timothy E. *Music and Mythmaking in Film: Genre and the Role of the Composer.* London: McFarland, 2008.

Schreibman, Myrl A. "Memories of Max: An Archival Interview with Max Steiner. Part 1." *Film Score Monthly,* January/February 2005, 24–27.

———. "Memories of Max: An Archival Interview with Max Steiner. Part 2." *Film Score Monthly,* March/April 2005, 22–26.

Slowik, Michael. "Hollywood Film Music in the Early Sound Era, 1926–1934." PhD diss., University of Iowa, 2012.

Smith, Jeff. "That Money Making 'Moon River' Sound: Thematic Organization and Orchestration in the Film Music of Henry Mancini." In *Music and Cinema,* edited by James Buhler, Caryl Flinn, and David Neumeyer, 247–71. Hanover, NH: Wesleyan University Press, 2000.

———. *The Sound of Commerce: Making Popular Film Music.* New York: Columbia University Press, 1998.

———. "Unheard Melodies? A Critique of Psychoanalytic Theories of Film Music." In *Post-Theory: Reconstructing Film Studies,* edited by David Bordwell and Noël Carroll, 230–47. Madison: University of Wisconsin Press, 1996.

Smith, Steven C. *A Heart at Fire's Center: The Life and Music of Bernard Herrmann.* Berkeley: University of California Press, 2002.

Sullivan, Jack. *Hitchcock's Music.* New Haven, CT: Yale University Press, 2006.

Thomas, Tony. *Film Score: The Art and Craft of Movie Music.* Burbank, CA: Riverwood Press, 1991.

———. *Music for the Movies.* 2nd ed. Los Angeles: Silman-James Press, 1997.

Timm, Larry M. *The Soul of Cinema: An Appreciation of Film Music.* Upper Saddle River, NJ: Prentice Hall, 2003.

Wierzbicki, James. *Film Music: A History.* New York: Routledge, 2009.

Winters, Ben. *Erich Wolfgang Korngold's "The Adventures of Robin Hood": A Film Score Guide.* Lanham, MD: Scarecrow Press, 2007.

———. "The Non-Diegetic Fallacy: Film, Music, and Narrative Space." *Music and Letters* 91, no. 2 (2010): 224–44.

History of the Boston Pops Orchestra

Bachman, Ron. "Behind the Scene at Evening at Pops." *Nine,* June 1989, 34ff.

"Boston Pops Members Reveal They Hated Fiedler, His Music." *Journal Inquirer,* 10 August 1984.

Boston Pops: The Story of America's Orchestra. Boston: Boston Symphony Orchestra Inc., 2000.

Clendinen, Dudley. "At 100, the Boston Pops Still Packs Them In." *New York Times,* 1 May 1985.

Daniel, Peggy. *Tanglewood: A Group Memoir.* New York: Amadeus Press, 2008.

Dickson, Harry Ellis. *Arthur Fiedler and the Boston Pops: An Irreverent Memoir.* Boston: Houghton Mifflin, 1981.

Dyer, Richard. "Boston's 'Other' Pops Orchestra." *Boston Globe,* 15 June 1986.

———. "Lockhart, Stars to Shine for Boston Pops' Season." *Boston Globe,* 4 April 1995.

———. "Remembering the Pops Maestro." *Boston Globe,* 11 July 1979.

———. "Stars and Stripes Forever and Ever." *Boston Globe,* 28 April 1985.

Fiedler, Johanna. *Arthur Fiedler: Papa, the Pops, and Me.* New York: Doubleday, 1994.

Holland, James R. *Mr. Pops.* Barre, MA: Barre Publishers, 1972.

Howe, M. A. De Wolfe. *The Boston Symphony Orchestra, 1881–1931.* 1931. Reprint, New York: Da Capo Press, 1978.

Hughes, Allen. "Arthur Fiedler, 84, Conductor of Boston Pops 50 Years, Dies." *New York Times,* 11 July 1979.

Johnson, H. Earle. *Symphony Hall, Boston.* 1950. Reprint, New York: Da Capo Press, 1979.

Kupferberg, Herbert. *Tanglewood.* New York: McGraw-Hill Group, 1976.

Laber, Bob. "Recording the Boston Pops." *Instrumentalist,* April 1992, 28ff.

Laning, Humphrey. "New Pops Era Recalls Another 50 Years Ago." *Boston Globe,* 1 May 1980.

Ledbetter, Steven. *100 Years of the Boston Pops.* Boston: Boston Symphony Orchestra, 1985.

McLellan, Joseph. "Pops Puts Emphasis on Masses." *Washington Post,* 18 July 1985.

Moore, Robin. *Fiedler: The Colorful Mr. Pops—The Man and His Music.* Boston: Little, Brown, 1968,

Rockwell, John. "Exponent of Populist Music." *New York Times,* 11 July 1979.

Stearns, David Patrick. "Music That's Light on the Baton: USA Orchestras Enjoy a Pops Explosion." *USA Today,* 26 April 1985.

Stebbins, Richard Poate. *The Making of Symphony Hall, Boston: A History with Documents.* Boston: Boston Symphony Orchestra Inc., 2000.

Symphony Hall: The First 100 Years. Boston: Boston Symphony Orchestra Inc., 2000.

Wilson, Carol Green. *Arthur Fiedler: Music for the Millions: The Story of the Conductor of the Boston Pops Orchestra.* New York: Evans Publishing Company, 1968.

Interviews, Articles, and Essays on John Williams

Anderman, Joan. "Endlessy Devoted to His Music." *Boston Globe*, 11 May 2010.

Archerd, Army. "John Williams Preps for *E.T.* Redux." *Variety*, 14 March 2002.

Aschieri, Roberto. *Over the Moon: La mùsica de John Williams para el cine.* Santiago de Chile: Universidad Diego Portales, 1999.

Audissino, Emilio. "John Williams, *Star Wars* and the Canonization of Hollywood Film Music." In *Il Canone Cinematografico / The Film Canon*, edited by Pietro Bianchi, Giulio Bursi, and Simone Venturini, 273–78. Udine: Forum, 2011.

———. "John Williams, the Boston Pops Orchestra, and Film Music in Concert." In *Cinema: Critique des Images*, edited by Claudia D'Alonzo, Ken Slock, and Philippe Dubois, 230–35. Udine: Campanotto, 2012.

———. "'Se l'avventura ha un nome, questo dev'essere John Williams': Le musiche di *Tintin.*" *Filmcritica* 61, no. 620 (December 2011): 518–26.

Bazelon, Irwin. "Interview with John Williams." In *Knowing the Score: Notes on Film Music*, 193ff. New York: Arco, 1975.

Bennett, Ray. "John Williams, Composer." *Hollywood Reporter*, 8 March 2000.

Berthomieu, Pierre. "John Williams: Planètes symphoniques." *Positif* 430, December 1996, 72–73.

Bond, Jeff. "God Almighty! FSM Finally Talks to John Williams." *Film Score Monthly*, January 2003, 10–13.

Booth, William. "Shark Attack?! John Williams Liked the Sound of That." *Washington Post*, 5 December 2004.

Bouzereau, Laurent. "Interview with John Williams." CD booklet of *Close Encounters of the Third Kind*. Arista, 1998, 07822-19004-2.

———. "Jaws." CD booklet of *Jaws: The Collector's Edition Soundtrack*. Decca, 2000, 467 045-2.

———. "John Williams Interview." CD booklet of *E.T. The Extraterrestrial*, expanded edition. MCA, 1996, MCAD-11494.

———. *The Making of "E.T. the Extra-Terrestrial."* Documentary, MCA Home Video, 1996.

———. "When You Wish Upon a Note." CD booklet of *Close Encounters of the Third Kind*. Arista, 1998, 07822-19004-2.

Buhler, James. "*Star Wars*, Music and Myth." In *Music and Cinema*, edited by James Buhler, Caryl Flinn, and David Neumeyer, 33–57. Hanover, NH: Wesleyan University Press, 2000.

Burlingame, Jon. "A Career of Epic Proportion." *Los Angeles Times*, 3 February 2002.

———. "Energizer Jedi: John Williams' Music for the *Star Wars* Trilogy Keeps Going and Going." *Hollywood Reporter*, 15 January 1997.

———. "From Hollywood to Boston: An Interview with John Williams." In *The Boston Pops: The Story of America's Orchestra*, 19ff. Boston: Boston Symphony Orchestra, Inc., 2000.

———. "John Williams Talks *Jaws*." www.horror-movies.ca/2012/08/john-williams-talks-jaws. Accessed 3 April 2013.

———. "Master Class: Williams Earns Himself a Spot in Pantheon of Composers." *Variety*, 29 November 2005.

———. "Why Stop at 43 Nominations?" *New York Times*, 15 January 2006.

Burton-Hill, Clemency. "John Williams, the Music Master." *Financial Times*, 17 August 2012.

Byrd, Craig L. "The *Star Wars* Interview: John Williams." *Film Score Monthly*, January/February 1997, 18–21. Repr. in Cooke, *Hollywood Film Music Reader*, 233–44.

Caps, John. "John Williams—Scoring the Film Whole." *Film Music Notebook* 2, no. 3 (1976): 19–25.

Cariaga, Daniel. "Clearing the Air." *Los Angeles Times*, 3 August 1984.

Catalano, Peter. "John Williams to Leave Boston Pops." *Los Angeles Times*, 21 December 1991.

Christy, Marian. "Conversations: John Williams' Pursuit of Excellence." *Boston Globe*, 4 July 1989.

Colburn, Michael J. "John Williams Returns to Bands Where He Began 50 Years Ago." *Instrumentalist*, June 2004, 12ff.

Dalton, Joseph. "Hollywood's Music Man at Play on a Classical Stage." *New York Times*, 21 August 2003.

Delacoma, Wynn. "Williams: From Celluloid to CSO." *Chicago Sun-Times*, 28 November 2003.

Dobroski, Bernie, and Claire Greene. "Pass the Popcorn: An Interview with John Williams." *Instrumentalist*, July 1984, 6ff.

Downie, Leonard, Jr., and Stacy Jolna. "Boston Pops Goes Hollywood." *Washington Post*, 11 January 1980.

Dyer, Richard. "And a Good Concert, Too." *Boston Globe*, 30 April 1980.

———. "At the Pops: Williams' Farewell." *Boston Globe*, 9 July 1984.

———. "A Birthday Score for Williams." *Boston Globe*, 30 May 2002.

———. "Boston Pops in Classiest Form." *Boston Globe*, 30 June 1982.

———. "Composers Learn Film Music from the Master." *Boston Globe*, 20 August 1998.

———. "An Enduring Love for Music, Movies." *Boston Globe*, 23 June 2002.

———. "Gala Tonight Launches Pops' Star-filled Season." *Boston Globe*, 7 May 1991.

———. "Getting Ready for a Big Date." *Boston Globe*, 22 April 1986.

———. "*Hook, JFK* Are the Latest Hits with the John Williams Touch." *Boston Globe*, 19 January 1992.

———. "Inside a Recording Session with the Boston Pops." *Plain Dealer Magazine*, 19 July 1987.

———. "John Williams Begins 10th Year in Tune with Pops." *Boston Globe*, 7 May 1989.

———. "John Williams Bows In." *Boston Globe*, 11 January 1980.

———. "John Williams: Bringing Hollywood Magic to the Boston Pops." *Ovation*, June 1983, 12–15.

———. "John Williams Casts Spell for *Potter* Score." *Boston Globe*, 11 November 2001.

———. "John Williams Considers Prospect of Writing Opera." *Boston Globe*, 15 September 2000.

———. "John Williams' Final Bow: After 14 Years, the Boston Pops Conductor Is Too Busy to Look Back." *Boston Globe*, 20 December 1993.

———. "John Williams Is New Pops Maestro: A Musician's Musician." *Boston Globe*, 11 January 1980.

———. "John Williams Listens to the Song of a Tree." *Boston Globe*, 2 July 2000.

———. "John Williams: Making Movie-Music History: *Schindler* Composer Is Up for Fifth Oscar." *Boston Globe*, 20 March 1994.

———. "John Williams: New Horizons, Familiar Galaxies." *Boston Globe*, 4 June 1997.

———. "Latest *Star Wars* Score Is an Emotional Adventure." *Boston Globe*, 6 June 2005.

———. "Lights, Camera, Pops! Maestro John Williams Revs up for the 98th Season." *Boston Globe*, 3 May 1983.

———. "Making *Star Wars* Sing Again." *Boston Globe*, 28 March 1999, reprinted in *Film Score Monthly*, June 1999, 18–19.

———. "Mix Design and Mystery, You Get a Pops Maestro." *Boston Globe*, 10 January 1980.

———. "The Music Man: John Williams Writes the Sound Track for America's Make-believe." *Boston Globe*, 7 October 1990.

———. "A New Recording Contract for Pops." *Boston Globe*, 14 December 1989.

———. "Orchestrating a New Pops Season." *Boston Globe*, 4 May 1982.

———. "Pops Japanese Tour: A Rousing Start." *Boston Globe*, 28 November 1987.

———. "Pops Star: The Legacy of John Williams." *Boston Globe*, 12 December 1993.

———. "Pops' Williams to Retire in '93." *Boston Globe*, 20 December 1991.

———. "Pride and the Pops." *Boston Globe*, 5 May 1987.

———. "Q&A with John Williams: Pops Conductor Talks about His New Beat." *Boston Globe*, 27 April 1980.

———. "Reluctant Williams Remembers Early Stage Foray." *Boston Globe*, 12 October 2001.

———. "Sound of a New Era—Bravos All Around." *Boston Globe*, 22 January 1980.

———. "Sounds of Spielberg." *Boston Globe*, 24 February 1998.

———. "Where Is John Williams Coming From?" *Boston Globe*, 29 June 1980.

———. "Williams and the Art of Pops." *Boston Globe*, 20 December 1991.

———. "Williams and the Pops March on to Japan." *Boston Globe*, 13 November 1987.

———. "Williams is Candidate for Fiedler's Job." *Boston Globe*, 6 January 1980.

———. "Williams is Ebullient on Pops' 100." *Boston Globe*, 1 May 1985.

———. "Williams Is a Force, as Usual, in Visit to Pops." *Boston Globe*, 28 May 1999.

———. "Williams Makes a Stirring Debut with the BSO." *Boston Globe*, 30 August 1993.

——. "Williams, McCourt Make Music, Words Soar at Pops." *Boston Globe*, 6 June 2000.

——. "Williams Passes Tests with Flying Colors." *Boston Globe*, 24 January 1980.

——. "Williams Poised for Pops." *Boston Globe*, 26 April 1981.

——. "Williams Polishes Stars at Pops Event." *Boston Globe*, 15 May 2001.

——. "Williams, Pops Go to the Movies." *Boston Globe*, 29 May 2003.

——. "Williams, Pops in Harmony." *Boston Globe*, 19 August 1984.

——. "Williams Reflects on *Angela's Ashes*." *Boston Globe*, 28 January 2000.

——. "Williams Renews Contract with Pops." *Boston Globe*, 22 December 1981.

——. "Williams Says Pops Well-tempered for Upcoming Season." *Boston Globe*, 1 May 1988.

——. "Williams Soars on New Score." *Boston Globe*, 7 May 1999.

——. "Williams to Stay on as Pops Adviser." *Boston Globe*, 4 February 1994.

——. "Williams Talks of Pops' Past, Future." *Boston Globe*, 19 July 1990.

——. "Williams' Touch on *A.I.* Lingers." *Boston Globe*, 6 July 2001.

——. "The Williams Whirlwind: Dinosaurs, Sinatra, CD: His Busy Final Year with the Pops." *Boston Globe*, 9 May 1993.

——. "The Williams Years: Knowing What Counts." Concert program of the "Opening Night at Pops: A Gala Celebration for John Williams," 12 May 1993. Boston Symphony Archives, Symphony Hall, Boston MA, 33ff.

——. "With Donen, Williams, This Pops is Tops." *Boston Globe*, 22 May 1996.

——. "The Wizard of Film Scoring Tackles *Harry Potter*." *Boston Globe*, 18 May 2001.

Elley, Derek. "The Film Composer: 3. John Williams, part 1." *Films and Filming* 24, no. 10 (July 1978): 20–24.

——. "The Film Composer: 3. John Williams, part 2." *Films and Filming* 24, no. 11 (August 1978): 30–33.

Espey, Raymond. "Meet John Williams: Space Music Superstar!" *Space Wars*, November 1979, 38–40.

Fanto, Clarence. "Hooray for Hollywood, Boston Pops-style." *Berkshire Eagle*, 19 July 2001.

Farber, Stephen. "Mr. Pops." *Dial—WGBH Boston*, July 1983, 9–12.

Feather, Leonard. "From Pen to Screen: Johnny Williams." *International Musician* 67 (April 1969): 6–7.

Fenwick, Henry. "A Close Encounter with John Williams." *You: The Mail on Sunday Magazine*, 2 October 1983.

Ford, Beverly, and John Impemba. "John Williams Quits Boston Pops." *Boston Herald*, 14 June 1984.

Galloway, Paul. "Airman Composes Way to Movie Career." *Beacon*, 27 August 1954.

Gensler, Howard. "Pops Tops: Conductor John Williams Dreams up His All-time Fantasy Lineup." *TV Guide* 39, no. 32 (August 1991): 14.

Gladstone Brooks, Valerie. "Top of the Pops." *Westin Magazine*, June 1985.

Gonzalez, Fernando. "Orchestrating *Indiana Jones*." *Boston Globe*, 18 June 1989.

Goodman, Peter. "A Great Little Visiting Band." *New York Newsday*, 11 June 1986.

Goodson, Michael. "Yes, There's Life after Fiedler." *Boston Sunday Herald*, 27 January 1980.

Gorfinkle, Constance. "John Williams Now in Tune with His Players." *Patriot Ledger* (Quincy, MA), 10 August 1984.

———. "'Light Stuff' is Hard Work." *Patriot Ledger*, 15 January 1985.

———. "Why John Williams Changed His Mind." *Patriot Ledger*, 8 August 1984.

———. "Williams Miffed by Hiss from Pops Orchestra?" *Patriot Ledger*, 14 June 1984.

Grace, Bob. "John Williams: Scoring Big in the Movies." *Houston Chronicle*, 13 November 1983.

Holden, Stephen. "Boston Pops Plays Songs of Films." *New York Times*, 7 February 1991.

———. "Composing Music for Clattering Wagon Wheels or Zooming Spacecraft Is more Complicated than It Sounds." *New York Times*, 7 February 1990.

Holland, Bernard. "Boston Pops Conductor Resigns Post Abruptly." *New York Times*, 14 June 1984.

"Indiana Jones and the Ultimate Tribute." *Empire*, no. 208, October 2006, 69–101.

Jennes, Gail. "The Boston Pops Gets a Movie Composer Who Doesn't Chase Fire Engines as Its New Boss." *People Weekly* 13, no. 25 (June 1980): 47–48.

Jurgensen, John. "The Last Movie Maestro." *Wall Street Journal*, 16 December 2011.

Kalinak, Kathryn. "John Williams and 'The Empire Strikes Back': The Eighties and Beyond: Classical Meets Contemporary." In *Settling the Score: Music and the Classical Hollywood Film*, 184–202. Madison: University of Wisconsin Press, 1992.

Katz, Larry. "Dr. Hollywood & Mr. Pops." *Boston Herald Magazine*, 28 April 1985.

———. "John Williams and the Future of the Pops." *Boston Herald*, 5 May 1989.

———. "New Pops Chief Needs Time to Broaden Range." *Chicago Tribune*, 31 January 1980.

———. "Pops Needs a Leader for 100 Year." *Boston Herald*, 15 June 1984.

Keegan, Rebecca. "John Williams and Steven Spielberg Mark 40 Years of Collaboration." *Los Angeles Times*, 8 January 2012.

Knight, Michael. "Boston Pops Names Successor to Fiedler." *New York Times*, 11 January 1980.

———. "John Williams Opens Season with Pops." *New York Times*, 30 April 1980.

Ledbetter, Steven. "John Williams: Six Decades and Counting." In concert program of the "Opening Night at Pops. A Gala Celebration for John Williams," 12 May 1993, pp. 27ff. Boston Symphony Archives, Symphony Hall, Boston, MA.

Lehman, Phil. "When Capitals Collide: Maestros Slatkin and Williams Join Forces for a Series of Film Music Festivities." *Film Score Monthly*, February 2003, 12–13.

Lerner, Neil. "Nostalgia, Masculinist Discourse, and Authoritarianism in John Williams' Scores for *Star Wars* and *Close Encounters of the Third Kind*." In *Off the Planet: Music, Sound and Science Fiction Cinema*, edited by Philip Hayward, 96–108. Eastleigh, UK: John Libbey Publishing, 2004.

Libbey, Theodore W., Jr. "Disks Attest to the Versatile Talents of John Williams." *New York Times*, 27 February 1983.

Livingstone, William. "John Williams and the Boston Pops: An American Institution Enters a New Era." *Stereo Review* 45, no. 6 (December 1980): 74.

Lowman, Rob. "Film Composer Williams Scores Hit at the Bowl." *Los Angeles Daily News*, 16 July 2001.

Lumsden, Carolyn. "Pops Conductor, Angered By Hissing Exists Stage Left." *Gardner News* (MA), 19 June 1984.

Malone, Chris. "Recording the Star Wars Saga: A Musical Journey from Scoring Stage to DVD." Version 1.4, 2012. www.malonedigital.com/starwars.pdf. Accessed 2 April 2013.

Mangan, Timothy. "Composer for the Stars." *Gramophone* (U.S. Interview), May 2006, A3ff.

———. "The Movies' Music Man." *Orange County Register* (CA), 7 July 2002.

Maremaa, Thomas. "The Sound of Movie Music." *New York Times Magazine*, 28 March 1976, 45ff.

Matessino, Michael. "John Williams Strikes Back." CD booklet of *The Empire Strikes Back*. BMG Classics, 1997, 09026 68773 2.

———. "A New Hope for Film Music." CD booklet of *Star Wars: A New Hope*, BMG, 1997, 09026 68772 2.

McCosker, Sylvia. "*Star Wars*: Opera spaziale: La musica di *Star Wars*." In *Guida completa a "Star Wars,"* 107ff. Rome: Elleu, 1999.

McKinley, James, Jr. "John Williams Lets His Muses Carry Him Along." *New York Times*, 19 August 2011.

———. "Musical Titan Honors His Heroes." *New York Times*, 18 August 2011.

McKinnon, George. "Williams Answers Spielberg's Call for Music." *Boston Globe*, 13 May 1983.

McNab, Geoffrey. "They Shoot, He Scores." *Times* (London), 25 September 2001.

Medrek, T. J. "Pops Honors John Williams with *Star*-Filled Birthday Party." *Boston Herald*, 30 May 2002.

———. "*Star Wars* Suite Is Williams' Light." *Boston Herald*, 27 May 1999.

Merluzeau, Yann. "A Conversation with John Williams: From Schindler's List to the Cello Concerto." *Cantina Band* 18 (Winter 1994/95): 2–5.

———. "An Interview with John Williams." *Soundtrack!* 12, no. 47 (September 1993): 4–9.

Meyer, Nicholas. "Star Wars and Music." CD booklet of *Star Wars Trilogy*. Arista, 1993, 11012.

Miller, James. "John Willams' Lucky Seven." *Boston Globe*, 11 August 1998.

———. "Keeping Time with John: Inside the Tanglewood Film Music Seminar." *Film Score Monthly*, October/November 1998, 20–21.

Miller, Margo. "The Tradition that Cost Pops Its Conductor." *Boston Globe*, 15 June 1984.

———. "Williams to Resign as Pops Conductor." *Boston Globe*, 14 June 1984.

———. "A Wonderful Choice." *Boston Globe*, 11 January 1980.

Montgomery, M. R. "John Williams' Quiet Side." *Boston Globe*, 18 March 1981.

Moormann, Peter. *Spielberg-Variationen: Die Filmmusik von John Williams*. Baden-Baden: Nomos, 2010.

Moss, Peter. "A John Williams Triumph at Bowl." *Herald Examiner*, 15 September 1984.

Moss, Stephen. "The Force Is with Him." *Guardian* (London), 4 February 2002.

Oatis, Greg. "John Williams Strikes Back, Unfortunately." *Cinemafantastique* 10, no. 2 (Fall 1980): 8.

Oestreich, James R. "Schubertizing the Movies." *New York Times*, 30 June 2002.

Oksenhorn, Stewart. "The Man Who Loved Conducting." *Aspen Times*, 16 July 2004.

O'Neill, Catherine. "Making Music for the Movies: Composer John Williams Discusses the Delicate Alchemy of Film and Sound." *Chronicle of Higher Education* 9 (July 1979): R14–15.

"Orchestra Shocked at Williams' Decision." *News Tribune*, 15 June 1984.

Ornish, Laurel. "The Two Sides of Composer/Conductor John Williams: Leaving His Mark in Hollywood and in Symphony Halls." *On the Air Magazine*, May 1994.

Owades, Stephen H. "Williams Good Choice at Helm of Pops." *Cincinnati Enquirer*, 15 February 1980.

Page, Tim. "Fade In: Soundtracks' Starring Role." *Washington Post*, 19 January 2003.

———. "Williams Rejoins Pops." *New York Times*, 3 August 1984.

Paiste, Denis. "Boston Pops Tradition Lives On: John Williams Reflects as He Begins His Final Season at Helm." *New Hampshire Sunday News* (Manchester), 9 May 1993.

Palmer, Christopher. "The Changing World of Film Music." *Crescendo International* 10 (April 1972): 8ff.

Pfeifer, Ellen. "A Diary of the Pops Decision: How John Williams Got the Job." *Boston Herald American*, 13 January 1980.

———. "From Star Wars to Boston Pops." *Boston Herald American*, 5 January 1980.

———. "A Legend Replaced with a Goldmine." *Boston Herald American*, 11 January 1980.

———. "Passing the Baton." *Boston Sunday Herald*, 9 May 1993.

———. "Play It Again, Maestro! John Williams Signs Up for a New Hitch." *Boston Herald*, 21 December 1982.

———. "Pops Get Better Every Year, Says Eager Conductor." *Boston Herald*, 8 May 1991.

———. "Williams: 'I Never Intended to Conduct in Public.'" *Boston Herald American*, 28 April 1980.

———. "Williams Tinkers with Audio, Video." *Boston Herald*, 15 August 1997.

———. "Williams to Pop into Retirement." *Boston Herald*, 21 December 1991.

Pincus, Andrew L. "Boston Pops Booms under Williams." *New York Times*, 9 August 1987.

Ponick, T. L. "Movie Music Raised to Its Rightful Place by Composer." *Washington Times*, 3 December 2004.

Pushkar, R. G. "From *Star Wars* to the Boston Pops." *American Way*, January 1982, 16ff.

Reed, Josephine. Transcript from a radio interview with John Williams. *Art Works*. National Endowment for the Arts, 2009. http://arts.gov/audio/john-williams. Accessed 2 April 2013.

Rockwell, John. "Concert: John Williams and His Boston Pops." *New York Times*, 24 January 1980.

———. "Traditionalist for the Pops: John Williams." *New York Times*, 11 January 1980.

Rodman, Ron. "John Williams's Music to *Lost in Space*: The Monumental, the Profound, and the Hyperbolic." In *Music in Science Fiction Television: Tuned to the Future*, edited by K. J. Donnelly and Philip Hayward, 34–51. New York: Routledge, 2013.

Rothenberg, Fred. "Boston Pops Alters Concert Look in Wake of Video Revolution." *Orlando Sentinel*, 16 July 1983.

Rothstein, Edward. "'Star Wars' Salutes a Brave Old World." *New York Times*, 31 January 1997.

Safford, Edwin. "Pops Irritated Busy Williams." *Providence Journal*, 20 June 1984.

Scheurer, Timothy E. "John Williams and Film Music Since 1971." *Popular Music and Society* 21, no. 1 (Spring 1997): 59–72.

Seiler, Andy. "Williams Adds Musical Magic to *Harry Potter*." *USA Today*, 13 November 2001.

———. "Williams Shapes More Music for *Star Wars*." *USA Today*, 13 November 2001.

Shaw, Arnold. "John T. Williams." *BMI*, February 1972, 6.

Shone, Tom. "How to Score in the Movies." *Sunday Times* (London), 21 July 1998.

Smith, Tim. "Film Composer John Williams to Make Baltimore Conducting Première." *Baltimore Sun*, 1 June 2013.

———. "Maestros and the Movies." *Baltimore Sun*, 19 January 2003.

"*Star Wars: Episode I—The Phantom Menace*: John Williams Interview." Videotape, Sony Classical, 9 April 1999.

Stearns, David Patrick. "Maestro of the Mainstream: Williams Scores with Pops and Hollywood." *USA Today*, 3 August 1992.

———. "2 Emmys, 4 Oscars, 15 Grammys . . . But, Hey, Who's Counting? Not John Williams, Hollywood's Most Honored Composer." *Arts & Entertainment*, February 1993, 21ff.

Stewart, Richard H. "We Didn't Drive Williams Away." *Boston Globe*, 8 July 1984.

Swan, Annalyn, Abigail Kuflik, Lea Donosky, and Ron LaBrecque. "Boston Strikes up the Band." *Newsweek*, 21 January 1980, 85–86.

Terry, Kenneth. "John Williams Encounters the Pops." *Downbeat* 48, March 1981, 20–22.

———. "John Williams Has Close Encounters of Another Kind." *Pan Am Clipper* 22, no. 4, April 1982, 43ff.

Thomas, Bob. "Williams Looks Backward in Composing Score for New *Star Wars* Movie." *Nevada Daily Mail*, 12 May 1999.

Thomas, David. "King of Themes." *Sunday Telegraph*, 13 July 1997, 48–50.

———. "Point Blank: The Total Film Interview: John Williams." *Total Film*, September 1997, 74ff.

Thomas, Tony. "A Conversation with John Williams." In *Film Score: The Art and Craft of Movie Music*, 326ff. Burbank: Riverwood Press, 1991.

———. "Interview with John Williams." *Cue Sheet*, March 1991, 6ff.

Tichenor, Mary-Jane. "A Tanglewood Extravaganza." *Boston Globe*, 12 July 1997.

Townson, Robert. CD Booklet of *Empire Strikes Back: Symphonic Suite from the Motion Picture Score*. Varèse Sarabande, 1980, VSD 5353.

————. "John Williams." CD Booklet of *Great Composers: John Williams*. Varèse Sarabande, 1999, VSD-6047.

Tylski, Alexandre, ed. *John Williams: Un alchimiste musical à Hollywood*. Paris: L'Harmattan, 2011.

Tynan, John. "John Williams." *BMI*, Spring 1975, 42ff.

Vernier, David. "Magnificent Modern Maestro." *Digital Audio*, March 1988.

von Rhein, John. "Interview with John Williams." *Chicago Tribune*, 27 January 1980.

Waters, Jen. "NSO Scores with Hollywood." *Washington Times*, 1 February 2003.

Wessel, David. "The Force Is with Him . . . 'Rich Is Hard to Define.'" *Boston Globe*, 5 July 1983.

Williams, John. "John Williams on Star Wars." Liner notes of *Star Wars*. LP album, 20th Century Records, 1977, 2T-541(0898).

"Williams Returns to the Pops with His Evolutionary Plans." *Enterprise*, 3 August 1984.

Wolf, Matt. "The Olympics Offers John Williams Another Heroic Challenge." *South Coast Today* (MA), 21 July 1996.

Wood, Daniel B. "Bang-Up Centennial at the Pops." *Christian Science Monitor*, 30 April 1985.

Zailian, Marian. "John Williams: Master of Movie Scores." *San Francisco Examiner-Chronicle*, 18 July 1982.

Zarroli, Jim. "Pops Conductor John Williams Rescinds Resignation." *Morning Union*, 3 August 1984.

Index

WISCONSIN FILM STUDIES

John Williams's Film Music: "Jaws," "Star Wars," "Raiders of the Lost Ark," and the Return of the Classical Hollywood Music Style
Emilio Audissino

The Foreign Film Renaissance on American Screens, 1946–1973
Tino Balio

Marked Women: Prostitutes and Prostitution in the Cinema
Russell Campbell

Depth of Field: Stanley Kubrick, Film, and the Uses of History
Edited by Geoffrey Cocks, James Diedrick, and Glenn Perusek

Tough as Nails: The Life and Films of Richard Brooks
Douglass K. Daniel

Dark Laughter: Spanish Film, Comedy, and the Nation
Juan F. Egea

Glenn Ford: A Life
Peter Ford

Luis Buñuel: The Red Years, 1929–1939
Román Gubern and Paul Hammond

Screen Nazis: Cinema, History, and Democracy
Sabine Hake